WHAT
REALLY
MATTERS

WHAT
REALLY
MATTERS

12 Perspectives on Living

E. Jane Oyer and
Herbert J. Oyer, eds.

The Stephen Greene Press
Brattleboro, Vermont

This book has been produced in the United States of America.
It is designed by Irving Perkins Associates, and published by The Stephen
Greene Press, Fessenden Road, Brattleboro, Vermont, 05301.

Library of Congress Cataloging in Publication Data
Main entry under title:

What really matters.

Includes bibliographies.
1. Aged—Interviews—Addresses, essays, lectures.
2. Aged—Attitudes—Addresses, essays, lectures.
3. Aged—Biography—Addresses, essays, lectures.
4. Success—Addresses, essays, lectures.   I. Oyer, E.
Jane.   II. Oyer, Herbert J.
HQ1061.W45   305.2'6   81-6225
ISBN 0-8289-0443-X   AACR2

To Aunt Alice Moyer, now eighty-plus, whose mature perspectives and wisdom in the golden years continue to enrich the lives of many.

CONTENTS

ACKNOWLEDGMENTS

WE express our appreciation and gratitude to the twelve famous people who so graciously and generously taught, inspired, and encouraged us with this project. Their accumulated wisdom provided the substance for the book and without their meaningful contributions it could not have been developed.

THE EXPERTISE, guidance, and wisdom provided by our editors, Wilbur F. Eastman, Jr. and Mary Metcalf have been of tremendous value in the completion of this book of interviews. Working with them has been professionally and personally rewarding.

WHAT
REALLY
MATTERS

INTRODUCTION

THIS book of interviews with noted older people is meant to be precisely what it is: a book of interviews. We chose as subjects people who have achieved, who were old, who are still active and concerned. We explore with them attitudes toward what we feel are significant aspects of living.

So much of today's printed material about the elderly emphasizes the problems associated with aging. Here, we seek to highlight the productivity and continuing contributions of our select group so that we may show the positive side of growing old. Through talking to these committed, interesting people who bear witness to their own individual lives, we see that aging need not be a liability, but can be, in fact, an asset. For as we grow older, our interpretations of life are enriched by experience and graced by wisdom. It is our intent to share the experience and the wisdom we gained from our meetings with these unusual people. We hope to refresh and stimulate and surprise.

As we talked to these older people, we asked them to reflect, to consider their lives in the light of certain common human concerns. "How important is the family?" we asked. "Is there some special person who influenced the course of your life?" "How do you feel about aging, about goals, about love and hate?"

We went on to explore religious and moral principles, to ask about sources of strength in times of need, about secrets of living. Too, we asked if they felt it was harder or easier to be young today than it was when they were growing up. Their answers and musings are here to absorb and ponder.

How, it may be asked, is "old" defined? Suffice it to say that the government (through social security legislation) has provided an arbitrary cutoff point at age sixty-five: a chronological definition. Another alternative might be a demographic definition: based on the life-expectancy data of a given country, for instance. Yet another might take into account a man's or woman's ability to participate in the ongoing stream of events: a functional definition.

One of the myths associated with the elderly is that they are all alike. Contrary to popular thought, older people do not constitute a homogeneous segment of the population. Their abilities, values, experiences, and attitudes vary as they do within any group. The things most often held in common are two: the state of retirement and chronological age.

Still another myth is the one which suggests that an older person is not "with it," is unable to appreciate the world as it is today. Actually the elderly of today have had greater diversity of experience than any other age group in recorded human history. They have moved from horse-and-buggy days to a time of interplanetary travel. They have witnessed the birth of the wireless and have seen and heard Neal Armstrong speak to the world from the moon.

Change has been part and parcel of their lives, a given, and they alone know how they have dealt with it, how far they have come.

Because of such myths—and many more exist about aging—respect for the elderly has diminished in the United States and in many other industrialized countries. The elderly have been viewed as nonproductive members of a production-oriented, materialistic society. In developing countries, however, advanced years bring status, and the elderly are often decision makers.

Now, we are glad to say, the tide seems to be turning. There is evidence that attitudes are changing as a result of the demographic revolution that has occurred since the turn of the century. In 1900 in the United States, 4.1 percent of the population was

65 years or older (about 3 million persons). In 1981, approximately 11 percent (over 24 million persons) are over 65 and it is projected that by the year 2030 there will be almost a 100 percent increase to 46 million persons. Clearly, older persons are, and will be, making a significant impact on social policy.

We hold that the wisdom of these and other elders is an untapped resource, one of great value, and one that ought not to be ignored. It is our hope that the reader who meets these twelve remarkable people through these pages will come to realize, as we have, that this important storehouse of human capital is a life-enhancing force, a bright spot in an uneasy world.

RICHARD H. AUSTIN

RICHARD H. AUSTIN, Secretary of State, Michigan, has had diverse experiences. Born in Alabama, May 6, 1913, the son of an itinerant coal miner, he moved with his family to Detroit after his father's death in the early 1920s. First in his graduating class at Cass Technical High School, Austin managed to help support his widowed mother while he earned his Bachelor of Science degree in Business Administration at Detroit Institute of Technology. He went on to become a certified public accountant and to found his own accounting firm.

A long-time community and civic leader, he was listed by Ebony magazine in 1970 as one of the 100 "most influential Black Americans." He holds an honorary degree from Detroit College of Business; Michigan State University presented him with a Distinguished Citizen Award. He and his wife of over forty years, the former Ida Dawson, live in Detroit. They have one daughter, Hazel.

We met Richard Austin at the Treasury Building in downtown Lansing one sunny, gusty March afternoon. Now serving his third four-year term, the trim, handsome, self-assured Secretary greeted us with an easy smile and made us welcome. His book-lined office, furnished comfortably with a great desk, pull-up chairs, and a sofa, proved a relaxed and cheerful setting for our conversation.

7

How important is family life?

I think family life even in our day is important to an individual in establishing some base from which to project a life—out in the community, out in the world—a base to which a person can always return and look to for the consolation or even praise that might be needed. And I think that a person who doesn't have a family connection can be a very lonely person and very often lose direction because there are times when we question even our close associates as to whether they have our interests completely at heart. But, somehow, you always feel that the people in the family have your interests at heart. You can always look to the family as the last resort—when all else fails. I think I can appreciate family a lot more today than I did as a younger person when it was a much greater influence . . .

My father was a coal miner who migrated from the coal fields of Alabama to the coal fields of Pennsylvania. He was an itinerant worker. I think by the time I was twelve years of age that I had lived in seven or eight communities—just like a preacher's son. Only the preacher has a house waiting for him and he also has a constituency. As a coal miner's son, you very often land in communities where you are ostracized. People don't accept you—in fact, are quite suspicious of you, and you never really become part of the community.

The only thing we had was family, small as it was, and it was a very small family—father, mother, three brothers. But my father died when I was eleven, and then mother had to become the head of the family. She brought us out of Pennsylvania to Detroit, so Detroit has been my home since 1925.

I'm married to a lady who is part of a big family. She had something like ten brothers when I married her. She has eight brothers living today. I can certainly have a greater appreciation for the family tie watching these people, who are extremely close. The remnants of my family are not that close today. But these people, her folk, really are. They have adopted me. I always point out that the wife and I have been married for forty years because any man who has seven or eight brothers-in-law as neighbors is going to be kind to their sister. And these people meet regularly and discuss family plans. They take trips together. But I must say that one of the subjects they discuss when they meet is "What is brother-in-law doing now?"

IS IT IMPORTANT TO SET GOALS?

I think it is important to set goals, but it is not easy—especially for young people who have had little or no experience in pursuing goals outside those ordinarily pursued by students and children. I'm talking about career goals, for the most part. And they dominate our lives when we reach maturity—however early we reach it. One reason goal-setting is so difficult now is because society changes a lot faster than it did when I was younger. It was pretty easy to predict what your lifestyle would be after a given number of years of pursuing a certain goal. Today many job situations and opportunities disappear within a short period of time. Although you might have your heart set on a particular goal, it just might not be available by the time you are ready to assume the responsibilities of that goal.

I think that as young people set goals today they should be more concerned with the basic needs—communicative skills, the ability to read, and I'd say acquiring some standard credentials such as a degree of some type in some field. Even more important is to have the skills to shift the emphasis of one's goal as the need arises! There has to be flexibility in our planning today, because a person will find even if he or she pursues a single goal, even if he or she is in a single career for life, that it is necessary to retrain and update all the time. Sometimes the jobs and the careers change so much that if you look back, you will find that you are virtually in a different career. So, *flexibility* is very important!

HOW SHOULD ONE DEAL WITH PFOPLE WHO OPPOSE ONE'S POINT OF VIEW?

Frankly, I think that the best way to deal with people, those who oppose your point of view, is to listen to them, and then examine your own point of view in the light of what you hear. Examine it objectively! You might be wrong! The other fellow's point of view just might be the right one. And I think that's the first thing to understand—that is, that there is the possibility that you could be wrong, that the other fellow is right; so listen, and analyze your own position very carefully. If you find that the other person is right, then even though you might not be quite prepared to accept that point of view, at least learn to work with the other individual with the understanding that there are some differences in the way in which you approach things.

If you find that your views are so different that there is no opportunity for working together, then it is probably best to have that type of understanding from the outset rather than to try to develop some type of relationship that is just going to be filled with suspicion.

As for communicating with others, there are two ways in which I usually think of communication. One is just expressing views, exchanging ideas. But expressing views doesn't always get the message across. If the message is important enough, it is equally important to make sure that you *are* communicating—that you understand each other. So, I think communicating means understanding as well as expressing views. Misunderstandings develop because one person told another person something without realizing that person didn't fully understand. So there wasn't communication!

WHAT ABOUT THE LOSSES THAT OCCUR IN LIFE?
HOW DOES ONE BEST HANDLE THEM?

Some losses in life are relatively easy to accept, and there are others that are not very easy to accept because when you suffer those losses they mean the loss of options or alternatives that might be available. And sometimes a loss means that you have made a gross miscalculation somewhere in your life and you don't know where—and it can leave you adrift. Those are the hardest sorts of losses to accept.

But I think most losses can be borne if a person just adopts a mature attitude. For example, some losses have to be expected in the course of one's lifetime. They are bound to occur. There are going to be happy times and unhappy times. I suppose it's pretty much like that Alcoholics Anonymous slogan, You have to know the things you can do something about and the things that you can't do anything about, and, I think the third part of it is, you have to learn how to distinguish between the two. Pursue those that you can do something about, then, of course! Those that you can't, just learn that you can't and accept that gracefully and maturely. One must know how to distinguish between the two.

If you have been in politics and have run for office, you can understand this more than most people. A great deal of effort goes into running for an office—not only on the part of the candidate, but also on the part of the candidate's supporters. A lot of effort and a lot of hopes ride on the outcome of an election. And to run and to lose, especially by a close vote, is extremely difficult to take. You are just haunted by the little mistakes you made, the things you could have done . . .

WHAT ABOUT FEARS AND ANXIETIES?

We should try to analyze our fears and anxieties—try to determine why we have them. Very likely we will find that it is a matter of anticipating losses or successes. If we find that the source of our fear is a nagging doubt that we can succeed in something or that something is going to go wrong or has gone wrong, that we are unprepared to face a situation that is bothering us at the time, then it is best to try to analyze the circumstances and appreciate the basis of the fear and the anxiety. I think you can deal with it if you can do that. You can handle it maturely.

I am somewhat reluctant to talk about fears and anxieties because I very often, just at hearing something for the first time, will begin to develop fears and anxieties when I haven't even thought about it. It is just, you will excuse the expression, the gut reaction that you get when somebody says something to you. Immediately your stomach turns, but I think it is best to be mature, to listen and try to analyze the basis for the fears and anxieties. Then proceed.

WHO WERE THE PEOPLE YOU THINK OF AS MOST INFLUENTIAL IN YOUR LIFE?

When I was quite young there isn't any question but that I was greatly influenced by my parents and my immediate environment. I think as I grew older, I began to have some appreciation for the limitations of my family leadership; it became necessary for me to rely on people outside the small family circle. And I would say that teachers became influential in my life.

As I advanced in my classes from high school into college, various work associates, and, to some extent, church leadership people, became important. I say to some extent because in my youth, I did not have the opportunity to spend much time in a church situation. But *one* of the persons who made the most profound impact upon my life was a minister who took an interest in me—knowing full well that I was not a regular churchgoer to his church. He just took an interest, and that interest was exceedingly important to me!

Is there any event—local, national, or international—
that influenced your life?

I have to admit that it was events, family circumstances, that pretty much dictated the course of my life and career. Just by way of example, in early life I had a desire to be an artist—just loved to draw! I'm not suggesting that I had any talent for it or that I had any great promise, it was just my desire.

When I reached high school I was persuaded that as a high school student in Detroit I should prepare myself with a good technical education—one that would be useful in the auto industry there. So I aspired to become a tool and die maker. I attended Cass Technical High School and just loved that school environment. I was a fairly good student—well, top of the class when I graduated. But I had absolutely no thought, no desire to go to college at that point. My viewpoint was purely vocational.

My father was deceased. I came out of high school in 1931 in the depths of the Depression, and survival was the key word of that time. Career? That was something for other people! Our main concern was to try to stay alive, to keep the family together. So, frankly, I put training for work, vocational training, ahead of any career plans or higher educational goals. I remember that the principal of my school tried to induce me to go to college and become a teacher. He thought I would have made a pretty good teacher. But I wasn't interested. I was a fair athlete, also.

Track was my sport. So the coach at Wayne University approached me one day shortly after I had graduated from Detroit Institute of Technology. He visited me where I worked and asked me if I would come to Wayne. This was the College of the City of Detroit at that time, and he asked me to become a member of his track team. He said he would see what he could do to help me along financially. Well, I told him that the idea appealed to me, but I had a younger brother who was due out of high school shortly, and if he could wait until this younger brother came out of high school to take over my job, I would consider taking him up on his proposition. I know it sounds funny now.

Jobs were not easy to get. I had a widowed mother and three brothers, and it was a matter, frankly, of trying to keep the family together. And I was really interested in doing that. I had an older brother who wasn't quite so responsible, so I truly became the head of the family, and that's why I had to be more sensitive.

I went to Wayne for about a year on a scholarship arrangement. But the family didn't fare so well, so I abandoned the scholarship. Incidentally, while at Wayne, I pursued engineering using the training from Cass Tech. Cass Tech was actually training me for an engineering career although I was mainly interested in the vocational aspects of it. As a matter of fact, I wanted to go to trade school, and I couldn't get into trade school.

Now, one of my classmates was Emil Mazey. He, my wife, and I graduated from Cass Technical High School in the same class. We joke about this, about his going into the factories and organized labor. I tell him that I got sidetracked. I wanted to become a tool and die maker and they forced me to go to college. While I was out in the field of work, someone gave me a book-keeping job, and I became interested in accounting. So, when I left Wayne, I attended night school to study accounting, and I got my degree in accounting and went on to become a CPA—certified public accountant. But I told this little story so you could understand just what I meant when I said that *conditions* and *circumstances* dictated the course of my career. It was not the type of career planning young people usually make when they determine they are going to become a doctor or a lawyer and then pursue it. I didn't feel I had the means to do that.

I don't regret the influence of circumstances and conditions on the course of my career, but I'll admit that with better planning, I probably could have done more with the equipment that I had to work with. I should have gotten a great deal more basic training than I did. Sometimes I think I'm traveling on short rations.

My motivation was survival, then it became one of planning

and wanting to achieve. As I got into accounting, I discovered that in Michigan there had never been a black certified public accountant. So that became a goal.

I became the first black to become a CPA in the state of Michigan. That is an interesting story—how that was done—but I don't believe it really has a place in this discussion. It became a goal, and there were a number of obstacles that had to be overcome in achieving that goal.

HAVE WRITERS EVER INFLUENCED YOUR THINKING?

I am constantly influenced by writers. I don't read a great many books of a profound nature. I read some professional publications, some fiction, some light reading; I do that constantly. And I try to read a few books that I feel are designed to have a direct influence upon one's thinking and the direction of one's life. I'm being constantly influenced by the writers that I read! I know that I was influenced by what I read when I was younger, and I am still being influenced, so it's not a matter of some *one* writer who made that profound impact. I think it's just been a matter of trying to read enough so that I am influenced by people who have time to pull ideas together with the thought of helping folks. And I want all the help I can get—even now. So I'm reading one or two books even now that I find very fascinating.

One book that I'm finding extremely interesting is a book written by Judge A. Leon Higginbotham, a federal judge on the circuit bench out of Philadelphia. It is entitled *In the Matter of Color,* and what he attempts to do is to trace the legal history of blacks in this country from the time they were first brought over in ships. What were their legal rights at that time?

Interestingly enough they had more rights when they first arrived than they did after having been here for a hundred years. They arrived about the same time that indentured people arrived from Europe. You will remember that James Oglethorpe cleaned out the prisons in England—I think it was England, and brought the people to Georgia. Those people ultimately became, of course, the citizens of Georgia. Well, blacks arrived about that same time, and all indentured servants were given pretty much the same treatment. But as time went on it was concluded that because of the color of the skin of the black he could not be assimilated. Therefore, he had to be treated differently—as inferior.

But slave laws were then passed to define the subjugation of the blacks, and of course those of us who are familiar with the most recent course of history know that the struggle has been to change those laws so that blacks are treated somewhat equally, regarded equally.

The way people are treated usually has some basis in law. Custom dictates law, and then law has an influence on custom. They fortify each other, so you change the law. Minds may not change, not all minds, but ultimately it becomes accepted as the norm. Judge Higginbotham spends quite a bit of time reviewing the struggle of the colonialists in this country seeking their own freedom from England. He goes into the writing of the Declaration of Independence by Thomas Jefferson and the adoption of that instrument, and uses some of the very lofty language from it. But when you read it, you can't help being moved and impressed—". . . all men are created equal and endowed by their Creator with certain inalienable rights." But they didn't mean blacks. They *didn't mean* blacks! And there was a Supreme Court decision in the 1850s in which the Supreme Court justice wrote an opinion which said that blacks have no rights a white man is bound to respect and that the Constitution had to be amended to correct any misunderstanding.

The main point that Higginbotham is trying to make is that if we are going to understand, and again this is a matter of how you deal with those whose views are different from yours, if we are going to understand the forces that keep us apart, then we've got to look back into history. We can't assume that history never existed . . .

I think that it would have been unthinkable fifteen years ago for a black man to be elected statewide to an office like this. I don't regard this office as center stage, so to speak, in comparison to the governor's office or some of the others, but I regard it as an important opportunity, and I accept it that way. I'm very proud to hold the office, to accept the responsibilities. But at the same time I'm realistic enough to know how the influence of this office compares to the influence of an office like the governor's. There is just no comparison.

HOW DO YOU FEEL ABOUT GROWING OLDER?

I accept it with, let's say, mixed emotions. I'm not happy to be growing older, but I am resolved. And sometimes I even feel a certain amount of relief that I'm beyond a stage where I must endure some of the things that are expected of younger people. For example, I'm very pleased that I'm not expected to shoulder a rifle and take the life of some other people or fight for my life. I'm not suggesting that you might not encounter a situation where you would have to do it. But at my age it surely isn't expected on a continuing basis, that is, being a member of the armed forces.

On the other hand, the sadness is that I know that physically I just don't have the resources and the ability, facility, or capability of achieving some of the things that I could have much earlier. I know that my body is coming apart, biologically, and I also feel my options running out. As a young person there are just *so many* directions in which you can move. As you grow older, you're restricted, greatly restricted. And I think that's the sadness that I feel.

I don't have grandchildren of my own, but I'm part of a family where there are young people everywhere; somehow, there is satisfaction in helping them to move along as an extension of yourself.

I think our government has reached the point where it accepts responsibility for the economic survival of people who have lived useful lives. A person who has worked is entitled to social security, hospitalization; in fact, these means of survival for older people are available whether they have lived useful lives or not. I think this is a very long step forward for government as it relieves young people today of a burden—of having to plan their lives around concerns for their children and for the welfare of their parents. I don't believe that children, as a rule now, have any great pre-occupation with the welfare of parents because parents are out of the way and pretty well taken care of. If they haven't managed on their own, at least their basic needs will be met—maybe not in the manner in which they might want, but at least they'll be met. That relieves young people of a burden that you had and that I had that they don't have.

I was always concerned about my mother and her welfare. Fortunately, her later years were lightened greatly by the benefits available to her under social security. So, young people are pretty much free to do with their lives what they wish. It's easier for them to be flexible, too, about career changes. And our society is such today that they have to be prepared for changes, as we discussed previously.

So, I think the best way for young people to prepare themselves for old age is to lead their lives in such a way that they maximize whatever opportunities are available. *Then* when they reach older age, whatever mistakes they have made, they can accept. They can always say—sure I made some mistakes, but I think I did the very best I could under the circumstances. That's the greatest satisfaction. But it would be a horrible feeling to grow old and suddenly realize that you have wasted great opportunities—wasted a life.

So, I think it's a matter of making sure that you are not haunted in your later life by wasted opportunities. There is no need for it.

DO YOU THINK THAT LIFE IS MORE DIFFICULT FOR OUR YOUNGSTERS
TODAY THAN IT WAS WHEN WE WERE YOUNG?

In some respects it is more difficult. It would have been difficult for us to manage in today's milieu, today's society, but I think youngsters are better prepared for the changes, the shifts that we are finding in our society and the rapidity with which changes are occurring.

I think maybe it's best to say that these explosions of knowledge, the scientific and technological advances, have created a style of life which older people have difficulty keeping up with. But younger people have grown up with the changes, they've seen the changes occur and it becomes a part of them—part of their lives.

They don't become as attached to some of the institutions we did either. Some of the institutions perhaps had a value, but had outlived their usefulness and we didn't realize it.

The whole society is more complex. This is the age of specialization, and it's difficult to realize how complex our society is when we can spend a day sitting at a desk performing a chore that required some training but which doesn't influence the production of food or clothing, and yet, when we have done a day's work at whatever we are doing, we expect to have transportation to get home. And, when we get home, to find food on the table and schools for the children.

Only a complex society is able to reward us with our fair share of the fruits for this very specialized chore that we are performing. Fifty years ago people wouldn't have felt secure in that kind of society. They would have felt—look, I've just somehow got to stay close to the land, and see the fruits of my labor. But when the machinery breaks down, it's a great cause for concern. Because now when the machinery breaks down it has a much greater impact than it did back in those days.

ARE THERE MORAL OR RELIGIOUS PRINCIPLES THAT YOU FIND
IMPORTANT? WHAT IS YOUR SOURCE OF STRENGTH
IN HOURS OF GREATEST NEED?

I find both of those questions difficult. I think all of us have religious and moral principles by which we live. Even if those principles are amoral or atheistic, they are still of a religious nature or moral nature. I think that my basic tenets probably center around the Golden Rule more than anything else. It's just a matter of treating other people about the way you want to be treated and being quite religious about it. And, frankly, I am!

I was taught that great harm will come to you if you steal—that's taking something that doesn't belong to you. No matter what the circumstances are, there are going to be times when you're entrusted with someone else's property. Perhaps it's trite, but again it's a matter of very, very religiously guarding the principles which govern your life as well as those you would expect to guide other people.

Very often you are going to be disappointed, you can't always be sure that everyone lives by the same code. You can't be sure in walking down the street and meeting someone, especially at night, that this person is not going to try to mug you. But I certainly would not think of ever mugging anyone that I meet on the street—that's my moral code. And it does help me because I just feel that most people think the way that I do. Occasionally, I'm going to encounter someone who is going to abuse his or her freedom. But if I had this feeling of "doing in" anyone I could, of taking advantage, full advantage, of everyone I meet at every opportunity, then I'd be very unhappy, ultimately because of this selfishness.

There are times in life, even for people who run for political offices and who hold political offices, when one must determine if one is skirting the line on these principles. But then you have to ask yourself, am I being dishonest? When this campaign is over, win or lose, is it going to be on my conscience? And it will be on your conscience if you have misled folks and know darn well you can't deliver. So, I think that it is a matter of adhering to your principles, to the guidelines you normally follow. It's not always easy because you're going to be encouraged from time to time to tip over the line by people who just think you ought to for their benefit—people who supported you—people who claim a close allegiance to you and who expect you to do something for them, and who very often will make you feel obligated. And I think that's where it gets difficult—when your closest friends tempt you! But you have to have a code by which you live; if you don't, you are going to be lost.

DO YOU HAVE ANY THOUGHTS ON SECRETS FOR LIVING A
GOOD AND LONG AND HAPPY LIFE?

Reverend William Work who was the Executive Director of the Lansing Area Council of Churches came to the State Administrative Board, the top administrative body for the state of Michigan, about a month ago and delivered an invocation. He often comes to our meetings. Before we begin our deliberations, we usually have a minister come in and give us some words of wisdom. On one occasion he delivered this prayer; he couldn't find an author for it. I thought people getting along in years might enjoy it.

A PRAYER FOR TODAY

*Lord, Thou knowest better than I know myself that I am
growing older, and will some day be old.*

*Keep me from getting talkative, and particularly from the
fatal habit of thinking I must say something on every
subject and on every occasion.*

Release me from craving to straighten out everybody's affairs.

*Make me thoughtful, but not moody;
helpful, but not bossy.*

*With my vast store of wisdom, it seems a pity not to use it all—
Thou knowest, Lord, that I want a few friends at the end.*

Keep my mind free from the recital of endless details—
give me wings to get to the point.

Seal my lips on my many aches and pains. They are increasing,
and my love for rehearsing them is becoming sweeter
as the years go by.

I ask for grace enough to listen to the tales of others'
pains. Help me to endure them with patience.

Teach me the glorious lesson that occasionally it is possible
that I may be mistaken.

Keep me reasonably sweet; I do not want to be a saint—
some of them are so hard to live with, but a sour old
individual is one of the crowning works of the devil.

Help me to extract all possible fun out of life. There are
so many funny things around us, and I don't want to
miss any of them.

AMEN

I especially like the third line from the last: "Teach me the glorious lesson that *occasionally* it is possible that I may be mistaken."

REFERENCES

Anonymous, "A Prayer for Today." Delivered before the State Administrative Board, Tuesday, February 5, 1980 by Reverend William Hubbard Work, Executive Director, Lansing Area Council of Churches.

"The 100 Most Influential Black Americans," *Ebony* (May 1979), pp. 34–38.

Higginbotham, A. Leon, Jr., *In the Matter of Color: Race and the American Legal Process*, New York: Oxford University Press, 1978.

MORARJI DESAI

MORARJI DESAI became Prime Minister of India at a particularly turbulent time in his country's history. His long experience in government prepared him well for his tenure as Prime Minister in the sensitive months following the ouster of Indira Ghandi from the post.

Born February 29, 1896 in Gujarat State, Desai has been in government service since 1918: Minister of Revenue, Minister of Commerce and Industry, Bombay State; Minister for Finance, Government of India (under Prime Minister Nehru). He has also served as chancellor of Gujarat Vidyapeeth University, Ahmedabad, and of Jawaharl Nehru University. A member of the independence movement of the thirties, his strong commitment to freedom led to imprisonment and detention on a number of occasions.

Desai assumed responsibility for his family (three brothers, three sisters, mother, grandmother) early: he was only fifteen when his father, a teacher, died. Nonetheless, he managed to provide for the family, marry, and obtain his education. Hardship and sacrifice have not been strangers to him.

One warm morning we visited the Prime Minister's residence, a gracious old house known locally as the "P.M.'s bungalow," and were shown into a formal sitting room with floor-to-ceiling win-

23

dows which overlooked a beautiful garden. Desai, a large, soft-spoken man in a white suit, soon arrived to welcome us with a broad smile and an outstretched hand. Shortly, he led us down the hall to his comfortable, well-used study.

WHAT CAN YOU SAY AT THIS POINT ABOUT THE IMPORTANCE OF
THE BASIC FORCES OF LOVE AND HATE IN THE WORLD TODAY?

Well, hate is destructive and love is constructive. Hate hurts even more the person who hates than the person who is hated. Whereas for love it is quite different. Love supports the person who loves and also the person being loved. If man can give up hatred, he can rise to any height, because hatred restricts the ability to think clearly. It does not allow one to think of the good of others.

Hatred is not only of men, but also of things and situations. Whenever one hates, one is not able to maintain an objective point of view. His view is governed by hate and not objectivity. It is very destructive and in no way is it advantageous and, therefore, to be eschewed.

But it is easy to hate and it is difficult to love. This is how the whole scheme of things works. All good things are difficult to achieve; and bad things are very easy to get. Take, for example, dirt. Dirt accumulates if only you close your eyes and do not bother about it. It goes on accumulating. If you want to keep clean, you have to make an effort all the while yourself. The moment you relax, the dirt accumulates. Therefore, one has to cultivate the habit of cleanliness and require things to be kept clean.

The whole difficulty in the world is selfishness. Materialism, a preponderance of materialism. Materialism is necessary for man. I cannot say that materialism is not necessary. Matter does matter because the body is matter and soul is the spirit. If there is no soul left in the body, the body is empty. It has no value. But the spirit is never without value. It has always a value. There is a more lasting value and that is the soul, the spirit, and not the body— that is matter. And yet, the spirit has to function through the body. Therefore, the body has also got to be looked after. But it cannot become the sole concern as it has become at present.

We made our mistake in this country in the reverse way. We think only of spirit and neglect matter. But for ordinary man this concept is too difficult to grasp.

We, therefore, draw inspiration and wisdom from the *Bhagavad-Gita* * which I consider the essence of all wisdom. There is nothing which is not in there somewhere. It is said that the person who understands or who has knowledge, knowledge in the sense that he acts on it and not merely as an encyclopedia, must show it in his life, in his actions. That person should not create a doubt in the mind of the person who does not understand, by giving him all kinds of wise advice on matters that he is not able to grasp. It has no value for him. The one who has knowledge should, by his own example, show him what can be done.

When a teacher teaches through books only, he is not effective, but when he teaches through his life, he is very effective. That is why in our country, education was imparted by teachers who were independent. They never approached the state or anyone else for help. Students maintained their schools, known as Gurukuls, and the students who came, came irrespective of their position in life. For example, Krishna belonged to the ruling family, but he and Sudama, a poor Brahmin, were there on equal terms. There was no difference between them. And they worked for the guru and the guru worked for them, and that is how he imparted knowledge to them. Then the rich and poor left afterwards; they became close friends.

That was the education in those days. We cannot bring it back in the modern world, but we can bring the substance of it. The essence of it we can bring, this relationship between the teacher and the taught, and between the teacher and the govern-

* A Sanskrit dramatic poem forming part of the *Mahabharata*.

ment or society in general. We, therefore, put the teacher at the highest level. We put him in line with God. But if he is like that, then he will be like that. Teachers claim to have that position, but sometimes they don't want to behave like that. That is what is creating the whole problem here in the world. Teaching is a mission because the teacher affects the lives of young people very greatly. Both love and hate are taught and the influence of the teacher is tremendous.

Everything depends upon the ways of life of the teacher and that is what has affected me most. I am the son of a teacher. My father was a teacher of *Anglo-Vernacular* School, teaching from I to IV Standard of English, and he was drawing a very low salary. This was, of course, more than sixty years ago—sixty-seven years now. But he never worried about it, and he never taught me at home. He was equally interested and helpful to every student. He never showed me any special favors.

My father was so independent that he did not get any promotion for six or seven years. His students used to revere him! Even after completing school and being in a good position in life, they wouldn't sit down in his presence. They would stand. That was the respect they showed for him. One of them became the private secretary to the Maharaja of the state, and one day came to see my father and requested him to go to the king with him so that he might get my father a promotion. Father immediately told him, "I depend not on the king, but on God. If He wants to give me a promotion, He will give it to me. I am not going to the king to solve my problems," and he did not go. Once the Maharaja came to inspect my father's school without informing him; a surprise inspection! When he came my father was teaching. Father simply saluted the king and continued his teaching. After a while the king went away, and my father did not see him go off. When his friends asked him why he did not, he said, "He came without telling me, I received him, and he went away without telling me. Why should I go after him? For the students I am more than the king. What a bad example I would have set for them, the students, had I gone after the king!"

WHAT ABOUT THOSE WHO THROUGH LIFE HAVE OPPOSED YOUR POINTS OF VIEW?

I always try to recognize that those who oppose my points of view have also their own views. If in life everyone held the same points of view, I would consider all of them to be idiots. Only idiots will agree on everything! Men with wisdom are bound to have different views on some matters. They may agree on some matters and in others they may disagree. Therefore, when our views are opposite, we should try to understand each other, and if in the process we can come to some agreement, it is better. If I am not convinced about another man's views, then I must go on my own. But then I must also respect him, for this is the only way one should meet an opponent's view. Otherwise, it creates arrogance in one. What right have I to say, "You are wrong and I am right," when you have an equal right to think that you are right and you are not convinced by me. Somehow, when I do not accept the other view, my colleagues say that I am rigid or obstinate. That is the opinion of those who are not able to get what they want from me. They say I am very rigid and very obstinate. But they forget that they would be called rigid by my standards as they do not accept my view.

I met an editor of a newspaper one day who opposed me. I was for prohibition, and he was very fond of the bottle, and he wrote persistently about me, although I was not in office then. Then he came to see me. We were friends otherwise. I asked him, "Why do you call me rigid? What is the definition of rigidity or obstinacy? One can be called rigid or obstinate only if he persists in maintaining his view even when he sees it is not right. Then you can call him rigid or obstinate. But if a man sticks to his own views because he thinks he is right, you can call him *firm* but you can't call him *rigid*." He had no reply to this. "Do you consider me rigid because I believe in prohibition?" I asked him. He immediately saw the point and said, "I am also rigid then because I am anti-prohibition." "When you call me rigid because I have not accepted your point of view, and you have not accepted my point of view, are you not rigid?" He accepted my view and wrote accordingly in the next issue of his paper.

HOW DO YOU FEEL ABOUT GROWING OLDER?

Growing old is nature's law. One cannot say that "I won't grow older." You cannot fight God's law; you must abide by it. The body does become weaker even if it looks all right. Years have their effect on everything in the body, but the mind improves if you lead a clean life. Wisdom is the result of experience and not intelligence. Therefore, when you grow older, you get wisdom. But everybody does not get it. Everybody does not lead a clean life like that ordinarily.

We have a saying in Gujarati: "Sathi Buddhi Nathi," meaning, "At sixty, one loses his sense." That is true only for a person who leads an unclean life. The person who leads a proper life becomes richer by experience, and the mind also becomes better. You may lose your memory to some extent, that is for details, but then you develop a selective memory, and some things you remember much better. So there is a compensation in everything.

The person who tries to follow the truth, to live a truthful life, gets it for himself. But when he forgets that he is growing older and does not adjust, he must pay the price. But there is one phenomenon which has taken place in the world after the last war. This is not noticed by many people. Before the last war, two-thirds of the world was governed by one-third of the world. The two-thirds was in subjugation, and it was an age of submission. Children also submitted to their parents' view. They didn't challenge them. That is what was happening.

After the last World War, things changed. The spirit of dissent has come in because the world has become free. Except for very few countries, the world is free today; nobody is governing anybody, and that has contributed to freedom and spirit of freedom. The spirit of freedom is useless without the right of dissent. If you are not free to dissent, how then are you free? Therefore, the right to dissent now is recognized especially by our young people. They want to dissent. It can become an obsession, however—that one is independent only if he dissents. That should not be the case.

The elders think that they are wiser because they are older. That is also wrong. If they are wiser being older, and better in their thinking because of age, then younger people ought to listen to what they are saying and appreciate it. If they don't agree, then they must do what they like. Thus, the relation between older and younger people should be one of trying to understand each other, trying to benefit each other, and not simply going against each other.

Old people think the young are useless, and the young think that the old are useless because of the generation difference. How can there be anything else except a generation difference between a father and son? Because there is a difference, what is the quarrel between a father and son? There is bound to be a difference because they are father and son. The interests for the welfare of both is the same. If that is borne in mind, then each one will benefit from the other. And therefore, on the other hand, the young man also must respect experience, and he can then do whatever he thinks is right. He need not do what his parents tell him. He must not be insulting. He should say, "I am sorry I cannot do this." Then the relations will be quite normal and natural. This is what we have to achieve, and we can achieve it only through education. The older people must set an example. They must be wise enough to show that they have patience, and are tolerant, and try to understand the points of view of the younger person. Young people are impatient. That is the sign of youth, and there is no real sense of responsibility. Therefore they are bound to act like they do. However, if older people try to behave properly, the young-sters will respond accordingly.

DO YOU HAVE REAL HOPE FOR MANKIND?

I am an incurable optimist! I refuse to give up hope! Under no circumstances have I ever felt even a little despair. I have passed through all kinds of stages. As a young boy, I have passed through a penniless state. I lost my father when I was fifteen. I was the eldest in a family of nine people, and the whole burden was on me. There was not a farthing of income. But I did not give up in despair or frustration. It was at that stage that I had decided not to incur debts and not to beg for help from anybody. If help came, I would take it with gratitude, and with a resolve that I would transfer that help some day to someone else so that I earned it. That has left me without any despair. That has left me with hope. That has left me happy under all circumstances, and I have passed through all kinds of things.

DO YOU BELIEVE IN DIVINE LAW?

My faith in God is complete. I believe that everything happens in accordance with His law; however, it is up to us to make an effort. What happens is in relation to all other things. I believe in the law of action. None can really harm anyone else. None can harm me; none can give me anything. I can get only what I have earned. Whatever actions I have made, I reap the results of them. I cannot avoid them. Every new action is in my hands. I am not helpless in that way. God's law thus leaves me in full volition. As you sow, so shall you reap. That is why we believe in life, birth, and rebirth, a belief that is peculiar to this country. Throughout the world also, some people are beginning to believe it. I say this be-cause of the simple reason and logic that if you believe in God then God is impartial; otherwise he ceases to be God. How can He be kind to one and unkind to another? Why should three children be born differently from the same parents with different capacities? If God is unkind to one and kind to another, then he ceases to be God. Injustice is not enduring and God is enduring.

The universe goes on without any disturbance. If there is any disturbance, we can estimate it, we can know it. It is all according to law. If it is not so, how could a man have gone to the moon? It is because man knows the laws and acts on them. Therefore it is a *law* which is perfect.

I cannot avoid the results of my own actions in the past. They have their own consequences. Any action gives a result of some kind. When you plant one tree, it may give fruit in three years; another in ten years; a third one may give instantaneously; and one may not give at all. All this happens according to some law. Likewise no one can hurt me even if he kills me. For I am supposed to die and that is why he kills me. He couldn't have done that if I were not to have died. Any number of bullets aimed at me will not kill me if I am not to die. We see this in life. For example in war some people get several bullets, but do not die, and some die of shock only. Whatever happens is all according to a law.

I believe that your coming here is according to that law.

ALL THINGS THEN ARE SUBJECT TO LAWFUL EXPLANATION?

That is the only reality. Everything else is destructible. God alone is indestructible, because He is the only truth. Each man has the prerogative to know Him if he exerts himself and tries to know.

We also believe that man and an insect are subject to the same law. Man becomes an insect when he leads the kind of life that befits insect status. After undergoing this he again comes back. It is only as a man he is able to know truth. Man can know the truth; therefore, man is superior, but he does not always behave in a superior way.

Freedom comes only from complete faith in God. That faith gives me freedom from fear and freedom from pessimism along with complete optimism and goodwill for everybody. But it takes time. It took several years for me. I grew greatly in faith when I was detained for nineteen months, because I was alone. People often go mad when they are all alone, but I got wiser and as a result got my passions completely under control.

DO YOU HAVE ANY ADVICE ABOUT ACHIEVING A LONG LIFE, A HAPPY LIFE, A PRODUCTIVE LIFE?

Well, it is of no use to advise anybody. I always believe that advice should never be given unless it is asked for. Anybody who gives advice without its being asked for makes himself look foolish. There is a story about it in the *Panchatantra*.* This is an ancient book here and a storehouse of wisdom. This is copied everywhere, Aesop's fables and others are based on it. It contains a story, showing how advice should not be given unless asked for. There was a monkey who was shivering in the cold as he was sitting under a tree and trying to warm himself by catching fire-worms. He thought he could warm himself by that, though that was foolish.

There was a weaver-bird sitting on the tree nearby under which the monkey was taking shelter, in its fine cozy nest. The small weaver-bird had a very fine nest. The bird saw the monkey and felt compassion and pity, and began to say: "My friend, why are you not doing something for yourself?" "Don't bother," said the monkey as he brushed him aside.

After a time, again the weaver-bird had compassion and began to tell him: "You are stronger than I; your hands and feet are mighty. I have a small, warm nest, and I suppose you can make one also." The monkey, angered by the free advice of the bird, went up and destroyed the nest!

This is what happens when you try to give advice. I read this when I was sixteen years old. That is why I do not believe in

* An ancient collection of Sanskrit fables.

giving advice. But I would only say that young people, if they try to follow truth and try to utilize the great energy which youth possesses for doing good to others and not being selfish, then they would really serve their own selves much better. There will be far more joy and happiness and no frustration. If they lead a life which will be useful to others and not harmful to others, they derive benefit for themselves.

If I keep you happy and smiling, I cannot help but smile. If I annoy you and I try to smile, my smile will vanish. It is only by making other people happy that one ensures one's own happiness. Young people, not having any experience, cannot see this quickly, therefore if they can be given this through education I am quite sure they will grasp it. Nobody wants to be unhappy. Everybody wants to be happy. That is the common trait of all human beings and even animals. But when a person does not know what happiness is, then he reaches out for something which is not happiness. Therefore one should define what happiness is.

Nobody can deny that happiness is a condition inside and not outside. If you have a peaceful mind which is not disturbed by anything, then you enjoy life richly. The world is full of disturbance, but in that whole disturbance you can remain peaceful by trying to exude that peace for other people's benefit. Inner peace. Whatever way you can achieve peace, achieve it! It will be good for you!

Is it more difficult for young people today than in the past?

Life at any time can become difficult; life at any time can become easy. It all depends upon how one adjusts oneself to life. One is not born by one's own volition. It is chosen by one's own karma (actions).

In any condition you can be happy. Even with excruciating pain you can be happy. I have undergone this myself. I had herpes here on my head about six months ago. Herpes you know are very painful. They were on a most vital and tender part. It lasted for about a month. I did not allow anybody to know. I went on doing my work. In the parliament I went on replying. They never realized and they never saw. My own people did not see them for a few days. I didn't tell them. One day I had taken off my cap and they saw the eruptions. Even now there is a little scratching sensation. But that does not worry me. It is a part of my own life and is a result of my own actions.

So sometimes in pain, too, one has to be happy. For what is to happen will happen. Once I had a plane crash. It came all of a sudden. But it did not move my pulse faster. That is how I was literally tested by God. I look at it like that.

This is further exemplified by Ramana Maharshi, whom I met in 1935 when I had gone to see three sages—Aurobindo Ghosh, Ramana Maharshi, and Mahatma Gandhi. I went just to find out what was the attraction of these three people. Now with Ramana Maharshi, I was impressed more because he was a person who was a "realized soul" (at one with God). I sat with him for about an hour. I did not ask him anything and he did not tell me anything. I had no questions in my mind. There was complete peace in his face. I saw a joy which I have not seen on anybody's face. I saw it many times in Mahatma Gandhi, but not to that extent. Then Ramana Maharshi was suffering from cancer and they began to treat him. He must have done something in the past and he had to pass through the bout with cancer. He could not avoid it. Then they operated upon him. When they cut him open, he did not take any anesthesia and he kept on smiling. That is what a man can indeed do. That is in our capacity. It cannot be given by anybody, you have to earn it. If I have to go to America, I have to go myself and cannot go vicariously through anyone else.

I am going away tomorrow for about three days, otherwise I could have met you again. Had you come to the Gandhi celebration at Ahmadabad, I could have met you every day.

WHAT ABOUT THE IMPORTANCE OF FAMILY?

One must go to the purpose of man's life if family life is to be realized in its proper perspective. Man's main purpose in life is, in my view, knowing the truth of life and, for those who believe in God, to know God; that alone can make man a fully perfect man. How is that to be known? Man also has intelligence. He therefore understands that his happiness will be guaranteed and ensured only by guaranteeing happiness to others. If I am in a happy company, I am bound to be happy; I shall not be unhappy. But if I am happy and I make all others unhappy or I am surrounded by unhappiness, my happiness would disappear.

A family is a very closed group. Parents and children have a natural attachment. Therefore, if they learn it, appreciate and develop that attachment properly, that lays a foundation for serving each other, and other people as well. Therefore, family life is of greatest importance. If parents are served and respected by their children, then the children will prove their gratefulness for the kindness shown by the parents, because without the help of parents they could never have grown up.

We had a joint family system where thirty, forty, or even as many as fifty people lived together. Brothers, parents and their sons, parents' brothers and their children, all lived together, and they lived in such a manner that anybody who lived in the family earned according to his capacity. All pooled their earnings; the head of the family saw to that. And all partook of the facilities equally. That is the very best form of communism—a nonviolent communism. When this is truly accomplished one cultivates the spirit of being useful to other people. To my mind, that is the most important aspect of family life. This is natural in this country because we have been brought up in that tradition.

We consider parents as God. If we satisfy our parents fully and worship them in our heart, then and then only do we repay the debt we owe them not only for being brought into this world but also for bringing us up and in so doing suffering many inconveniences.

Children do not grow up without the mother suffering a lot, and the father also exerting much energy because of them. But this is forgotten by the children in your system. Here in India, however, I have found that a son who does not respect his father is not respected by his own son. For the behavior of a child is learned from the parents. If I tell a lie and I ask my son to tell the truth, he will not tell the truth because he will follow what I am doing and not what I am saying.

All this is the result of family life, because good parents realize that they must not do anything which serves as a bad example to the children. Of course, modern life is different and yet the truths are still important.

A family doesn't always remain as a group, but they eventually come back together. Now there is an advantage in that. I lost my father when I was fifteen, and we were four brothers, three sisters, my mother, my grandmother, and my wife. I was married at the age of fifteen—and we did not have any income. But we were brought up in my grandfather's, my mother's father's house. It was a large family. There were about fifteen or twenty of us there. Could this have happened if there had not been a respect for one another? When the family is a solid unit you don't require social-welfare schemes. It manages itself automatically. Therefore, if we reduce the social-welfare schemes and increase the importance of strong family ties, I am quite sure it will help a lot. Human society will benefit a great deal. But this must be done by understanding and not merely by ritual. When you go by ritual it gets broken up.

The strength of family should be taught in schools. Even in the class they then will behave like a family with the teacher. That is the conception of family in this country.

Is communication important?

That is a matter of temperament. It depends again on past life. But it is far better to communicate to others and not to keep anything bound up within oneself. It has got to be conveyed to somebody else, and one is not fair to the other person by restricting communication. What you think and what you say may be very important to his decisions. One must not however try to impinge or impose on the other person; but this again depends on temperament. Some people are more communicative than others. But those who are not communicative suffer from "heart trouble" later on because they go on having tension within, because it doesn't come out. A man who gets angry and bursts out doesn't get "heart trouble." But if a man is very angry and suppresses it instead, he gets "heart trouble." It is the tension which is responsible for this, and tension is the result of suppression within oneself. So one should not engage in suppression, rather one should try to see that he does not think thoughts that must be suppressed. One should have nothing to hide. Then only can you be truthful.

What about fear and anxiety?

Anxiety is mostly a result of fear, and fear is the real enemy of man. But I believe that the largest fear complex is in this country. That is why we are not able to behave as we should behave in our life, because of fear. Fear is most illogical. Reason cannot remove it; only one's own determination and realization can remove it.

I was a coward until I was sixteen. Therefore I know what it is. I could not stay in one room alone. I could not go out after evening alone anywhere, and if anybody told me something I could not say anything to him. I was afraid, afraid of all kinds of imaginary things. However when I lost my father and the whole family burden fell on me, that burden itself took away my fear because I *had* to act for other people. The change in me was unbelievable to many people.

I consider fear the greatest enemy of man. We rule the animal world because animals are afraid. If a horse or bullock realizes that he is stronger than man, can a man drive him? He will drive you! But one must work on his fear, make him afraid, and then you can drive him.

Therefore, when we are afraid, others can drive us. Hence fear has to go. And I have found that fear goes away only when your belief in God is complete.

One may be afraid of losing something. It may be money, it may be reputation, it may be affection, it may be some item, it may be an advantage; but these are all fears, and once one becomes afraid, then he tries to defend himself by any means to get rid of that fear.

Jealousy comes from fear. When a person is not afraid of these things and free from fear and the results of it, he then can arrive at truth. Truth and fearlessness go together. Unless you are fearless, you cannot be truthful, and unless you are truthful you cannot be fearless.

One should not be afraid, even of God. You should not fear God; you must love God! When you are afraid of God, you are also trying to deceive him. That is what fear does. Love removes fear and there is no question of fear.

Abraham Lincoln was the most fearless man as president. It was he who kept the United States together. I put him at times above Mahatma Gandhi. In some matters, not in all matters. Lincoln remained truthful. He accepted office and then remained truthful. Mahatma Gandhi did not want to accept office because he said: "I will have to compromise with truth." I argued with him that if those who believed in truth do not accept office, someone else will fill the office. Government will always be there. Only liars will take the leadership roles, and then what can we expect of that government? Therefore those who want to pursue truth must not run away from it, but pursue it without fear.

Pursuit of truth can prove to be a real test and one might get dirty in the process. If you see a man lying in a pool of mud, how

will you save that man without going inside and getting dirty?
You have to save him. That means go in and get dirty, save him,
and then wash yourself. If you don't go in because you will become dirty, then you won't save the man. You cannot always hope
to keep yourself clean by avoiding things which pollute you. You
can keep yourself clean only if you are clean within. Then you
are clean wherever you are, and the jobs you must do are a challenge to you. In the midst of it all, if you are clean then you are
true, and if you are true there is no need for fear.

One should never run away from a test. One should not invite a test, one should not invite a difficulty, but one should not
run away from a test, because the tests we are called upon to face
determine whether you have really got it or not. We can all claim
that we are very truthful, but the moment a little pressure comes
in, lies begin to creep in. It is only when pressure comes and one
remains truthful that one can claim to be truthful. And in remaining truthful one can successfully combat the fears and anxieties
that are bound to come.

Hardly one in several millions might be able to say that he is
really following truth. This should be explained to the students.
But the students will really learn about truth only when their
teachers set examples.

How important are international affairs to our lives?

There cannot be anything international without there being something national first, and therefore you cannot reduce the importance of nationalism by only preaching internationalism. I will
give you an example. I had a long argument with Mr. Kosygin in
the year 1968 when he visited us here. He began to argue with me
about some remarks about "communist brothers." I said that communists in this country have been divided. One element leans toward China and another toward Russia. He said that those who
lean toward Russian communism are good nationalists. They are
doing good, they are serving the people. I said, "I am sorry. I do

not agree." He said, "Why do you say that?" I replied, "Those individuals think more of Russia than of India. They go by your philosophy and not by ours and thus run counter to true nationalism and internationalism." He said, "How can I believe that?" But I put to him a straight question. I said, "Supposing a circumstance arises in which Russia is hurt and India gains. Will you then say 'Yes, I agree,' or will you first think of Russia or will you first think of India?" He appreciated my point. I said, "We need not be in conflict. But that can happen if I am true to myself. If I am true to my country then I will be true to others. That is why I am against adopting communism in India." He had nothing to say. He made no reply to me.

ARE THERE PEOPLE WHO HAVE INFLUENCED YOU STRONGLY?

My father, my mother, my maternal grandfather, and my maternal grandmother influenced me most in my childhood. Later on I was influenced by Mahatma Gandhi even more. But I was also influenced by people like Vivekananda, and more than that, his guru Ramakrishna Paramahamsa. Of course he passed away in 1885 before my birth, but I read a book on his life that affected me, and that concretized my ideas on religion and on God. That I owe to him. As I mentioned earlier, I have learned a great deal from Abraham Lincoln. There are several people like that from whom I learned several things, but that was only confirmation of what I had already learned. More confirmation comes as I act on what I have learned. I learned the most however from the *Gita*. That is a guide for me.

HAVE ANY PARTICULAR EVENTS LED YOU TO SUCCESS?

Success or failure is the result of your past actions. Efforts are our own. Therefore, whether success comes or failure comes really does not matter to me. What matters to me is whether my efforts have been correct and right.

Maintenance of freedom and success lies within oneself. Nobody can give you freedom or success. Nobody can take it away. One must be prepared to pay the price and that is why one must not be dependent on anything, either a person, or circumstances, house, or food, or anything! It must never be the case that I cannot do without it.

REFERENCE

Desai, Morarji, *The Story of My Life,* vols. 1 and 2, India: Macmillan, 1974.

ARTHUR S. FLEMMING

ARTHUR S. FLEMMING has an ongoing concern for social justice and has lived his life accordingly. Presently Chairman of the United States Commission on Civil Rights, his government service includes posts as Secretary of Health, Education and Welfare, Commissioner on Aging, and Chairman of the White House Conference on Aging (1971).

Born in Kingston, New York, June 12, 1905, he is a graduate of Ohio Wesleyan University and earned his law degree at George Washington University. He has been president of three educational institutions (Ohio Wesleyan, University of Oregon, and Macalester College), has been the recipient of many honorary degrees, and has headed the Oregon Council of Churches and the National Council of Churches in America.

We interviewed the forward-looking Dr. Flemming in his downtown Washington office. A vigorous, charming man who lives very much in the present, Flemming's energy, his sharp, intense glance, charged the pedestrian "government issue" surroundings with a sense of excitement and urgency.

43

How important is the family?

I have no hesitancy in saying that I regard the family as a very important institution in the life of our day and that a good many public issues should be examined to see if they tend to strengthen or tend to weaken the family. I think this is vital to issues in the welfare field. We should deal with them so as to preserve the integrity of the family as an institution and we shouldn't do anything that provides an incentive for the family to break up.

I feel that there is a very real need for government involvement in the welfare field so that it may help maintain the stability of the family. I appreciate the fact that we do have situations where families have been involved in the welfare system for maybe two and three generations, but this is often due to the fact that our society has denied them the opportunity for employment. We are not willing to the extent that we should be to accept responsibility for the fact that we have had practices in vogue or in effect that have resulted in such denials.

Most of the people who are on welfare would much prefer to have the opportunity to be involved in gainful employment, but those opportunities have for a variety of reasons been denied them. This of course is particularly true as far as minorities are concerned. This is one of the reasons why it's very, very important for this country to come to grips in a more effective way than it has with the issue of desegregation of schools, because as long as we have segregated schools, it means that some children and young people are being denied access to the educational opportunities which they need.

I am also a great believer in affirmative programs in the area of employment because unless those programs are developed, and unless they are implemented, a great many of these persons who have been discriminated against in the past will continue to be discriminated against and will not have the opportunity for gainful employment.

Older people are victims of discrimination, too. Many of them would welcome the opportunity for either full-time or part-time employment in order to augment their incomes, and to help them come to grips with the problems of inflation. But we have a great many employers, both public and private, who just assume that when people reach a given age they belong on the shelf and that it is not possible for them to engage in productive endeavors of any kind. I feel that the Age Discrimination and Employment Act is a very important act. I feel that it should be enforced more vigorously and effectively than it has been up to the present time.

The responsibility for the enforcement is about to be transferred to the Equal Employment Opportunity Commission. I believe that this will lead to more vigorous and more effective enforcement. Now of course these older persons are the victims of discrimination too, when it comes to the delivery of services. Congress, of course, tried to come to grips with that in the passage of the Age Discrimination Act of '75 which became effective July first of '79. The Commission on Civil Rights conducted a study in that area, held hearings, in fact. It became very clear to us that a good many services, financed all or in part by the federal government, are denied to older persons solely on the basis of their age.

One illustration is the area of mental health. The literature makes it pretty clear that twenty-five to thirty percent of the people sixty-five and over could profit from mental health services. Take, for example, a community mental health clinic. If you analyze the persons who are served by community mental health clinics, you would find that on an average in the nation as a whole, only three to four percent of them are people sixty-five and over. And we discovered in our hearings that a fair number of administrators of mental health services will justify this on the grounds that they have limited resources and that it is better to invest those limited resources in younger people or middle-aged people than in older people. In our report we took the position that a policy of that kind is in direct conflict with the Judeo-Christian concept of the dignity and worth of each individual. We also said in our report that this factor, which has been identified as "ageism," has worked its way into the administration of programs in very insidious ways. It is true in the administration of educational programs, such as those in the field of continuing education, that persons sixty-five and over get pretty short shrift.

We are already making some progress in challenging ageism in federal employment. Congressman Pepper has provided very effective leadership, and as a result Congress at the last session passed a bill which raised the upper limits of the Age Discrimination and Employment Act from sixty-five to seventy. Except for a few positions, the act eliminated compulsory retirement on the basis of age completely in the area of federal employment. We regard that as real progress.

Some of us have been very much opposed to personnel policies that call for retirement at a given age irrespective of the merits of the case. I often said that they really constitute a lazy person's device for dealing with what could be a difficult personnel situation. If you have a policy of that kind in effect, no one has to make a decision—the calendar will make it for you. If you don't have a policy of that kind in effect, then a person or a group of persons may have to make some rather difficult decisions. But they are decisions that ought to be made. A policy of that kind is in direct conflict with the concept of the dignity and worth of the individual. You can't reconcile the two at all.

For the last few months I have been chairing a national committee on careers for older Americans. We are about to publish a report dealing with some of the basic issues in that area and are also making some recommendations to both the public and the private sectors designed to open up opportunities for involvement on the part of older persons. We all know that noninvolvement leads to mental, physical, and I think spiritual deterioration. In addition to that, if we don't permit older persons to be involved, we deprive the nation of some very unique contributions. We are entitling our report: "Older Americans: An Untapped Resource."

We emphasize that this resource can be tapped and suggest why it should be done.

Older persons do have problems and as Commissioner of Aging for five years, I worked with those problems and I know that there is a lot that remains to be done. But I am afraid people in this country are at the point where, when you use the term "older person," or talk about older people, they think about problems. In reality many of them are a valuable resource.

I feel that we fail to use older persons to the extent that we can and should . . . as trainers, for example. Our top problem at the present time in the employment area is the unemployment of teenage persons and particularly teenage minorities. Many of the teenagers who are unemployed come out of families, going back to our earlier discussion, that for two or three generations haven't known what it is to have someone employed—gainfully employed. Consequently, they are complete strangers to the world of work. Not only do they need training in terms of skills, but they need to be motivated; they need to be brought to the place where they understand the way the world of work actually functions. For example, many of them really don't know what you mean when you are talking to them about reporting to work on time—or being on time for a particular assignment.

That point was impressed on me by the late Walter Reuther, whom I knew very well back in the sixties. We worked together on starting the National Urban Coalition, and at that time the automobile industry was trying to open up opportunities for minorities and young people in minority groups. And he said that they very quickly became aware of the fact that many of these young people just did not comprehend what people were talking to them about as far as the world of work was concerned. So he conceived of the idea of taking some of the older members and having them function as buddies for the younger people.

Initially they went to their homes in the morning to make sure that they were up and ready to go to work, or, if they had a telephone, they called them, but many of them, of course, did not have telephones. And then, they stayed with them, during the course of the day, to help them to make adjustments. Well, the government through CETA (Comprehensive Employment Training Act) is making an investment in the training of these unemployed young people. And once again, who could be of greater help to many of them as trainers or trainer's assistants than the older persons? There are so many opportunities of this kind to tap this resource, and we haven't done a very good job of it as a nation up to the present time.

ARE GOALS IMPORTANT?

All I can say is that as I went through high school, and as I went through college, I had twin interests. One was in government, the other was in the work of the church. And as a practical matter, when I graduated from Ohio Wesleyan, I hadn't yet decided whether I was going to go to law school and in that way find my way into government, or whether I was going to go to theological school and find my way into the ministry.

It wasn't until the summer after I graduated that I decided, initially anyhow, to come here to Washington to pursue a course that I hadn't even thought about a month or two prior to that. I noticed that there was a new undergraduate school that opened up in the fall of '26 at American University and I thought that maybe they might be interested in someone who could coach debate. I had a great interest in intercollegiate debate at Ohio Wesleyan. I wrote a blind letter and got a response saying, yes, they were interested and that if I were interested in pursuing a master's degree, they would compensate me by giving me my tuition. So, I came here and coached debate, took a Master's degree in international law, and wound up staying at American University for about three years. I also taught a course in government during that period.

Then I had an opportunity to go with David Lawrence on what was then the *United States Daily* and is now the *U. S. News and World Report* as a reporter. Actually I had done a fair amount of work in that area. I had worked a year between high school and college as a reporter on my hometown newspaper. And I was a stringer for Columbus papers when I was at Delaware. So I put in five years with him as a reporter and as an editor of a current events publication.

But during that period of time, I decided to go to law school on a late-afternoon-and-evening basis while I was working. And I did it with the intention of going back to New York and going into practice with my father, who had a very attractive practice back there. I thought that doing that would probably open up opportunities for me to run for an elective office and get into the field of government in that particular way. Before I finished my law degree, I was invited to go back to American University to head up their School of Public Affairs. And that's what introduced me to the field of education.

One of the programs, in fact the main program I developed was one designed to help train government people in personnel administration and in organization and management. As a result, I was thrown into contact with the key people who were working in the field of personnel administration. So in 1939 a vacancy occurred on the Civil Service Commission and my name was suggested to President Roosevelt. He decided to appoint me to that post. That started me on my government career and, as you gathered, from there on out, I've just kind of shuttled back and forth between governmental administration and educational administration.

I maintained my two interests all through my life. I have always been active as a layman in the Methodist church and I have always tried to participate to a very considerable degree in the life of whatever local church I was associated with at any given time. Then as time went on, I became interested in the ecumenical movement. When I was still on the Civil Service Commission, Charlie Taft, who was then the president of the old Federal Council of Churches, asked me if I would become the first chairman of the Department of Church and Economic Life of the Federal Council of Churches. I agreed to do so. And that introduced me to that particular area and led to my being elected a vice-president of the National Council of Churches when it was created in the early 1950s. Then when I came back into government, I couldn't give as much time to that activity. But in the sixties I went back to the National Council of Churches as the first vice-president and then later became president. I have tried to work at that other interest of mine all the way through. I have found it to be very helpful and very rewarding, and obviously there has also been an interrelationship between my two areas of interest.

Have any writers been important to you?

Well, it's hard to single out any particular ones. Obviously, I have done a good deal of reading in the field of government. I suppose I could go back a good many years and say that Dr. Leonard White, who was the first professor of public administration in the country and served at Chicago University, and who was one of my predecessors on the Civil Service Commission, influenced me quite a bit in that area. So did Charles Merriam, who was one of the leaders in those days in political science.

But it is more the general reading I have done that has had an impact on me. I've done some reading in the field of government, and I have always read a good deal in the field of religion. I have been influenced by various people in the area of religion. I've always been very much interested in the unique role that Norman Peale has carved out for himself because, as you know, he is a graduate of Ohio Wesleyan. When I was president there, he was on the board and we were very close friends. At the same time, of course, Ralph Sockman, another graduate of Ohio Wesleyan, was on the board and he was having an outstanding ministry in New York at Christ's Methodist Church. And then there were Methodist ministers whose writings influenced my thinking a good deal. The fact of the matter is the people that hear me speak know that quite often I will go back to sermons that have been preached on the text "Thou shalt love thy neighbor as thyself," and which stress the fact that this commandment doesn't obligate us to like our neighbor because that's a feeling that's got to come from within— we can't be commanded to do that. It clearly doesn't obligate us to approve of everything that our neighbor says or does. But, it places upon us a common responsibility never to pass up an opportunity to help our neighbor achieve her or his highest potential.

When I was Secretary of HEW I was responsible for a White House Conference on Children and Youth, and I was responsible for the first White House Conference on Aging. When I gave the closing address at both of those conferences, that was my starting point. And when I gave the closing address at the second White House Conference on Aging in 1971, that was again my starting point. I know that I have tried to apply that interpretation of the commandment very, very frequently as I have taken a look at issues that confront us in the economic, the social, and the political realms.

HOW DO YOU FEEL ABOUT GROWING OLDER?

I think it is very, very exciting, and I really enjoy every minute of it. I think it's something that people should look forward to. I hope that our society can get itself organized in such a way that people really *can* look forward to it. I appreciate that I have been fortunate. I'm in my seventies and have had the opportunity for continued involvement in a significant way; not all people have that kind of opportunity. I really think that *that* in many respects is the most serious problem confronting us. Because, as you probably know, the statistics show that on an annual basis, the suicide rate for persons sixty-five and over is very high. And I have often felt that there was a correlation between that and slamming the door in the older person's face and saying, "You're through." Whether it's through a compulsory-retirement policy or in some other way—there are so many ways that society has for getting that message across.

Of course, as I talk with my fellow older persons, I say that I'm going to do everything that I can to try to get society to open up an increasing number of opportunities for involvement. Then I say, but when these opportunities open up, as older persons, we must take advantage of them. And I point out that it's very easy for older persons as well as any other group of persons to adjust to society's stereotypes. If society says that at sixty-five you're supposed to go on the shelf and rock in front of the television set, a lot of people are very apt to adjust to that particular stereotype. Once they have made that adjustment, they really don't realize what is happening to them and it's hard for them to get out of that kind of rut.

Then, I'll illustrate that in a couple of ways. I'll say that I've heard older persons in the church when approached and asked to do something, say, "Look, I've done that. Let a younger person do it." Whenever an older person says that, that older person is contributing to the stereotype. Then I also say that I've read the parable of the judgment a good many times and its command to take care of those who are hungry, and those who need clothing, and those who are in prison, and those who are ill, and I have yet to find anything in it that says we're to pay attention to it *only* until we are sixty-five that after we're sixty-five we can forget about it. It seems to me it's an obligation or a responsibility that stays with us until the last day of life.

But involvement is the key; we need to prepare to continue to be involved. I mean we need to do whatever it is necessary to do to ensure that we are going to continue to be involved in life in a significant way. Now this may mean we want to plan for and prepare for a new type of career—and a new career doesn't necessarily have to be in full-time or paid employment. If older people want to volunteer to do it, because of the satisfaction that comes from a regular, systematic involvement in a worthwhile type of activity, we should make it possible for them to contribute. And of course, the organizations that depend on volunteers are just as apt to be guilty of ageism as employers—public or private. They are just as apt to overlook this resource that older persons represent.

My contention is that if an older person is interested in pursuing a new career, that older person should have available counseling, training, and placement resources. We have no doubt in our minds these days that as people plan for a first career, they should have the benefit of these services. I feel that when persons plan for second or maybe even third careers, they should also have the benefit of these services. And unless society makes that kind of investment, it isn't going to get the return from this resource that it should get—or could get. But you take our educational institutions, typically they don't make very much of an investment in either counseling, training, or placement for older persons.

I think in many respects our institutions of higher education are the worst sinners in this area of dealing with older persons because they have had these compulsory-retirement provisions, and they've enforced them vigorously. And so often they have done it in a very-coldblooded way. Many of them have not even continued to provide office space, secretarial help, or anything of that kind. The retired member of faculty can just feel that he is out—that he is not a part of the operation any longer.

Just think of the role retired faculty members could play in the whole area of counseling. Of course, many of them could still be teaching their favorite course and so on, but they are needed as counselors also. This brings us back to this concept of bringing the older person back to help younger persons. The Edna McConnel Clark Foundation made a grant out in Los Angeles to get a program under way in which older persons serve as teacher aides in the Los Angeles Public School System. And of course, those older persons are thrilled with the opportunity and the public school system is just overjoyed with the kind of results they're getting. Older persons are often able to relate to some of the younger people in a way that the younger or middle-aged teacher finds difficult. I mean there's so much that can be done along this line with and for older persons.

You take most of our educational institutions—they could use additional counselors. I realize they don't have enough financial resources. But think how they could supplement their counseling programs with the use of older persons—sometimes on a paid basis, and sometimes on a volunteer basis. We don't even give the older person a real opportunity to volunteer her or his services to the educational institutions that he or she served for forty years or so. We don't get organized in such a way because if you're going to get volunteers, you've got to be very specific about what you want them to do. You've got to provide staff support and so on. And here is a resource that every educational institution in the country has available to it. It's an untapped resource.

WHAT HAS BEEN YOUR GREATEST SOURCE OF STRENGTH WHEN YOU WERE IN NEED?

I have always put a great deal of emphasis on spiritual growth and development and I feel that that is very, very important.

DO YOU THINK THAT YOUNG PEOPLE HAVE A MORE DIFFICULT TIME TODAY, GIVEN THE SHIFT IN STANDARDS AND MORALITY?

It's hard for me to generalize between now and then. They may be confronted with some problems to a greater degree than young people were fifty or sixty years ago, but it seems to me the same basic issues confronted people as they were growing up in the twenties as confront them today. Now there are different manifestations of those issues, and the way they confront people today in contrast with then may differ somewhat. But I feel that the opportunity of seeking for and discovering the spiritual truths is present today just as it was fifty or sixty years ago. Those opportunities may manifest themselves in a little different way now. I happen to be active in the Foundry, United Methodist Church where the pastor is Ed Bauman. For twenty-one years he has had a television ministry, too. As I listen to him and as I notice reactions, including those of our own grandchildren, it seems to me that the opportunity that they have of listening to him, of being taught by him is equal, and probably may be even somewhat greater than some of the opportunities that we had some years ago. This minister has profited from the scholarship of the last fifty years, and it is reflected in his presentation. But he is still dealing with basic truths, and applying them to today's issues. He may have different issues to which he is applying these truths.

Of course, I'm now nine years away from the campus, as I left Macalester in '71. I spent seven years at Oregon and three years at Macalester, and that was a fairly hectic period as far as the educational world was concerned (from '61 to '71). However, I didn't leave the campus after those ten years with any feeling of pessimism at all. I had what I regarded as great experiences with the student leaders and I was very positive in my convictions as to the contributions they were going to be able to make to life. And I'm living long enough to know that some of those feelings were correct. I'm watching them make those contributions.

I'm wary of making generalized statements about now and then. In fact I think the older I get, the more I'm inclined to stay away from generalizations. I'd much rather deal with specific situations. Of course in the field I'm working in now, the civil rights field, I find that you're constantly combatting generalizations which are not supportable. But that's hard to get across to people: the fact that they are not supportable.

HELEN HAYES

NOW over eighty, Helen Hayes, America's "First Lady of the Theatre," is still busy, still involved, even though she says she is retired. Her theatrical career is part of the collective memory of generations of theatregoers—her name went up in lights when she was twenty-one, and by that time she had already appeared in many productions to high praise.

She starred in such plays as Dear Brutus, Mary of Scotland, Victoria Regina, Mrs. McThing, Skin of Our Teeth *and* Harvey. *Her performance in* The Sin of Madelon Claudet *earned her the Best Actress Award from the Motion Picture Academy of Arts and Sciences. She has been president of the American National Theatre and Academy, honorary president of the American Theatre Wing, and holds honorary degrees from Hamilton College, Smith College, Columbia University, and Princeton University.*

Miss Hayes, dressed in a cream shirtwaist dress, greeted us one summer day at the door of her lovely white frame house in Nyack, New York, the home she shared with her husband, playwright Charles MacArthur. We sat down to talk in a charming living room which overlooks a gently terraced descent to the Hudson River.

We chatted about changing times, old-fashioned ways and

wisdom, and the seeming need of each generation to invent and
reinvent the wheel.

On wisdom

I have always felt that the Orientals had a lot more wisdom than
we in their relationships with the various ages because they have
had ancestor worship, which I suppose is wrong, but we have
youth worship and that's just as wrong, isn't it—to go overboard
in either direction. However, I was disheartened to see that the
Orient is now fighting against this reverence for the elderly—did
you know that? They are breaking down this whole tradition and
I think it's a shame because when I was in Korea, and I spent a
month there in the early sixties—in Seoul, I was impressed with
their sense of respect for and reliance upon the elderly for a lot
of things. I'm sorry that it's going out because now this will make
it harder for us to reestablish that relationship between youth and
age where both ages can contribute something.

You are very lucky to be teaching this era of youth instead
of mine because we were a frivolous lot. When I was young, we
really were not as thoughtful and as penetrating in our thoughtful-
ness as these young people today.

You see, I don't think it is the real youth that is opposed to
or disregards the elderly today, because I find that young people
are forever asking me for help and advice and even just to meet
me. I went out, for instance, to Notre Dame to receive the Laetare
Medal—that's their highest award, you know. And it's a ram-
bunctious graduating class there. They're mad!

Gracious, I was surprised—I had never seen this before. I love
it because I think it's great fun, and I think they should enjoy their
big moment. All the other universities take commencement so
seriously. Well, the ovation they gave me, these youngsters, and I
thought, how do you know who I am? You couldn't possibly really

be connected with me except in the sense that my name rings a bell and you think that your mothers or somebody might have known about me. But youth is really paying attention to the elderly now. Thank the Lord!

How important is the family?

Family? I think it's all-important, but that's a big generalization, isn't it? However, I have to qualify that after I've made such a bold statement. I have two grandchildren who have grown up in a broken family. My daughter-in-law walked away when they were both very young—which is a thing that's happening now more and more. My son was heartsick. Oh, to have his children taken from him—it was just heartbreaking. He said to me, "Mom, I don't know what I did, I don't know what I did. I didn't do anything wrong." But they just want something different from what they have, and I don't understand the girls today, the young women. However . . .

It seems epidemic. I was just in California and what do they do when a thing gets epidemic, really unbearable? They form a committee! So they formed a committee to look into this situation because eight out of every nine marriages break up in California. Can you believe it? Eight out of every nine break up, so there you are.

A sense of family was there with me within the past. I had family, you see. My grandmother lived with us and sometimes my mother was impatient with the idea of Graddy* saying, "Now what time will you be back and what time will you come in?" "Mother, I don't know!" You know, that sort of thing, but those are superficial irritations and they don't alter the fact that it's a unit and it's an important thing to have that. And of course, it was

* Miss Hayes writes in her autobiography that in the days when she grew up, grandmothers were always available for extra duties. She goes on to say that ". . . Graddy looms large in the first scenes of my childhood. Everything about Graddy Hayes was warm and safe and loving."

heaven for me because I had my grandmother and she was so important to me.

However, I meant to clarify the qualification I made about this—my bold statement that the family is all-important. My grandchildren, my grandson is now eighteen, and my granddaughter, fourteen. He has finished his first year at the University of Denver. He is a fine young man and I couldn't be happier than I am with him, and so is she, a lovely girl of fourteen. And they grew up in this crazy, broken-home atmosphere where they lived from the time my daughter-in-law walked away with them. They have lived in nine different homes. Nine homes—in ten years. That's a lot, perhaps it was a little longer than ten years, possibly eleven. And then I have a goddaughter who grew up in the same terrible, (what seems to us terrible) situation. She is so strong and self-reliant. I think maybe it is like throwing the child into the water and making it swim. I think children get thrown into life and they just have to do something about it—have to find a way to get through it. I guess it perhaps has to do with whatever they are made of inside.

But I have seen some children, oh, I don't know how many, of course, my profession has long been practicing divorce as a way of life, unfortunately, but I've seen a lot of children—divorced children, of divorced marriages—who come out strong.

The family is all-important because it's a joyous recollection and it's a strengthening one, I think. I'm strengthened. I've been strengthened by crises in my life, by the recollection of my family and of the way we got through suffering and loss and so on. I had a model to follow in that.

Do you feel encouraged by what you see in the world today?

You'll never get me to say I'm discouraged about the human race. I believe in the human race and I think it's going to weather all kinds of setbacks. As for the forces of hate and the forces of love—

there are more forces of hate, I suppose, or else they are just more noticeable. God knows you cannot look at a newspaper without feeling that there is something very much more, ah, much vaster than anything I ever saw in my youth or dreamed of, but the world is much more populated. It's much more crowded, and we have, of course, the same old clichés. We have better communications, and we hear more than we did when I was young. So I don't suspect that the situation has worsened having read what it was like in Barbara Tuchman's *A Distant Mirror*, about the calamitous fourteenth century, the Middle Ages. My gracious, it's too bad that we are not farther ahead of that than we are, but we are somewhat ahead of it—we have come a little ways. At least people protest the lack of humane treatment of their fellow man. People do mind it and hate to see it on the news. But it still does happen.

ARE GOALS IMPORTANT?

I think they are all-important too, like family. I think it's tremendously important for people to set goals. I think to drift along and just take what comes and pray that it'll get better all the time, that you will get better and better things, I think that's, well, it's like gambling your life, isn't it? It's like shooting the dice. I prefer to *invest* in myself rather than gamble.

DID YOU HAVE ASPIRATIONS FOR YOURSELF?

Yes. Well you see, it grew upon me. I didn't have to yearn to get on the stage. I didn't have to yearn to get roles or to advance in my profession because all of this happened automatically. I must have been very good when I was little because every time I did anything I was seen by someone, or, someone in the company promoted me. I was being promoted by people who saw me all the time so I didn't ever have to go out and struggle to advance. It just happened. And you know that I was the youngest star in the history of the American theatre—at twenty-one my name went up.

Now they become stars earlier than that. But at that time I was the youngest star ever to come along.* Now, end of autobiography. What I had set in the way of goals was not the achievement of a place in the theatre to get my career going. My goal had to be to be the best I could in this career which was handed to me on a silver platter.

But I had goals, and I couldn't bear not to be the best I could, and you know that that very same passion and fixation about perfection and the best I can reach—excellence is the word I'm looking for, not perfection, because I don't suppose anybody could aim for that, or get near it, but excellence—that passion has caused me to retire now from work because I haven't been satisfied with what I've been doing since I've been on the screen. I don't like myself. I don't like what I see and it isn't what I've aimed to do. I just never did learn how to do what I found acceptable on the screen. I never learned it. Started too late, perhaps.

The legitimate theatre? I did reach that goal once or twice, and a fine thing it was and a happy moment in my life. But when I had to leave the legitimate theatre, I tried to make do with films— I can't do that anymore because that isn't what I want.

The film I did with Fred Astaire† I liked. That came closer than anything else I've done in this second career I took up when I went on the screen at the age of seventy, or whatever it was. That was all right, that one. So I decided to stop there. I haven't done anything since except for one little thing for PBS,‡ but that's for a cause, not performance as such.

But anyway, I started learning after I became a star. I started taking drama lessons, singing, voice lessons, posture—I worked like

* Miss Hayes first appeared on stage at age six.

† Miss Hayes and Fred Astaire starred in a film called *The Upside-Down Family* for commercial television. The story was about an old man who had a serious heart attack and the couple's struggle to maintain their independence.

‡ *Miles to Go before We Sleep.*

a crazy thing from about the time I was twenty-one. I started taking all these courses.

Somebody said to me once that there is no limit to what you could do if you were six inches taller or whatever he said. And he told me in no uncertain terms that I was limited by my size. Well, I wouldn't acknowledge a limitation so I just aimed at being tall, and I finished playing the tallest queen in history, Mary Stuart, Mary of Scotland, you see. I just would not be a cute, little ingenue, you see.

How do you react to people who oppose your points of view?

I get frustrated and flustered and often very unpleasant, I think. I'm nervous about fighting for things. As I told you earlier, I didn't ever have to fight for things. So, when I have a point of view that differs, I get excited and frantic. But of course I would advise someone else to keep a cool head. And first learn everything they can—the two sides, or the other sides—however many sides—it might be octagonal—of the situation. Try to fathom, try to peek at all the sides. That's hard to do. I try it, but I don't know whether I've made it.

How do you deal with loss?

Well, mine is a very personal thing. I don't know how I could pass it along, but I'm just fortunate in believing in an afterlife. I just believe in it. I once listened to a priest—he strengthened me so in my belief because I didn't feel sure that I had the right to have such a belief—or to take for granted that I was right—say that he had been discussing life after death with a young man. The young man said, "Oh, Father, there is no use in my trying, I can never believe as you do in life after death because I don't have your faith." And the priest said to him, "But you do, you have a very strong faith. You have a faith in your belief that there is no life after death. I have a faith in my belief that there is." Isn't that interesting?

Well, that strengthened me. I thought I choose to believe this and I shall have faith in my belief. Now, once you have convinced yourself that that is possible—I don't feel bereft. I don't feel that my Mary is all that far from me or all that inaccessible to me and I often think about her. She is there in my mind all the time. I see her in my mind's eye every minute. And as for Charlie, I laugh with him as much as I did when he was here. All of them—all of the people who have left me through my life, I have them with me.

I learned another thing—I learned most of my things, any wisdom I have, from other people—we should all pass it on to each other: a mother came to see me who had lost a child with polio soon after Charlie and I had lost our daughter from polio. She asked if she could talk with me. I was a little reluctant—I just hated to go through the torture of it. But she helped me so. She gave me such strength because she told me, when I asked how she was getting on, "I'm all right, I'm getting on all right, but my husband is having a bad time because he keeps saying, 'Why should it happen to us' and I keep saying, 'Why shouldn't it happen to us? Why should we be chosen out of everybody else in the world to be spared? Nobody else is.' " And you know if you accept that, that you give your love, your whole heart to a mortal being, you have to accept that it's going to end sometime—on earth.

As YOU LOOK BACK INTO YOUR LIFE, WHO HAS INFLUENCED YOU?

Oh, the people who have influenced me—I have been influenced by so many. Of course, the most active one about influencing me careerwise was my mother. Because all of her dreams, all of her yearnings became realities in me and she really guarded me and my career. And she guided me toward that aim for perfection—that aim for excellence that has bedeviled me and dogged me all my life.

It's kept me from ever resting on my laurels, and she aimed me toward that. She was tireless and she had good taste. That's the best thing of all—she really had good taste. And she left me with some little sayings that were quite wonderful.

I remember, after I had achieved stardom (or had it thrust upon me—that's what really happened, it was thrust upon us), that my mother resented it because she didn't think it was good for me to have my name in lights that early. The producer refused to listen to her and that was that—she couldn't do anything about it. "Helen," she said (she heard me complaining about something to do with the director or some other person who was creative in the production), "Helen, you let the lighters light, and the writers write, and you act—that's your job."

I never did fuss around with those things and try to interfere with the design of the costumes. I was always a costume designer's delight because I never told them how to design my costumes.

I'm an actress and they are specialists in their field. And they were chosen to work in whatever I was appearing in. They were chosen because they were excellent in what they did, so I let them do it. But that's something my son and I were discussing about Pacino last night. I read aloud from the *Times* the terribly heartbreaking review of *Richard III*. This young man had been a great success in *The Godfather*, Al Pacino. Well, he came back and worked in a play and showed that he is a bona-fide actor—not just a screen personality, but a real actor. I forget what the play was, but he did it last year in New York. Now he comes in with Shakespeare—as director, star, and producer, I think, and it's not good. This man on the *Times* said if only a director had been there to help him.

Isn't that too bad? Isn't that sad? It's a—my son and I were discussing that—it's a very fine line into being too malleable, being too giving and too open to suggestion. One can try to do too much, and there it is—it just defeated him.

My mother influenced me to just rigidly stay in my own field, and to accept help. Oh yes, I like to accept help. I don't give in on some of my ideas, but I like help. My mother was a help, then, and I worked with a series of great stars in my profession who were very fine, very good, and very intelligent. I must say that was one thing we had over the present day. These were great ladies and gentlemen, but that's kind of old-fashioned talk, ladies and gentlemen, isn't it? Out of fashion.

But William Gillette, for instance, opened up Mark Twain for me. He had been a friend of Mark Twain's when he was young. William Gillette, who wrote the play *Sherlock Holmes* and another called *Secret Service*, was a great matinee idol of his day. And I played with him when I was a girl—played his daughter in *Dear Brutus*. Oh, he opened up the whole of Mark Twain to me. And before that, when I was a young girl of eleven or twelve, John Drew opened up Kipling because he thought I would enjoy Kipling's jungle stories.

Someone else opened up Conrad, Joseph Conrad—and Emerson, a producer gave me Emerson. The first producer I ever had gave me O. Henry, and I learned New York from O. Henry. And New York can't ever phase me. I know it's kind of run-down and dirty now and I know people say, "Oh, this dreadful city," and they get no pleasure out of New York. But I have the pleasure out of New York that I first learned from O. Henry's stories, and there are traces, many traces of it left. And it still has a heart as O. Henry said. There is a heart in New York. And I like it for that.

So all of these people—producers, stars, my mother, my grandmother, and my dear father were very influential in my life. My dear father taught me such patience and delight in small things. He delighted in so much—just going out to hunt for black walnuts in the autumn. I look back on that with great joy. . . . and going out and cutting the first arbutus in the spring and all of these things my father loved, and I loved them along with him—and going to baseball games on a weekend.

Everybody just poured treasures into my life.

How do you feel about growing older?

Um, I did that, I haven't got much farther to go, have I, unless I join the centenarians? I'm eighty now.

Yes, I am eighty, and I know it all the time. I know it in my knees, when I rise from a chair, I don't sp-p-r-ring up as I once did. I don't regret my eighty years because they have given me an opportunity to be around at a wonderful time in our country's life. I lived in Washington as a child, as you may have read in my book, and that was a city of such peace and charm in those days and even now it's an exciting city. I like it for what it is today. But I love to remember it when it was charming and peaceful.

I have a lot of memories. I can sit for a long time and not be at a loss because I have those memories. I'm never bored because I have those. I heard a wonderful story the other day, and I've been practicing it—about a man who was an admiral, I think, in the Navy Air Force—or captain, captain.

He was captured—the longest-held prisoner in North Viet Nam. He was the longest in prison. And for two-and-one-half years when he first went in he was in solitary confinement and he spoke to no one. His cell was so small that he couldn't move about at all. And he was just a thing sitting there—just a thing. And someone asked him (someone who had met him reported this to me) how he got through that. He said he began back with the first memory he could conjure up and went through his whole life, over and over, to see if there were another thing he could remember—all through those first two-and-a-half years—right through his life, everything he could remember from the first thing to the present. And it kept his mind alert and alive and kept him from going mad. Isn't that amazing? Well, Alfred Lunt told me when he had lost his eyesight and he could no longer enjoy watching the television which he had taught himself to enjoy (because it's not— it wouldn't have been Alfred's taste), he said, "You know, Helen, I just sit like an idiot remembering." And he said, "The idiot part of it is that I giggle all the time and people would be alarmed walking in and seeing me chuckling to myself." He said, "I thought of something to do with you the other day, and I was laughing heartily out loud—I don't know what it was—when we played together." However, this is a common thing that happens as you get older, that you can call upon that store of memories. And it's very nice. So it's a good thing when you are young to make some good memories, isn't it? It's a wise thing.

An awful lot of young people, at least the ones that make the newspapers, seem to be trying to blot out memories. They are trying to pull a veil across their lives by going into unreality or fantasy. I don't understand this, so that's why I think it's time that somebody advises them that they'll find very good use for those memories in the attic trunks of their minds. But aside from that, this sounds awfully righteous, but it's just practical—I think it's practical, not just righteous, storing up for the future things that you are proud of having done, not only in your work, but also in your relationships with those with whom you come in contact. Just be happy, do things you will be happy to remember such as "I did this for her" or "I did this for him," and it's a nice feeling.

Is it more difficult for young people to cope with life today?

Yes, I think so. They have been given a lot more responsibility. They have the earlier vote, they have—decisions have come much earlier to them, and competition is much stronger. There is fierce competition now in the world. And I think that those who stumble and those who don't get through the harshness of growing up and developing in today's world, I think that we shouldn't be too hard on them. I don't think we should condemn them because it's a difficult world to grow up in because of its being so crowded. I don't think it's that our morals or anything else have deteriorated to too great an extent, but it's just mobs—and especially youth has to contend with all these crowds of young contemporaries.

I suppose that if I knew anything about statistics, I would probably know that churchgoing has fallen off, that there is a deterioration of moral fiber. I suppose that's so. But then you have to say, well, what's moral and what isn't? I happen to believe a certain thing is moral, but I don't know that that proves that it is. I don't believe in people living together—these young people living together without marriage, because I don't think it's just entirely moral. I think it's very bad for people to deny responsibilities. I think if you are going to have the advantages of a mate, you jolly well ought to take the responsibilities of it. And I think that's important to your whole fiber.

DO YOU HAVE ANY SECRETS FOR ACHIEVING A LONG LIFE, A HAPPY LIFE, A PRODUCTIVE LIFE?

No, I don't. I just bumble along, singing a song. What was that old song? Well, I don't know. I'm not—well, I don't have any philosophy to speak of. I've never worked at having one anyway. Some little stray bits have probably planted themselves in my mind, but I just do the best that I can, and I don't know anything else to do about it.

And as for having a long life, I have never worried about the length of my life—really, I haven't. I distress my companion by saying, for instance, well, I nearly got on that plane. Yes, that fatal plane. I was staying with Lynn Fontanne and I was due to leave on Thursday, the day before the crash of the American flight number 191 to Los Angeles from Chicago. I was up at Genesee Depot with Lynn and she wanted me to stay over one more day. She is alone up there. And I said, "Lynn, it's coming on to the Memorial Day weekend, and it'll be too crowded—they'll never let me get on that Friday plane." Well, she said, "Don't you want to try, don't you even want to try?" And that did it. I just had to try. So, I phoned and they said no, they couldn't possibly let me on.

But now I believe I'm here for some good purpose. I don't know what it is—maybe this interview. But when we all stopped shaking, poor Lynn was phoning here to Nyack, and phoning Los Angeles, saying, "Oh, what did I do? I tried to kill you." I know she was really upset, poor soul, and my companion was shaking when Lynn had called her here and said I tried to get her on that plane. Yes, Vera began to shake. (Miss Hayes's companion is a charming lady called Miss Vera.)

Then I said, "Now look everybody, after eighty glorious years and about two seconds, maybe, and it's all over." What's wrong with that? Well they all think that's terrible of me, but I don't think it is. I don't think you should try to live forever—who cares to live forever? People are so frightened of the adventure of death. And I rather look forward to anything new.

Well, death is part of life—one can't deny it. And then people who fight age—who try to erase the physical look of age. I've just come from Los Angeles where everybody looks the same as they did thirty–forty years ago. It's unbelievable! They've all had face-lifts and all kinds of things, you know. And my contemporaries looking many years younger than I. And I think, well, does it make you feel any better inside? I don't know.

I sound awfully perfect. No, I'm telling you my philosophy, but I'm not telling you I always follow it. And I said I didn't have any philosophy, so I'm not telling you my philosophy. I'm telling you what I'd like to do and how I'd like to be.

But I have read of people who will tell you and be able to put in very concise and very clear terms how they have worked out their lives and how they feel about the pattern of life—how to create the good life. I don't think I know anything about that. I mean I don't think I consciously have said, now this is the way I'm going to do it. I really haven't. But I do know that certain things I shun—like trying to keep young and trying to fool the world about my age and fearing death, because I think that only came into our lives in the Victorian era. For a long time, you know, death wasn't all that spooky. It was when Queen Victoria went into that long mourning for Albert that everything got changed. People began to wear lockets with their lost one's hair in them and the whole thing became sort of heavy and strange and mournful. But before that I think we were more wholesome in our attitudes.

It is a short journey through this world, relatively short, and why waste any of it worrying about bad things. I don't want to be a Pollyanna, and I want to be angry about some things that I feel I should be angry about—and I can be angry, like the Irish. But I think to waste time by trying to cover up your age and cover your mortality or pretend that you are not aging is futile and it's time-consuming. Not for me.

I've wished sometimes that I had lived in Korea because I was so impressed there that the elderly go into gray garments. They wear these beautiful, long gray garments and well, sort of witches' hats with pointed crowns and big brims. That is the uniform of the elderly. Sometimes when I go out shopping and all the clothes are made for the young, slender figures, and I'm trying to get something that I can put on, I wish to heaven that we were all in a uniform after fifty—or even earlier. They have kept us alive longer, and they had jolly well better accommodate us. Yes, with fashions and all kinds of things.

Thank goodness I have had the common sense to realize that my losses and my unhappinesses were not remarkable—they weren't greater than anybody else's. It's just that when you are famous these things are unknown. I remember when I went out for a walk—when I went out for the first time in public after Mary died, and I was walking down the street. As people went by me all looking bright and going about their business, their lives, I looked and I thought, I wonder how many of you have gone through what I'm going through now. And once I thought that, I thought, Damn it! You've come through it and you're walking, and you're going about your business. . . .

REFERENCES

Hayes, Helen, with Funke, Lewis, *A Gift of Joy*, New York: M. Evans, 1965.

Hayes, Helen, with Dody, Sandford, *On Reflection: An Autobiography*, New York: M. Evans, 1968.

Hayes, Helen, with Loos, Anita, *Twice over Lightly: New York Then and Now*, New York: Harcourt Brace Jovanovich, 1972.

MAGGIE KUHN

THE founder and leader of the Gray Panthers, advocates for the aging, Maggie Kuhn is herself a dynamo. Forced to retire in 1970, she has dedicated herself ever since to overcoming ageism.

Kuhn worked professionally for the YWCA and for twenty-five years with the Presbyterian Church. Now she serves, too, as liaison for various agencies and the Gray Panther Movement: National Hospice Board, The Memorial Society of Greater Philadelphia, and the Senior Services Law Center in Boston.

One fiercely hot, muggy day we went to see her in Germantown, Pennsylvania. We had to wait a bit; she was having a visa photograph taken—a trip to Australia was in the offing.

We were greeted by her "family of choice"—her secretary, and a young couple, both graduate students. We waited in her office and sipped iced tea and chatted.

A breathless Maggie appeared, sank into her desk chair, and though her appearance suggested she was delicate, even fragile, the strength and energy of this tiny woman who travels some 100,000 miles a year on lecture tours soon became apparent.

WHAT IS THE IMPORTANCE OF THE FAMILY?

Well, I feel that the family is very, very important—that the family has certain built-in interrelationships and support systems that are necessary to the survival and well-being of people of all ages. I've been very much interested in the rather recent development of family history. You know there is a person, Tamara Harevan, who teaches at a university in Worcester, Massachusetts, who has done some very interesting work in tracing the development and the social and societal changes affecting the family. She is a very interesting woman and has written good stuff. I was in a conference with her and was very impressed with the work she was doing. There are vestigial remains of the extended family that we overlook, and there is a good deal of evidence that families still—that family members, those that are still alive, keep in touch with each other. And the family has turned to its members (even though people may not live under the same roof) for different kinds of help—for counsel, for financial help, for a certain kind of continuity.

I like to think that there can be a new understanding of tribalism—you see the family is related to the tribe. The extended family was tribal—and I like that. You see the family in my time got off the track when it went so entirely privatistic and individualistic—just me and mine! The tribe is not like that. The tribe is societal and personal. And we've forgotten that—and that can be explored and that is the dimension of the future that I am very much interested in. You see, the tribe is great—the tribe is great!

Now I was born in my grandmother's front bedroom—and I grew up in an intergenerational household. My father was one of the old guard in the Bradstreet Company, a credit agency, and he was one of the bright, bushy-tailed young men coming up in the credit-agency field. He was shunted all over the country to do this and that—and to move this and that. And we had home base with my grandmother. And while my father was moving around and uprooting, y'know there was just a certain kind of continuity provided in my grandmother's house.

I think this intense privatism that looks at the family in terms of its own, narrow self-interest is a threat to the family. And I think that the nuclear family is in deep trouble. I believe that. And look at the divorce rate! Look at the growing numbers of single-parent households!

And there are all kinds of improvisations—single parents getting together—single parents and their children getting together. You see, there is this deep yearning for support—for the family—for the tribe. The tribe that endures. Now, I feel that I have outlived my tribe. I have second cousins and two first cousins —whom I don't see. We are fond of each other and we communicate by phone and occasionally by letter. We know where we are, but there is little visible support in that setup. But I have here in this house a family which I consider to be my support system. And I think that many women, because we are the survivors in our society, have to find that kind of alternative to institutionalization. I think it is just terrible the way people "paint themselves into" institutions—again looking to the institution to provide the framework that the family once did. But the institution is regimented and awfully paternalistic—even the ones that are built under church auspices are highly paternalistic.

So, many institutional arrangements are prevalent today—and every denomination has built them—Philadelphia Presbytery is building another one—there are four already and a large nursing home. And I've approached several of the ministers and have said, "Why don't you put some of that money—and it's going to cost between five and six million dollars, and that money is being contributed by the churches, they are being assessed for that—into maintaining people in their own homes."

They *are* the congregation, for heaven's sake! You see I think that the family in the tribal, extended sense can be reconstituted in

two places today, (a) in the worshipping community—in the
church and the synagogue, some of the congregations see themselves in that light—not many, because you see it's so privatized;
and (b) in the community college or the continuing-education
movement where learners of different ages go to school together.
I was the commencement speaker for Antioch-Philadelphia, and
Antioch was graduating last month 400 older learners. And there
were a grandmother and a granddaughter in the same class, and
there were two sets of mothers and daughters getting Master's
degrees together. I talked about that in the commencement address, and I commended them—and said to the audience, "You
ought to be thinking in conscious terms of how you reconstitute
that kind of intergenerational interaction."

Now, I believe that the "family of choice" can be the family
of the future—of family members who come together not on the
basis of marriage but on the basis of common goals and shared
resources. That kind of a family has limitless possibilities.*

DO YOU HAVE ANY OBSERVATIONS TO MAKE ABOUT LOVE AND HATE?

Well, I think that there is some sound evidence that suggest love is
indispensable—and love, for my money, is not a romantic matter
—it goes beyond that. It may have a first flush of romanticism, but
it embodies friendship, and community; I think the loving relationships that endure in families are based on friendship. Now my
mother and I were friends. My father and I were not friends.
There was always the authority matter.

But from my point of view, from the familial point of view
and also in terms of the marriage relationship, marriages endure

* Maggie Kuhn shares her duplex with a secretary and a young couple, both
of whom attend a seminary.

when the partners are friends and companions and have an enduring interest in basic things that mean much to both partners. And I think that love between members of a community like ours is an enduring thing. Now we may separate, y'know, I expect that we will, but we have enriched our lives and contributed to each other's well-being in a loving relationship. And, there is always some tension. That's a part of it—but how you *deal* with it is what counts.

I think children have to have companionship and dependable relationships in order to grow. And I tremble for the future of so many children who have never had that—and how do you give it to them? I think the foster children's movement has shown that loving foster homes can indeed help and heal.

You see we have made goods, y'know, if you've got a lot of stuff—that in our society are assumed to be an expression of love and an evidence that you care. From my point of view it's a very materialistic transaction. It's like buying a slave, it's like buying a wife, it's like buying, y'know, into any kind of business arrangement. So we have made goods a substitute for good living in every way. Now just one more thing before we leave the family. I have been very interested in a definition offered by the American Home Economics Association. They defined the family in their national convention in 1975 and we have paraphrased it and have adopted it as ours for the basis of our shared living. The family is a unit in which (as the American Home Economics Association says) "two or more persons share resources, share goals and lifestyles, and decision making over time." And a family is a group that one comes home to. It's that network of commitment and decision making that transcends marriage, adoption, or any other blood or legal ties—that's a family. I think that's the basis of the family of the church or of my family. Now, that's the definition I have accepted. And from my point of view, that definition will endure. And the nuclear family, the extended family, and the tribe can fit into it.

Is it important to set goals?

Well—there must be a goal at every stage of life! There must be a goal! And the goal that is going to be really satisfying is the goal that transcends your own survival. Just staying alive and getting ahead is not a good enough goal.

What about handling conflicts in viewpoint?

It's very hard and there is no easy formula, and I think that you can't generalize too much because so many situations differ, and interactions and personality and chemistry are all so complicated. But my theory has been that you need to know your ground, and you need to know the facts, you need to do your homework before you shoot from the hip—and then I'm ready to shoot, y'know, and go right to it, but I always try to be informed. I don't always succeed in doing that. And I try to find out what the other point of view is based on, too—y'know, where are their groundings and what is the basis of their position, what social analysis have they made, and so on. And I think I have had some modest success in that. I think that another way to deal with the sharp conflicts is not to be afraid of them. I feel that there can be some very creative thinking coming out of the creative use of controversy. Nobody is going to think exactly as another person does: if we all thought alike, it would be very dull.

But as you interact with the other and as you let your difference come out, and be honestly expressed, there can be some interaction and some modification of views. It takes a lot of patience, and certain kinds of people just do not have it. And we have seen that in our movement. Some people are just absolutely poison to each other, and no matter how long they are in conflict, just *nothing* is going to come out! You don't have the time or energy to let that go on and destroy. So what you have to do is to gently remove and substitute, with some other goals. The Gray Panthers have used two kinds of strategies to deal with differences, or opposing camps, that have worked well up to this point—y'know this is a changing world and they may not work tomorrow.

But (a) I have found that within the enemy's camp there is always somebody who takes a different view—who dissents, for example, within the AMA. Within any group you can name there are insiders who want to change things but who cannot change unless they are linked with outsiders. And we can be the responsible outsiders that give them support. And they can tell the outsiders things that the outsiders would never find out. Never!

Now (b), the second strategy is one in which you build coalitions. And I'm not impressed with great crowds. I'm a devotee of Schumacher—small is beautiful. And a small group of people with their heads together, with a sense of community, can do more than the mass can. A mass can be manipulated, a mass can be easily swayed. It takes a hell of a lot of energy to stir up a mass—but there can be reinforcement and we have built our movement on small groups. We are not a mass movement and we probably never will be.

We have used the coalition and we have used the intergenerational efforts. And the reason that our analysis is good is that we have within our group of young Panthers people who are based in the university community who know how to do research, who are first great scholars, thinkers, and writers. Dale* is one of them. He's an excellent writer! And an excellent analyst! And you link what he can do, and the new knowledge that he has access to, with things that I have experienced, and others who are older, and you've got a good, solid analysis.

WHAT DO YOU HAVE TO SAY ABOUT LOSS?

Well, my life has not been one joyous, happy picnic. I've worked very hard all my life. I've had demanding jobs that I have really put myself into. I've worked hard! And I don't expect to stop. I

* The young seminary student who lives in her duplex.

push myself every day, and I'll continue to do that. The things that have given me the greatest joy and the greatest enduring satisfaction have come out of deep tragedy, and I'm grateful for that. And I think for all of us—our finitude, our predicament, is that of loss and separation. In many instances the losses outweigh the gains, and for a time in my life this was true. But in retrospect, the things that were most difficult and most painful for me to do day by day, were the things that have given me strength and have given me a certain insight that serves me well today.

My brother was a tragic person, and there were only two of us. He was three years younger than I. He was emotionally unstable, sick, very sensitive, very bright, and very troubled. *Never* happy. And I took care of him.

He was hospitalized in a mental institution for a long time, years. And then he was released in his old age to my house and this was his room.

So this room has many awful memories—and joyous ones. He sat in the big chair right there for practically two years. He had a heart condition and he couldn't lie down. He resented what I did because he wanted me with him. And to do what I felt I had to do meant constant conflict with somebody that I loved. Irreconcilable conflict!

And I learned in this long period with Sam what mental illness is, what depression is, what despair is. Oh, wow, I know, and that knowledge gives me a certain assurance in doing what we have done with nursing-home reform, with the President's Commission on Mental Health, and innumerable other things. I know! And that, that certain knowledge and the ability to triumph over it is something I'll be eternally grateful for.

WHAT INNER RESOURCES HELPED YOU?

Well, I suppose an abiding faith—I'm not, I'm not a pious person but I have a deep ethical sense that I've never lost, and an abiding hope.

How have you dealt with fears and anxieties?

Fears and anxieties are our common lot. There's no escaping them! But some people are destroyed by them—immobilized by them—so many are. But they don't have a goal! That makes a difference—or they don't have any sense of the future. This was one of my brother's problems. He had no future.

How is change affecting our lives?

Well I, maybe oversimplistically, think that the Third World and our relationship with it gives the thoughtful person cause for a devastating critique of the inappropriate use of technology.

And, our deification of technological advance leaves a great deal to be desired—and I don't advocate going back to the dim ages. But we have come to worship technology as an absolute god. We have come to worship it! And we have made it a substitute for things more real.

You see, we are foisting it on the people in the developing countries—we have tempted them with it and truly ravaged them. We're doing that in South Africa—we're doing that wherever we have exported nuclear-power plants and all that stuff. We've made our industrial progress a sign of their progress. Every developing country wants a great big airport. Every developing country wants a great big power plant.

I was so distressed—it was almost two years between my visits to China—I was so distressed with the way in which the Chinese government was seeming to open its door to all the big corporations here in America that were just waiting to leap in with all of our machinery—with Cokes and all the rest of it. I could just see McDonald's golden arches opposite Mao's tomb. I'm sure that's about where they would choose to put them!

WHAT SHOULD WE BE SHARING WITH THE WORLD?
WHAT SHOULD WE BE EXPORTING?

Oh, you see, I think that we really *have* something to give. For example, England and some of the other countries are dealing with racial-justice questions for the first time, and they don't know what the hell to do. They've got racial violence and tension. Well, we're still living with that. Our society is still racist, but there are ways in which we have dealt with it that the others have not yet developed.

And I think that the way in which we have integrated and built upon the rich ethnic strains of the many groups that have come to this country could be shared. Other societies are much more homogeneous than we have ever been and have more difficulty in dealing with racial differences. But it seems that the bottom line with us as far as sharing is concerned is to share that which is most profitable to us financially.

You know, one of the dreams that I have—it's only a glint in a few of our eyes at this moment—I wish that there could be some very substantial efforts made to radicalize the very top echelons of the great corporations and to bring into their thinking some matters of ethics. I think some very, very important theological and ethical insights ought to be shared with those people. And if they are not informed about such things—then I would like to see stockholders' revolts, really, led by clergy and responsibly informed laity. I would love to organize stockholders' meetings! I may try that some day.

I've had some very interesting conversations with some top management people—all too few, actually, but it's been a real challenge. But theirs is a deep, subconscious, inarticulated sense of uncertainty. You know the corporations are under fire, particularly the oil corporations, and the justification of their being, their doings, and their policies is an ethical matter.

Well, I think that my two grandmothers influenced me a lot in childhood and my mother's oldest sister, who was a widow and who lived with us, was a great influence in my life. She was a loving person and taught my brother and me to read long before we went to school—we read all kinds of stuff. And she was a suffragette—marched and made speeches, and demonstrated, y'know, and she told us about it. Yes, she was very influential in my life. And there were also a couple of teachers who were very influential. I was an English major and a sociology major and there were people in both of those fields who opened the world to me, and taught me that I had a head. I think that people need to know that, that one can think and think in a disciplined way.

And I'm glad that I went to a woman's college. I think it was good for me to be in touch with women who were good teachers and good thinkers. And I can understand the women working as they did in the sixties and early seventies to desegregate the men's schools and to enroll in Princeton and in the other bastions of male supremacy. Nevertheless, I think that there was an awful lot to be gained by attending a good woman's college, with my peers and my sisters.

I also think of one of the first women with whom I worked in the YWCA, Grace Mayette, I'll never forget her—and Rhoda McCoullough. Both of those women were very radical—radical feminists, radical in their economics. Grace Mayette was a socialist —an out-and-out socialist. She was very low-key and very soft-spoken, very quiet, y'know, but very effective! And she was a mentor of mine in many ways.

WHAT WORLD EVENTS WERE IMPORTANT TO YOU?

Well, I think the crash, the stock market crash affected our family destinies a lot. It reinforced my need to work. And at that time I was involved in a very serious love affair and it made me realize, well, y'know . . . and then I was working for one of the big stockbrokers, Webster, Stone, and Blodgett, and that was really something, too, because they had very serious setbacks—and my father had a lot of losses. Everybody did.

And I was convinced that what I had to do was to get on and work! So during the great Depression I worked in the YWCA and worked with low-income women who had little or nothing. That was a very, very important experience for me. It gave me a social insight that I never would have had without it, as a person in a middle-class family that was comfortable. We had everything that we needed and wanted. We did everything and lived in a nice house, y'know how that is. The social difference in the way I lived and the way in which the young women with whom I was working in the YWCA lived was just enormous! What poverty!

WERE THERE ANY WRITERS THAT STRONGLY INFLUENCED YOU?

Yes. Lincoln Steffens—I think he influenced a lot of people in my peer group. I was an English major, you see, and I was very much interested in the great dramas that dealt with social protest and social comment. Hauptmann and Sudemanns' dramas of poverty and alienation were powerful! I'll never forget them!

And in growing up, *the* book that I have drawn on again and again is Mills's book on *Sociological Imagination.* I've used that in all kinds of speeches. And it has been a very important basis for my social analysis—the interaction between the person and the public. You can't separate them.

HOW DO YOU FEEL ABOUT GROWING OLDER?

In my thinking, my old age is the flowering of my life. It's a culmination—it's a putting into perspective the pain and the tragedy and making of them great things, great events. I celebrate life every day and my hope and dream is that others will do so as well. For that ought to be the way!

I think that at every age there has to be a *purpose* in life—
that's basic. And as a result of having a purpose I think there has
to be a substantial understanding of one's own history: what
you've seen and done and lived through. I've said to people who
were sick or who were very anxious about the thought of getting
sick, "Look, how many times have you been sick in the past?"
And they usually respond, "I really never thought of that." I say
to them, "How many times have you had measles or some other
communicable disease?" And I say, "Well, I've survived that and
I have also survived three bouts with cancer." And I try to tell
them that they have a lot of experience in survival.

DO YOU THINK YOUNG PEOPLE HAVE A MORE DIFFICULT TIME TODAY?

Oh, I do—much more difficult! There are so many more choices.
Middle-class kids have so many options that they are confused.
Many are. And many of them are so unconnected with enduring
things that they feel that they have no future! Some of the very
gifted kids that were involved in the anti-war movement (and we
know so many of them because that's how the Gray Panthers got
started) are very cynical and disappointed.

I think that educational institutions have a tremendous responsibility today to help young people to make connections with
those things that endure—with history—you see we teach history
so poorly in grade school and in high school. I never cared a hoot
about history until I was in the later years of college and then
graduate school. I didn't think it was relevant. It was a battle
somewhere! And you had so many guns and so many people were
killed. I think that young people need to know about the history
of the places where they live. And I love the idea of living history
and of oral history and of life review and the interconnection between the very young and the very old. I feel these things can
play an important role in education today. And I do not think the
rigid segregation of peer groups that begins in nursery schools is

in the larger public interest. It is not going to correct the present anomie and disengagement of this present generation of kids.

Like the kids who live in a housing project near here, which is a troubled place. Mostly black kids live there now. Many, many kids. Mothers are on welfare with some rent subsidy, and the absentee landlords in New York own it and aren't giving anybody anything; they only collect the rent. The kids' summer sport is breaking the windows of the vacant apartments. Some of the apartments are vacant on the top stories, so it takes quite a lot of aim. That's awful. And another favorite sport is breaking pop bottles on the street. They are not bad kids, but there is no place for them to go.

No goal! No goal! I would like to see some people harnessing the energies of all those kids and building solar greenhouses—back of all these houses. Or getting kids to work in the gardens. I sometimes despair of the future for these young people.

IS THERE HOPE FOR MANKIND?

Well, I think vestigial remains of the past can be reconstructed and provide some kind of continuity, but we've not provided any kind of unemployment benefits for those kids.

You see, I think kids need to be taught to work, and given a challenge to work. The son of one of our colleagues here in the office is attending a seminary where he is pursuing a Master of Divinity degree and is working with a group of these people. He has taught them about ecology, building solar greenhouses and things. They have made a seminar room in a basement and the little kids give lectures on their projects.

Now kids could be taught all kinds of things about animals. They could be taught how to love and care for and raise them instead of tormenting them. We are fortunate to have two veterinarians who are wonderful and are our cats' doctors. I've talked with them. I've said, "If you only had time to come around to the Housing Improvement Association and teach those kids about animals." And Dr. Wall said, "Maggie, I wish to God that I did have time, but I don't." But maybe someone ought to subsidize him while he taught the kids how to take care of animals.

Those kids want something exciting. Dale, another of our seminary students, has been working in prisons—several of our student members of the Gray Panthers are working in prison reform. We have some older people who are involved as well. The federal prisons are terrible! And so many of the people are sucked right back into crime because when they get out, there is nothing exciting to do. I have been told by one of the workers that several of the prisoners with whom he has been working would like to go deep-sea diving—you know, adventurous, dangerous. We give them some damn little mamby-pamby job . . .

We could do a lot more for them. But when we encourage people who are well educated, who are the former teachers, to move into condominiums in Sun City, and in Florida, and this new Cathedral House that a church has built out on Ridge Avenue . . . it's complete separation. I've fought them. I'm very hard on them. And they say, "Well, we've worked hard and we should have this leisure time." And I say, "Well, that's your choice. I think it's a very selfish choice." And they don't like to hear me because I make them feel very uncomfortable. And I want to.

Young families, you know, single-parent households, need somebody—some bodies, as advisors and companions.

DO YOU HAVE ANY SECRETS FOR A LONG AND HAPPY LIFE?

I think the secret is to keep moving and doing. And the secret is, I reiterate, to have a purpose.

ARE THERE ANY PARTICULAR MORAL OR RELIGIOUS
PRINCIPLES THAT HAVE GUIDED YOU?

Yes, the eternal wonder of life and the wholeness of the whole creation. And one of the things that I've been thinking and talking about in the last year is that *age* is a universalizing force. It's a common human experience that everything that lives shares. And if we had different funeral practices our bodies could be part of a nitrogen cycle that could replenish the earth. The continuity of the nitrogen cycle, the seamless web of nature, and the creation that the creator of all life provided for the nourishment of people and animals is to me a wondrous thing! And the sad thing is that it is so endangered.

I'm a member of the board of the Philadelphia Memorial Society and, internationally, of the Continental Memorial Society. And they have been working to reform funeral practices—to get funeral directors to scale down their prices to enable people to be buried in plain pine boxes. Simple. And not to prettify and glorify the corpse, but to celebrate life and the history of the person who has died. That's what ought to be, you know, a memorial, a remembrance of that life. And memorial societies are to some degree effective, but the funeral industry is very lucrative. They give a hard sell! There were hearings last year clear across the country —perhaps a year-and-a-half ago—on funeral practices. I testified in those hearings and they showed how exploitative they are. Often people who have lived very modest lives seem to have to have a great funeral.

Now when our Toby died—well, our cat, Toby, died on my lap. And, oh, I just felt awful! He was very sick toward the end. And the vet came to see him at the house. Isn't that dear? He made calls on Toby. He tried very hard to save him, but he couldn't, and Toby died. We buried him in a flower-covered box under the azalea bush in the back yard. This was three years ago. And last year the azalea bush was never more beautiful. And we said, "Wow, that's Toby!"

And I think of that as an appropriate way of replenishing the earth. Now that, to me, is the whole creative order about which I feel so deeply . . . and I get so angry when I think about nuclear fission and those defoliants we used in Viet Nam. I view them as a crime against the Creator. They are a misuse of the creation. And one more thing about the moral and the ethical. In my old age I feel more and more concerned about the Old Testament. I read it and I like to hear Old Testament preaching. I don't go to church very often. I do some preaching myself on occasion, and I always preach from the Old Testament.

Because the faith, you know, the adoring prophets, and the continuity, Abraham and Isaac, the great heros of faith—I think they speak to me in my old age. And the sense of justice that is so clear in the Old Testament—I think our society has lost much of this sense of justice. We are as strong as we are in the Gray Panther movement because of the Jews who are in it. Some of them are not practicing Jews, but they come out of that great tradition—just as scholars with whom you are associated come out of it. Now in the Gray Panther movement we have downplayed any religious conviction. Rather it is a kind of broad, ethical base that holds us together, and people come from many religious backgrounds—and from a humanist point of view as well.

I think there is the potential for a great gathering of the elders of many tribes coming together and affirming a new kind of peace and justice and humanness for the world. There is the possibility of making the international year of 1982, when there is to be a world assembly on aging sponsored by the United Nations with the central theme of a just and peaceful world, a focal point for this. But, oh dear, there is the danger, if you look at the present politicizing of the elders, that we are just going to be another vested-interest group. You look at the silver-haired lobbies, and you've got silver-haired lobbies in many of the states wearing their big gray-power buttons of which they are so proud . . . and that means more power for us, us old folks!

I say, "To hell with that, that's going to do us all in." And it's very hard to get that message across because we are special-interest in our thinking. And what's more appropriate than an old folks' lobby? It's going to be difficult to build that, thank goodness, because we're so diverse. But I tremble to think of that as the future—just a lot of selfish old folks.

Such people are not the elders of the tribe. And I think there is so much we can learn about the role of the elders from other societies, from the Messiahs of Kenya, for example, who have a special role for the elders. And in China we can learn from the veteran workers who gather every year to remember the past, the bitter past, reminding them that their revolution of development must go on. Now that's a very different situation from being sure we've got our pension and so forth, which we also need of course, but that's such a little piece of it. It's settling for so small a gain.

I think there has to be a new lifestyle that reinforces public mass transportation. I don't have a car any more. I miss it. I've put a lot of money we've earned and some I had saved into the Gray Panthers movement. That's the way we got it started. Most of us that were in on the beginning of it funded it ourselves. We got no grants. We believed in it.

I changed my will just two months ago and these two houses I'm leaving to the Gray Panthers to do whatever they want with them—sell them, live in them, use as an academy, or whatever. But I think we have got to develop a new lifestyle. The young have helped us.

REFERENCES

Hessel, Dieter, *Maggie Kuhn on Aging*, Philadelphia: Westminster Press, 1977.

Mills, Charles Wright, *Sociological Imagination*, New York: Oxford University Press, 1959.

SAMUEL LEVENSON:
DECEMBER 28, 1911–
AUGUST 27, 1980

EDUCATOR, humorist, writer, the warm and wonderful Sam Levenson grew up in Brooklyn, one of ten children. His death, some months after he granted us an interview, saying he didn't know why we had asked him, leaves our world poorer. What follows, we feel, is a gift, a special legacy:

"I'm not really a wise man—except for the thing that proves my wisdom—you find as you get older the less you know, the less certain you get about things—and that is a kind of special wisdom. I hesitate more about making judgments than I ever did before in my life. Yes, I'm more aware of the unknowns. I need time more now—you fight for time more as you grow older, because you know how you need time to make movements, decisions, you know how you form an opinion. When you are young, they come quickly. Time is very precious as you get older, and it's not ordinary clock time; it's life time. I make my own distinction here. I hate clocks on walls anyhow. I've done TV and I've found that they measure only when you start to talk and when you stop. But they don't measure the quality of anything—they only measure beginnings and endings. The in-between doesn't count."

ON VALUES . . .

I was asked something recently. I was doing a TV interview
largely to plug a new book, and a young boy who I judge was
about sixteen or seventeen got up and said, "What do you think I
should be reading at this point in my life?" And I said, "Well,
what are you reading?" And he said he was reading practically all
the new novels. And I said, "You know, it will probably sound as
if I'm preaching to you, but I don't think you will ever understand what it is to live in the twentieth century unless you read
the Bible." And he said, "Well, what do you mean?" I said,
"You've got to know the roots. If you know the roots you will
know the branches and the blossoms, you'll know where we are
living. Otherwise you have no roots. You can't start at the top. I
think you should take time out, with a teacher, because it's difficult, and read through and find out what these values are that we
live by which fundamentally do come out of the Bible. We are
Bible people. Not everybody is religious, but whether they are
religious or not they must realize that they are living by a code
that is a biblical code, fundamentally."

The boy looked at me, and said, "You know, I had never
thought of that."

I said, "I'm not selling you anything. I know I had to go back
and reread the Bible because I was getting it about third-hand.
Everybody knows about the Ten Commandments. You know the
line, "If everybody obeyed the Ten Commandments there would
be no eleven o'clock news."

So, as I got older, I had to go back and pick up a lot of
literature I should have read as a young person. And among the
things that I felt I needed to read more of was biblical literature,
just for the value systems that this literature has left to the world—
aside from the stories, the great prophetic wisdom, and so on. It's
a fact that wherever I go in America now I'm aware of the fact
that ours is a *religious* country. It's still a *religious* country!

The wisdom I believe in (not my own wisdom necessarily)—the things that I believe are wise . . . Man is a survivor, and if he has survived so long there must be some rules which keep him alive—otherwise this race would have been exterminated by now—died out! There is something to know about staying alive. There are so many more of us now than there were before.

At one time I thought I could *pursue* happiness. I feel now that it is a mistaken method of achieving a rich life. You cannot pursue happiness! I stopped pursuing it. I found that for a lot of people who were pursuing it, they got their happiness mixed up with a lot of other things like fun, like the Pepsi generation, and trying to make bubbles fly and all that.

I think that at this point in my life I am pursuing truth, and justice and compassion, and peace, and I find that the more I pursue those, the more content I am with myself. When I pursued happiness, I was never really content!

There are other values that I think are more important. Happiness is a by-product. You cannot pursue it by itself. All the other things will produce a state of euphoria, the joy of being alive and aware and responsive to life, a wonderful experience. But the pursuit of happiness doesn't do it. I try to teach it to my children. But I'm afraid that they are still pursuing happiness. I say to them, "No, don't, it doesn't pay off." There are too many tranquilizers being sold that contradict the theory that you can achieve happiness on earth.

ON THE FAMILY . . .

It appears to me that the family is not just eroding today, but that it is crumbling. Erosion is a very slow process, but not so with the family—it is really crumbling. It's like the ceiling suddenly giving way. There were a lot of invisible cracks which we didn't pay much attention to. Now the chandelier and the ceiling are really coming down on us, and a lot of people are getting hurt. They are getting hurt very badly. And it hurts me a great deal because I have a profound faith in the biological, the religious, and the spiritual need of a family.

I think the family is basic to all nature—no matter what aspect of nature you look at you will find a male, a female, and an offspring. That's the way it works. You know plants work that way and atoms, they found out, work that way with positives and negatives. Everything seems to produce another of its kind. The family seems to be the one basic kind of relationship that runs through all of life. Now that makes it of very fundamental import.

I'm one of the fortunate ones, and I talk always from the fortunate position. I call myself the privileged poor. You know, I never felt unwanted, rejected, or anything, because the size of the family in my opinion has nothing to do with the quality of life in that family. You can have a very large family and not be living well. You can have a very small family that's full of hatred. It's the emotional relationship that's between people that makes a family. There is a commitment to each other.

I believe very strongly in the quality of sacrifice that keeps a family together. Not how much I can get out of it, but how much can I contribute to it. I have a line in one of my books that says that the family is like a bank and if you take out more than you put in, it goes bankrupt.

Now as I extend that feeling—for example—my mother and father brought ten children into the world and raised us with comparative ease because their values were clear! A family is not a luxury, it's a necessity—it's not optional! You *must* have a family! You can't *live* alone! That's what I was taught.

Marriage is not doing well today because, in a sense, it's optional. I was raised to believe that marriage was compulsory, so that the whole race could perpetuate itself, so that there would be children who would in turn perpetuate themselves and that way the faith could be perpetuated and life would be perpetuated. But as for the family—it was the *strongest* single element in my life and it has stuck with me—the family! My mother used the word if we did anything wrong, a wrong by her standard. Maybe you got into a fight with a kid or whatever it was, she used a *we* in scolding. She said *we* have been put to shame! Not just *I* was responsible.

Yes, and I say—where did they get the wisdom to know that we owe each other dignity and respect and that we must not let down the name or the good reputation or the good fame of the family? Anyone who broke with that brought shame to the family. Always the question was: "What are we going to say to the neighbors?" If you got a "B" in conduct, what are we going to say? *We!* How shall *we*, not how shall *I* explain it. You're in this too, was the thought.

All of our lives it was always *we*, even when the brothers went off and got married it was still *we!* I have several brothers that have died in recent years, but the rest of us are still in constant communication with each other as a family.

I believe I know the fundamental difference between privilege and underprivilege (and I don't know why they use the word "privilege," I never felt that life was a privilege—I was born into it, you know). But I know what underprivilege is—if you don't have a family, that to me is the height and depth of underprivilege! A family in which there is much quarreling and dissension breeds in the child all kinds of emotional havoc. That to me is underprivilege. See, privilege is not the money in the family. There's a line I don't think I have ever used in any of my books, "I was not a poor child. I just didn't have any money."

Love really wasn't overtly expressed—not heavy on the kissing, not heavy on the hugging, but an abiding concern. You knew that they were interested in you at all times. If you were in trouble, they were there! If there was anything to rejoice about, they were there!

I think the family is a kind of natural club that you are entitled to belong to without being rich or aristocratic or with any special letters of recommendation. One is simply born into a family automatically—it's a primary gift of the universe. For the universe itself is a family.

The family is in big trouble now, but I think it's going to come back because society won't be able to work without it. It can't be done. I am completely convinced that much of the unhappiness in the world today is because people are taking the concept of family too lightly and thus are rendering it unstable. I think it should be kept in a strictly classical form wherein each member has a role to perform.

That thinking does not conflict with, let's say, women's liberation or anything. The role of the parents is to *teach*, to *feed*, to *nurture*. The role of the child is to *learn* from these parents how to live. It's no different in a nest or in a cave or anywhere else. This is fundamental to lions, tigers, as well as human beings! What would happen, and it does happen, to a cub left alone in a cave? It dies. Now my feeling is that no matter how old you get, you can still die without family.

On love . . .

I think the primary human value is love. But there are varieties of love, you see. And I think that one of the greatest disasters of this era is that we have equated "love life" with "sex life." Investigators of the topic inquire about your "love life" when what they mean is your "sex life." There is love of nature, love of mankind, love of country, love of family, love of beauty, love of just doing things for people—just being helpful! There are some people who are tremendously gifted just in being of great service. I think that I could list about a hundred different variations of human love. The total adds up to life itself and it begins to fall apart when any of these breaks down. You can live with some small breakdowns, but the more breakdowns there are within these little love patterns, the more shattered life becomes.

You find if you go to a mental institution that you will meet people who have lost their *love*. And when they lost their love, they for all intents and purposes lost their life. When they lost their love, they became suspicious of the whole world. I got that idea from the fact that I remember my feelings when I got lost one time as a child. I couldn't find my mother or my father. I knew what it was to be for a few minutes without a mother or a father—and that I might not ever have one again. I was lost! I'll never find them again! Such terror is greater than any other terror I have ever known in my life. That's terror!

On hate . . .

I think it's been encouraged too much. I think that instead of assuming the blame as a sinner or an evildoer, we have been encouraged by therapists to find other things to blame for what's wrong inside. And I think that can develop into a hate of a lot of things, and a lot of people and a lot of institutions.

If I as a boy would come up from the street, and say to my mother (I use Mother as an illustration because she represents thousands of years of folk tradition), "Louie hit me." (Now I expect a mother today would call a PTA meeting to find out why "Louie hit me.") *My mother* would look at me and say, "Why didn't he hit me?" And I would say, "What?" And she would say, "Funny thing, I went down to the street five times today and nobody hit me. How come they're always hitting you?" And she would walk away and leave me to figure out if *maybe* there was something I had done that brought this on. Perhaps I had put myself in this position—maybe I *deserved* to get a sock on the head.

On opposing points of view .

I was asked about that when I was giving a talk shortly after what happened at Kent State University—the deaths. There were a lot of mixed feelings. Some people said, "Well, those kids were playing with fire, they deserved what happened to them." Most people, however, seemed to feel very unhappy about what had happened. And somebody said, "What would you do, Mr. Levenson, if you saw all this violence?" Now, I'm Jewish and yet I said, "I can only think of one answer—what would have Christ done? Would He have carried a weapon as a reply or would He have walked to them and held out His hand as in the traditional stained-glass window pose, and said to them, 'Look, I come to you with naked hands and love. Talk to me. I love you.'" See? We're only here for a short time. Is there no way we can communicate in love? Let's try for love. As simple as all that. "Let's try for love." And I really mean *love*.

For example, when you folks walked in, I had never seen you before—but I already have the feeling we have known each other for a long time and I trust you, and therefore I cannot hate you. I have no reason to hate you—none whatsoever. And again—if I start quoting the Bible again it's because I was raised on it—I think the greatest teaching in the Bible is, "Thou shalt love thy neighbor as thyself." It doesn't say you have to like him, but it doesn't say you have to hate him, either. But if you can only like him, you have a very good chance of loving him. But if you don't like him, you have a very good chance of hating him.

It's tough. I've raised two children who are not pacifists, I've never used that word with them, but I was terribly unhappy if I saw them raise their hands against another kid. I just can't take violence. "But he hit me." So, I would kind of try to intercede and say let's try to get some sort of principle here so you won't feel as if you have to try to use violence against each other. There must be some other way—there's got to be an alternative. There really is only one alternative to hate and it is to love a person. Do you expect me to love Hitler? How could I? How could I? At best I can say that if he had been loved enough in his life, he wouldn't have been the Hitler we have known.

Because even in my case, I was a slum kid, and many who have grown up in the slums have written volumes and volumes about the horror of the slums, but I saw the violin lessons, and I saw the kids who went on to school, and I saw the sacrificing mothers. How come I saw all this? Somebody must have taught me that.

On goals . . .

I think that having no goals is a mistake—I would say that the parent should set goals at least until the child is about twelve or thirteen. Now by the time they get to college, they should at least know the tradition from which they come—the values they have inherited from their family. At that point they have a right to set their own goals and develop their own values. There is also an old proverb which my parents used to use that says there is a great difference between a heretic and an ignoramus. If you want to be a heretic, be a heretic; but don't be an ignoramus! *Learn! Know* why you choose the goals you choose!

I got married—and even then I carried my parents' goals into my own home. With my own children, I have found that their goals are reflecting new directions—the direction of much more free will and much more freedom of choice, and they have so much *more* to choose from.

In college my first two years were fixed—I couldn't move one inch out of the way or one credit out of the way. I had to have Latin, I had to have math, I had to have my science, and so on. But you know that in most colleges in America today a kid can pretty well take what he likes. So that there has been a change now. Are we requiring that students set goals or just list preferences? There's a difference.

The first goal is to learn to love, I believe. The second is self-sustenance. Nobody should be dependent upon others for his food. He's got to work! And I believe that work is one of the great goals. I was told in college that this was the Protestant ethic, but I thought it was the Jewish ethic until I was twenty-seven. Work! Work! The great line of my father's was, "If you ever need a helping hand you will find one at the end of your arm."

So to me that was both a goal and a value. I believe in sacrifice as a goal. I've told my kids, there is probably no one-hundred-percent achievement of any goal. If there were we would all be Phi Beta Kappas, or we would all be one hundred percent in something. One must not expect perfection, but always aim for it! You must not become frustrated or fall apart if you hit an eighty or a seventy-five.

I have noted that a lot of seventy-fives and eighties do *very* well in real life. And that mark is no absolute prognosis of what this person is going to be, because I think *Who's Who* is full of people who never got beyond seventy or eighty. We don't know. We don't even know their IQs. It would be interesting to find out how many dumb-dumbs there were who became leaders. So, I don't believe that freedom of choice is the greatest value for children or youth. I believe that they have to concede some of this in the name of peace. As one lives with others one has to concede some freedoms. I find some kids today who say that they are free persons and can do anything they like. I don't believe it! I don't believe in that kind of freedom! There is a difference between freedom for all and a free-for-all.

ON PEOPLE WHO WERE INFLUENTIAL . . .

My parents. And then I had a teacher. Intellectually, my greatest teacher was Professor Benardet, who taught us how to study—a college professor. Now, I'll let you in on the big secret. If you write a book—how do you write a book? You don't write a book. You *study* before you write a book.

He gave us a course of the novel. I was majoring in Spanish. One novel for the whole class, one book for the whole term. Now, he said each one of us was responsible for one character in the book. You're responsible for Mr. so-and-so, you're responsible for his wife and so on.

What did he mean, "responsible"? He said, "It is very easy, but you need a shoe box." And we said, "What do you need a shoe box for?" He said, "Tonight's assignment is to get a shoe box and some four-by-six cards. It's a marvelous method and I've used it to write everything I have ever written." Benardet's method. "Now," he said, "every time your character's name is mentioned, you have to answer three things and write them on the card: What does he say about himself? What do people say about him? and what does he say about others? Whenever his name comes up you have got to put it on a 4 by 6. You have to follow him through the whole book. Then once you've got all, say 180 cards, you have to classify them and find out if he really has genuine ideas on different subjects or is he just talking. If he has nothing to say it will show up because these ideas will not hold together. It's like a scientific experiment. How much data can you produce to indicate that this man has a position on a particular topic—that he has something to say?"

Now when each one of us did each character and when we put them all together we could see the construction. He called it the *organic method*. You saw the construction of the novel, you found out who was truly a character with definite ideas, and who just had notions. If he had real ideas they would stand up. You could draw a premise, a thesis out of what this man said.

Now when I did my latest book I did this and also when I did my earlier books. I took cards and sat right in my mother's kitchen. I put on cards utensils, mops, closets, everything had a card. Her ways. What did she say when you walked into the house? What did she say when you walked out of the house? How did she pray? What was her relation to God? Mama and God, Mama and floors, Mama and kitchens, Mama and windows, and then out of this I was able to determine who she was.

Then when people read it they said, "Yeah, it's true!" They'll never know that I sat *four years* with cards in my hands before I started out to write one line. And to him, Benardet, I owe a great deal, aside from his general respect for learning. To this day if I read a newspaper I'm almost classifying what I read on 4 by 6's in my mind. He was the greatest intellectual influence in my life—

and in a lot of other people's lives as well. He taught others who yet taught others. There is a whole school of people all over the world who are disciples of Professor Benardet.

When he retired, they gave him a dinner and he got up and began to recite a poem from sixteenth-century Spanish literature. And do you know that about three hundred people went along with him and recited the whole poem from memory. I said to myself, how often in the world does this happen? They *all* knew it! It was like an anthem that came out of all his students—the things he had taught us. That was the greatest teacher I ever had! He is still alive, he's still grumpy, and when I write a book, I send him a copy and he will grade it. He will send it back and say, "You can do better than this!"

Another is my brother Michael, to whom I once dedicated a book—he and my little grandchild missed each other as he died when she was born. His life is an example of the unforeseeable, the unpredictable. In a house in a ghetto, on the East Side, in Harlem —we lived in all the poor neighborhoods—an artist was born. That was Michael! And I saw the miracle of a kid who grew up and said to his Orthodox mama and papa, "Don't feel too badly for me, you're not responsible for me, don't worry, I'll get along, I must paint!"

My father had to ask him a simple question like, "What do you mean, paint?" Well, he was very understanding of my parents. He said that he must paint pictures. The next question was, "How are you going to make a living?" He said to my father, "I don't know." The next question was, "How can you do something from which you are not going to make a living because who is going to feed you?" He said, "I don't know, but I must do it!"

Now here—see the beds, see crowds of people sleeping, see the whole family, some going to school, some working, a mob of us eating good peasant food and in the corner is this nut, Michael, standing there with this canvas, painting pictures. He never made big money. He taught painting at Rutgers. He retired only about two years ago. He was the art critic for the *Newark News*, a very learned man who never went to college—he just worked at painting. And he won a scholarship and he lived in Paris for five years. And he impressed me, for I saw that a man can be none of the things that the world expects that he is going to be, and yet he can say to all his brothers, "Fellahs, I have lived a richer life than any of you, and I haven't earned a nickel!"

On growing older . . .

I have little nightmares—like of dying. I don't know where I'm going, but I believe that the universe is eternal and I will somewhere fit into the universe—I don't know exactly what particle of matter I may *be*. Or maybe I will be just some particle of mist floating around somewhere. But I do believe that life is eternal, and that I'm part of it.

Spiritually, I feel stronger than I have ever felt before. I know my mind, I know myself. See? But suddenly I realize that I'm not young anymore. I used to be able to say, "Well, I'm eighteen. I'll go on forever." Now, forever is beginning to shrink a little bit, and I do get scared sometimes, and I say, "Gee, now it's no longer forever—now it's only years." And in some ways I'm not as confident in myself as I used to be. I used to take on big projects—say it will take me five years to write a book. Now I say "Five years— do I have five years to sit down and write a book?"

The advantages are only that I am much more courageous now. I have lost my fears. You know, I ask, what harm could anybody do? I'm going to die anyhow. You know, what are they going to do, stick a toothpick into me now? Nothing hurts that much anymore because I know that the big hurt is going to come soon. And now I have the *courage* to speak up. I was never a great radical and all that. But I'll try to illustrate.

We have a great books course at my temple. We've been reading books for years—a good group. And I'm not afraid any longer to let the most *foolish* ideas surge up, and say, "You know what I'm thinking? I'm thinking something I would have been ashamed to say when I was twenty because I would have thought people would have laughed at me. I have no more shame." I respect my mind. I think I have accumulated some kind of a treasury which I can draw on now. I'll tell you a wild one to illustrate my sheer courage.

I was invited to a St. Patrick's Fordham University alumni reunion. The St. Patrick's parades were finished and everybody was happy and it was great. And I was the guest speaker. Fine! The place was full of monsignors and it was really delightful. And it got to me and I talked about family again, which is one of my favorite themes, the family of man. Family! And I got around to my mother who did slap, my father who did exercise corporal punishment and all that, see? But she never let me hit anybody else. That's a rotten kid who raises his hand against another kid, and if I told my mother that so-and-so hit me, I was crucified, really crucified.

Now this is something I have not put down yet, but as a Jewish kid coming through a non-Jewish neighborhood, on the way to school they were looking for us—plain, simple, childish prejudice! Once they grabbed me and put me up against a heavy school fence, you know, like a big, heavy chickenwire fence. And two kids held my arms apart. And you know what they did? Pulled down my pants, so the whole world could see I was a Jewish kid. I'll never forget the fear, the trauma . . .

Well, I said, this is the time to tell it. And here I was surrounded completely by Catholics. And I said this is what happened to me. And they didn't know what to make of it. I said, "I don't want you to feel guilty. I'm telling you the truth. We're grown-up now. Let's be honest with each other."

And after the incident against the fence I went home and told my mother. She said, "All right. God will protect you. Don't worry. God in his judgment knows what's right, and if you suffered, God will make all things come out right in the end."

And I said, "You know, that that is the basis of the Sermon on the Mount—you know, 'Blessed are those that suffer for righteousness' sake for their reward shall be in heaven.' " And I turned to the Fordham Alumni audience, and said, "Only at my age would I dare to say this. Is it possible that Jesus learned this from his Jewish mother?" That's what I mean by no longer being afraid.

And do you know what the answer was? "Of course." So I said, "You see, we both have Jewish mothers. We *both* have Jewish mothers. And don't raise your hand against the other, you know, your reward will be in heaven. Don't worry. And then there was general applause that suddenly there had been a recognition of a truth that Jesus at his mother's knee and I at my mother's knee had learned from a Jewish mother to be a good boy and to behave.

Now as a youngster, I would not have had the courage to tell this story—and that's one of the advantages of maturity, *real* maturity, to be able to trust your instincts and your ideas, see? And be open about them—it's a wonderful feeling! There comes a time, *only* when you are mature, that you can stand up.

You know, you make your greatest demands on life when you are young. I think what I have done is cut down the list of my demands on life as I grow older. I don't demand to be able to run up three flights of stairs, and I'm not disappointed that I can't because I've already told myself, "You're not going to be able to do it." I don't demand to eat all the goodies I would like to eat because I know that after a certain age they're not good for you. So you start cutting down on the list of all the things you could do when you were young.

Get used to the idea that you can't—that there are certain things you can't do! You can't go from one party to another—in my business I could go to a different cocktail party every night. So, I learned to say, you know, you will wear yourself out much faster. Cool it! Cool everything!

To keep from getting ulcers and possibly heart disease, and other things, learn to compromise more with a lot that life demands of you. Let's say, for example, that I'll be a big earner, if I sell a million copies of the book—everybody's going to clap. But by this time I say, so I won't sell a million copies. It's more important that I survive. It's more important that I stay alive longer. I've found out I don't *need* everything they tell me I need. So I cut down the list. I'm watching TV and some guy comes on and says, "Run, quick, and by some gum . . ." And I say, "Get out of here, leave me alone, I don't need so much." I really don't. I don't need as many shoes, I don't need as many clothes. It isn't that I'm going to be poorer. My spirit is richer than it ever was, but I have cut down on the list of *things* that the world thinks that I ought to have as a success—and I don't need them. And it's as simple as all that.

If I were to lose all the *things* I have in the world, first, I would still be me, and second, I would still be ahead. Because I had nothing to begin with. And we run a very simple home, Mrs. Levenson and I, trying to keep alive, trying to grow older, by not taxing ourselves with the goals, the ambitions of an eighteen-year-old. And you know, I don't need them. I'm almost sorry. I watch the eighteen-year-old, and I say, "He is killing himself." I know— I did it at eighteen too. But now I have cut down.

You know, when opportunity knocks on the door, I don't answer. You can keep your opportunities. I have had enough opportunities. I know what I want. And it gets simpler and simpler. There are about four or five *things* I need in my life. I need a good record player, I play the violin, so I need a violin. My wife plays the piano, so we need a piano. I need to be able to sit down and eat a meal, and believe me, it doesn't have to be steak, a nice piece of chicken or fish or something is wonderful. I need to take off my shoes, relax, read a book, and that is really all I want, you know.

But life plays dirty tricks on you and this is where growing older has its great discomforts. The children grow up, and instead of their being no longer a burden to you, if you are a loving father, *all their problems* are also your problems. So that whereas I have given up all my problems, I am very much concerned with the lives of my children. When they are in trouble and their marriages don't do well, or something like that, I get very, very unhappy.

It's a different kind of unhappiness. Materially, they are all doing fine. But I don't find them happy.

It's a terrible thing to say, but I think I had a happier childhood and a happier youth than youth has today. Yes, I think that I had a happier youth than youth has today! And one of the reasons is that I had fewer options. It was all so simple. You graduated. You went to work. You got married. You had your children—it was all so easy. You could handle it. But if you pick up the *Dictionary of Occupations* you know there are about two-and-a-half million different occupations a kid can go into.

And you can go on to college forever—and before you can finish, they come up with a new degree, and a new curriculum, and then you can go on with that—then it shoots off on another branch, and a kid can go to college forever! There's a funny joke where the kid has a B.A. and an M.A., he's got a Ph.D., he's thirty-two years old—and the only thing he hasn't got is a J.O.B. And it isn't that he doesn't want to work, but the fields keep expanding. In the sciences, for instance, there's more, and more—it's forever! And I've watched my children. The demand is made upon them to keep up with all the new, the new, the new—and now that we have worn out this world, it's space, and they're going to go on to space!

And just when I thought I could just sit down and take off my shoes, I find that my children get into many problems in a very complicated world. And because I love them, because I try to be a good father, because I believe in the family, I find a lot of heartache in watching their agonies.

It's a deep concern. The major source of whatever unhappiness I have in my life is my children's problems rather than my own.

ON SOURCES OF STRENGTH ...

My parents. We majored in adversity! So, you know, you couldn't expect things to get much worse. I had one sister. My mother gave birth to nine sons and one daughter. And when my sister got married there was no long lecture on sex education. My mother just told her, "Expect the worst and you'll never be disappointed." Now, that's fundamentally how I feel. If I write a book and it didn't work out—maybe I wanted it to be on the best-seller list for twenty-seven years, you know—I would just say to myself, "Don't *expect* so much. Who gave you the right to expect so much." So, I don't expect as much.

It's an attitude. I will define my successes and failures, not the world. I'm not going to be made unhappy by their ideas. I've never gone hungry. I've talked a lot about poverty, but I've never gone hungry because we made do, we made do, we made do! We were great make-doers! And I make do with everything. I mean that in all sincerity. I have a home and a car and everything, but if you took it all away from me, you wouldn't leave a man with a broken heart here crying. I'm still *me!* I'm alive! I'm thinking! I'm breathing and I'm talking to people—my mind is functioning. I'm a very wealthy guy but my material possessions are only of secondary importance.

On religious and moral principles . . .

You get your training fundamentally in the family. I think that is the greatest school there is. I think going to school is a form and a formula that is required of civilized people. But my mother and father taught us affection and taught us love and taught us ritual; and yet I am not a religious man in the sense that my father was. My father was a ritualist. "It is written that . . . And this is the way you do it." Orthodox forms were very important. They were beautiful and they were colorful. I still love candlelight and I love holidays and all that, but I am of another time and another generation, and to me the line that "man was created in the image of God" is a purely spiritual concept. I don't think of it physically. My father really meant it—arms, hands, legs, feet. I think that there is a Supreme Mind that operates the universe and that that Mind is interested in me. And very often I have taken the attitude, it's a switch on that political line "Ask not what your country can do for you, but what can you do for your country"—I've gone so far as to say, "Ask not what life can do for me, but what can I do for life?" How can I enhance life?

Now I have quietly in the back of my mind been working on a book which will fill a gap if I can only do it right. I find that the one subject that does not run through our education is *morality*. It should be like a river that runs through all our education, all subjects everywhere. What is the moral purpose of this? What good can this do for humanity? You know we have developed all kinds of curricula but nobody puts it all together—maybe by accident you take a course in morality or ethics if you can get it.

But I have felt that I wanted to start from the beginning and that the first reading should not be "Jump, Dick, jump," but rather "Love, Dick, love." And start right from the bottom with the four-letter words like give, hope, care, kiss, help—those are the words, these are the building blocks with which youngsters should start. And I'm going to do a textbook which will either be a big nothing because people think it is pure corn, or it will be successful.

Some time ago I began to let my mind run free, and I said I'll see what happens. "A" doesn't have to stand for alligator. Why is it always in the picture books as an animal? You know, "Z" is a zebra, "L" is a llama. So I sat down and I said, "What would happen if we said 'A' stands for 'all of us,' and you develop that theme. And 'B' stands for 'bad.'" Now I know that it's hard to define "bad," so I said, we all do bad things. They are bad simply because they are not good. Do you know what I mean? It's better to do good things, because if we do good things we all feel better, you see? If you want to be bad, I could give a lot of words that begin with "B." You can bite, you can battle, you can bump—give a whole list of "B" 's.

It's just a matter of facing the fact that it's better to live peacefully with others, but instead of presenting a big concept like that in such a book, simply explain that you don't really feel good when you are bad. You feel better when you are good. So let's try "G" is for good, "L" is for love, "O" is for old, and there I would say that you should know what old is because you are going to be old someday. And I would say, we *all* must learn to be old, etc.

The problem with me is that I'm a humorist, so I'm expected to be funny. So I ran into Clifton Fadiman, who is an old friend of mine and I respect his judgment. He said, "Sam, it's great, but you had better write some humorous commentary with it using examples out of your own life to prove that good is good or whatever stories you would want to tell." Tell a little story to illustrate— sort of a contemporary Aesop, you know. I am kind of excited about the concept and it is nonreligious. And the reason it is nonreligious is because I have never seen as much ill will as there is between religious denominations. It would defeat its own purpose if written from a religious perspective. One church would say, "What do you mean by prayer?" They can't even agree on what prayer means. Not only do they disagree on whether or not they should pray, they don't even know what it is. So, I'll include an introduction which will say that I'm going to keep away from that, and you can have your own fights outside.

Do you know what I'm going to call the book? *Love Letters.*

And what do you do when you get to "Z"? "Z" stands for zero. I'll say that zero is just a circle with nothing in it. Now the world is also a circle, but it has a lot in it. And a lot of what's in it depends upon what you put in there. See? That's the difference between a zero and a world.

You know I turned to my wife and I said, "I hadn't the vaguest notion that this was going to happen, but there again you have got to trust that mind of yours. Let it go, let it ride." What do you do with "X"? How many words are there that begin with "X"? Well, I thought the only word I know is x-ray. What can you do with x-ray? How wonderful it would be if we could all see into each other, past the surface, into where the heart is. And the idea began to take off. And I would say you can't do it for yourself. You must do it for me, and I must do it for you. You have to develop an x-ray vision and tell me about me and I'll tell you about you.

MORE ON GROWING OLDER ...

I think that since old people are not generally respected—the saying is "They are taken care of, but they are not cared for"—they become a nuisance to humanity in many people's minds.

I have been to a Lutheran convention where they took me to a home, and I have never seen any more dignified treatment of older people. But when a reporter or anybody asks me my age, I refuse to answer. Not on grounds that it's going to incriminate me. I say, "What am I doing?" If I am adding to life, then I am young even though my age might be seventy-five. I'm still contributing to life. I am young. All people can contribute to life. You can be ninety and as long as you don't feel you have nothing left to say or do—that's death, a living death—you will feel young. I have sat with ninety-year-old men and you just say to them, "C'mon, get off it, you have just said something to me that has given me a whole page to write about," and the ninety-year-old man says, "What did I say?" And I told him what he said to me, that it was so profound. A couple of them I put in the book, you know, like "You're never too old to learn something stupid." In other words, what I'm saying is, "Am I acting alive?"

Am I acting alive? Do I look alive? If so, then I'm alive! Don't put an age number on life. I refuse to let them number me because there are implications. Suddenly you can't do this. You're eighty, you certainly can't do that! I don't believe a word of it! I saw Pablo Casals working at ninety-one and ninety-two. He drove me up the wall. He played the passion according to St. Mathew, and I had never heard such art. The man was ninety-two with a big towel around his neck. The secret is *do* and keep on *doing!*

On the international situation . . .

I think we are at the crossroads between two fundamental ideas. It's either "Can I" or "Can *we* make it alone?" Or is that an ancient concept—can I make it alone? We must make room for *we*—only *we* can do it, the collective world. It's the individual versus the collective world. And it doesn't frighten me to say that in America we need more emotional and moral collectivism in the sense that we had it in the beginning. Remember? "*We* the people," not *I* the people, not *me*, but "*we*." That kind of collectivism, emotional, educational, social, is a healthy thing—but only under freedom!

I could operate nicely in a free collective, but I couldn't operate in an enslaved collective. It has to be voluntary—our voluntarism versus their "compulsarism." Everything that's not forbidden is prescribed, you know, is the way their line goes. I feel at this point that my freedom is being taken away. It's not being taken away by *my* country, but it's being taken away by great sections of the world who say to me now, "You are a failure, your system in America is a failure." Theirs, they say, is a better one and the future of the world lies in socialism. So far we have had no proof of their success! And I have a line which says that "the value of a country can still be measured by the number of people trying to get in versus the number of people trying to get out."

Now I feel free. I do not mind the restrictions that are put upon me in the name of the total good. O.K. I'm willing. I'm a very sentimental guy. I'm a success, but I do not hesitate at all to share. We have shared time together here, we have become friends, we have talked. I will share anything I have in the world, and I feel richer for it. It's a great experience. And the older I get, the more willing I am to share everything. I have told that to my children. I've said, "You know, I had nothing. I've earned a little money and I've put it aside. It's really for all of us. I'm not handing it over to you, but I want you to know that I didn't think of myself alone, but of us as a family. It's for all of us that I have worked."

And I also let them know that if something should happen,

that if I am in trouble, then I expect them to sustain me as I sustained them. Otherwise we are not a family—not even friends. I told them they had better come through, because I'm telling them now that if I should get sick and should run out of money or be in trouble, I don't care where you get it, you're going to take care of me—because I did it for you!

I wouldn't hesitate. And my son said there was no question about that. No question about my daughter either. No doubt about that. Yes indeed, for if it's really a family it's not *I* or *me*, but rather it's *us!*

REFERENCES

Levenson, Sam, *Everything but Money*, New York: Simon & Schuster, 1949.

———, *In One Era and Out the Other*, New York: Simon & Schuster, 1973.

———, *You Can Say That Again, Sam!*, New York: Simon & Schuster, 1975.

———, *You Don't Have to Be in Who's Who to Know What's What*, New York: Pocket Books (Simon & Schuster), 1979.

ROLLO MAY

PSYCHOANALYST, lecturer, writer, Rollo May was born in Ada, Ohio, April 21, 1909. Author of Love and Will *and many other books, May earned degrees from Oberlin College, Union Theological Seminary, and Columbia University. He holds honorary doctorates from several institutions, and his distinguished work has won many awards, among them the Ralph Waldo Emerson Award and the Distinguished Contributors Award of New York University.*

We met in Dr. May's contemporary home in Tiburon, California, a ferry ride away from San Francisco. The walls of his living room were hung with paintings, and a window wall gave way to a spectacular view of San Francisco Bay. May, a lean man with penetrating eyes and a wonderful smile, was dressed casually in slacks and sport shirt.

How important is the family?

Well, I don't think there is any doubt that the family is going to persevere in some way or another. I don't think in my case, at least in my family, that it is technology so much that affects the family. I think it is more a loss of the sense of community—everybody is on his own. I think it is psychological, religious, and ethical. Obviously the family is disintegrating.

We had six kids in my family and had a very tough time. We had a difficult time maintaining morale. Our family had in it about everything that disintegrates a family. We dispersed to the far ends of the country, and our parents were divorced. I am very fond of my two brothers. But the only one who has what might be called a family is my brother who married a Roman Catholic, and he is a Catholic, too. He became a Catholic after they got married.

But there is no doubt at all that the family by and large is going through a transition, and I think the great experiment of the communities on the part of youngsters is, first of all, to try to resuscitate the family, and secondly, to find a substitute for it if necessary.

There was a community set up about seventy miles up the road from here called Forestville. Some of my dear friends participated. Now these kinds of families are very difficult to sustain—they always peter out. I thought that this one would last about five years and it did. They don't have a purpose beyond themselves whereas an ordinary family does. In the ordinary family there is a structure—mother, father, youngsters, and the mother and father almost always put some kind of purpose into the family whether it is verbalized or not. They want their children to be well educated, good Christians, well liked, and successful. I think parents usually do that—and if parents don't do it, the children seek it somewhere else.

Now these communities are organized and lived in by small groups and, it seems to me, perform a very important service for the rest of us. Most of these communities don't succeed, but they have shown the importance and significance of community living. And they demonstrated that if you don't have a family, you can create one. You have got to have your support group.

In my family we teased each other, sometimes rather cruelly, but we supported each other. Nevertheless, teasing can be a substitute if you haven't got anything else for communication. So, I am not really pessimistic about the future of the family. I think it is going to continue. I don't really expect that some new kibbutzim or some other sort of thing will take over. But there will have to be some kind of community—maybe several small families living together. We have out here in California quite a lot of this—what you might call the enlarged or extended family with two or three young women parenting all the children and their husbands out working.

The tremendous change in this modern world has resulted in a loss of the basic elements and symbols that are essential to human life. They absorb the excessive anxiety and the guilt. We don't have them in our day. Everybody is as though he were wandering alone and not quite knowing the road—swimming alone, for instance, in this bay. This is why we have a lack of commitment— no mooring posts. Commitment ought to be given by the family, and if it is not, it has to be given by some community of sorts, some support group. If that fails, then we have the really alienated individual who will wander from pillar to post, perhaps be psycho- analyzed a number of times, and often turn out to be wandering as much at sixty as he did at twenty. I don't think our culture can support this. But there will always be some people like that. For the general run of people we have to have form. Often the most productive people are these strangers or estranged people, but that cannot do as a sound foundation for people, cities, or nations.

What do people learn about integrity? The family has to be the channel. We learned that integrity was an important value.

WHAT ABOUT LOVE AND HATE?

There are a number of platitudes that I could express about love and hate, but your readers are going to know those anyway. I think the importance of love and hate resides in the fact that they both always have to exist together. And I think the idea that we can produce a world of love is not only nonsense, but dangerous.

I used to be taught that idea in Peoples Church in East Lansing, Michigan, back when I was going to the university and when I was on the faculty there for a couple of years. I was the student director at the church and we believed then that we had made progress in getting over hate and generating more love the same way you made progress in the Olds Motor Company. As there would be gradually less and less hatred, people would be less warlike.

We were all pacifists then. We had Norman Thomas and others come out and talk. I remember that once we had a big League of Nations meeting in the student-union building there at Michigan State and some guy who headed the League of Nations organization made a big speech. We were all sure there would be no more wars. We students were absolutely *certain* there would not be. We thought that love would enlarge without hatred, and I think now that this was absolute nonsense—but not quite absolute, because it still has ideal-power. But essentially it's nonsense, and, I believe, or at least I think that this belief—that we must always be on the side of love—is one of the reasons that Hitler triumphed. As a result of the influence of that belief, we didn't really believe in this country what was going on.

When I graduated from Oberlin I went to Greece. I lived in Europe for three years. I certainly learned a lot over there about tragic things. I learned about the tragedy of life. Back at Michigan State we never believed that at all. I think one has to have a tragic point of view in his idealism—otherwise he is going to be dangerous.

Love and hate are as necessary for each other as night is to day. Confucius has this to say—that you not only must love well, but you must hate well. And I don't think that love increases as hatred goes down. I think that both love and hate increase as human beings become more sensitive, more aware, more conscious. The moral standard is not measured by how much you love other people. But the good man, in my mind, is the man who is most sensitive to and conscious of others. He is aware of the effect his actions have.

Now this means also that sensitivity and consciousness are the basis of love. Love without sensitivity and consciousness is nonsense. It's like that of a dog or a cat—it's not human. This is why sin is a part of the classical religions as most of us in our day understand them. We think of such concepts as sin, evil, and the devil as symbols of hate. Incidentally, I don't believe in a devil. But I do believe in what I call the diamonic—that is, using one's potentialities in a nonintegrative way. This is what I like to call the diamonic, and that means power.

But when it is used nonintegratively, it becomes vicious. Temper, the ability to get angry, is a good thing. It is very much present in all creativity. But to lose your temper is diamonic, destructive.

Now these very same potentialities (the diamonic), when used integratively, change and do become positive. They give us zest in the same way sex does. The constructive aspect of the diamonic is love. Or you could say that the destructive aspect of love is the diamonic. Perhaps that's a better way to put it. So I am interested indeed that when countries go to war, they still do so for reasons that people just don't understand. I think most of us are barking up the wrong tree—trying to figure out the causes of war. But you know, it's a very strange thing, after a war, we generally become sensitive and help the very people that we fought.

During World War II the Japanese were thought of as devils and the most evil, slinky people you ever saw. As soon as the war was over, our attitudes changed. And they changed intensively— which means that what we repressed, the constructive views, could only come out after the peace treaty was signed. The changing relationship between Germany and America is a very good example, too.

DO YOU THINK GOALS ARE IMPORTANT?

Goals are essential as a means of aiding the commitment of the total person to whatever he is devoted to. Without goals there is no integration. As a psychoanalyst, I can see that—because you integrate the personality around and toward some goal.

WHAT ABOUT DEALING WITH OPPOSITE POINTS OF VIEW?

Well, I think the best approach is to listen. The others will have some truth on their side in what they are saying. I can't think of any possible statement in the world that doesn't have some truth in it. But it is also amazing how listening to somebody else dilutes the negative in what they're saying. It's quite amazing how flattering listening is to the person with whom you are communicating.

In therapy it is obvious. Carl Rogers was quite right in his contention that the listening is the most important thing. We often find in psychoanalysis that people we work with have never been really listened to by anybody—and that's why they're there. There's no way of avoiding confrontation and the confrontation that is most constructive is the most direct. I mean that I don't think we should hesitate a bit to debate our point of view. I love the English parliament for that reason. These guys get up and spiel away often for the fun of spieling. But there comes out of it some very skillful debate points—and I think a very skillful government. It's not doing so well now, but I don't think it's their fault. They were tremendous at one point in time when they practically ruled the world.

You've probably seen over the TV and radio some of Winston Churchill's confrontations with other speakers in the House of Commons; he was an excellent debater. I didn't like debating much as a college sport, but I do think that the listening, which means taking seriously the other person's view, and then opposing it as you think important, are contributions to both of you—to you and to the person you oppose. He learns something from your confrontataion that he otherwise wouldn't have learned at all.

I think people in academe are so concerned about their own status, their own prestige, and the prestige of their ideas that they tend sometimes to become dogmatic—as though one could preserve one's idea by shouting loudest about it. Academics also tend to hide their ideas. Paul Tillich once said that he and Martin Heidegger, who were among the best philosophers in Germany and taught at the same school, never spoke to each other. They taught for three years at the same school! I think the school was in Frankfurt, but they never once spoke to each other. Now there is in Germany a great deal of pride about not interfering with somebody else's point of view, but Tillich said he thought that was not a constructive thing. However, after he left that university he often talked with Heidegger. Now in our country we do a little better. However, I do believe there is a problem here, and that is, the need various people in the academic world have for status, which takes an intellectual form. This need has a great deal to do with the dogma that is born of it.

The best way to make an idea tighter and better is to get friends to examine it. Many don't dare do that.

HOW DO YOU DEAL WITH GREAT LOSS?

I believe that a living conception of fate is a very important thing in anyone's conception of life—what the Greeks call fate.

Now you and I had no choice whatever in what family we were going to be born into—that's one aspect of fate. I would define fate as characteristics of life that can't be influenced, that nothing can be done about. Now I'm quite aware that Shakespeare thought it was not in our stars, but in ourselves. Sure, a great deal is, and whatever is, then it's our task and our interest to do what we can. Well, certain things simply cannot be changed. You can do a little bit about how long you'll live, maybe add six months by staying away from cigarettes. But you cannot change the fact that if we can effect change, it is only in a technical sense. Let's take where we are born, we have no choice over that at all. Part of the value of living is in a struggling against fate, and if fate weren't there, living would have infinitely less value.

I remember my tuberculosis—I had TB for about five or six

years. I was a cripple for over ten years. My thirties were entirely absorbed by tuberculosis. I had a fifty-fifty chance of living or dying. I did not begin to get over it until I made up my mind that the doctors were not going to cure me. They didn't know much about it anyway. I was the one who had the disease, and I had to consider it an aspect of fate—an aspect which I had decided to shift as much as I could to guilt. Now guilt is fate that you can do something about—or that you should have done something about. For example, people would write me letters when I had TB saying it's terribly unfortunate that you've got this disease and I'm very sorry for you. That didn't help much. What did help was when someone like the Catholic priest from a nearby monastery came around and sat down beside me—we were just friends. With him I could ask, what was happening in my life (that I contributed) that led, partially at least, to this TB? And God knows there was. I worked too hard and this and that. I worked days at the university and nights to get my doctorate, or vice versa. But one can take one's losses. I shouldn't say *can*, because it is awfully difficult. I have a very dear friend who died a week ago in the southern part of the state and that is an ache in my heart. There is nothing in the world to do with it. Sure, I could take a Librium or a Valium or what not, and if it gets too hard I always can. But it's just part of fate and I think it turns out best if one bears as much of it as one can. I mean I could take a Librium every four hours and not feel much of any of it. B. F. Skinner used to say that when somebody you love dies, the best thing to do is to move out of the house, clear away all signs of the other person. And then you will feel less grief. Now, if I ever heard a cockeyed sentence by an intelligent man—I know Skinner and I like him, but he can get off the awfulest bromides—because then you will lose all the value of the grief.

Now what is life without grief? The ancient Greeks had a great deal to tell us. I don't know if you know the poem by Mathew Arnold, "Dover Beach"? Well, it's a great poem, it's his best, and I think it's a great thing. In any case, it tells how the ocean is heaving in and out of the stones, and Sophocles once heard it in the Aegean and know that it was the eternal voice of sadness. Now in any case what Arnold was talking about, as the Greeks knew very well, was that there was an eternal note of sadness, an eternal note of grief, an eternal note of, well, pain, suffering. And I think that it is most growth-producing for a human being to absorb, to take, to experience the unavoidable grief.

We all feel it. It used to be allayed by the religious emphasis. You see, very close to what I am calling fate was the will of God. Well, not exactly the will of God, but what Providence decreed or something. In Ibsen's play, *Peer Gynt*, they got in a big storm in this ship and they realized they couldn't do a thing and they yelled, "To prayers, to prayers." The fact that you go to prayer when you're completely helpless means that you do project on God some aspect of fate. Maybe He can change it. And this used to be done, I think successfully, by a number of intelligent ministers back, say, in the nineteenth century—or maybe some not so intelligent ones in holding the revivals. But now we don't have anybody to do it, and I think that this is one of the reasons for our dilemma. All we have is the old Book of Common Prayer that talks about how we like sheep have gone astray, and so on. I think these emphases did provide a very healthy basis for life in that they helped people to a frame of mind which enabled them to take losses and to expect them.

HOW DO INTERNATIONAL PROBLEMS AFFECT US?

I think they make a great difference. I think of the results of the Viet Nam War, and I am one who believes we lost the war. One of the results we've seen, so long as we have eyes to see, and we do not forget, is that one country cannot war with another without also warring against itself. And this is a shift in human history.

In the nineteenth century it was quite possible to send an army to fight someplace and win or lose. Now it's not. Because the world, it seems to me, is like a human being in that conflicts don't go on just outside ourselves. They go on inside ourselves. I think we had no business there at all—it was a great tragedy that we went into Viet Nam in the first place. But we went in there on nineteenth-century psychology and we simply couldn't win. Now that's not by accident; it is that history and the development of technology have progressed to the point where what happens in Washington is going to have repercussions in Peking, in Tokyo, and in every other capital. I think that's one of the things that I like about Carter. He realized that if you can get Egypt and Israel, the Middle East, together, it will have vast repercussions on how we get along in America. I think it will not only have vast repercussions on our oil, but also on the factions in America. I would say that the longer I live the more I am convinced that what happens in other countries affects me—there but for the grace of God go I; for whom the bell tolls, it tolls for thee. I think that I would put it to students in terms of historical change; the thinking of the nineteenth century—which is each country for itself and the devil take the hindmost—will no longer work. If Russia were to attack China today I don't think there is a chance for a contained war. We contained it in a little country like Viet Nam only by the grace of God.

We have to live from here on out in a planetary world rather than in a world of nations. In order to get to that point, the undeveloped nations have to find themselves as nations, which means that they will be over-nationalistic for a few years. But I think it's necessary for the rest of us to realize that what goes on in any capital affects other capitals.

WHO HAS BEEN IMPORTANT IN SHAPING YOUR LIFE?

The man who has influenced me most of all is Paul Tillich.* Tillich and I were very close and dear friends for some thirty

* Dr. May wrote a biography of Paul Tillich: *Paulus*, New York: Harper & Row, 1973.

years. He was the wisest man I ever knew and also the most sensitive. He taught me all kinds of important things. My learning comes chiefly from Tillich. *The Meaning of Anxiety* comes chiefly from Tillich. Perhaps I shouldn't say chiefly, but among the people who influenced me, he was chief.

And of course it's necessary, if one's going to be at all accurate, to bring in one's parents if they were around long enough to be an influence—God knows they are going to do it in one way or another. My father always believed in me. He was not a very successful man, but he had the idea (he was in YMCA work) that it was good to train youngsters to take their own initiative later on. And when he'd be building a porch on the house (he and I working with a hammer), he would ask my opinion on what board to put where. And of course I would think of giving my opinion. Now I hope he didn't follow it because I didn't know a damn thing about such things, or not very much at least, but I liked to work with him. And the important point is that he would do things that would show a kind of respect for my ideas, my individuality. I think that was very helpful. My mother, who was a very sad and disturbed person, had a terribly bad temper, was very excitable, and couldn't get along with anybody. She had been an orphan and she had a great deal of courage. Now I think of her as having a good deal of courage. In psychology I have always been among the shock troops, although I haven't chosen to be. I just seem to find myself way out front because that's where I think the significant problems are. But when I'm introduced to others as having courage, I always think of my mother, for she fought her way through life like a tiger and half destroyed us kids en route; but if we survived, it seemed we would survive as strong people.

In psychology Alfred Adler was my first teacher and he, I'm sure, influenced me most. But then existentialism has always been my philosophical home. Existentialists talked my language on lots of stuff. They certainly influenced me.

I would put success in quotation marks because we don't know. I mean if I die tomorrow, will I have had any influence or not? I think that really what success means as you use it, might be called notoriety, or that one is well-known. Now I'm well-known. But whether or not I'm a success we have to leave to God. I think that some people are great successes and we have never heard of them. Well, certainly the fact that I was born in the twentieth century accounts for the fact that I've shifted from religion and theology to psychotherapy and psychology. Because I think that the psychoanalyst and psychotherapist occupy the role that the priest used to occupy during the Renaissance and even later on.

If you had troubles in those days you went to a priest or a minister and nowadays you don't. You go to a therapist of some sort. I'm not making a value judgment as to which is better. I think the former is much better, but I'm not trying to say that. I think that one of the great problems in psychology is that we try to straddle two quite different realms. The damn science has become warped by virtue of this fact. We try to have one foot in creativity and in caring for people (which were always the concerns of religion and philosophy) and the other in empirical studies. Those to my mind are irreconcilable and totally different approaches. Now the first involves empathy. The second must *not* involve empathy because if it does it will be screwed up. I was born in the twentieth century when all of this was in flux. I was in the ministry for a couple of years, and I liked it and became a psychotherapist. I've never regretted that. But also I've never regretted having the theological training. I find it tremendously useful. Going to Greece had a great effect on me. Meeting Adler had a great effect.

The last World War resulted in a great influx of German scholars into this country; they influenced me tremendously. Tillich was one of them. Kohler* was one of them. The arrival of

* Wolfgang Kohler was a psychologist who was born in Estonia and came to the United States in 1935.

these scholars in New York in that period was a tremendous thing. It was a stimulating period. Many analysts came from Europe as exiles. Erich Fromm* was one. These people were great sources of wisdom. You know, I never thought how important it was until just now. I am vaguely working on an autobiography. What I am saying now gives me a lot of new ideas. New York used to be a vital, fertile place, and I think it was largely because of these good scholars who were most often German. They happened to be German, but others were French, Italian, God knows what.

WHAT WRITERS AFFECTED YOUR THINKING?

I would start with the Greeks. Aeschylus I would put at the very top, and Sophocles, and Euripides. Their writings have influenced me tremendously—more so than Shakespeare, well, more so than any modern people. Every time I read *The Oresteia*† I catch fire. In a negative sense, Lucretius in *The Nature of the Universe* had an impact. I never agreed with his theory of the universe at all, but I think he writes absolutely beautifully and this has affected me.

A course in Greek inspired me. We had a seminar in the library with about fifteen people. We sat in the front of the library around a table and there was a Greek vase in the middle of the table. I had just come from my hometown up in Michigan and I had never seen anything like it. My family was not what you would call cultured. And I used to sit there day after day thinking I had never seen anything so beautiful. How is it that human beings can make such a thing as that? And I developed a kind of reverence for ancient Greek art. This was tremendously valuable for me and led to my going to Greece where I saw all of the rest of it.

* Erich Fromm, a psychoanalyst who was born in Germany, came to the United States in 1934.
† Aeschylus's most famous surviving tragedy.

How do you feel about growing older?

My main concern is that I won't have enough time to finish up the books that I want to write. There are about four or five of them. And I don't have any problems with the aging illnesses—I don't hear terribly well, but I never have heard terribly well. I often think it's because I'm an introvert. I'm not much interested in hearing some of the stuff that you have to hear. But I want to be able to write. I want my faculties, especially my intellectual faculties. The memory deteriorates somewhat when you're around my age. Well, I hope that the rest of my brain will continue to bubble and continue to have the zip that is necessary in writing. I seem to have no problem with the zip when I'm asked questions. This seems a very good way to turn me on. But I do hope that I don't lose any of my intellectual faculties.

The growing older itself means that—let's say, I have about ten more years to live. I expect I will live for fifteen or twenty more, but in any case, let's be conservative about it—die at eighty. What I regret most is that I would leave my friends. I'd be leaving the people that I knew, the people that I love. I don't particularly regret being mortal and I think I would rather be mortal than immortal because the gods always got bored to beat hell. But I do regret having to say good-bye to everybody. That would be the real problem for me.

The brain research that seems to be going on over in Berkeley does indicate that there is no actual organic deterioration associated with aging. There seems to be little doubt about that now. If you can keep your spirits up, your brain will be all right. Then it's mostly a matter of psychological commitment. But also, there is such a thing as wisdom, and it often seems to me that the wisdom is connected with the fact that the older we are, the more we forget the details of the present day. I notice that when I go downstairs with a cup of tea. I'll put it down someplace and I won't remember where I put it down. Well, it's perfectly irrelevant whether I put it on the stove there, or on this table, or whatnot.

The irrelevant things drop out and the things that are not irrelevant become more important. The thoughts you have as an older person are more significant than any you've ever had in your life. What I'm trying to say is that's why they always had the old men run the tribe. Their sense of judgment, their sense of significance was greater even though their memories had gone to hell.

We in this country have lost our appreciation of wisdom; perhaps we are getting it back to some extent now. I think it's a tremendous thing. The Academy of Independent Scholars that Boulding* is organizing addresses the matter.

Is there hope for mankind?

Yup. But I think the question is wrong. You have to ask about hope in the technological sense. You mean that you hope the race is going to go on—I don't know, and you don't know, and nobody knows.

The question of whether people are going to live together effectively and integratively with each other is subsumed under the planetary perspective. But I would ask, is there hope for values? Is there hope for creativity? If you can be creative, intensively, you are apt to live for quite a long time. People die because they have lost that, and their enthusiasm goes with their creativity, business people particularly do this. Let's go back to art history. The men who could really paint, painted a long, long time and lived right on until something happened.

But now I would ask the question about hope, not in terms of technical problems, nor in terms of people getting together (because they've got to do that or we are going to be defunct), but in terms of values, in terms of capacity to love each other (which also means a capacity to hate each other), capacity to appreciate each other, capacity to value the original contribution of African

* Academy of Independent Scholars, organized by Kenneth E. Boulding in 1979, is located at Academy Building, 970 Aurora, Boulder, Colorado 80302.

tribes. All of these things would really comprise what I call civilization: the capacity to save the Parthenon—I don't think it's going to be saved, but the statues are indoors and they're going to be saved—and the capacity to appreciate music, as well as the capacity to create music and art. In some ways we have seen our capacity to appreciate diminish over the past ten, twenty, thirty years. I'm very much a modern artist, but I also know that modern art is partly not devoted to beauty. But if you want to see beautiful things, you don't go to a modern-art exhibit. You go to an ancient-art exhibit or you go to see the French impressionists. You don't go to modern art.

Over there on the wall, the lower one—now that's an excellent painting. I wouldn't say that if I wanted to look at beauty I would look at that. I would look at mine above which is a much simpler thing. Or I would look at this one over here, which is a drawing I made up north here a while back. Or that one over there which is a drawing of pine trees, a pastel. Now, the one over there is by my daughter. I have girl twins and they are both artists and my brother's an artist. Our family is entirely artists and psychologists. My son is a psychologist and so are a couple of nieces, and I'm very much a part of the art world.

I know that the art during the past couple of decades has been mostly for the purpose of shocking—all sorts of strange things—a white piece of paper with a frame around it, a toilet seat with a frame around it. Now what they're trying to do is to get people to listen, and to hear, and to see. And that may diminish, I mean people's ability to see, and to hear, and to have music, may diminish. God knows that TV, and rock and roll, and all sorts of that kind of thing do not foster it. There might possibly be hope in everybody dying. I don't happen to think so, but there might be. T. S. Eliot once said that his prayer would be for God to teach us not to hope, for if we hope, we would hope for the wrong things. Now this is very much to the point. People who have lived in the past thirty, forty years have tended to hope for exactly the wrong things—prosperity, making more money, winning the war.

Do you think it is more difficult for young people today?

If I were to say anything, I would say less difficult. Because there is more learning, there is more information. You take the sexual problems, which I had quite severely in my teens and early twenties. Apparently young people today are much more aware of sex. Back when I grew up nobody would even talk about it. Now they read about it and they see movies about it. Whether or not that's good is a real question, but I think it's a little better. I think that the positive aspects outweigh the negative aspects by a little bit.

But I really don't know whether it is more difficult or less difficult for young people. Maybe the very difficulties that I had to fight are partly responsible for their success. It's very hard to tell that, you see. If people were going to turn out to be a Lincoln or someone like that, I wouldn't want them to stay back in the nineteenth century so that they could.

There is in young people, many of them, at least, a latent hostility. And this comes out of what we were talking about earlier—that the society has lost its myths and its symbols. It is as though everybody is an orphan and kids notice this first of all. There is no structure by which they can relate to God, if you want to use a religious symbol. There is no structure by which they can deal with their guilt. Now all these things are set out in the open, and what it does is make young people very mad.

They are also quite angry about the fact that (at least around here) their parents lead such high, wide, and handsome lives and never stay home to be with them. This seems to be the cause of some of it. A TV man who came up here to study this place says that's his impression of the young people to whom he has talked.

Well, in that sense it's more difficult to grow up nowadays than earlier.

Are there ways to achieve a long, happy, and productive life?

It's not done by secrets. It's done by good hard work and devotion. That's the way to a productive, happy, and long life—joyful is a better word than happy. Happy sounds placid—it's a by-product of joy.

Are there religious or moral principles you consider important?

The two things go together. One is integration of the self, pulling oneself together (so difficult for young people without the symbols and structure), the other is commitment. These two values underlie others—they operate together. You have to have one to have the other. We put meaning into life by virtue of our capacity to experience joy, a creation of our power. It depends upon how much we put into our experiences: power, creativity, love, joy.

What have been your sources of strength?

I think that a great source of strength is belief in the values one holds. You need to hold to some central values. We have the choice: Do we want meaning in life or not? Life will reflect *our* meaning. There is a powerful tendency to love a person back who loves you. The matter of love comes to me as the strongest thing you can muster. I am also a great believer in solitude.

Modern society needs its older people. It's suicidal to waste the wisdom of the older generation.

REFERENCES

May, Rollo, *Love and Will*, New York: W. W. Norton, 1969.

———, *Paulus: Reminiscences of a Friendship*, New York: Harper & Row, 1973.

———, *The Courage to Create*, New York: W. W. Norton, 1976.

———, *The Meaning of Anxiety*, New York: W. W. Norton, 1977.

———, *Psychology and the Human Dilemma*, New York: W. W. Norton, 1979.

C. C. MEHTA

A distinguished professor, playwright, and translator, C. C. Mehta has lectured at colleges and universities all over the world. In 1927 he left his studies at the University of Bombay to become a volunteer in the Bardoli Satyagraha movement, a group which worked toward self-rule for India.

For many years a close associate of Mahatma Gandhi, Mehta participated in symbolic demonstrations such as a 24-day, 241-mile walk protesting the British Salt Tax Law, in which a group of 78 volunteers walked to the sea to show the Indian people that British laws must be broken in order for India to attain self-rule.

Mehta also translated for Gandhi, and, when the great leader was jailed, carried on his work, with others, through the publication of an underground newspaper. The eighty-year-old Mehta recalled, with tears in his eyes, his part in the committal of Mahatma Gandhi's ashes to the rivers of India.

We met Mehta one hot October day at the New Delhi apartment of a friend, Mr. I. Patel, former assistant to Sardar Patel and Prime Minister Desai. As a slow-moving ceiling fan stirred the air, we began to hear something of the life and thought of this man whose needs are few and whose inner peace is evident.

IS THE FAMILY IMPORTANT IN TODAY'S WORLD?

In the modern social structure, one cannot live an isolated life, unless he chooses to be a saint who renounces the world and lives alone in the caves or on the mountains. But even there, all of nature is his family. Birds, trees, and rivulets give him company. Therefore, the oldest Vedic concept of "Vasudhaiva Kutumbakam," which says the entire world is one family, should hold true.

The family is an important and useful unit. There may be a few most negligible heartbreaks during one's course of life, but by and large, both the losses and the gains, sorrows and joys are worth sharing by each member of the family, which gives every one much comfort and warmth. A little adjustment here and there makes life worth living. Kalidasa, the great classical poet-play-wright, states in his play *Shakuntala*, "Sorrow divided among the close ones becomes bearable." This is quite a practical truth.

Moreover, angularities of extreme individuality get rubbed off in a family and consideration for others grows. Children get affection and learn to sacrifice, help, and adjust. Childhood and old age need a looking after and a protection. Above all, egotism, the worst enemy of mankind, is kept in check and one is gradually led to expand from "I" to "WE" and thence to "THEY" and "ALL OF US."

WHAT EFFECTS ARE THE FORCES OF LOVE AND HATE
HAVING IN THE WORLD?

Since time immemorial all saints and prophets have advocated "Love thy neighbor as thou loveth thyself." The supreme truth holds its own ground even today. If need be, we may add "Love thy enemies," which may give good results. Hatred should have no place in any progressive society. On the contrary, forces of love have achieved wonders. The problem is how far one can go to put this in practice. But one has to try, if one aims to better the world. Absence of love begets hatred, jealousy, animosity, conflicts, wars, and destruction. Too much emphasis on intellect has killed the heart in the modern world. Love is sacrifice and synthesis; hatred is selfish and destructive.

How important is it to set goals?

Absolutely necessary! Otherwise, life will become blank, aimless, and adrift—a rudderless boat. A goal must be determined according to one's inclination and inward strength. It may be art, or the service of humanity, or carrying out research in science or in any field of knowledge. "Hitch your wagon to the star" or "Have the desire of the moth for the star," in this age of sick hurry and divided aim.

What is the best approach to those who oppose your point of view?

Certainly stick to your convictions; the best approach is persuade the opponent with all humility. Patience at times yields good results; intolerance is harmful. Listen attentively to all the views of the opponent. Then, go slowly and prove your case, put forth all your advantageous arguments supported by logic and facts, experience and knowledge, reading and reflection, and hope for the best. See that no ill feeling is bred in your discussion. Let the ideas clash but not the hearts.

What about communicating with others?

Keep all your windows open in order to receive winds from all directions. In the modern world, communication is the key point of progress. There are two aspects: 1. If you do not know, you may be considered ignorant or a fool; 2. If you happen to know, you may be considered clever, learned, and knowledgeable. Communication helps to break various kinds of barriers, establish contacts, and widen the field of knowledge and understanding. Communications established with the outer worlds of the moon, Mars, Venus, Jupiter, and Saturn help us to know them better; we get a fuller idea of the whole solar system. The spiritualists and the yogis claim to communicate with the higher and the divine powers and with the Almighty. The media may change, but communication will always remain an all-important functional entity in the world at large. Communication is an antenna for all the five senses, for the mind and soul; communication enriches life. Ignorance of peoples and nations is a curse. It is always beneficial to know and understand more and more people and more and more nations; then, realize that national barriers or walls between man and man are false, illusory, and non-human. By doing so, you remove crabbed and confined thinking and feeling. You become a citizen of the world. Caste and creed, race and nationality, then, do not matter much. I have moved almost all over the world and met people of different races, religions, and nations. And now I feel, "what fools these mortals are" when they quarrel over such things as power, possessions, land, boundary, raw materials, and so on when they know that they are not going to live, at the most, more than about a hundred years. Hence, it is the greatest need to have communication with others.

What have you to say about loss?

The self that suffers loss should concentrate on and look to the widening circumference of the not-self with fortitude and hope. The human being as he advances in life must develop the sense of detachment. The main losses are of two kinds: deaths of dear friends and near relatives—loss of love; and of possessions in terms of money and power. If you have developed the sense of detachment, you can easily pull through successfully in all situations. If you have not acquired that detachment, you should weep out your losses. Moreover, if you have inner strength, you can fight them out and lift yourself above them.

How about fears and anxieties?

Develop confidence in yourself. Faith in yourself should be the guide. As a matter of fact, one should try to develop one's nature in such a way that one becomes more and more fearless in almost all walks of life. If you have conquered fear, the anxieties will disappear. And if you have faith in God, you are bound to strengthen your own faith in yourself. This works wonders.

There is another way out. Analyze your fears and anxieties and know their causes. If they are genuine, then try to remove the causes or meet them with fortitude and positive thinking; if they are not real, then rub them off as you do the teardrops from the eyelashes.

Who has most influenced your success?

It would be difficult to define my success. Yet, I can state that what I am today is due to the First World War and the Gandhian Movement, which sharply differentiated the concepts of violence and nonviolence; they influenced me to lead a simple life, that is, to have minimum wants and lofty thinking. Primarily there were two teachers, both of them in the high school—one Mr. C. R. Munshi and the other Mr. M. K. Mulani—who imparted discipline in our studies and games. Later on in the twenties, Sardar Vallabhbhai Patel taught us how to develop disciplined thinking and life. Sardar Patel had a unique practical sense— perhaps the sixth sense, the third eye, quick and sharp. We learned a lot from him while being with him, working with him, and reading with him. That was sufficient in later life to help us face life and its problems squarely and successfully.

There was also another personality who influenced me during

my twenties. Strangely enough, I was lucky to witness the performances and meet the divine dancer Anna Pavolova for fifteen days continuously in Bombay and that infused in me the lifelong love and respect for the theatre. Moreover, the nonviolent Satyagraha Movement brought me in good contact with Gandhiji, who helped to develop in us a great sense of sacrifice, devotion, purposefulness, and a love of truth and mankind as a whole.

WHICH WRITERS, PAST OR PRESENT, AFFECTED YOUR THINKING?

Mahatma Gandhi for clarity and simplicity of thought and writing. I was lucky to have edited his paper, *Navjeevan* when he was in jail. I was also much influenced by the French writers, particularly A. Dumas and Anatole France. For writing plays, my first contact with *Saint Joan* of Bernard Shaw, translating it and staging it during my twenties, gave me a deep insight into play construction.

HOW DO YOU FEEL ABOUT GROWING OLDER?

I feel happy at eighty, as I have learned the golden lesson of eliminating tension, and of always keeping calm. Every age has a goodly wine. I do not bother about the advantages or disadvantages of old age since they are there in every age. Only your viewpoint counts in the matter. At the same time, if you can develop a sense of humor, good cheer compensates for much that you lose by growing older.

The great writer and thinker, Seneca, observed: "There is no cure for old age." I think that is very good advice and one should always remember it. Moreover, I avoid hanging on to the past, which, in fact, to a great extent, shaped my present; I live richly and fully. Physical age has not proved a handicap to my mental age.

If you have failed in your duties toward your health while growing older, begin at once. There is no timetable for undertaking a few simple exercises daily. What you need is to keep your body supple and to keep your mind alert with regular work. From the practical point of view, it is always best to keep the three things clean—the mind, the chest, and the stomach—all for physical and spiritual health. Moreover, be prepared to experience and face the truth of, "from ever-lasting Nay to everlasting Yea." And with faith in God, learn to practice with regard to everything in life, not my will, but "Thy will shall prevail."

Do you have "hope" for mankind?

I do not think that I have any hope for mankind as long as the powerful nations are harboring hatred and fear and running the arms race. That is the surest way to destroy this beauteous earth and all things on it. In spite of all the religious organizations in the East as well as the West, some mad politician, one day, will destroy most of the human beings and other good things. I am convinced of that at least. If I look at it philosophically, I feel that the whole world is a stage and we are merely players in the divine play of the Supreme Being.

Do you think that life is more difficult for young people today?

This is a question of relativity; it would vary according to one's belief, experience, and the social status in which one lives. Yet, I can say that physical life is less difficult for the young today. They have better comforts, dress, food, variety of joyous activities, longer span of youth—i.e., the life of the senses. The life of the mind for them, however, has become more difficult and worse. The easy way of life in the young years today will certainly make it difficult for them to face the problems of old age. The young today should not take to the easier and more comfortable way of life.

ARE THERE "SECRETS" FOR ACHIEVING A LONG LIFE?

First of all one must have God's grace for this. We Indians believe in a divine destiny to a great extent; "There is a divinity that shapes our ends, rough-hew them how we will." However, if a young man wants to have a long life, he can certainly do so by controlling and economizing his breath and reducing the waste of his vital fluid, the semen to the minimum; he must practice the Patanjala Yoga; he must keep his mind, chest, and stomach clean; he must eat less and have fewest of desires and fewest of possessions; he should not allow the cancerous goiter of egotism to grow. For an eternal life or to become a Jivanmukta—who can put on and put off life, he should realize the Kaivalya Samadhi—the attributeless Brahman.

ARE THERE SOME RELIGIOUS AND MORAL PRINCIPLES YOU HAVE FOUND TO BE EXTREMELY IMPORTANT?

What you understand by religion is a foreign thought to us. The word itself is European. The Latin and the Greek thinkers differ in its definition. St. Augustine accepts both of the meanings and uses them in both the senses. One is "to take up," i.e., "to be gathered," i.e., to observe the science of divine communication. That is what Cicero also said. But Servius held: "to bind," meaning relationship. From this, most European religions have come to mean a fixed relationship between the human self and some non-human entity, which may be the sacred, the supernatural, self-existence, or simply God.

In India, the religion starts from one's own self. Look within and know "That Thou Art," or "Aham Brahmasmi." Principles of simple living, high thinking, keeping the ego subdued, of sacrifice, of being helpful to others, of having affection for man and the world, I have found to be important in my life.

Dr. Radhakrishnan defined religion as a way of life for us. I have learned to keep myself clean, free from pride and greed, and not to allow the heart to be killed as the intellect grows. I have also learned to live, to love deeply and widely. Moreover, when I have not been able to realize the divine, I have at least not allowed myself to become a dehumanized devil. I have learned to pursue one great goal of art which has enriched my life, I have learned to be my own police in order not to become an enemy of the man and the world within and without.

WHAT HAS BEEN YOUR GREATEST SOURCE OF STRENGTH?

Faith in God and an optimistic outlook. "If winter comes, can spring be far behind?" and "There is a silver lining to every cloud" are the ideas that strengthen me.

WHAT ABOUT THE FUTURE?

It seems that the experience and wisdom of older people will have a marked influence upon the future society since the extreme individualities of the young have not brought about the necessary constructive benefits.

Peace in the world seems to be a distant dream, possibly a mirage. Yet, if the superpowers and their dependent small powers honestly give up war and the deathly weapons as the means of solving the problems in the world, peace may come.

The vast developments in the fields of communication and transportation have not fully reached all corners of the world. If these available means are used with tolerance and understanding and some other measures such as free movements in all countries of the world, real cooperation and help for one another, disarmament, healthy rivalry, peaceful means of solving all kinds of conflicts, truthful reporting, and so on are taken, it is likely that we shall have one world government with a better life for all peoples.

CLAUDE D. PEPPER

CLAUDE PEPPER served as United States Senator (1936–1951) and, since his defeat in the 1950 senatorial election, as congressman from Florida. Born in 1900 in the Dudleyville, Alabama area, Pepper was educated at the University of Alabama and at Harvard Law School. A champion of the elderly, he leads the House Select Committee on Aging; in fact, he had just come from conducting a committee hearing when he met with us.

Memorabilia line the walls of his Washington office, ranging from a picture of Orville Wright's biplane to a photo of Neil Armstrong's moon walk. There is also a framed letter from Franklin Delano Roosevelt in which FDR thanks Pepper for seconding his nomination to the presidency at the Democratic National Convention in 1932. This letter provides some reassuring evidence of the continuity and history which "the senator"—as he is still called by some of his friends and colleagues—embodies.

Pepper was warm and relaxed as we talked, despite the pressures of his work and his evident concern for his wife, ill in Florida, whom he planned to visit that afternoon.

I feel that it is an important unit of society and I think it is the predominant source of influence upon the young who grow up to become members of a family. I know that my mother and father had a great deal of influence over me. My father was a farmer, merchant, and law-enforcement officer. My mother was a noble, wonderful lady of great character and courage who brought me up in a country church called County Line Church between Chambers and Tallaposseh Counties in Alabama. I was born in Chambers. My father was superintendent of a Sunday school and my mother played the organ—one of those organs that you pump with your feet. She was rather talented in music, my father was good at singing, and so the two of them were active in the leadership of the Sunday school. I was just a little tot beginning to run around in the church, but I remember going to prayer meetings.

So they had a profound influence on me and I think ordinarily a family does have an influence for good or bad upon their children. I hope in most instances for good. I know in my case it was for good.

Well, I believe in love and I believe in it as a great motivator in one's life. I think that the impact of hate upon one's life is a grievous one. It's negative. It's corroding to the spiritual being which harbors it. Right now my wife is terribly ill and it's my love for her that makes her illness an extremely exacting thing for me— it's a very difficult experience.

Love for my mother, father, brothers, sister, love for the things that are important in the world, the spiritual values of life, love for friendship and worthy people, noble people that I have been privileged to be associated with mean a great deal to me. I have always tried to live an affirmative life, and I've tried to be an advocate of doing good, of helping people.

I sometimes have a little temper, and it was taxed when a man defeated me in one of my campaigns, taking me out of the Senate with a vicious, unscrupulous, and very brutal campaign. Well, it hurt me to be deprived of the privilege of service in the Senate and of being chairman of the Foreign Relations Committee and all that. But I have not wanted to contaminate my soul by enduring hate even for that man who did me such a grievous wrong. So I've tried to make love one of the great motivators of my life, and I know that love has meant a great deal to me.

DO YOU THINK YOUNG PEOPLE HAVE A MORE DIFFICULT TIME TODAY?

I think so because they have so many more temptations. For example, now they have the automobile, you know, and when I was growing up the automobile was still a very rare thing, relatively. Most girls and boys didn't go out in automobiles in the evening and stay out until all times of the night. The morality of the day was different from what it is now. The rules of behavior were different then from what they are now.

Now an individual, for example, a girl, has a great many more temptations and risks than the ordinary girl growing up in earlier times. But the style of life is so different now and the world is so much more complicated. There are so many advantages that didn't previously exist. But the problems of the world are also multiplied over what they formerly were. On the other hand, it may be like being constantly bombarded by noise. You get to the point at which you finally can tolerate it. And it may be that we develop strength of character and wisdom by being able to endure successfully the vicissitudes and the dangers of the present. However, it is a more complex world than it was when I was growing up.

HOW ABOUT OLDER PEOPLE?

Well, older people have always been granted a certain amount of respect in general and have had a certain amount of influence over young people, especially children and grandchildren. But now older people have come to occupy a far more important place in society than they once occupied. Today older people work longer. They hold positions of influence and responsibility. Mr. Louis Harris testified before our committee the other day and pointed out that the trend today, for the first time, is for people to continue to work and to hold their positions after they are sixty-five years of age. And now we've got about 24 million elderly people in the United States—I mean sixty-five years of age or older. They are about eleven percent of the population and are increasing as a percentage of the overall population. By the year 2000 there will be a much greater percentage of elderly people. Older people are going to retain their influence and their positions of authority and responsibility longer than they ever have before. So, as to their role—they are important politically, they are important economically, they are important spiritually to the country. The role of the older person today is becoming more and more important.

How important are international affairs to our lives?

The world has progressively become more and more interdependent. Events that at one time did not affect this country, today do affect it. Before the age of the automobile, electricity, and the energy consumption that we have today, what happened in Iran was not very important to the United States. But now what happens in Iran may cause a man or woman to lose his or her job in the United States. Right now the big companies are curtailing the availability of fuel to their agents. It may be that we will be denied the opportunity to drive our automobiles as we formerly could— all because of a revolution in Iran. And what happens in another part of the world may lead to a war in which we are involved in one way or another. With the Korean War, for example, we lost about 50,000 men and another 300,000 were wounded.

Today the inflation that we have is affecting the lives of all people and is to a large degree traceable back to that Viet Nam War. It happened on the other side of the world. Today if China invades Viet Nam or if Viet Nam invades Cambodia or North and South Yemen get in a fight or they have a revolution in Iran— those events may actually affect the standard of living of millions, if not all the people in this country. We are living in a much smaller, a much more interdependent, interrelated world than we did in the past. For example, formerly, with the United States separated from Europe by a wide ocean and from Asia by a wider ocean, and having no large nations on our northern and southern borders, we were relatively free from attack. And now within thirty minutes probably all of the major cities of this country could be wiped out by Russia with nuclear weapons. We live under that threat now. Today the world is very intricately inter-related and interdependent.

Is it important to set goals?

I think young people should strive to settle in their minds a life objective. I know they tell a story on me and it's basically true— that when I was twelve–fourteen years old I said that Claude Pepper would someday be a United States Senator. Some of them have it that I carved it on a tree in the area where I lived in East Alabama. Actually what happened was when I was thirteen– fourteen years old I would go up to the office of a justice of the peace who was a friend of my father in this little town of Penfield where I grew up. He'd let me use his typewriter and let me read his books at night, and some nights I'd be there till ten or twelve o'clock, just sitting up there by myself, reading some of these books or writing on his typewriter or dreaming about the future. And one night I went back to a room across the hall from the room where I worked, usually the library, and I took a pencil and I wrote down, "Someday Claude Pepper will be President of the

United States." I didn't make it to the presidency, but I did become a United States Senator. And I always wanted to be a United States Senator.

When I was in college or in law school at Harvard, the boys whom I ate with, some of my close friends, used to call me "Senator" because I would always argue that I'd rather be a United States Senator than a Justice of the Supreme Court. And I assumed from my youth that I was going to be a lawyer and I just gravitated right on to that.

It's pathetic to me for a youngster not to know what he or she wants to do. They just want to get a job. They don't know whether they want to work in a bank or grocery store or somewhere else. I knew that I wanted to go into politics early in life.

How do you feel about growing older?

Well, in my instance the transition has been so slow and so gradual that I just haven't abruptly passed from a life of activity into a life of inactivity. That is, even now, I walk faster than most people who walk with me. I can still play golf, but when I'm here, I'm terribly busy. I do a long day's work. So I'm not like I was when I was on the cross-country team in college; I can't run that far that fast. At the same time I think that people should not think too much about it—just keep on living a normal life as long as the Lord gives them the privilege to have a life—and just don't worry about whether you are sixty-five years of age, or, as I am, seventy-nine. Imagine if I just sat around and moped and said, "Well, I guess if I'm seventy-nine, I don't guess I can live much longer." I try to keep from thinking about that. I keep busy, I've got a lot to do!

So what I would advise is to try to keep healthy in a sane and sensible way. And try to keep your life moving ahead just like it's been all the time, asking the Lord to give you more years of delightful activity and meaningful contributions to make to life.

WHAT DO YOU CONSIDER YOUR GREATEST SOURCES OF STRENGTH?

Well, I believe very strongly in prayer. I believe in what one of my professors in college once said: "Learn to draw upon the invisible forces of life for your strength." Those could be friends, relatives, or God. Right now my wife is very ill. I pray very fervently for her survival, her recovery, and I have always had a great deal of help from the strength of inner forces that have been a part of my life.

NORMAN VINCENT PEALE

UNLESS he is off speaking elsewhere, Norman Vincent Peale preaches Sundays at the Marble Collegiate Church in New York City as he has for forty-eight years. With his wife, Ruth Stafford Peale, he edits and publishes Guideposts, *a monthly, interfaith, nonprofit magazine read by millions.*

Born in Bowersville, Ohio, May 31, 1898, Dr. Peale was educated at Ohio Wesleyan University, Boston University, and Syracuse University. He has won countless awards for his devotion to worthy causes and holds honorary degrees from a number of institutions. The Power of Positive Thinking, *a familiar inspirational work, is probably the best known of the many books he has written.*

The busy, sparkling-eyed Dr. Peale, whose schedule would intimidate many, years younger, welcomed us warmly to his homey office at Marble Collegiate Church, and there, surrounded by a gallery of photographs of his friends and acquaintances, we began to talk about his life and work.

WHAT DO YOU HAVE TO SAY ABOUT LOVE AND HATE?

Well, of course, the other word for Christianity is love. It's a philosophy of love. If you could define Christianity in one word

153

it would be love, because that's the basic element. I once talked to a minister in North Carolina who entertained Karl Barth, the famous theologian, at dinner one time.

He is a great mind. At dinner, according to Reverend—the name skips me for a minute—a young professor of theology from a local theological school said, "Dr. Barth, could you define in one sentence what Christianity is?" Well, Barth, according to my informant, sat back and said, "Yes, I can do that." And he said, "I would give you a sentence from an old hymn that my Swiss mother used to sing when I was a small boy—'Jesus loves me this I know for the Bible tells me so.' "

Now—if a lesser intellect had come along with such a simple definition it would have been looked upon with scorn. But he was great enough to be simple and rudimentary in his appraisal of Christianity. I, myself, feel that Christianity is a science. It's the science of the application of love. And that is what has kept it going for 2,000 years in a world that still, unfortunately, believes in force and the balance of power. You know that sophisticated people don't use the term "balance of power," but they surely practice it in all international affairs. And they haven't yet caught up with the idea that love can be practically utilized. And I maintain that Jesus was the greatest scientist that ever lived. He had formulas which work always under appropriate circumstances. And one of them is, "Thou shalt love thy neighbor as thyself"—you shall love your enemies and be kind to those that spitefully use you. The thing about all this is, *it works*—and therefore it's pragmatic. And it is not illusory, or poetic. But still, supposedly sophisticated generations look upon this as fantasy.

I don't know why it is but humanity still believes, apparently, that you can get more by being mean and vindictive and hostile, than you can by being otherwise. I don't believe they think that philosophically, but in practice . . .

One thing that I'd like to say before we get too far along on this matter of love. I was quite startled within the past two years to have my staff here in the church tell me that whenever we receive a group of new members into the membership of the church—say, for purposes of illustration, 200 at one time—that of that group at least 150 would be single persons—either widowed or divorced or never married—young and old. Now, when I began my ministry in this church forty-eight years ago it was pretty much a family church, although because of its situation a large number of visitors were present every Sunday out of the hotel population in New York City—but if you received a group of members it was Mr. and Mrs. Smith, Johnny and Helen—two kids, a mother and a father. Presently, well over half—maybe seventy to eighty percent are single people. Now on Manhattan Island, I'm told—or I read it somewhere—one-half of the population is single. The same thing is true in other cities. For example, I know a church in Houston, Texas which has a building given to what they call "singles ministry." And the same thing is true in Dallas, and throughout the country. Now we are adding a minister to our staff whose sole job is to minister to single people and their particular problems—right here in Manhattan.

Now what does this tell us about the love process in the United States—in urban centers at least? And what does this say to us about the family unit? America grew up on the family unit. I think you can establish that definitely. What is all this doing to the family—a very important question which we mean to explore? It's a great field for sociological study.

I was riding in a taxicab here in New York City with the most hostile, crude sort of man—profane! And I commented that it was a nice day. He grunted at that and he was really mean. So I said to myself, "This man is worried about something. He isn't feeling well—there is something on his mind." So I noticed on the little board where his license was posted that he had a long, beautiful Italian name—and I said to him, "My friend, I notice that you are Italian." And he said, "Yeh—so what—what about it?" I said, "Well, you know, I've been in Italy a great many times, I love Italy," I said, "There's a quality in the sunshine that's different— it's golden—it's salubrious—it's a magnificent place." And then I said, "Did you ever stop to think that the Italian language is probably the most musical of all languages—even the town names—Padua, Salerno, Capri—aren't they beautiful?" And he said, "Yeh, yeh, that's right, they are." And then I said, "Your name, it has the same melodic flow to it—it's beautiful." And he said, "Gee, I never thought of that before." Well, all of a sudden he was a different man. And when I got out of the car he practically shook hands with me! It was loving him, and it was also treating him as an unusual human being—with esteem. It was getting down to his national roots.

We struggle with the complexities and avoid the simplicities.

How important is it to set goals?

That is a cherished theme of mine. Do you know of a man named Bob Richards? A former Olympic star. He was a pole-vaulter, I believe. He later became a preacher. He was teaching a Sunday school class, he told me, in a Texas town where he apparently lived. He said to the class, "You know, you kids, have you any ideas of what you could become?" He said, "If you set a goal, something you want to be more than anything else, and you put it down on a piece of paper very simply so that you can understand it, and then memorize it and say it over to yourself every day and even mark down a date when you want it to happen—then all of the forces of your nature will conspire to make it happen." So there was a little dumpy, fat girl with great big heavy glasses. She jumped up and she said, "I am going to be the greatest woman tennis star." And the class laughed. "Look at you!" Well, she became Billie Jean King.

I have a home in the country as well as in the city—in a little town up in New York State. One day a little boy stopped me on the street and said, "Can I speak to you a minute?" I said, "Certainly." He said, "I want to get somewhere, I really do." I said, "That's great, the motivation and an impulse—that's the beginning of your getting somewhere. But tell me, where do you want to get?" Well, he said, "I haven't figured that out yet. I don't know exactly, but I just know that I want to get somewhere." And I said to him, "What would you like to do more than any other one thing?" And he said, "Oh, I have never given that any real thought either." "Well," I said, "what can you do best of all— of everything you can do, what can you do the best?" "Oh," he said, "I don't know, I can't do anything very well." I said, "Here you tell me now that you want to get somewhere, but you don't know where you want to get, and you don't know what you like to do, and you don't know what you can do. Now you go home and pray about this matter and think and then you come back to me and you write down where you want to get, your top priority. Answer those two questions, and then put down another thing— *when* you want to get there. And come and show it to me. Then we'll do business." After some time, he showed up. He had it down, exactly what he wanted to be. Now he was a boy who hadn't had much education and he said he wanted to be a foreman of a certain plant doing a certain kind of job, making a certain kind of product, and I am glad to report that *is* what he is.

It has to be a sharp, clearly defined, specific goal. Most people don't get where they want to go because they are not sure where they want to go. And they have a fuzzy goal. It has to be sharpened down to a fine point. You write it out on a piece of paper, and if you have got a shirt pocket like this, carry it with you.

I carry a lot of stuff in my pocket. Yeah, that's my filing system and I keep things in there and take them out and read them until they are threadbare, then they're in your head!

There is a deep tendency in human nature—it's called, scientifically, "imaging" or "visualization." The power of the projected image. Somebody said that there is a deep tendency in human nature to become precisely like that which you constantly imagine or "image" yourself as being.

People will ultimately take you at your own self-appraisal. If you go around telling yourself you are a worm others will believe it too. I remember when I was a small boy, I was so shy. I had the most enormous inferiority complex, and I was reticent, and I was what they used to call bashful. They don't use that word much anymore, but it means abashed.

I would tell myself that I didn't amount to anything and I never would and all that. Finally I began to realize that people were agreeing with me.

It is a fact that you project what you are. Now there is the superegotist—a person who thinks highly of himself but actually is just trying to compensate. But that isn't reality.

I had a father who was both a medical man and a minister, I mean, doctor of medicine and an ordained minister. He used to say he was a paradox. From him I first got this idea of the relationship of religion and psychiatry/psychology, because he practiced that. As a minister he knew that mental reactions of people were very important. He used to tell me, "Norman, don't go skulking through life. You will never go any further than you can see yourself." He said, "You must have confidence in your dreams. You'll never go any higher than you can dream, but you can go as high as your dreams." And my mother used to emphasize the same thing.

I think they knew that they had a sensitive, scared kind of a boy on their hands, and my father was a very rugged type of guy and my mother was very gentle and sensitive. And the two of them together were just right! Conrad Hilton told me one time that his father said to him that if you want to get anywhere in the world, *work!* And he said his mother said to him that if you want to get anywhere in the world, *pray!* And so, he said, he decided to blend both of them. He worked and he prayed.

There was a professor at Ohio Wesleyan and I cannot tell you his name, but I can see him as plain as day. He kept me in after class one day, and he sat there and he looked at me, and said, "You know, I can't figure you out. You know this material, but you don't know how to communicate it. You don't know how to give it back. You don't know how to organize it. You are just no good at all." And he said, "That is a pity, because you have the ability to do it." He said, "Why don't you?" He gave me quite a lecture.

Well, this infuriated me, and I decided I was going to check out of that college right away, but as I was doing so, I decided to go back and really clean up on this professor. But I decided against it because he was about six-foot-four and weighed about 225 pounds and I decided that wouldn't be wisdom.

So I got to thinking about it and how right he was. And, I don't know whether it was exactly that day, or a few days later, on the fourth step from the bottom of Grey Chapel at that university I decided to quit being a negative, scared, inferior person. I decided I was going to change and be something different. And being a very religious boy, I asked the Lord to help me. I told Him I didn't want to be this way anymore, and it was then that I began to read everything I could get my hands on about the power of the human mind, the way humans can think their way to a better category of life. Out of that experience emerged, I'm sure, my later book on the power of positive thinking. Because I wrote it first for myself, because I needed it: Norman Vincent Peale was in a mess. So I had to work my way out of it and I did it through the process of spiritual conversion plus mental change. And he, the professor, applied a motivational technique to me, and he did it right. I look back at him now with great thankfulness.

I used to work for a man named Grove Patterson. He was editor of the *Toledo Blade* and also editor of the *Detroit Journal.* And I worked for him on the *Journal.*

He was a metaphysical thinker. I had never heard of a metaphysical thinker up until that time, but he was that as well as being a very prominent Methodist. But he was way ahead of the Methodist theology of his time. He used to talk with me about what a young person could do with his life if he decided what he wanted to do with it, and then proceed to change it accordingly. With Grove Patterson the way you thought was of extreme importance. He believed that you created your life out of your thought processes. That idea later came to assume great prominence in my own thinking. I firmly believe that that's the case, so I owe Grove Patterson a great deal.

ARE THERE ANY PARTICULAR WRITERS
WHO HAVE INFLUENCED YOU?

I owe a great deal to good old Ralph Waldo Emerson, and to Thoreau. I would say that those two of the old school have not been excelled by any modern writers in wisdom or understanding. In my developing earlier years they were very important to me.

I always did read a great deal of biography. I think I have read about every biography that has been published. Fortunately, or unfortunately, I am a fast reader, and I can take a biography and find what I want in it without poring over every word. I undertook one on Queen Victoria some time ago. It was about 700 pages. I'm sure I didn't read the 700 pages, but I think I sized up Queen Victoria.

HOW DO YOU FEEL ABOUT GROWING OLDER?

Well, I'll tell you, I don't like it! I would rather be, what would I rather be? Forty, because at forty you have natural energy, plenty of it; and yet, you know, I do more work now than I did when I was forty—by far! I love this world and I don't like the thought that comes to me occasionally that I am going to have to leave it because I would be very unhappy not to know what's going on. But maybe I'll know more about it than I do now.

I had a little thing happen to me one time that helped me a lot. At that time I think I was sixty-five and I had just turned sixty-five and this disturbed me—sixty-five. I was making a speech to a big convention in the Sherman Hotel in Chicago which at that time had one of the largest ballrooms in the United States, and the owner of that hotel, the chief owner, I don't think he owned it all, but he owned most of it, was Frank Bering. Frank at that time was eighty-five years old and he ran this hotel. He was the executive and he operated it himself. He was there running this big convention. And I knew Frank very well because he came from the same small town in Ohio where my mother and father came from. So,

I said to him, "Frank, I've been watching you operating this big convention in this big hotel. How old are you anyway?" He said, "Son, what do you want to know that for? Of what importance is that?" He said, "Isn't your room all right in the hotel?" I said, "Yes, everything is perfect." "Well then," he said, "what difference does it make how old I am?" "Well," I said, "I know how old you are anyway because you went to high school and graduated in the same class with my mother." "Well," he said, "if you know that why are you asking?" He said, "Why have you age on your mind?" And then he said, "Young man, let me make you a suggestion, *live your life and forget your age.*"

Now Frank ran that hotel until he was about eighty-seven, when he moved to Palm Springs. And I always maintained that if he had kept on running that hotel until age ninety-five, he would have lived at least that long. He died shortly after he moved. But that one statement, *"Live your life and forget your age,"* sticks with me.

I went out and made a speech in Toronto the other night and the man who introduced me had to tell the audience how old I was. And he said, "You just watch him—do you think you could do it at that age?" Well, so that made me demonstrate what an old person could do. And I told him afterwards, next time you introduce me, leave out the age. I walk out there and I give them a message and it doesn't make any difference how old I am.

You mustn't think age. You think—"Thank God, I've got this wonderful day and I'm going to fill this day full of meaning." Then you should go to bed early and get a good night's sleep. And you should keep your weight down because of that old saying, "It's a lean horse for a long race." Old people that I know who are thin do better than fat old people. And then I believe you should walk two miles every day—or three or four.

Of course, I do think heredity may play a part in good health. A reporter asked me not long ago what my secret was. He had heard me speak for nearly an hour on one of these programs and spoke to me afterwards. He said, "How do you get that much energy at your age?" So I gave him all this business about two miles, three miles and proper food, keep the weight down, and so forth. "Well," he said, "anything beyond that?" I said, "Yeah, it's a passage in the Bible: 'They that wait upon the Lord shall renew their strength, they shall rise up with wings as eagles, they shall run and not grow weary, they shall walk and not faint.'" That is one of the most practical aging formulas that you can possibly have.

WHAT REAL HOPE IS THERE FOR MAN?

I think that anybody who believes in God and Jesus Christ has got to have an optimistic view of the world. Now there are some religious people who believe that the world will get so bad that it will finally come to an end and Jesus Christ will return from heaven and pick up the remnant that is left. And they claim that they get this out of the Bible. I've lived through several warnings that the end of the world is at hand. Not long ago a man wrote a book about the great planet Earth, and he said it's pretty close in coming. But I've lived quite a while and I haven't seen the end of the world yet, and I believe that Almighty God who created the whole business is trying to work out something here.

Now of course he may have made a great mistake in giving man free will because man wasn't that trustworthy and didn't exercise his will in the right way. The animalistic side of him seemed to triumph over the mental and spiritual side. But man is still trying to evolve and evolution is a long process. Perhaps the kind of man and woman who can build the kind of world that we idealists dream of may not have been completely fashioned yet. But I believe that *we* will create that kind of person. That's what I've been preaching about all these years and I wouldn't have done it unless I had believed in it.

It's a good thing, you know, that the newspapers report bad news. A very good thing! Because if they headlined good news, then, that's when we really ought to get worried. Because bad news is a departure from the norm. If a dog bites a man, that is not news, but if a man bites a dog, that is news. Now, if suddenly the paper comes out with "Found, A Good Man," that would be devastating! But the fact that the paper doesn't come out with that kind of a headline means that there are lots of good people.

Incidentally, I have started a radio program called "The American Character"—and it's only ninety seconds, five days a week. It is sponsored by International Telegraph and Telephone and the idea is to tell good stories about people. Well, anyway, people told us (the doubting Thomases) that we would never find enough good stories to keep that program going. We have now done about 250 of them and we find that one sprouts a dozen— deeds of love, sacrificial love, where people put their lives on the line to save somebody. In other words, we are trying to bring good news up against the bad news, but I don't want to do too much of that because I want to keep it in the same balance that it's always been in.

WHAT HAS BEEN A SOURCE OF STRENGTH?

My greatest source of strength? . . . Well, from a human point of view that's been my wife. My wife is an anchor in all times of storm. She never loses faith. I had to get my faith the hard way, she was born with it. And I go down into discouragement easier than she.

DO YOU THINK THAT LIFE IS MORE DIFFICULT FOR YOUNG PEOPLE TODAY?

You know, I think life was more exciting when we were young. None of us ever thought of going very far away from home. I remember watching the Baltimore and Ohio railroad train when I was a small boy and I wondered to myself if I would ever get to Cincinnati, you see. Finally I got there. Then I began to wonder whether I would ever get to Cleveland.

We had to make our own fun. We didn't have television that

we could turn on. We had to work with the other kids and there-fore, we had to be more imaginative. We did things that now, I presume, would be considered corny. But it was wonderful. And there was the future out there. The future was great. We hadn't been infected by pessimism or by cynicism in those days. We didn't have so much of the world thrown at us. We lived in little towns, dimly we knew that there was a place called Paris or London in some faraway place. But you know, so far off! So remote!

We didn't have so much to process. So I feel a little bit sorry for young people, what they have to cope with. Then we had a moral code that was clearly defined and we knew what was right and we knew what was wrong. And we were supposed to do right, and not do wrong. And if we did wrong, we knew it was wrong and we didn't try to kid ourselves and rationalize it away. And when you went out with a girl, you were going to have a good time, but you were going to be decent. You might hold her hand, and you might even kiss her goodnight, but as far as any-thing beyond that, that was incredible and inconceivable, you see. So you were protected by a pretty definite morality.

Now today, a girl or a boy has got to struggle against a very permissive situation. And that's hard to cope with. Very hard to cope with! We didn't have that to bother us. Now that doesn't mean we were all angels, and many times young people of my generation strayed away from morality. But they knew they were wrong if they did.

DO YOU SEE ANY SHIFTS AWAY FROM PERMISSIVENESS?

Oh, absolutely! That's the great thing about what Emerson called the pendulum theory. If a pendulum swings over just so far, then human nature revolts. They've got to have it better again. And then the old pendulum of human opinion starts swinging back in the other direction. Now if it could stop about halfway, at about a normal point, instead of swinging way over the other side, then we could be happier because we know if it gets way over to the other side, in due course of time, people will get tired of that and it will swing back to the other side. So if it could swing back to a position in-between, we would be safer.

There is a saving quality in human nature; after a while it gets sick of its own rottenness. You can't live with it any longer. It has to be cleaned up again. What language that is, "It's got to get cleaned up"—it has to become cleaned up. So that's one thing that gives me hope for humanity. Right now I think we are moving away from degraded attitudes that once existed. And one sign of that is the *immense* interest in spiritual guidance that we find today.

In my boyhood days there was not hostility against control and maybe that wasn't all that good, I don't know. But young people have got to question the older generation's activities. I mean that's inherent. There would never be any progress if they didn't.

The survival quality which Almighty God has built into people is a tremendous thing! We can live through almost anything. I don't see why anyone growing older should lose faith in the world, or in the people, or in society. I just don't! If they do it's because they have allowed themselves to become embittered by something. But the philosophy of optimism suggests that at long last the good of life will overbalance the evil thereof.

REFERENCES

Gordon, Arthur, *Norman Vincent Peale: Minister to Millions*, Englewood Cliffs, N.J.: Prentice-Hall, 1958.

Peale, Norman Vincent, and Blanton, Smiley, *Faith Is the Answer*, Carmel, N.Y.: Guideposts Associates, 1940, 1950, 1955.

Peale, Norman Vincent, *The Power of Positive Thinking*, New York: Prentice-Hall, 1952.

COLONEL HARLAND SANDERS: SEPTEMBER 9, 1890– DECEMBER 16, 1980

COLONEL SANDERS, founder of the fast-food restaurant chain, Kentucky Fried Chicken, was born in 1890, and began his incredibly successful business when he was sixty-six. Reason enough for him to tell people, as he did, "Don't retire when you reach sixty-five. Maybe your boat hasn't come in yet." Ninety and still going strong when we saw him a few months before his death in December 1980, he maintained with characteristic spirit that he wanted to live to be a hundred. Though he didn't reach the century mark, his nine energetic decades remain an example of a life lived to the fullest.

We met Colonel Sanders early one morning at the headquarters of the KFC Corporation in Louisville, Kentucky. Patterned after a southern mansion, the building contains handsome furnishings and is decorated elegantly. A gracious host, the Colonel appeared in his customary white suit with the diamond stickpin in the lapel, and showed us into his first-floor office for our conversation.

ON THE FAMILY . . .

I think that's a most important thing! That's what America is built on. Yes, that's the foundation of America. It was founded on families that were close together, and lived for a purpose.

I don't think parents take the interest in the children that they used to when I was a kid. I still live up to a whole lot of things that my mother taught me when I was growing up. Of course she was a widow, you know. Daddy died when I was five years old and I think of the hours, the evenings we used to spend at home, you know. We would bring home a library book and I always used to like to read about somebody like Admiral Dewey or David Farragut or some of those fellows. Their military lives—I always liked that. Mother would read those library books to us, you see, and point out how nice it was to be a man like that . . . accomplishing something and doing something that was worthwhile! And she was always against smoking, and I have never had a cigarette in my lips, because Mom told me never to smoke. It would grow on you, she said. Playing cards? She didn't want us to ever learn to play cards, because a couple of her brothers, she said, were found by their mother way over in an old house in the country that was vacated, you know, and a bunch of boys would meet there. They got to gambling, you see, gambling and drinking. And she didn't want us to ever fall into a thing like that. The idea was that if I didn't know cards, I wouldn't drift with that kind of bunch.

And she didn't allow us to drink coffee. We drank teakettle tea. That would mean taking the old black teakettle off the wood stove, filling a cup with hot water, putting in a spoonful of cream and I suppose sugar, and we called that teakettle tea. And that was what we kids drank; but she drank Arbuckle's coffee. Funny, but she didn't want us to ever drink coffee. And I hardly ever drink coffee today—hardly ever.

It's interesting and it shows how a fellow can take an interest in kids—pointing out the way they should conduct their lives as they are growing. I think kids do better when someone takes an interest. I think they have better health, live longer, and everything else.

I remember one time when we were to observe Sunday quietly and my brother and I slipped out and started to dig up sassafras root. My brother accidentally got hit on the head with a hoe— and then Mom caught up with us, y'know. And I stole one watermelon one time from a neighbor farmer and he told Mom about it—and y'know I haven't even liked watermelon since then!

In terms of the family—I think that when it is close it is a better life.

ON LOVE AND HATE . . .

I've been wondering what motivated the present ruler in Iran to be so bitter and hateful to America. Is it because he was such an enemy of the former ruler, the Shah who had him in exile so long? He beats everything I ever heard of for hatred. It's something to see those mobs and the way they all have their fists clenched. I can't see how they can develop such hatred!

As to love, I see it—in our family and in our neighbors. Why I have a neighbor out here who lives right next door to me that I just think the world and all of—just as much as I would if he were my own boy! And he seems to appreciate things. You have got to have some appreciation for the other person before you can love, I think.

ON SETTING GOALS . .

Well, I didn't do such a thing. I just took everything as it happened. And the only goal I've had is hoping I would live to be a hundred, and could stay active and well during that time. And, I

kind of keep my habits along that line, so that I feel that I can live
to be a hundred.

On Secrets for a Good, Long, and Happy Life . . .

No, not really. But I've had a happy home life with my wife,
and am happy with my work and my employer. And a funny
thing . . . about prayer . . . so many people talk about praying,
about prayer that will give you this or give you that. My prayer
has always been to recognize God for all the things that He has
already given me, and what I am enjoying! I think that's the greatest thing of all. And, so to pray to ask for something—I don't do it.

On Opposing Points of View . . .

Well, I guess I have never had much occasion in all my days to
try to win somebody's friendship. It's important not to become
antagonistic when different views are expressed by others. On the
other hand it's better to show by example what it is that you believe, and I think that is a great deal more convincing.

On People Who Were Influential . . .

Not a single individual that I know. Just the characters that I've
read about in the books, don't you see? I've always liked inspirational and success stories for what reading I have done. And I
always hoped that someday I could match some of the characters
I read about. And you can only do that by giving all your time
and all your thought to what you are doing and be honest in it in
every phase. Integrity is the greatest thing in the world to build
upon! You need it for building a certain product, or whatever . . .
  I remember David Farragut whom I read about when I was
in school. And he did some daring things and they were successful.
And naturally you just love a man like that, you know.

But today—I don't know that I can pick out a particular person. Many of our people are politicians and are not sincere in what they are undertaking. Of course some of our inventors and people like that have really been great and they are an inspiration for you to try to be as great as they are someday.

ON GROWING OLDER . . .

I'm enjoying it because I have got all the life behind me—pretty nearly ninety years now! And I have had my ups and downs. And I sometimes wonder if I had my life to do over—well—I'd do the same thing that I did. The hardships were not any harder than they needed to be, by Jove, to qualify to keep on going. And one has to remember that every failure can be a stepping-stone to something better, particularly if one analyzes what has happened, one can build upon the experience.

I think it is wise for people to stop and study what they are doing—what dissipating they are doing. They constantly hear it every day, through some source, the dangers of smoking and the use of tobacco. And we've got the evidence that it is dangerous. I just heard the other night on the TV that lung cancer is increasing greatly, particularly in women now. So it is obviously not good for women to smoke—not good for anybody to smoke as a matter of fact. But you can't stop a one of them, by golly!

The important thing is for people to take good care of themselves, and to work. For if you keep working at your job you are going to stay mentally active and that's going to be good for your brain. I've never been a fiend about money. I have always had the slogan—"There's no use in being the richest man in the cemetery, 'cause you can't do any business from there." So I have passed on hundreds, actually thousands of dollars, against a few million, and maybe good sense should have dictated that I should have kept it, but I guess I'll be able to make it all right to the end.

ON YOUNG PEOPLE HAVING A MORE
DIFFICULT TIME TODAY . . .

No, I wouldn't think so, not if they have ambition, determination, and a willingness to work. Child labor laws have spoiled our youth in this country! They never learn to do a job for anyone else because they have to be past school age before they can work.

Parents aren't teaching kids how to work. They're going partying themselves and they kind of leave the kids to the baby-sitter. When I was a kid we lived over there on a farm in southern Indiana. I was, say, six years old and my little brother three, and my little sister was born two months after my papa died. Mom sewed for the neighbors and sometimes she had to go quite a distance away. I remember how she used to go to sew for several days at a time. This family had a big family of girls. She made dresses for them for school and anything like that they wanted done. She left us kids at home. I was the oldest there with my little brother and sister and we knew better than to burn the house down. We didn't have any baby-sitter—nobody to watch after us.

When I was seven years old there on the farm Mom went three miles away to Henryville and lived with her brother that week and peeled tomatoes down at the canning factory, don't you see—making her some cash money in the fall of the year. She left us three kids out there on the farm. I took a notion I wanted to bake light bread one evening. So I set my yeast and made my sponge and baked off the prettiest bread you ever saw. Well we were so elated over it we took this little two-year-old sister—carried her that three miles across the field and the woods to Henryville to show Mom that loaf of bread that I'd baked.

Well, I had real pride in what I had done and I tried to do something right, you see. But doggone it they don't do that today. Put you in charge of a baby-sitter—and if they're turned loose they are liable to burn the house down. You reckon kids are different than we were then? It might be that we were dumber and our minds were not as developed as they are today.

I think that parents are going to instill principles in you when you are growing up and if they don't instill them in you, you are not going to have them. My driver is now going with a young lady whose father and mother have separated, and she's living with her grandmother and she doesn't go with any of the other kids there in Shelbyville. She goes to church regularly every Sunday, goes to prayer meeting and got him going to prayer meeting with her now. And she is an influence for the good.

ON SOURCES OF STRENGTH WHEN
THE GOING GETS ROUGH . . .

Dependency on God. That's been a first order of strength to me. And when I started this chicken business, for instance, I promised God Almighty that if it could make good, I would also. Everything that I had in the past had played out. When I manufactured an acetylene-gas farm-lighting system, Delco came along with their electric system for farms. That put me out of business. It didn't die for any fault of my own. It was just a time for a change, you see, and therefore I lost out. I also had a ferry system between here and Jeffersonville. I organized that ferry company and was interested in that for years. Then they built the bridge across the river to Jeffersonville and my ferry had to quit.

The only thing that hasn't quit for me is this chicken business. It's something that takes care of the need when people have to eat, you see. And something in that line is good. I have always had an inclination to experiment with food and make it better.

As I said, I had the ferry system and then the bridge put me out. Then I went to the service station, don't you see, and eventually put food in the service station. Will Rogers made the statement in 1930 that life begins at forty. Well, my first forty years had been in a little of everything. I had railroaded, I had soldiered.

Of course now the first job I got was when I was ten years

old. My mother hired me out to farming and I got two dollars a month and my board. The farmer fired me that first month. My mother gave me a tongue-lashing—didn't whip me or anything. But what on earth was I ever going to amount to? Her oldest son— the only thing she had to depend on for any help in the future. And to think I was of no account, couldn't hold a job at two dollars a month. What would I ever amount to? Well, I made a resolve then that I was going to amount to something if I could. And no hours, nor amount of labor, nor amount of money would deter me from giving the best that there was in me. And I have done that ever since, and I win by it. I know.

I had to do it. You see, my step-daddy kicked me out of the house when I was twelve years old. So I have been out in the world ever since with a sixth-grade education. I've been handicapped over that? No use being handicapped over education because persons in those days who had the ambition to get an education, got one. I just didn't have that kind of an ambition.

You take the young folks of today. When a young man wants a job, why he asks what are the side or fringe benefits, what vacation time will I get, and do I get paid for it, and all those things— instead of getting that job and seeing what he can do with it.

I have a young man who worked for me as my driver and travel companion. He graduated from the University of Alabama. Well, some of these young fellows look at me, you know, as being a marvelous success, and they come and ask me what they should do to make good too, like I have. But I told him one thing, be sure you don't look at the hours you work, look at what you have got to do and whether you can do it, and then do it the best you can. And don't be afraid to put in a few extra hours.

He got a job after he drove with me for two years with a bank in Birmingham, Alabama, the second largest bank there. He is a vice-president of it. But he was put in charge of the mortgage department, mortgage loans. He would go down there every morning at seven o'clock. When the bank doors opened at nine he had been there making comparisons and analyzing the cases for two hours so if he did have a transaction of some kind in his department, he would be prepared. So he had just been advancing like nobody's business. They have been sending him to special courses and giving him advances in pay. It's just been wonderful. And he does it by putting in all these extra hours, and he doesn't mind them either. He says he sees what needs to be done.

On retirement . . .

I can't see that at all. I mean, I get pleasure every day out of my work. You've got to like your work. You've got to like what you are doing, you've got to be doing something worthwhile so you can like it—because if it's worthwhile, that makes a difference, don't you see?

And I never think of vacations. I had one vacation when I was seventy-eight years old—two weeks. And that was because I thought I had quit the company at that time. And during those two weeks the advertising department took hold. They sent two of their men over to Banff, Canada, in the mountains there where I was taking my two weeks vacation. They sent these two men there to kind of court me back into the company, and I have been here ever since. I have never quit since I took those two weeks. I enjoyed it, but that's the only vacation I have ever had in my life.

The week before last I was down in Panama and Costa Rica, had the greatest time in the world with those people, don't you see. They were enthusiastic to meet me, and I to meet the little kids. The little kids will give you more inspiration than anything else in the country. They are one of the greatest assets. You know I heard my grandfather say, "Once a man, and twice a child." So you love children and be sort of childlike, and then you get to be a child yourself. I guess I am maybe even more interested in children now than I used to be.

"Once a man, and twice a child"—when you are young and again when you get old.

Children are nothing but love—from the time they come into

the world. Love and love is all they have known all their lives. And if you love children, they are going to love you back. Love begets love. And they can tell whether you are genuine or not. There was love in my family, don't you see. I can't understand parents who would beat children as they do, you know.

On retirement villages where there are no children . . .

Well, it seems like some people are drawn to those centers because there is something in their lives, their line of entertainment, that they find in those places. They may find good companionships with other older people. And there are some people who are in pitiful, pitiful condition in those places, don't you see. But some people go in and buy themselves a home and enjoy golfing and fishing and all. But now that never appealed to me at all. Because I wouldn't sit along the river bank waiting for a fish to come along and bite my hook for anything in the world. I don't know whether I've got what he wants, in the first place, and I don't know if there is even a fish in there or not. So I think it's just foolishness and an absolute waste of time to fish. I would rather go to the fish market tomorrow and get the fish after the fisherman has caught him. Golf—you can get just as much good exercise at work if you work at your own job as you would by trotting around over a golf course. It might be nice once in a while, but so many people when they get to playing golf, want to live like the Joneses. They think it's great to be carrying golf clubs and be showing off like that. But the business man, he had better be in his own little business right then. I know many a business suffers because the head of the business is out on the golf course instead of at his work. He ought to be able to discern the time to do certain things.

On opportunities for young people today . . .

Well, I read an article in *Fortune* magazine about two or three years ago that there had been 500 multimillionaires made in the five years prior to that publication. And it told what they had done and how they had done it. So it evidently is there. I can't conceive of all those things, but I know how to take care of my own business. I know it well and know that I can put someone in a position to make a success with it, enjoy life, and have a good, wholesome income. And that's my responsibility to see that all that goes. Everything has been worked out for them, so when you become a franchise, you have got something that is a guide. All the figures and problems have been worked out.

For instance, a predecessor to whom I once sold an interest in the company conceived the idea that it would be good to sell the flour that breaded the chicken. All right. It had been mixed in the kitchens with the herbs and spices. They went to having it mixed in Texas. Well, I had had an experience already at the beginning of this thing—after I had been going for about two or three years. A flour company noticed that I used quite a bit of flour, so they proposed that they mix my seasonings with the flour at their mill. They said that they had the big mixing machines to do that with. And it wasn't such a pleasant thing for the franchise to mix in the kitchen either because it makes you sneeze your head off (all the spices, don't you know). So, I thought that would be a nice thing to try.

So, I fixed up 100 batches of the seasoning which would make several thousand pounds of the flour. The flour company was going to put it out wherever I had a franchise. All I had to do was notify them and they had a local man there to stock that flour. In about ninety days, I began to get calls from all over the country. "What have you done to your seasoning?" I said I haven't done anything but send it out to be mixed. So then I got to reasoning about what had happened. That seasoning is ground just as fine as the flour. In all that flour—twenty-five pounds of it to twenty-five ounces of seasoning—the seasoning had lost all its light, aromatic oils because it was separated from itself, don't you see? But before when it was all together in a bag the flavor was all there.

And so I quit that immediately. When a later executive started mixing it down in Texas, I told him what my experience had been back in the early days. You see, I had worked out so many of those problems like that. But he didn't listen. He wanted to sell the flour.

Well, there are so many things I don't understand as much about—for instance nuclear materials. You know that we have had many nuclear plants throughout the country that have worked very well, but when you find the human element coming in and jobs being neglected, the problems develop. You have to watch it. It seems to me that once we get nuclear plants established, we get that energy almost free. I think we are going to have to have it.

But I would like to comment on retirement for a moment. I am against forced retirement. When a man reaches age sixty-five, he might be having a very successful life. He probably has become an executive or a junior executive and has a pretty good job. But if he is sixty-five years old and has a mother and daddy, they are bound to be about eighty-five or older, and they will have reached a period in their lives when they are going to need some assistance in all likelihood. Many of them have not been able to accumulate a fortune or enough to live by. So that fellow who is being forced to retire today might not only be responsible for taking care of himself during his retirement, but maybe also his mother and dad and possibly some other members of the family. So it just isn't right to force anybody to retire.

When the Lord put old father Adam here, he didn't tell him to retire at age sixty-five. He told him to work until he returned to the dust, and that was about 700 years later, wasn't it? So there is just no key to advance why you should be forced to retire. Let a man work as long as he wants to work if he can deliver or if his work is commensurate with the pay he receives. But if he should be forced on into retirement, out of that sixty-five years he will have had the chance to observe so many different things that have happened, that he can surely pick something out of that experience and still find enough to busy himself and keep going. I have heard that the average life of the retiree is only three years after he retires. Some die within a year's time. I know we had a banker friend here who died just after he retired, and he was a lovely fellow. There are just so many examples like that. So, I say, let a man work as long as he wants to and can do it and deliver his value and services.

On older people having bigger say in government one day . . .

I believe they will. We just had a big election here, you know. We elected a new governor. Now his opponent did not make a very good showing at the polls, but it might make him determined to enter a whole new field. Will Rogers said, as I mentioned before, that life begins at forty. I was just forty when he said it, so I guess that's why it made such an impression upon me. That's when I took stock of all that I had done, and didn't want to go back to any of my former jobs. But I took note of what the country was like at that time. I found that I had this gas station and I had this drawer full of old pistols and watches and everything that they would come and hock for a few gallons of gas, you know, and never come back. And you are going to have to eat. You can go for two days or so without eating, but you are going to have to eat sometime, so I made my resolve that I would stay with gasoline and food. Because people are going to have to have gasoline if they have to sell their mother-in-law's chicken to get it, don't you see?

BENJAMIN M. SPOCK, M.D.

DR. SPOCK has been the "baby doctor" for so many that he is practically an American institution. People who are today middle-aged reared their children with the book in hand, and Baby and Child Care *is still widely used.*

Spock, born in 1903, has had a distinguished career as practicing physician and as a teacher at medical schools: Cornell, University of Pittsburgh, Western Reserve University. He has also been associated with the Mayo Clinic, Rochester, Minnesota.

In the sixties, Spock became involved politically with the problems of nuclear energy and the Viet Nam War. In 1972 he was the Peoples Party presidential candidate. Today, the six-foot-four writer-physician-activist maintains a busy lecture schedule.

We met at his contemporary home on Beaver Lake in rural northwest Arkansas.

How IMPORTANT IS THE FAMILY AND WHAT IS ITS FUTURE?

It is the most important aspect of human nature, basically because almost everybody grew up in the family. These are the first important initial relationships, and it's one of the strongest impulses in human beings to try to grow up and then recreate the situation of their own childhood. They want to give to children of their own what they received as children. I think this is the reason that those people, the skeptics who see the end of the family, are very premature.

Obviously the family is different in every society and the family keeps changing, especially in a society as changeable as ours. I believe myself that it's good that people who think of marriage as a ball-and-chain have decided to live together without the ball-and-chain. However, they are going to find the same difficulties living together without marriage as those people do who have gotten married. Just as soon as the relationship is achieved, then there is the danger of negatives. Anyway, I don't see that as very disturbing. I do think it's also good that some young people are deciding that they don't want to have children. In the past practically everybody thought that if you married, you had to have children because you want to be like everybody else. The woman wanted to be like her sister and have a child and the man wanted to show that he could be a father, too. So a lot of children were created without much love being in store for them. My personal impression is, though, that a lot of young people who say they wouldn't bring children into a world like this, or that they are never going to get married because that would ruin a good relationship, quietly get married later and, a little later still, they have children.

In other words, the declaration that marriage is outmoded and the declaration that it's wrong to bring children into such a world—those are protests of youth, and are not lifelong decisions. They are developmental rather than historical. They don't represent a change in society but a certain stage of growing up.

Is love learned in a family?

Sure. Children, especially in the three-to-six-year age period, are playing the parts of parents all day long. They call it playing house. You be the father, and I'll be the mother and this smaller child will be the baby—or this doll will be the baby. If you listen, you will hear the parents' voices and attitudes. Many years ago when I was a visiting professor at Madison, Wisconsin, I took some medical students to a nursery school and we watched a bossy four-and-a-half-year-old teaching doll care to a three-year-old. She undressed the doll, bathed the doll, and dried the doll and put it in the crib, all the time saying to the three-year-old, "See dear, see how I do it, dear? Watch me carefully." And after ten minutes of demonstration she says to the mousy three-year-old, "Now dear, you try." So the three-year-old comes forward and starts and the four-year-old says, "No dear, not like that, dear. Now watch me more carefully."

This is the voice and the attitude—the sickly-sweet condescension—of the mother of that four-and-a-half-year-old, and the four-and-a-half-year-old has already learned most of what she will learn about child care. Then when she is twenty-four-and-a-half she'll be talking to her child in exactly the same tone of voice. So that's right, the family is where you learn love and hate and most else of what you learn, too.

How important is it to set goals?

I have two reactions. The first is that people move toward their goals (especially if they are not middle-class and if they're not brought up in an ambitious family) gradually without necessarily thinking about them or putting them into words. For instance, take medical students. Some of their early goals in terms of choice of specialty are very unrealistic; they have no idea what the field will be like. Medical students characteristically change their ideas of what specialty of medicine they want to practice as they go on and see it. That's the way it should be. That's why I approve of Antioch College's so-called cooperative program where you work for three months and study for three months, and work for two months and study for two months. Education should be much more realistic than it usually is and, specifically, it would be good for everyone to have a chance to try out the different occupations that appeal to him.

If you are not talking about occupational goals, but moral goals and social goals, I'm skeptical that people really decide much by thinking about them. Either you do continue to identify with your parents in your moral goals, social goals, or you rebel against them for a while, then quietly come around to them again. In other words, I think it's a process that goes on mostly unconsciously. One is influenced very much by, first of all, the parents and then later, as one becomes a youth, one is influenced by teachers and peers.

One of the problems of American society, as I see it, is that for many people goals are strictly materialistic ones. I see ours as a very materialistic society. The spiritual goals are very dim for most people and I think that this is a sickness of our society and I think that it's going to get worse. Of course one never knows exactly what it was like in previous periods, but I think that religion particularly and the moral concepts derived from religions were buoying and orienting for people in an earlier time.

But now, for a majority of Americans, religion, it seems to me, doesn't have much directing force. It is a place to go on Sunday to show that you're on the right side, that you're one of the good, responsible people. But as for living by Christianity from hour to hour or the rest of the week, I don't see much sign of that. In fact, I think much of our behavior in this country is quite anti-Christian. One of the wittiest things that's ever been said is "Christianity is a great idea. Too bad it was never tried." I assumed that it was science that mainly shot the foundation out from under religion at least as people feel it.

The morality that I was brought up with was a very fierce morality! Fierce in the sense that it was intensely taught with strong disapproval of everything that wasn't just right, by my mother, particularly. I tried all through adolescence and youth and young adulthood to shuck it, but I realized after a while that you can't shuck it and I think I have ended up just as moralistic as anybody.

There is a tendency in people as they grow older to deplore the fact that things are not like they used to be. So I warn you that my morality may be due primarily to age. But I do see as I travel around and see other societies that Americans are increasingly lacking in spiritual conviction and in a moral sense. I see *that* not as the whole cause of our problems, rather a part of our problem. I envy those societies where they still have a strong conviction about what each individual is there for. Back in earlier times in other parts of the world, children were raised for the glory of God, they were raised to serve the family, and they were raised to serve their nation. One sees that this gave a shape to life. But here in America all you raise people for is fulfillment and it is assumed that fulfillment means earning more than your parents did, and getting to a higher level of prestige in your job, and having more pleasure than the parents did. The English social anthropologist, Geoffrey Goren, said that in the rest of the world a father says, "Son, you're lucky to have been born into this family, we've been respectable citizens, we've done our work and we have no serious troubles of any kind. You will be fortunate if you turn out in a way that justifies your being in this family and *your* job will be to contribute to the family." But in America, a father says to his son, "Son, if you don't do better than I have, I won't think much of you." This is turning the pyramid of respect upside down.

You can see why we have gotten to this, because we all came here to forget the traditions in the old country and each generation has surpassed the last. So new generations keep looking hopefully to the children. Parents sacrifice with the assumption that the children will profit from this and go beyond the parents.

Go beyond them materially?

Yes, and also educationally. But the education is to enable them to succeed beyond their parents, materially. Education in the United States is not to become a wiser person, and certainly the teacher, though he is considered essential, is not really respected as he is in many other parts of the world. We make jokes about professors in this country, absent-minded professors, that are chasing butterflies.

Which people have influenced you most?

Obviously it was mostly my mother, against whose tyranny and intense morality I and my brother and sisters all ground our teeth through adolescence. I'll tell you a few stories.

When I was a senior in college, I went to the Bureau of Appointments at Yale to get a summer job. I was now entitled as a senior who had been on the varsity crew—which was glorious, in those days, in fact we won a gold medal in the Olympics—and as a certified social success having been elected to Scroll and Key, I was entitled to a cushy job. (I had worked the previous three summers as a counselor in a small crippled children's home in Connecticut and earned fifty dollars a month.) They gave me a job as a tutor-companion to a rich boy in Southampton. So I came home quite pleased with myself, and my mother said, "I'm ashamed of you! You've taken a job as a nursemaid." So, biting off my nose to spite my face, I went back to the Bureau of Appointments the next day and said, "I want the most unpleasant job you have here." They offered me a job they said nobody else was interested in, at a place called Frontier College in Canada, where you teach English and Canadian customs to immigrants to Canada. But in order to earn their respect, you work with them ten, twelve hours a day. They sent me to the Canadian Pacific Railroad out of Winnipeg where I worked on an "extra gang" with about forty men. Real hard physical labor on the tracks. The regular workday was ten hours and they usually worked overtime. I never could do the overtime. I was exhausted with the ten hours. Then I was supposed to teach them English and Canadian customs in the evening. Well, it turned out that they weren't really interested or at least that I wasn't an inspiring enough teacher.

Another story. In World War I we were meant to conserve wool and my mother and father conceived the idea that I could wear one of my father's cast-off suits that he was tired of. When I saw this suit my heart sank. My God, it was nothing like what any young fourteen-year-old would wear. Instead of being tight, it was loose, and it didn't have any cuffs on the trousers. Instead of being a sporty weave, it was iron grey with a very fine lining—suitable for a banker or a mortician. And I said, "I can't wear that. Everybody will make fun of me" (which they did). And my mother said, "You ought to be ashamed of yourself worrying about what people think about you. All you have to know is that you're right!" Well, I didn't believe her, but it's obvious that in the end I came around to her view.

I was trying to think in conventional terms of who influenced me in medicine. I guess Freud influenced me a great deal but I didn't come to that until much later. Somebody gave me Cushing's book about the life of Osler to read before I went to medical school. It was the most discouraging book I ever read. Osler was the first professor of medicine at Johns Hopkins. He was very distinguished. He wrote a textbook that was used a good deal. He loved science from the time he was a small boy, went down to ponds and got algae and looked at them under a borrowed microscope. But I had never been that interested in science. Also he believed that a doctor had no business marrying until he had made a great success of himself. Osler was well-known and received guests from all over the world. He married at the age of forty because he needed someone to preside at his dinner table. He loved old people. And I never liked most old people. (I still don't.) So I thought I was completely unfitted to be a physician. Osler didn't influence me. I just felt it was too late to turn back because I had signed up at Yale Medical School by then.

When it came to opposing the war in Viet Nam, a professor of sociology at Western Reserve University named Sidney Peck, led what was called University Circle Teach-In. This group got together for lunch on Mondays and Sid Peck's clear thinking and activities really impressed me a lot. Through Sid Peck's example, and through the example of the young people who were opposing the war in a more and more radical way, I gradually changed my politics, I changed my personality.

The Viet Nam War was tremendously influential! I really did change! Members of my family said, meeting me a couple of years after I'd been active, "What's happened to Ben?" I really was a very cautious person and always said "on the one hand," "on the other hand," and thought very carefully. At a press conference I spoke in a very slow, measured pace, obviously thinking twelve thoughts for every one that I let out, considering its pros and cons. Well, I changed into a much more outspoken, much warmer person, and became much more approachable. I was also radicalized quite thoroughly in my politics.

I really traded occupations twice. I was first a practitioner in New York City. Then *Baby and Child Care* came out, and that was what got me invited to the Mayo Clinic for a special project, the Rochester Child Health Project. And it was that that got me invited to the University of Pittsburgh to build a Department of Child Psychiatry and Child Development. That took me to Western Reserve University in Cleveland where I went as a teacher in the new curriculum, which assigned a family to each student within a month or two of his starting medical school. This was a drastic innovation, almost a revolution in medical education because all of medical education in the twentieth century and the last part of the nineteenth century was founded on the idea that it was only after two years of laboratory work that you were allowed to see a patient.

How do you feel about growing older?

I don't really recognize that I'm growing older. I know it intellectually, but in terms of my sense of myself, I think of myself as being just a few years out of college. Part of the reason is that I've never stopped being active. If I had really had to retire as most academic people have to retire at sixty-five, at least in the medical schools, if I'd had to retire suddenly and go into tilling nasturtiums, I probably would have gone into some kind of depression. But in the two years previous to retirement, I was becoming more and more in demand as a speaker to undergraduates. I spoke in six universities per week, day after day, and week after week, and month after month. I kept that up for eight years. And each university would mean about four or five appearances. Arrive in town by noon, and there would be a press conference at the airport. There would be lunch with a student committee, and then I was often asked to teach a class either in history or in political science or in child development. I would be available to students later in the student lounge, and then there would be dinner with students. There would be a talk from eight to nine and questions and answers from nine to ten and then, as the wording often went, "We'll repair to the student lounge now for those who want to ask further questions." And usually 100 people would follow. At eleven the students would say, "Now we're going to Professor Jenkins's where we can really relax." Well, they could relax, but I couldn't relax because I was the speaker. These were students who wanted to know, "Do you think I should go to Canada or should I go to jail or should I . . ." The point I am making is that I have never had to face retirement. This was a much more exciting life than I had ever led as a professor. I was never particularly popular as a professor, I was perhaps average. But this was heady stuff. Undergraduates were so eager to hear somebody older who was emphatically on their side that when I would go into the auditorium, I would get a standing ovation every single night for six or eight years. And then when I would finish my talk, I would get another standing ovation. Boy, that's great stuff for a professor! I talked to somewhere between six and eight hundred universities.

This is where a lot of the change in my personality came from. I myself would naturally have become more and more intolerant of the young as they got into the more casual clothes—casual is putting it mildly, raggedy, dirty clothes, long hair, things like that. I'd never appear in public without a blue suit with a vest, a gold chain across my vest and a very high collar with a pin under the tie. This was an essential part of myself. But when young people came and met me in droves and figuratively threw their arms around me I couldn't say, "What about your hair? What about your clothes?" Well, I was forced to admit that the soul was the important thing, and that appearance was utterly unimportant. After a few years of it I used to ask, "Do you think I ought to change *my* appearance?" And they said, "No, no, be yourself." You know, that's part of the tolerance of youth.

For eight years I was constantly with undergraduates who welcomed me as a friend and supporter.

The demands have gradually tapered off. I get probably ten percent of the invitations I used to get.

ANY ADVICE ABOUT GROWING OLDER?

I'd offer the traditional advice that people ought to have some interests. I think it's true that many people, at least in this country—I guess it's true in most countries—have only one or one-and-a-half interests. For men it's their work, and sooner or later they have to get out of that. And for women, it's raising the children and sooner or later the children go away. So, obviously, it has to do with having some interests aside from one's main occupation. I've never had any problem there. I've loved sailing for a long while. In Cleveland I took up ice-skating because I liked the idea of having some exercise. I have been interested in politics since I was a young man.

Keep an open mind! Most people hate new ideas. They want

to get into a groove as early as they can. If they are going to be lawyers, they want to get into the lawyers' groove, and be with the lawyers' group. If the lawyers belong to a country club, they want to belong to that country club too, erase their individuality as soon as they can by conforming in all respects. And new ideas? They don't want to hear any ideas except the ones that belong to the group in which they aspire to becoming a success. New ideas anger them, they really do!

YOU HAVE SAID THAT MAN IS IN TROUBLE, THAT IS, MANKIND IS IN TROUBLE. DO YOU HAVE HOPE?

I see our species as one that's capable of great nobility and creativity, and on the other hand, as the most hostile and murderous of all the species. We accuse animals of animal behavior. It's nowhere nearly as bad as human beings behave—not only in making enemies out of a whole national or religious group, but going to war and trying to slaughter them all. The great majority of murders, however, are committed in the family. I was shocked and amazed when I learned that fact. Something like three-quarters of all murders committed are committed in the family.

This is a reason, it seems to me, for working for the betterment of a country or for the world. I mean people's potentialities are there. They love to dance. They love to act. They love athletics. They love to create in several dozen different ways. They are potentially kind. They feel good when they are working cooperatively with others. I think that the greatest problem nowadays is that man got so smart that he invented weapons that are capable of erasing the whole species and all other species from the earth. But it's very clear that man hasn't got the political wisdom to run a world that can avoid war.

In the United States it's the communists that are at fault for everything. Of course, in the Soviet Union it's the capitalists who are to blame for everything. I would call that the paranoid aspect of human nature. And because of this paranoia I think there is within the next hundred years, at least a fifty percent chance that the world will disappear in a nuclear holocaust of some kind or other. The ironic thing is that paranoia is based on guilt, that you blame other people for your own hostility and aggressiveness.

Americans say we mean well toward the rest of the world, that we believe in letting people determine their own national choice—which is absolute nonsense. We went halfway around the world to Viet Nam because we decided that we wanted to have a big military and commercial base in Southeast Asia.

The reason that we project our own hostility and aggression is because we feel guilty in admitting that we are hostile and aggressive. So we say *we* are peace-loving, it's *they* who are trying to take over the world. So we have to take it over to keep them from taking it over. I thought the most amusing and yet horrifying recent example was finding these 2,000 Soviet troops in Cuba. The United States has something like a million troops ringing the Soviet Union and China. And yet, we think it's absolutely outrageous that the Soviet Union has 2,000 troops in Cuba. What could 2,000 troops in Cuba do to the United States? I still am very political. I'm still bitter about the Viet Nam War.

I think the interesting thing is that after having been enemies of China and enemies of Germany and Japan, we can make friends with those countries after a decent number of years go by. But we cannot forgive two little countries that worsted us. One of them was Cuba (Bay of Pigs), and the other one is Viet Nam. It's the fact that they're little countries and they beat us at our own game! This is why our hostility to those two countries is unrelenting. No president, no matter how much encouragement he gets from business dares to judge that we should grow up and treat Cuba like a country.

Anyway, I think the chances are very great that the world will blow up, because we now have weapons that can destroy the whole world, but we haven't got the statesmanship. But I think it's worth working to try to save the world! I'm against nuclear power. I think if you get enough Americans to realize how dangerous nuclear power is then maybe they'll realize that nuclear weapons are a thousand times more dangerous than nuclear power.

Do you think that it is more difficult to grow up today?

Perhaps. Perhaps not. One problem that youth has is too many choices of occupation. In colonial times in the United States, there were fewer choices. You could be a minister, or you could be a physician, or you could be a farmer. But this was the choice for the people who went to a university. Think of the occupations that are available now. It's clear that the more choices, the more disturbing it is to young people, especially when combined with the lack of any common values.

I had great hopes in the sixties and early seventies that youth had found answers that would simplify life for all subsequent youths. I was particularly impressed by two things with which they were concerned. Many of them said, "Why do we have to get into senseless competition and work all our lives with this dog-eat-dog kind of system? Why not work cooperatively in the spirit of brotherly love?" I think that's a great idea and that's why I'm a socialist and particularly deplore the ferocious competitiveness in the United States. The other idea they expressed was "Why try to compete in acquiring possessions and making a show of your possessions? Why not see how simply we can live?" These were the reasons they tried farming, they turned to the crafts, making leather belts and so forth. But it's clear that the impetus behind all that, the real impetus, was the dismay caused by the war in Viet Nam. And just as soon as the United States pulled out of Viet Nam, most of the protest, as you know, disappeared.

Now that doesn't mean that today's young people aren't as good as the previous ones. It's simply that the stimulus isn't there. The young people of the fifties were extremely materialistic. I remember public-opinion polls of college students. "What do you want out of life?" "I want a job that will pay me the largest amount of money I can find and I don't care what I do." Well, they weren't bad people. This was the style at that time. In the late sixties and the early seventies there was a style, it was more than style, a conviction, because of being threatened with being sent to Viet Nam to kill and be killed in a war that was absolutely senseless. They developed convictions, about sensible life goals.

I think there is always an intense rivalry between the generations that comes nearest the surface in the youth period. It seems that this is biologically determined and this is how the species has moved ahead—by young people having impatience with older people. (Freud would be able to point to the kind of dreams where the boy murders his father. It really is murderous at the unconscious level.) The young people figure, "Why, hell, with one hand I could do better than this." That rivalry frees them too of the need to be respectful, at least in a country where you're not required to be respectful. (It's different in countries where the middle-aged revere the old and the young people revere the middle-aged and the old people.) In America you don't fuss about the old, you've got to tolerate them, not revere them, because they support you and some of them are amiable.

WHAT IS YOUR GREATEST SOURCE OF STRENGTH?

Some psychoanalysts have said the thing that makes a person tend to be an optimist the rest of life is having been well fed and loved in infancy. And I think that's as good an answer as any though I suspect there are inborn differences in temperament that would have at least as much influence. There's a picture of me at one year of age which shows me full of beans. It's very clear I considered the world my oyster. I imagine that my general optimism was there at one year of age . . .

The pictures of me after one year of age show a rather worried-looking person. I think that this was due to my very dominating mother who was full of warnings of various kinds. She demanded total subordination.

When I was nine years of age, my father was invited by a

rich classmate to go abroad for one or two months. My mother wanted to send him pictures of all his children and herself to keep him from wandering from the straight and narrow path.

We were on an island in Maine called Vinalhaven and the pictures were satisfactory to my mother except the one of me. She said that I looked insufferably cocky. And she took all the trouble and expense of hiring a horse and carriage a second time to drive across Vinalhaven Island, it was perhaps five miles, in order to get a photograph of me taken that was more subdued.

I'm an optimistic person even when my political diagnosis is quite pessimistic. I have the feeling that I ought to go on working, but I also have a relentless sense of obligation. I've never been particularly aware of the feeling of depression. I think I've felt very guilty at times, and that's probably the closest I get to depression. I've noticed, that whenever I get anxious or guilty, the whole impulse is to become more active. I don't offer that as a prescription, I think that just happened to me.

There have been some crises, although relatively mild. When I was indicted by the federal government in 1968, that didn't bother me because I knew that Lyndon Johnson and his administration were wrong, not just politically wrong or militarily wrong, they were morally wrong! Part of that came from the fact that his administration asked me to support him in the presidential campaign in 1964 because he promised not to send Americans to fight in Asia, and I did enough on radio and television so that he called me up two days after the election. He said, in this humble-sounding voice, "Dr. Spock, I hope I prove worthy of your trust." And I had no idea that he would prove to be utterly unworthy of my trust, so I said, "Oh, President Johnson, of course you'll be worthy of my trust."

But in January '65, he suddenly escalated the war with the bombing of North Viet Nam and the buildup of troops. I only give that as an example of the fortitude that my mother gave me. (You don't have to worry what people think of you, even the president of the United States. All you have to know is that you're right!) So, this didn't bother me. I thought, since I'd now become a political creature, I've got him coming and going. If I win this case it proves to the world that I'm right. If I go to jail this will outrage millions of people in the United States and around the world, for which Johnson will take the rap.

I don't think I had any other very serious crises. My conscience has been the thing that's hard for me to bear, and I have to keep on a pretty straight and narrow path—not a conventional one. It's perfectly all right with my conscience to oppose the war in Viet Nam.

To write a book to help millions of parents—nobody can criticize me for that as long as the medical profession doesn't. I was scared of what the medical profession would say about the book because it was too newfangled. It went in for entirely new psychological concepts that had never been put into a book on child care by a physician before. And then it just told too many things compared to earlier books. Finally, a book review appeared in the *Journal of the American Medical Association* that said in essence, "It's quite a good book. Its only serious fault is that too often it says to consult your own doctor." Well, this is what I was worrying about—that I would be accused of usurping the doctor's role.

Do you think that older people are playing a more significant role today?

Well, there's gradually getting to be a greater proportion of them, but I don't see that they are playing a greater role. The shocking thing is that politically, very few Americans play any role at all. I think it's one of the disturbing things that only half of the people eligible to vote, voted in the last presidential election. I wonder what has happened to our country, our democracy, and what's going through people's minds. I *always* voted throughout my life—every time. My mind simply can't understand a person who says,

"What the hell!" or "Why bother." I just don't get it. I mean, it alarms me.

Older people could have a real influence, you know, if they wanted to get organized. Everything that I've learned politically, in general, is that what you need to do is organize and get people to play an active role. But, is that a job to get people stirred up to do something. Every once in a while there is a success that impresses me. I think of the war in Viet Nam. In the end, enough people turned against the war in Viet Nam so that Bobby Kennedy saw a chance of ousting Lyndon Johnson from the job. And Lyndon Johnson had to retire. That was an extraordinary achievement when you consider how power-loving and how powerful that man was. Young people said that nothing does any good because the war went on for four more years. Well, it was bad luck that the alternative was Richard Nixon, and it was bad luck that Richard Nixon persuaded our people that he would find an honorable end to the war in no time at all. Then it took four years because, of course, there was no honorable end.

WHAT ABOUT MORE ENERGY CONSERVATION?

I take the energy crisis very seriously and get impatient with those people who seem to feel that they are entitled to an inexhaustible amount of energy—like Americans generally who seem to feel that a 4,000-pound automobile is essential. In time people will be forced to live a simpler lifestyle, but, obviously, until that time, they are going to live it up.

Public-opinion polls report that most Americans think that the gasoline shortage is just some kind of plot. They think it's the oil companies trying to justify higher prices. And I am second to nobody in suspecting the oil companies. I think that they're the greediest poeple that the world has ever known! But it's perfectly clear also that oil is going to run out some day.

WHAT ABOUT COMMUNITIES FOR THE ELDERLY?

Well, since I've never identified with older people I can't talk with great authority. But my understanding is that some older people much prefer to live in an older persons' community. Other older people definitely don't want to live in an older persons' community. And I think that it should be possible for a person who gets old to lead the kind of life and live in the kind of place that he wants to. It would be intolerable for me as an old person to have no *power* over my own life, that would be absolutely horrible!

So, I think that the most important thing is for older people to have a choice, and the other thing is for them to have enough money so they can live in dignity and with some pleasure. That is another example of how thoughtless this country is in general, that only those who can throw their weight around get what they want and it's industry in general that decides how governmental money will be spent. Our country, that pretends to be child-centered, actually treats children very badly. And we're the only big industrialized country that doesn't have health insurance. And the income taxes are written very much for people with money and for industry. So, children don't get what they deserve and old people don't get what they deserve. Children can't organize politically, but old people could if they had the impulse—but there doesn't seem to be much of that impulse. It's because people have lived apolitically through their whole lives. America's credo is to leave politics alone, and go out and make your money.

REFERENCES

Bloom, Lynn Z., *Doctor Spock: Biography of a Conservative Radical*, Indianapolis: Bobbs-Merrill, 1972.

Cushing, Harvey William, *The Life of Sir William Osler*, London: Oxford University Press, 1940.

Spock, Dr. Benjamin, *Baby and Child Care,* New York: Meredith Press, 1945, 1946, 1957, 1968.

Spock, Dr. Benjamin, Reinhart, John, and Miller, Wayne, *A Baby's First Year,* Boston: Little, Brown, 1954, 1955, 1966.

Spock, Dr. Benjamin, and Lowenberg, Miriam E., *Feeding Your Baby and Child,* New York: Duell, Sloan & Pearce, 1955.

Spock, Dr. Benjamin, *Decent and Indecent,* New York: McCall, 1969, 1970.

DOMESTIC CORRESPONDENCE OF
DOMINIQUE-MARIE VARLET
BISHOP OF BABYLON
1678-1742

STUDIES IN THE HISTORY
OF
CHRISTIAN THOUGHT

EDITED BY

HEIKO A. OBERMAN, Tucson, Arizona

IN COOPERATION WITH

HENRY CHADWICK, Cambridge

JAROSLAV PELIKAN, New Haven, Conn.

BRIAN TIERNEY, Ithaca, N.Y.

E. DAVID WILLIS, Princeton, N.J.

VOLUME XXXVI

BASIL GUY

DOMESTIC CORRESPONDENCE OF
DOMINIQUE-MARIE VARLET
BISHOP OF BABYLON
1678-1742

LEIDEN
E. J. BRILL
1986

DOMESTIC CORRESPONDENCE OF DOMINIQUE-MARIE VARLET BISHOP OF BABYLON 1678-1742

EDITED, WITH NOTES, BY

BASIL GUY

LEIDEN

E. J. BRILL

1986

ISBN 90 04 07671 9

In memoriam
C. H. L.
1888 – 1966

CONTENTS

---

* Throughout this edition, the initials DMV refer to Dominique-Marie Varlet, Bishop of Babylon, 1678-1742.

PREFACE

At the term of this undertaking, which presents a largely unknown family correspondence of Dominique-Marie Varlet, bishop *in partibus* of Babylon (1678-1742), and which, it is hoped, will shed some light on Jansenism, its role and meaning, as it developed internationally until, roughly, the mid-eighteenth century, it is a pleasure to acknowledge the kindness of the editors and staff under whose imprint it appears, particularly of Professor Doctor Heiko Oberman, in charge of the distinguished series in which it is now included. Without such encouragement and advice as was most generously offered, the present volume would be considerably less attractive and perhaps even less successful in directing the reader's attention to ancillary details in the life of one man and, implicitly, to an important moral and psychological problem in the development of Western intellectual history over the last two hundred and fifty years.

Basil Guy
University of California
Berkeley.

INTRODUCTION

In 1974 the Bancroft Library of the University of California at Berkeley acquired from the Boston firm of Goodspeed's, Inc., a collection of letters and documents concerning Dominique-Marie Varlet (1678-1742), Roman Catholic Bishop of Ascalon and Babylon. (Though little-known today, Varlet was a French missionary and prelate who achieved some notoriety in his own time through championing what has since become known as the Old Catholic confession.) Efforts to trace the ultimate provenience of the collection have so far proved unavailing.

Of the seventy-five items in the collection, fifty-three are letters, both signed and unsigned, from Varlet to members of his family in France, whence the title of "Domestic Correspondence" supplied by the present editor. This collection of documents, written at irregular intervals from 1712 to 1739, contains sixteen letters dealing with Varlet's missionary activity, first in North America, then in Europe and the Mideast until 1721; thirty-seven others concern his family and personal anxieties following his establishment in the Netherlands, from 1721 until 1739, when he suffered the first of a debilitating series of strokes.

The remaining twenty-two items come from various sources. With one exception, they are legalistic in nature and deal largely with Varlet's inheritance, his death, and the disposal of his worldly belongings. The exception is number 63 which consists in two fragments of one page each containing geographical data which may have been gathered by, or for, Varlet around 1719 when he was preparing to journey to Persia, where his attempt to enter the See of Babylon and there occupy his rightful place as Bishop would end in ignominy.

The letters from Varlet are holograph; almost all are written on paper of uniform marking and size (approximately 22.5 cm × 18 cm.), folded three times in the same way, leaving generally a surface of about 11 cm. × 18 cm. for the address. At one time these letters were sealed with an imprint in wax that has, unfortunately, disappeared from all, though the signet undoubtedly represented the prelate's coat-of-arms. The other documents are by various hands, mostly notarial. All the items in the collection are in reasonably good condition, except for number 69, which is the much deteriorated copy of a document from the Claims-Court of the Châtelet in Paris.

Varlet's letters are addressed to his mother, née Marie Vallée, his brother, Jean-Achille, *procureur au Châtelet*, his sister, Marie-Anne, and her husband, Antoine Olivier, likewise *procureur au Châtelet*. The remaining correspondence is addressed uniquely to Antoine Olivier and emanated, so far as can be determined, from the collaborators of Varlet in the Netherlands, as well as from the notaries Jean-Henri Tremblay and Antoine Chastellain (Paris), Georges-Christian Qualenbrinck and François de Villiers (Utrecht), and from certain Dutch officials.

The Bancroft Library manuscripts are here published entire, and, it is believed, for the first time.[1] Unfortunately, even this limited exchange is incomplete, as witness numbers 39, 45, 47, 50 and 52, where reference is made to enclosures and previous letters of which there is no trace here. Nor does this selection contain replies to Varlet's missives or those of his agents. Despite such lacunae, however, the nature of the replies and the reactions of Varlet's family are nonetheless apparent from the "theme and variations" that can be followed from one letter to another, dealing in particular with financial settlements that might have contributed to the well-being and security of a generation, younger than Varlet, living in the French capital. The grasping attitude of these people may be one more proof of such niggardliness as is commonly said to have character-ized the class of *la petite robe* to which they all belonged. On the other hand, the prelate's patience and "otherworldliness" are patent in his let-ters.

Yet, however interesting this correspondence may be from the human point of view, it is still only part of a whole, the vast scope of which can best be appreciated through a perusal of the materials from the "Ancien fonds d'Amersfoort" now housed in the Rijksarchief at Utrecht,[2] and from those sources listed in the Bibliographies at the end of this edition. If publication of these few letters can spur a renewal of interest in the figure of Dominique-Marie Varlet as part of a future study which his role in eighteenth-century religious controversy demands, our purpose in editing them will have been well served.[3]

Dominique-Marie Varlet came from a family of the lesser nobility (but still of the *noblesse d'épée*), his grandfather having been for a time under Louis XIII the king's Lieutenant and Captain of the castle at Nanteuil (S. et M.).[4] His father, Achille, sieur de Verneuil, in company with

---

[1] Except for numbers 1, 6, and 47 (this last dated *31. xii. 1733*), published by Maximin Deloche in *Bulletin de la section de géographie*, xlv (1930), p. 39-66.

[2] See the *Inventaire de Port-Royal*, published by J. Bruggeman and A. van de Ven at the Hague in 1972.

[3] The next few pages follow in their outline and inspiration the *Nouvelles ecclésiastiques* of 8. vii. 1742 (Jansenist inspiration), Dupac de Bellegarde (militant Old Catholic point of view), C-B. Moss (ecumenical point of view), and B-A. van Kleef in *IKZ* (modern Old Catholic and to our knowledge the only full-scale study of Dominique-Marie Varlet available).

[4] See the Genealogical Table of Appendix 3, infra, *Documents du minutier central*, p. 85-278, passim, and A. de la Chesnaye Desbois, *Dictionnaire de la noblesse*, XII (Paris, 1868), under "La Grange."

Dominique's uncle, Charles, sieur de la Grange, was associated for some twenty-five years with the *Comédiens du roi* at the height of their popularity under Molière. He quit the troupe in 1684, however, having previously married and begotten a family. Some time before the turn of the century, Achille Varlet underwent a religious conversion and withdrew to an hermitage, which, according to the *Nouvelles ecclésiastiques*,[5] he had constructed with his own hands at Mont Valérien, immediately to the West of Paris. There he spent his days in orison and in mortifying the flesh until his death in September, 1709.

Varlet's mother, Marie Vallée, *Bourgeoise de Paris*, came from at least three generations of officials at the Châtelet, that body of notaries and petty lawyers who would, in the course of time, see their political power increase and, with it, an increase of the political role they would arrogate to themselves. Developing into and allying with the full-fledged *noblesse de robe*, this group is characteristic of the upward mobility of French society in the seventeenth and eighteenth centuries, illustrated in the case of Varlet's family by their several and important connections with the legal profession through his mother.

Outside the home, when still a youth, Varlet came under the influence of the abbé Jean-Baptiste Daguesseau, youngest brother of the famous Chancellor and jurist. Although this connection with another family of *la robe* is not to be overlooked, the important fact here is that the abbé was well-known for his piety and for the devout life he stimulated and encouraged in the parish of Saint-André des Arts. Thanks to the prompting of this spiritual guide, Varlet decided to take holy orders and set about preparing for his admission to the priesthood, manifesting in the course of his studies considerable susceptibility, if not exaltation, and great assiduity. At the turn of the century he entered that hotbed of Jansenism, the Oratorian seminary of Saint-Magloire, located on the rue Saint-Jacques near the present rue de l'abbé de l'Epée, and was made a priest in 1706. In the same year, he became a Doctor in Theology at the Sorbonne, writing a thesis on, and editing the work of, Claude Caille: *Quaestio theologica: quis solus habet immortalitatem.*[6]

After a brief period in which he served several churches in the Paris region, Varlet was named curate of the parish at Conflans-l'Archevêque (present-day Charenton), immediately to the ESE of the capital. There he was put into close relations with his rector, Cardinal de Noailles, Archbishop of Paris, a man known for his generous and pro-Jansenist sympathies. Although amply seconded by the Archbishop in his projects

---

[5] *Nouvelles ecclésiastiques*, 8. vii. 1742, p. 105.

[6] Bibliographical data on all of Varlet's works will be found in the first two sections of the Bibliography appended hereto.

for re-invigorating the spiritual life of his flock, Varlet found that some of his parishoners and neighboring priests did not share his zeal, were, in fact, attempting to thwart him at almost every turn, with the result that he resigned his charge. Apparently his disappointment did not last long, however, for he expressed to the venerable Archbishop the hope that he might have less difficulty in converting the heathen than he had experienced in trying to help people who were Christians—though in name only.

In 1711, through the offices of Jean-Henri Tremblay, *prêtre procureur*, a relative with connections reaching even to the family of the celebrated Marquise du Châtelet, Varlet became associated with the Société des Missions étrangères in the rue du Bac. The reasons for this new orientation and interest in his life are set forth by him in his *Seconde Apologie:*

> Naturellement ami de la retraite, du silence et du repos, je n'en sors pas volontiers, à moins qu'une grande nécessité ne me presse; mais alors Dieu me fait la grâce de m'y employer de grand cœur. J'avoue que les œuvres saintes abandonnées m'attirent extrêmement. C'est à elles que je me suis voué: c'est le seul motif qui m'a porté en Amérique. C'est le seul qui m'a fait aller relever la Mission des Tamaroas parce que personne ne voulait ou ne pouvait l'entreprendre. . . . Je me souviens que, il y a dix-huit ans, feu M. l'évêque de Rosalie [Artus de Lionne] nous exhortant à consacrer aux Missions étrangères, ne nous parlait ni de la Chine, ni du Tonquin, ni du Siam, mais seulement des œuvres abandonnées. Il ne voulait pas qu'on considérât les Missions sous une autre face: J'avoue que c'est ce qui me gagna et je n'aurais pas été si sensible à tout autre motif.[7]

After several false starts, Varlet set off for the New World in March of 1713. The mission to which he had been assigned was in the country of the Tamaroas, a tribe then living in the middle Mississippi valley, with their principal encampment near modern East Saint-Louis, Illinois. Since the French possessions in North America had just been divided for administrative purposes along the fortieth parallel into Canada and Louisiana, this mission was technically in the latter province and subject to a governor and clergy at Fort Louis, or Mobile, Alabama. (New Orleans had not yet been founded.) Arriving via Santo Domingo and Havana in early June, 1713,[8] Varlet was not able, for various reasons, to join his charges until April, 1715. During the next two years of his apostolate,[9] working the Lord's vineyard for the salvation of souls (not least of all his own), Varlet, full of zeal and enthusiasm, knew at last some of the consolations which the ministry is said to afford, finding the Tamaroas docile

---

[7] Dominique-Marie Varlet, *Seconde Apologie*, p. 421.
[8] *Not* 1712, as Garneau claims in his *Histoire du Canada*, I: 135.
[9] *Not* six, as in the *Nouvelles ecclésiastiques*, 8. vii. 1742, p. 105.

and apt—if not ready—for instruction in the white man's ways. (Their gentleness is what probably led to their extinction by the end of the eighteenth century, when they were overwhelmed by their enemies the Chickasaw and Shawnee.)

On the other hand, because of the struggle for power in which various religious orders were then engaged, not only in France, but abroad, Varlet sometimes came into contact with Capuchins, Recollets, and especially with Jesuits, whose views about the natives and their own respective spheres of influence conflicted with his. And so, the neophyte proselytizer knew once more some of the same difficulties and disappointments he had earlier encountered in his parish outside Paris.

Nonetheless, Varlet threw himelf into his work with more feeling than sense. By the beginning of 1717, the wear and tear of his labours began to take their toll, and he was required, in order to preserve his health—never robust, at best—to withdraw to Quebec, at that time the seat of French ecclesiastical authority in all North America. He went the more willingly as he had discovered a new cause to plead, that of the Indians already falling victim to "civilization." In this enterprise he was apparently successful, because he was named Vicar-General to the saintly Archbishop, Saint-Vallier, with responsibility for the myriad souls between the Great Lakes and the Missouri River. But in mid-1718, just as he was about to leave with three seminarians to resume his exciting life in the Mississippi valley, a packet from France brought news that he was to return to Paris, since, on the recommendation of the Mission étrangères and especially of one of his former teachers, now Director of the Seminary at Bordeaux, he was being considered in Rome for elevation as Bishop *in partibus* of Ascalon and co-adjutor to Pidou de Saint-Olon, Bishop of Babylon.

Varlet arrived in Paris at the end of 1718 and received the Brief of Pope Clement XI, dated 17 September of that year, naming him to the two Sees.[10] At the same time, letters from the Propaganda confirmed him in his titles, with the proviso that he be consecrated immediately, leave France forthwith, and proceed to take up residence in Hamadan (seat of the Bishops of Babylon) without further ado—all incognito.

Varlet was consecrated in the chapel of the Missions étrangères on 19 February 1719, with Matignon, the former Bishop of Condom, officiating, assisted only by Mornay, the Co-adjutor of Quebec, and another of Varlet's former teachers, the famous preacher Massillon, Bishop of Ciermont. There were no others present. That very day the new prelate learned of the death, on 20 November 1717, of M. de Saint-

---

[10] See the *Inventaire de Port-Royal*, no. 3626.

Olon, to whose See he therefore succeeded with full title, responsibilities and emoluments. Since further letters from the Propaganda were still urging him to make haste to leave for Babylon, Varlet prepared himself with all possible expediency and left Paris for Brussels on the first stage of his itinerary, 18 March, without paying the usual courtesy visit to the Nuncio nor even saying goodby to his family.[11]

After a brief stopover at Compiègne, Varlet arrived in Brussels during the evening of Saturday, 25 March, but had time only to say Mass on Sunday morning before resuming his journey. Thus, the incognito so forcefully urged on him prevented Varlet from paying his respects to the Nuncio in Brussels as he would have done under more normal circumstances, and this, with his earlier omission of a last visit to the Nuncio in Paris, is at the root of later difficulties in which the Bishop of Babylon was made to pay dearly for a seeming lack of respect and openness. Nonetheless, he apparently intended to abide by the strictures of the Propaganda, enjoining anonymity upon him, and sailed from Antwerp for Lübeck and Saint Petersburg. But bad weather and a change in orders for the captain of his ship forced them to land in Amsterdam, where Varlet arrived on 2 April 1719.

There he had to wait some days, including Holy Week and Easter, before being able to re-embark for Russia, whence he proposed to enter Persia via the Caucasus, the route through Turkey being closed. In a certain sense, as Varlet admits in the preface to his *Seconde Apologie*, this delay was as important to his career as his failure to consult the Nuncios, for somehow his presence in the Dutch capital became known, and several members of the local Roman Catholic community discovered his whereabouts and visited him.

Now, at that time, foreign priests were not allowed to say Mass in the United Provinces without special permission from the government, for which Varlet could not apply, since he was supposed to be incognito. One person (probably Jacob Krijs), claiming to have some influence with the magistrates, found him out, however, and asked Varlet to stay with him, since the Bishop of Babylon could celebrate Mass safely in his house. For want of any alternative, Varlet agreed. But in the course of conversations with his host and others, these men pointed out the parlous state of Roman Catholicism in the country, due above all to the lack of a head. (The last bishop, Pierre Codde, had been suspended in 1702 and

---

[11] See, for example, letter no. 13, *infra*. Earlier, Varlet had attempted to see the Nuncio in order to secure recognition of his title as Bishop of Babylon as soon as news of Pidou de Saint-Olon's death had reached him, but because such notification was not "official," his appointment to the full title could not be confirmed at that time. See van Kleef, *IKZ*, p. 150, n. 3.

deposed in 1704 because of his supposed Jansenism, and there had been no effective successor.) They also conveniently forgot to inform Varlet that the Pope had already charged the Nuncio at Cologne with serving the needs of Dutch Roman Catholics. Three appointees of this man had been refused admission to the United Provinces by the civil authorities who were inspired by a new-found sense of nationalism; indirectly their action tended to isolate the Metropolitan Church at Utrecht. Nor did Varlet's hosts explain that there were divisions among themselves, fostered by their own pettiness no less by the pretentions of the Papacy. Rome seemed bent on treating a religious body whose legitimate existence extended over a thousand years as a mere mission, because it lacked a bishop. But above all, these representatives of the Church were desirous of having the Bishop of Babylon confirm as many of the faithful as possible during his short stay. The Vicars-General and Chapters of Utrecht and Haarlem were particularly eager to urge this ceremony on him.

Recalling his earlier commitment to "les œuvres saintes abandonées" in seeking a career as missionary in Canada, and truly distressed by the situation of his co-religionaries in the United Provinces, Varlet felt that he could not refuse such a request. Without further consultation, he proceeded to confirm a number of candidates, mostly, as claim the *Nouvelles ecclésiastiques*, "des pauvres et des orphelins, qui ne pouvaient aller en d'autres pays recevoir un sacrement si particulièrement nécessaire aux fidèles d'une église affligée et dans un pays où la foi est exposée à tant de périls"[12] Thus, deeds inspired by charity and by a sense of duty became, when known to Rome, an act of insubordination and irresponsibility which could not be countenanced.

Varlet left Amsterdam 25 April 1719 and, after a rough passage, arrived at Saint Petersburg on 31 May. Following a brief sojourn in the newly-founded capital of the Romanoffs, he arrived in Moscow on 6 July, intending to reach the See of Babylon by sailing down the Volga to Nizhni-Novgorod, Kazan, Samara, Tsaritsyn and Astrakhan. Thence he would follow on land the Caspian coast from Derbent to Resht in modern Persia before crossing the Elburz Mountains and descending via Kasvin to Hamadan.[13] For reasons that will be explained shortly, Varlet accomplished no more than two-thirds of the journey, being halted on his way between Derbent and Resht at Schemacha.

Situated in the Eastern Caucasus, this city, the capital of Shirvan Province, was in Persian hands at the time, so that, after his arrival on 1

---

[12] *Nouvelles ecclésiastiques*, 8. vii. 1742, p. 106.
[13] See no 63, infra.

November 1719, Varlet awaited permission from the government of the
Shah to proceed to his destination. While in Schemacha, he conferred
with Isaiah, an Orthodox Bishop of Caucasian Albania, who encouraged
him in the belief that it would not be impossible to win the Eastern
Church over to Rome, if there were some way to deliver it from political
interference by the Moslems and especially if the effort were inspired by
those same sentiments which had moved Varlet to become an apostle to
the Indians in North America. But before this early ecumenical project
could develop, Varlet received, on March 1720, the visit of a Jesuit,
Father Bachou, who placed in his hands a letter from Barnabas, the
Dominican Bishop of Isphahan, dated 7 December 1719, claiming that
the Propaganda had declared the Bishop of Babylon suspended from all
functions of his office and jurisdiction as of 7 May 1719. The emissary of
the Bishop of Isphahan never produced the authority for the act of
suspension, so that the authenticity of the claim was never verified—nor
verifiable, though there is a brief from the Propaganda demanding obedience to the Bull Unigenitus dated from Rome 18 February 1719 (the
day before Varlet's consecration in Paris.)[14] So far as we are aware,
Varlet never received the text of this document.[15]

On learning of his disrespect toward the Nuncios in Paris and Brussels,
but without any realistic conception of the slowness of the posts nor of
how best to inform Varlet himself, the Propaganda had attempted, first,
to forestall his arrival in Saint Petersburg by alerting the Apostolic
Delegate to Münster and the Nuncio in Poland, through whose jurisdic-
tions lay his presumed itinerary, and, failing that, to halt Varlet in
Moscow through the good offices of the Polish ambassador to the Czar.
Second, on realizing the futility of such a chase where the quarry had a
lead of at least three weeks, the Propaganda sought to inform many of the
missionaries whom Varlet might encounter in the Middle East, invoking
their collaboration in suspending the Bishop of Babylon and delegating
authority to them in official briefs. Thus it was that the long arm of the
Church finally caught up with Varlet and made it clear to him that the
reasons for the suspension were primarily two: he had not seen the Nuncio in Paris to subscribe to the Bull *Unigenitus*, condemning the Jansenist
heresy, nor had he applied to the Nuncio in Brussels for permission to exercise his functions as a bishop in the United Provinces, outside his own
jurisdiction.

---

[14] See the *Inventaire de Port-Royal*, no. 3627, and Mozzi, *Compendio*, II: 69 (also his *Storia*,
II: 115).

[15] Despite J. Vidal in *Revue d'Histoire des Missions*, p. 364. Nor does van Kleef (*IKZ*, p.
157, n. 2) give the source for the text he quotes in this respect.

But even as Varlet was sojourning in Schemacha, and unknown to him, Dominican monks were occupying his residence in Hamadan and attempting to govern the See in his stead, in conformity with the dictates of the Bishop of Isphahan. If we are to believe Varlet's two *Apologies* and the protestations of good faith they contain, it is easy to see how this man of peace would have been false to his principles if he had decided to ignore the letter of the Bishop of Isphahan and had proceeded as planned. But since, as he himself claimed, he was "naturellement ami . . . du repos,"[16] he was probably the first to realize how devastating such an act might be, that there could only result from it scandal and dissensions which would have ended with the ultimate contempt of the Eastern Orthodox and those whom he would have wished to convert—after all, his one reason for accepting elevation and consecration in the first place. Furthermore, after careful consideration, Varlet decided that he would never be able to function effectively in his See because, suspended, the refusal of moral support by the ultramontane party there would make his task impossible.

On 6 May 1720, Varlet resolved to retire to Europe in order to seek redress and there justify his actions.[17] A Russian official who happened to be in Schemacha at the time, offered the Bishop of Babylon whatever help his good offices might afford, and so undertook to find him passage on a ship sailing to the Volga, to provide him with letters of introduction to the Orthodox Bishop of Astrakhan as well as to the court at Saint Petersburg, and to advance him credit for the return voyage. We should note the importance of this last gesture, since Varlet had by this time run out of personal funds for travel. And because of his suspension, he would never enjoy the emoluments from his title or diocese, his rightful income as Bishop of Babylon, and was, therefore, always in financial straits, reduced to seeking support from his family and friends.[18] This penury is implicit in the correspondence which follows and forms the pitiful, if tiresome, burden of his letters to unsympathetic relatives in France.

When at last Varlet returned to the United Provinces on 16 May 1721,[19] the principal members of the Dutch hierarchy pressed him to remain in their midst, at least until the obstacles he had encountered on the frontiers of Persia, and which served to isolate him from the mainstream of Roman Catholic life, could be removed. Because of his previous ac-

---

[16] Dominique-Marie Varlet, *Seconde Apologie*, p. 421.

[17] See the *Inventaire de Port-Royal*, no. 3753.

[18] An important issue. See especially van Kleef, *IKZ*, p. 84, n. 1; 85, n. 1; 92, n. 2; and 150, n. 3.

[19] *Not* in 1722, as Pastor claims in his *History of the Popes*, 34: 286; see letter no. 17, infra. The return journey was by land from Moscow to Dantzig, Berlin, Hamburg, and Amsterdam.

quaintance with the Church of Amsterdam and, again, because of his convictions about "les œuvres saintes abandonnées," Varlet felt that he could not legitimately refuse such an appealing challenge to his missionary zeal. He acquiesced and submitted to the will of a benign Providence. This arrangement offered the advantage of allowing him a necessary respite from his wandering and from uncertainty about the future, especially about the need to accept the Bull Unigenitus whose principles he did not approve (any more than he had approved the formulary of Alexander VII which he had been constrained to sign in 1702).[20] He thus ruled out the prospect of an immediate return to France, where the Bull would become the law of the land on 24 March 1730 with far-reching political consequences. Moreover, as Varlet says in his first *Apologie*, he feared

> le séjour de sa patrie, comme une tentation propre à affaiblir l'esprit de sa vocation; et il lui paraissait plus sûr de demeurer inconnu dans un lieu où rien ne l'obligerait de se communiquer beaucoup, et où il pourrait goûter les douceurs de ce saint loisir que cherche l'amour de la Vérité, et se remettre à l'étude tranquille de l'Ecriture, de la Tradition, et du Droit canonique, ses anciennes délices; [étude] dont il ne s'était distrait que par le désir d'aller chercher les âmes abandonnées.[21]

Varlet was well-advised in making this decision to remain in the United Provinces, for, after a quasi-secret return to Paris in June of 1721, word soon spread that the authorities were contemplating his arrest, or, even worse, were plotting against his very life. Examples of this sort of treatment were not hard to find in the milieu frequented by Varlet. Among those who had tasted of prison and were known to him were men like Quesnel, Codde, de Roquette, and D. Thierry de Viaixnes who would later be his secretary. Such threats also necessitated the use of pseudonyms, Varlet choosing on occasion to be called variously, M. Dumont, Dupont à Pozzo, Dupré, Dupuis or Gerson.[22]

At one point in the course of his visit *sub rosa* to France, Varlet sought safety and consultation at Régennes in Burgundy, the estate of Monsignor Caylus, the pro-Jansenist Bishop of Auxerre.[23] After various soundings of the clergy and police, with Caylus as intermediary, he had regretfully to abandon his homeland and resign himself to defending his

---

[20] See Appendix 4.

[21] Dominique-Marie Varlet, [Première] *Apologie*, Préface.

[22] On this important subject, see Taveneaux, *Jansénisme et politique*, p. 88-98, and the same author's *Jansénisme en Lorraine*, p. 584.

[23] Although such historians as E. Picot mention this consultation, they do not specify when it took place; yet on the basis of present knowledge, it can only have occurred in the summer of 1721.

name and actions from Amsterdam, where he at length returned in February of 1722, there to live out his days.

Thus the Bishop of Babylon took up residence in the United Provinces as had been proposed to him, devoting his time to study and reflection, utilizing his enforced leisure to meditate on the state of the Church in the United Provinces, no less than on his own salvation. At the same time, he did everything in his power to have his suspension withdrawn. In the first of a long series of tracts and polemics, he sought to convince the Pope as well as the Curia of his innocence, claiming that although he did not in conscience subscribe to the Bull *Unigenitus* and saw in it certain errors of dogma, he was ever ready to return to the See of Babylon, provided he were treated as he deserved and his name cleared.[24]

He pointed out further that when he returned to Europe from Canada he knew nothing about the Bull which had been promulgated during his absence in the New World (8 September 1713); that he had been ordered to maintain as strict an incognito as possible and therefore had not paid his respects to anyone; that, since the last directive from Rome had not reached Paris until after his departure and had not been forwarded, he could not possibly have reacted as he ought, nor even as he desired. Moreover, the form of his suspension and the manner of his notification were both highly irregular, the suspension itself not in accordance with the canons stipulating that a diocesan could not be arbitrarily suspended without a trial or other opportunity for self-defense.

After the death in 1721 of Pope Clement XI, the autor of the Bull *Unigenitus*, French friends of Varlet were of the opinion that the Bishop of Babylon might receive a fairer hearing of his case if he went again to France. But so dismayed was he by his recent experience there (or so wary), that he remained adamant in his determination on exile, and it is well he did, since on 29 September 1722, Cardinal Dubois, the Prime Minister, promised the Curia that he would have Varlet arrested and imprisoned when next he set foot on French territory.[25] Luckily for Varlet, the threat against him was never carried out, and Dubois died at the beginning of 1723. But the knowledge of such tactics merely served to confirm Varlet in his resolve—no matter how painful—to remain like Moses in sight of Canaan, "a pilgrim in a barren land."[26]

Meanwhile the Nuncio in Paris informed the Bishop of Babylon that if he would resign his See and return to France, he would be compensated with other benefices and pensions, enabling him to participate in the

---

[24] See the *Inventaire de Port-Royal*, no. 3757.

[25] See *Romeinse Bronnen*, nos. 689 and 715.

[26] The comparison with Moses is to be found in the anonymous Flemish poem *Ter Gedagtnisse van . . . Domenicus-Maria Varlet*, v. 395.

whole life of the Church. Varlet saw through the blackmail of such flat-tery as preyed on his baser instincts, and he rejected the offer out of hand, since, as he declared while paraphrasing the Bible, he did not wish to turn the House of God into a den of thieves.[27] At the same time Varlet obtained an opinion favorable to his case from a well-known French canonist, M. Gibert, supported by several theologians from Paris and Louvain. Van Espen, the most noted of these last, declared in particular that there was no precedent for such extraordinary treatment of a duly elected and consecrated bishop. Yet when Varlet revealed that, not-withstanding this opinion, he would never subscribe to the Bull *Unigenitus*, nor apologize for having administered confirmation at Amsterdam, nor resign his See, he closed the door on any such recourse as he or his friends might have desired or any such accommodation as could have been arranged.

The proofs he had invoked as justification did not fall on completely deaf ears and seemed to convince an ever-growing circle that he was in-deed the injured party, an innocent bystander, in a quarrel which was fast assuming untoward proportions, with the result that:

> les imputations qu'on lui avait faites disparaissaient; mais ses ennemis ne cédaient pas pour cela. Alléguaient-ils de nouveaux griefs? Point du tout. On reconnaît donc à Rome son innocence? Encore moins. On y trouve le secret de faire qu'un homme ne soit point innocent, quoiqu'il ne soit pas coupable pour autant.[28]

Varlet now realized that in order to redress his fortunes he would have to appeal to a future General Council of the Church as a whole. By such a move, he became allied with those avowed Jansenists who, refusing to acknowledge the Bull *Unigenitus*, or to subscribe thereto, had earlier set in motion the Appellant movement which was to complicate the situation of the Church in France during the eighteenth century and, perhaps as much as any other factor, lead to the idenfication of Jansenism as a political party.

Whatever Varlet's true feelings, the fact is that by omitting to visit the Nuncios in Paris and Brussels after his consecration, combined with his known resistance to signing formularies of any kind, his actions were in-terpreted as a refusal by him to acknowledge the supremacy of the Roman hierarchy (the Nuncios being both the personal and official am-bassadors of the reigning pontiff) and the validity of papal declarations. He was thus compromised as a thoroughgoing Jansenist though he did

---

[27] See *Matthew* xxi, *Mark* xi, and *Luke* xix.
[28] Dominique-Marie Varlet, [Première] *Apologie*, Préface.

not consider himself in this light until at least 1723.[29] Since, after all, he had not sworn to accept the Bull *Unigenitus*, to publish it, nor to see that it were put into efect—all primary considerations where the other Appellants were concerned (some 3,000 throughout France)[30]—what other conclusion could be drawn?

Varlet's own appeal, dated 15 February 1723, begins by claiming merely that the attacks and charges of which he was the victim were nullified by the fact that there was no legitimate cause (or *corpus dilecti*), since the lack of his signature to the Bull *Unigenitus* was only a pretext in his case and a secondary consideration in any event. He proceeds to demonstrate that the Bull is not without its logical weaknesses, is therefore unsuitable for publication and cannot possibly be the legitimation of an oath which, by reason of the errors in the text, would itself be erroneous and invalid before both the Law and the Church. In returning to the specifics of his own case, Varlet claims that the form of his suspension was null and void since the Bishop of Isphahan was incompetent to prevent him from entering Persia if the rules governing the canonical judgment of bishops had been observed. In this context, his next points are easy to understand—to wit, that no juridical procedure had been followed in suspending him, that there was no citation of his misdeeds which would lead to his suspension in due process, and that there had been no formal admonition to him personally before his suspension.

As is clear from this bald presentation of Varlet's case, he based all his arguments on form and not on substance. Yet we cannot help wondering why, if such be the truth, he did not stand his ground in Schemacha and attempt to enter Persia after first having pleaded in this manner, via correspondence, not with France, but directly with the Holy See in Rome. For how had the letter of censure reached the Bishop of Isphahan before Varlet arrived in the Caucasus, despite the distance and the difficulties of communication at that time? Whatever, these are the arguments Varlet would employ again and again to defend himself and which reveal, in part at least, beneath an innocent exterior, his contumacious nature.[31]

---

[29] See G. Lami's description of eighteenth-century Jansenists as merely opponents to the authority of Rome: ". . . sono Giansenisti i Gesuiti, i Francescani, i Vescovi, quasi tutti," (Vausard's edition of his *Lettres*, p. 190); or that of Father Fourqueveaux (quoted by van Kleef in *IKZ*, p. 82, n. 1): "Le jansénisme est . . . une dénomination qui change d'objet selon les lieux et les personnes et dont il ne reste de fixe que l'usage qu'en font ces Pères [les Jésuites] pour décorer ceux qui n'entrent pas dans leurs vues ou qui sont un obstacle à leurs desseins."

[30] The figure is from Préclin-Tapié, *Le XVIIIᵒ siècle* (Coll. Clio), p. 392. Earlier, even Pascal (Pensée 871, Brunschvicg) had given expression to this same sort of resistance, claiming: "il n'y a presque plus que la France où il soit permis de dire que le Concile est au-dessus du Pape."

[31] See the interesting quotation of texts from the Rijksarchief in van Kleef (*IKZ*, p. 150-159) with the act of his suspension (p. 157, n. 2).

In the spring of 1723, on 27 April, the Chapter of the cathedral at Utrecht elected Cornelis Steenhoven to be Archbishop of the Church in the United Provinces. They had carefully observed all the canons of ecclesiastical law and proceeded to comply with all necessary propriety in informing Rome of this election and in requesting confirmation of the new archbishop by the Pope. There was no reply (there would be none), and Innocent XIII died on 7 March 1724, leaving the Chapter and the ecclesiastical world in suspense. The new Pope, Benedict XIII, took no immediate action.

While the legitimacy of Steenhoven's election was being debated, there had appeared in Rome on 9 March 1724, over the signature of a conclave of cardinals, a letter against the Church at Utrecht and against Varlet in particular, couched in insulting terms of libellous intent. The Bishop of Babylon, whatever his other preoccupations of the moment, undertook immediately to write a *Plainte à l'Eglise Catholique* as well as a letter to Benedict XIII. These pieces, together with his first act of appeal, constitute the most important elements of his *Apologie*, published at Amsterdam in 1724.

With no response forthcoming from the Curia in Rome, and none of the bishops invited to the consecration of Steenhoven giving any indication of accepting, the Chapter consulted several prelates, theologians, and canonists in France and the Low Countries, with the result that on the advice of these learned men, the invitation to consecrate the new Archbishop was proffered to the Bishop of Babylon. There were recent precedents to explain this procedure both in France and Portugal[32] (not to mention Antwerp, where the incumbent had proceeded to make his brother Bishop *in partibus* of Rhodes to show his sympathy with Varlet and the Church at Utrecht).[33]

In his capacity as Bishop of Babylon, Varlet accepted and performed the ceremony at six o'clock in the morning on 15 October 1724, in the presence of the Chapter of Utrecht and members of the Church in the United Provinces. The deed was done. As C. D. Moss rightly claims,[34] the Church at Utrecht, though as yet she did not know it, had received her autonomy and begun her career independently of the See of Saint Peter. Unfortunately, the rite had been celebrated at Varlet's private residence in Amsterdam, and *not* in the cathedral or other consecrated place,[35] and this tactical omission, like previous ones regarding the Nun-

---

[32] See Neale's *History*, p. 248.

[33] This anecdote is related by Moss, *The Old Catholic Movement*, p. 123, and by van Kleef (with more circumstantial evidence) in *IKZ*, p. 173, n. 3.

[34] C. D. Moss, op. cit., p. 123.

[35] Contrary to the *Nouvelles ecclésiastiques*, 8. vii. 1742, p. 107, and Moss, op. cit., p. 123.

cios in Paris and Brussels, was charged to Varlet in the ever-growing list of griefs which the Roman Catholic hierarchy held against him.

On 21 February 1725, Benedict XIII issued a Brief[36] declaring the election of Steenhoven null and void and his consecration illicit and execrable, forbidding Roman Catholics to recognize him as their head or to have any dealings with him, and pronouncing the severest censures on the Bishop of Babylon and those in attendance. Great surprise greeted the Pope's accusation of false doctrine against the Church of Utrecht, an accusation which was patently untrue and unjust and which was repudiated on all sides in the United Provinces with great indignation.[37]

Although his first letter to the Pope had gone unanswered, Varlet felt it incumbent upon him to write a second in order to defend himself more fully and to vindicate his name and actions. This letter, dated 15 January 1725, along with another to the Curia from 23 March of the same year, marks the true beginning of Varlet's literary production, consisting largely in defenses and appeals, charges and counter-charges. The learned Bishop re-iterates time and again his devotion to "les œuvres saintes abandonnées" and the nullity of the procedure by which he had been suspended, so that the two points become a *leitmotif* in all his writings thenceforth. His attitude in these works is typical, demonstrating his clever sense of proportion in argument as well as his tacit recognition that any other defense would undoubtedly be subject to a more direct and damaging counter-attack. Yet however closely-reasoned and effective in their appeal to the intelligence, these works are a far cry from the standards of religious controversy set in the seventeenth century by Port-Royal and Pascal: neither the intensity nor the humour of the great stylist is here, though of "géométrie" there is more than enough. The modern reader should not therefore seek to be moved in reading this material, but, rather, only to be convinced through the rational purposiveness and insistent argument from bald statements of fact.

The death of Steenhoven on 3 April 1725 created somewhat of a stir, as the interested parties at Utrecht saw their labours in danger of being brought to naught and the patience or, ultimately, fatigue that had accompanied his election, elevation, and consecration in jeopardy. Despite such considerations, the Chapter met once more, and on 5 May 1725, elected Cornelis-Jan van Barchman-Wuytiers. Chosen unanimously because of his singular merit, the Archbishop-to-be was to prove worthy of the call, as may be seen by his immediate withdrawal to determine whether he should accept it or not. Once his decision was taken,

---

[36] For the text, see Mozzi, *Compendio*, II: 106.
[37] See Moss, op. cit., p. 124-25.

however, he followed the very same steps as had his predecessor: he wrote to the Pope to request confirmation of his election, at the same time forwarding his profession of faith and obedience according to the form prescribed by Pius IV in 1564. The Chapter, too, repeated its earlier efforts by writing to Benedict XIII on the same subject and for the same purpose: recognition of the election and of the right to full existence of the Church in the United Provinces. But, as before, no reply was forthcoming. After waiting for more than four months, invitations were again extended to French bishops, as in the first instance, and were likewise ignored. Nothing daunted, the authorities at Utrecht turned as before to the Bishop of Babylon. After inquiring into the regularity of Barchman's election as well as into his character and talents, Varlet declared himself satisfied and willing to officiate.

Before this could be done, however, according to Dupac,[38] Varlet was informed one day while visiting a priest at Naarden on the Zuiderzee that the captain of an unknown ship at anchor nearby would have the honour of his company at dinner. On receipt of his refusal, the ship hove to and set sail, and the Bishop of Babylon began to suspect that there had been a plot to kidnap him in order to delay or prevent his participation in Barchman's consecration. At about the same time, an attempt was made by M. de Montigny, the agent at Rome of the Société des Missions étrangères, to reconcile Varlet with the Papacy, but Varlet saw through the scheme of this erstwhile acquaintance and so avoided the trap he had so cleverly set.[39] Despite such threats, the consecration was finally held on Sunday, 30 September in the Church of Saint James and Saint Augustine at the Hague, at that time served by the Archdiocese of Utrecht.

Again the Curia at Rome reacted vigorously, and over the signature of Benedict XIII, published Briefs on 23 August and 6 December 1725,[40] declaring the election null and void and condemning those who had participated in the consecration. Unfortunately, partisan passion once more reared its head, and some of the terms of the condemnation were outrageously tendentious, if not simply incorrect. The Pope appeared ridiculous, not so much because of his glorification of "Divine retribution" in the case of Steenhoven's death, but because of the patently erroneous mention of "Doncker, the late layman," in whose home the consecration was averred to have taken place. It so happened that Theodore

---

[38] *Histoire abrégée de l'église métropolitaine d'Utrecht*, p. 332-340; other examples are put forward by van Kleef in *IKZ*, p. 193-194.

[39] For Montigny and samples of his two-faced correspondence, see *Romeinse Bronnen* and *Romeinse Bescheiden*, passim.

[40] Texts in Mozzi, *Compendio*, II: 110 and 113.

Doncker, who had, to be sure, attended the consecration of Steenhoven, was not a layman, but a priest, and was very much alive. Dupac, in one of the few truly droll moments of his *Histoire*,[41] recounts with considerable delight how, as in the condemnation of propositions from the *Augustinus*, papal infallibility backfired when Doncker, standing in his pulpit at Amsterdam, Brief in hand, asked his flock how the Pope, who had declared him to be dead, could expect his decrees to be accepted in good faith while Doncker himself was living proof to the contrary. Such manifestations of continuing resistance by the Dutch were soon criticized in an even more vituperative and discouraging attack, *Historia Ecclesiae Ultrajectinae*. This diatribe had been written by a canon of Malines, Hoynck van Papendrecht, and had appeared privately, without the *Imprimatur*. In it, the author pretends that since the Church at Utrecht lost its temporal right to existence (through the refusal by the Government of the United Provinces to let bishops named by the Popes enter the country after 1702), it had also foregone its right to spiritual existence. However overblown the argument and its presentation, this work has since attracted some notice and even the approval of latter-day critics.[42]

But all these polemics were more than Varlet could stand, with the result that he once more took pen in hand and composed his second *Apologie*. Introducing it with a "Preface" which is a sort of spiritual autobiography, as well as another protestation regarding his mistreatment as Bishop of Babylon, another appeal to a future General Council regarding the Bull *Unigenitus*, another *Plainte à l'Eglise Catholique*, a dissertation on the consecration of bishops, which defends quite naturally his own stance and actions, and several letters, some of which had appeared previously in the same intent and dealing with the same problems, he at length arrives at his declared topic. This second *Apologie* appeared at Amsterdam in 1727 and is as much a defense of the status and the rights of the Church at Utrecht as of Varlet himself. At the same time, this sturdy volume offers ample proof of Varlet's stubbornness and expertise in interpreting not only canon law but also Church history—as fine a testimony as can be invoked regarding Varlet's competency as a controversialist. To it may be applied the judgment of Colbert de Croissy, Bishop of Montpellier, regarding the first *Apologie*, "c'est une excellente pièce . . . dont je fais une estime particulière et dont j'ai été consolé et édifié en même temps. . . ."[43] The continuing encomium is also il-

---

[41] Dupac de Bellegarde, op. cit., p. 340.
[42] See Pastor, op. cit., 34: 285-292. For a more or less contemporary defense of the Church of Utrecht, see Van Espen, *Vindiciae resolutionis Lovaniensium doctorum* (Lovanium, 1726), Villiers, *Lettre d'un prêtre français* (Utrecht, 1754), and Dupac, op. cit., p. 327 f.
[43] Quoted by the *Nouvelles ecclésiastiques*, 8. vii. 1742, p. 107-108.

luminating, despite the source, which saw in Varlet's work only grist to the mill of the Jansenist Appellants in their quarrel with the Bull *Unigenitus*, and offers some understanding of why and how Varlet came to be famous in his own time:

> Cent fois j'ai béni Dieu en la lisant de ce qu'il donnait à son Eglise en votre personne un évêque digne d'un siècle plus heureux que le nôtre. Quel traitement que celui que vous souffrez! . . . Continuez, Monseigneur, à nous donner de tels exemples de vertu. Nous en avons un extrême besoin dans le siècle malheureux où nous vivons. Dieu vous a destiné pour de grandes choses; et ce que vous avez fait jusques-à présent, montre que vous avez répondu parfaitement à votre vocation. A Lui seul la gloire en soit rendue.[44]

In 1727, shortly after publishing his second *Apologie*, Varlet left his lodgings in Amsterdam to take up residence with the Carthusians and Orvalists at their houses of Schonauwen and Rijnwijk, the one within the second ward of the city of Utrecht, the other a nearby village to the East.

As if to give more weight to Varlet's protestations, a number of priests had undertaken at this time to escape from France to avoid signing a formulary and accepting the Bull *Unigenitus*. If, in the early part of the eighteenth century there had been fewer than one hundred such exiles in the United Provinces, they nonetheless counted among them the illustrious names of Arnauld, Quesnel and Pierre Codde. (Their numbers were to grow over the years, however, until the French Revolution and the *Constitution civile du clergé* in 1791 changed matters sufficiently so that some of them felt they could in conscience return to their homeland.) Early in 1725, some twenty-six Carthusians had withdrawn to Schonauwen because they had been unwilling to compromise their principles and had preferred exile to obloquy. They were soon followed by fifteen Orvalists from the famous Cistercian abbey in modern Belgium. But such was the attitude of the authorities, that, lest they be prevented from giving free expression to their commitment and cast into prison for insubordination, these last arrived at the village of Rijnwijk disguised as a squad of soldiers, while their predecessors had travelled to the Netherlands separately and incognito, using assumed names and false passports. Thenceforth, their two houses served as a refuge for emigrant Appellants, with that of the Orvalists at Rijnwijk becoming a favourite resort of Varlet. Both groups had placed themselves under the protection of Archbishop Barchman, and in September of 1725 issued statements in their own defense which were ultimately attacked and condemned. Not, however, before they had been congratulated by such as Bishop Colbert of Montpellier, while they received from France, via unexpected and devious channels, financial subsidies, when it was not simply a question

---

[44] Ibid.

of pledges of approval and moral support. If their arrival only complicated the situation among the local clergy, such was the nature of the struggle within the Roman Catholic Church that these acts in defiance of both cross and crown aroused considerable sympathy among the people and served only to publicize the case of men like Varlet, underlining the exemplary nature of his behaviour in the face of great difficulties.[45]

In the midst of this activity, Varlet did not cease from what he still considered his duty as a Christian, attending morning and evening services, persisting in this habit for as long as his health permitted. He thus became for his hosts, and for those privileged to observe his condition and to enjoy his company, a model of piety, unchanging moderation, and gentleness. But his charity was to know further tests.

After 1727, Varlet was aroused to new efforts by what, to some minds, has become known as "le brigandage d'Embrun," because of the high-handed manner in which the Bishop of Senez in France, Jean Soanen, had been chastized by a Church council for contesting any and every slight to Gallican liberties, as much as for his refusal to acknowledge the Bull *Unigenitus* and sign the formulary.[46] From his exile at La Chaise-Dieu, the injured prelate soon came to play the role of martyr to his faith by means of an extraordinary correspondence. As an Appellant himself, and as one who wished to retain his freedom of movement and maintain the rights of individual conscience, Varlet sympathized with the unfortunate diocesan. On 20 November 1727, he wrote to Soanen the first of several letters in which he underlined his protest against the irregularities in the proceedings at Embrun. Approved and signed by Barchman, Archbishop of Utrecht, this manifestation of Varlet's solidarity soon attracted favourable notice and the esteem of a sizeable portion of the French clergy.[47]

Though Barchman's *Imprimatur* was but one of the many public acts by which he showed his closeness to Varlet, their collaboration was not to last much longer. He died in the arms of Varlet at Rijnwijk on the morning of 13 May 1733. The Bishop of Babylon, along with the Chapter at Utrecht, was once more faced with the necessity of finding a successor, one who would resemble Barchmann as much as possible and who would be able to solve many of the problems facing the Church in the United Provinces. In addition to regularizing the situation vis-à-vis Rome, these

---

[45] On the Carthusians, see van Kleef, *De Karthuizers in Holland* (Rotterdam, 1956); on the Orvalists, see N. Tillière, *Histoire de l'abbaye d'Orval* (Orval, 1967).

[46] The literature on Soanen is enormous. The edition of his works by abbé Gualtier (2 vol., Cologne, 1750) is as good a place as any to begin. For a definition of eighteenth-century Gallicanism, see van Kley, *The Jansenists and the Expulsion of the Jesuits from France*, p. 25: "Gallican est la même chose que ce que l'on appelle Janséniste."

[47] See the *Nouvelles ecclésiastiques*, 8. vii. 1742, p. 108.

included dealing with the abuse of usury, which seems to have been flagrant among the clergy of the United Provinces at that time, and the cause of some perturbation.[48]

On 15-16 November 1733, Da Cunha, Ambassador of Portugal to the States-General, met with Varlet at the castle of Zeist, not far from Utrecht. Fénelon, the French Ambassador, was also present, and together they tried to convince the Bishop of Babylon that conditions had changed in France to a point where Varlet might profitably act on former offers of amnesty, return to his native land, and end his isolation and penury with further services to both Church and country. Obviously, Varlet's powers of persuasion in his letters to Soanen had not gone unnoticed, and he was thenceforth as much to be feared as admired. It behooved the authorities to have him on their side in the long-drawn-out political strife that eighteenth-century Jansenism was fomenting in the kingdom of His Most Christian Majesty, Louis XV. As before, however, Varlet remained steadfast at the cost of his material well-being. His intractable attitude was probably hardened the more by this second appeal to his baser instincts, for on 28 October 1734, he consecrated a third Archbishop for the Church at Utrecht, Theodore van der Croon.

The same year, 1734, saw the publication at Utrecht of Varlet's letter to missionaries in Tonkin on the Bull *Unigenitus*, on the hierarchy, and on the duties of a missionary priest. The last topic is treated most eloquently, though despite its beauties it is not of prime importance in the development of Varlet's ideas. Rather, we should consider the way in which the author here elaborates an explicit and very telling attack on those who approved the Bull *Unigenitus* and the reasons they were wont to invoke as justification for their acceptance of it.[49]

This letter was followed early in 1736 by another, directed this time against the point of view and outright errors which had appeared earlier in attacks against the Appellants and their cause. Printed at the end of a second letter from Soanen on the same subject, Varlet admits to sharing completely the views of the Bishop of Senez and criticizes in particular Father Le Courrayer's translation and edition of Fra Paolo Sarpi's history of the Council of Trent.[50]

Full of gratitude for the "miracles" which, since 1727, were said to have occurred in the Parisian cemetery of Saint-Médard on the tomb of Archdeacon Pâris, not to mention other "miracles" elsewhere in France

---

[48] See, for example, the many treatises on the subject in the *Inventaire de Port-Royal*, nos. 3337, 3642, 3737, and 3935-4093. Also Taveneaux, *Jansénisme et politique*, p. 164-183.

[49] See the *Nouvelles ecclésiastiques*, 28. i. 1735, p. 15.

[50] See the *Nouvelles ecclésiastiques*, 24. i. 1737, p. 13-15. On Father Le Courrayer, see Préclin, *L'Union des églises*, and Lupton's study, *Archbishop Wake and the Prospect of Reunion*.

and the Netherlands,[51] Varlet was at this time continually invoking their efficacity in order to defend himself, his fellow-believers, and their cause from the attacks of that section of the clergy which favoured the Bull *Unigenitus*.[52] In March, 1736, appeared two letters from the Bishop of Senez, one of which was addressed to Varlet. Once more, the Bishop of Babylon rushed to reply and produced a commentary (almost twice as long as the original) in which he declared himself opposed to the incredulous obstinacy of those enemies of miracles who reeked of apostasy and refused to believe that beyond the case of Archdeacon Pâris—though through his intercession—God can and does intervene in the affairs of modern man. "Ce n'est pas seulement à Paris et par toute la France que le nom et les reliques de M. Pâris sont en honneur, et que l'on obtient de Dieu des miracles par son intercession,"[53] claimed Varlet in a tone that would never descend to the level of vulgar diatribe, as was the case with others who shared his point of view. Yet, so far as we are aware, Varlet never did lower himself to such a level of discourse, not even during the crisis provoked in 1735 by Jean-Charles de Ségur, Bishop of Saint-Papoul, in retracting his excessive, anti-Jansenist stance which is also treated in Varlet's last-named reply to Soanen.[54]

But the work in which he treats most fully of the problem of Jansenist miracles and the conversions to which they are said to have given rise, is a letter to Colbert de Croissy, Bishop of Montpellier, dated 12 May 1736.[55] The multiplicity of palpable errors contained both in a pastoral letter of Vintimille du Lac, Archbishop of Paris, dated 8 November 1735, and in a scandalous petition of the *procureur*, Nigon de Berty, early in 1736, are the focus of Varlet's attack. Both are magisterially criticized by the author who here shows himself a past master in his use of the forms of disputation and rhetoric and in his knowledge of canon law. While repeating and adapting previous declarations which claimed to see the hand of God in the acts of Jansenist convulsionaries while decrying the infraction of Church rules and custom, Varlet extends the field of his criticism and launches into a personal attack against those authorities who were trying to make him subscribe to the Bull *Unigenitus*.

---

[51] All seemed to validate the Appellants' case. These miracles would continue in Paris, despite police intervention and the famous couplet of some wag, until roughly 1734. The couplet runs: "De par le Roi, Defense à Dieu/De faire miracle en ce lieu." See Barbier's *Journal*, Luynes' *Mémoires*, Montesquieu's *Pensées* and *Voyages*, Saint-Simon's *Mémoires*, and in the *Inventaire de Port-Royal*, nos. 5732-5795.

[52] See van Kleef, *IKZ*, p. 206-214, and Janssonius Beuning's *Geschiedenis*, p. 331 f.

[53] See the *Nouvelles ecclésiastiques*, 8. vii. 1742, p. 108.

[54] See the *Nouvelles ecclésiastiques*, 26. v. 1736, p. 81-82.

[55] See the *Nouvelles ecclésiastiques*, 7. vii. 1736, p. 124.

Amid such all-consuming tasks as sponsor of the Church in the United Provinces and defender of its interests (which he had come to identify with his own), Varlet suffered from a stroke in the autumn of 1739. Nevertheless, he actively participated in an intense—if local—quarrel over the choice of a Co-adjutor for the Archbishop which was not unrelated to the earlier and continuing quarrel about usury.[56] This did not prevent him, once the by-now familiar procedural formalities had again been initiated and again been ignored, from consecrating on 8 October 1739 yet a fourth archbishop for the Church at Utrecht, Pieter-Jan Meindaerts, probably the greatest of those he had so helped to enthrone. A series of strokes continued to plague him throughout 1740, until on Christmas Day of that year he suffered from a particularly severe one, curiously, at about the same hour as his comrade-in-arms and faithful correspondent, the Bishop of Senez, departed this life.

After this attack, Varlet's health and mind seemed to be seriously impaired, and he entered into a long decline. Despite such trials as are usually reserved for patients in his condition, the Bishop of Babylon continued to manifest those same virtues as he had amply illustrated throughout his life. He died "en odeur de sainteté" on 14 May 1742 at Rijnwijk, and it was there that a requiem was celebrated by Archbishop Meindaerts, followed by interment in a vault of the cloister of Saint Mary's at Utrecht. On 22 May a Pontifical Requiem was celebrated in the Cathedral of Saint Gertrude at Utrecht, with the Archbishop presiding. At the same time, appeared two commemorative poems, one in Latin and one in Flemish. All these manifestations bore ample testimony in their time and in their way to the special role and importance of Dominique-Marie Varlet who, as Bishop of Babylon, had become indeed "the Restorer so precious and necessary" to the Church of the United Provinces.[57]

In the rectory of Saint Gertrude's at Utrecht (now the Old Catholic Museum), there is an eighteenth-century oil painting of Varlet, the only extant portrait, and the one copied by Folkema for his later engraving of our subject.[58] It shows the Bishop of Babylon in relief against a somber background, arrayed in the splendour of his episcopal robes, sitting at a table on which there stands a crucifix, holding in his hands a scroll with

---

[56] See van Kleef, *IKZ*, p. 218-219, and the *Inventaire de Port-Royal*, nos. 3634-3769, passim.

[57] See no. 62, infra. For the two anonymous poems, see *Ter Gedagtnisse van . . . Domenicus-Maria Varlet*, and *In obitum . . . Dominique-Marie Varlet, Babylonensis episcopi*. The phrase "Restorer . . . " is from Moss, op. cit., p. 125.

[58] Reproduced in B-A. van Kleef's *Geschiedenis*, p. 111.

the words "Apologie et Appel." Whatever the artistic worth of such a presentation, it is still the face which rivets our attention. As analysed by Maximin Deloche with considerable delicacy and insight, we too may note there:

> Une physionomie placide, sans relief, empreinte d'une satisfaction naïve où prédomine une bonté confiante, accusée par l'épaisseur des lèvres, l'écartement de ses yeux moutonniers, la carrure lourde des mains. Rien d'imaginatif, ni d'énergique qui devrait, semble-t-il, répondre à la vitalité remuante que font supposer *a priori* ses aventures. Plutôt impression de force d'inertie, chez un faible par bonté, soucieux de sa dignité, mais incapable de travestir la vérité de façon quelconque.[59]

The discreet psychology of such testimony is of untold value, helping to set the stage for any appreciation of the man and his works through its refined descriptive and critical stance. The same sort of impression is to be had from a cursory glance at the following correspondence which confirms the outward and visible signs of the painting, while the inward and spiritual qualities of Varlet's mentality are revealed as simple and modest, perhaps even timid, lacking in broad perspectives, despite his training and experience. For, as a devout and fervent, nay, passionate, apostle of the faith, the zealot in him yet seems dormant, without sense of personal initiative or imagination, unless it be in the interest of his own self-preservation, though even here strictly controlled and imperturbable.

A modern analyst might say that the origins of this ambivalence are to be found in his spiritual inheritance: from his father (and the theater) a flair for *le beau geste*, while from his mother (and the legal profession) a tendency to querulousness and contumacy. To the former he owed that attitude which, after 1723, made him choose to be known as a Jansenist at a time when such a gesture entailed great risk to body and soul, maintaining that stance despite changed conditions to the end of his life; while from the latter derived certain turns of his written style as a Christian apologist, meriting in his own time the appellation of "the new Chrysostomos"[60] because of his defense of religious principles in controversy surrounding his own—and others'—actions. In light of such factors, Varlet developed a distinct personality, unloveable but yearning to be loved. Yet this temperament marked him as an easy prey, one better led than leading, though, as it happened, a leader in spite of himself. All this—and more—may be readily understood by means of a brief commentary on the rehearsal of his life and activity in the preceding pages.

---

[59] M. Deloche, loc. cit., p. 41.

[60] The figure of "the new Chrysostomos" is from the *Nouvelles ecclésiastiques*, 8. vii. 1742, p. 105, though it probably originated with Bishop Colbert of Montpellier, one of Varlet's earliest and most fervent admirers.

Though we are in possession of studies treating Dominique-Marie Varlet from a sympathetic, Old Catholic, or even ecumenical point of view, none has yet attempted to see him in another, important context, that of Jansenism. In light of our presentation, it should be clear that in the eyes of many, Varlet *was* Jansenist. But is it possible to find in his life and writings the inspiration, the activity, the effectiveness of a Quesnel or an Arnauld, not to mention Pascal? Or is our notion of Jansenism in the eighteenth century in need of refinement? Consideration of Varlet's position in relation to this important matter should allow us to obtain a nicer appreciation of the man, as well as a better understanding of his historic role in eighteenth-century Roman Catholicism, when religion is generally supposed to have become less doctrinal and more political.

Judging by his birth-date alone (1678), Varlet can be seen to have spent his youth between the dispersion of the "solitaires" (1679) and the destruction of Port-Royal (1710), a time when avowed Jansenists were actively persecuted and even harried out of France. In 1680 Arnauld, for instance, sought refuge in Brussels where Quesnel followed him in 1685. Although Varlet later regretted signing in 1702 the formulary of Alexander VII against Jansenism, the fact remains that he did accept it at the time and that, as a result, there was no obstacle to his advancement to the doctorate in theology at the Sorbonne in 1706. The period of his early curacies in the Paris region is not too well-known, but on the basis of certain remarks in the present correspondence, it is quite likely that whatever difficulties he encountered (and which necessitated moving from one to another of several parishes between 1706 and 1711) were largely the result of a naïve and callous flaunting of his position in the face of his undoubtedly poorer charges[61] and his idealistic, if misplaced, zeal in exhorting them to a higher Christian endeavour when they were primarily concerned with keeping body and soul together.

At last, of course, he did come into contact with Cardinal Noailles who, as Archbishop of Paris, was his rector at Conflans. This weak and impolitic man was usually considered to be tainted with Jansenism, since he ever showed himself well-disposed toward the movement, resisting the Bull *Unigenitus* and ultimately becoming an Appellant in the great upsurge of opposition to ultramontane pretention in the years 1717-1720. In him, Varlet may have seen the mysterious workings of Divine Providence, an exemplar whose life and teaching could only reinforce the inspiration he had earlier received from his father. Toward the end of the seventeenth century, it will be recalled, this man had joined a small company of hermits seeking, like himself, to renounce the world and the flesh

---

[61] See, in the postcript to letter no. 1, his remarks about debts to a carriage-maker.

by retreating to Mont Valérien where they became a living reproach to the ecclesiastical authorities of their time. The unorthodox nature of their quest and gesture necessitated dispersing them on order from Vintimille du Lac, Archbishop of Paris, in 1729, but not before their challenge to Christian witness—not to say: holiness—had been duly noted by the rank and file among true believers in France, nor before the future Bishop of Babylon had been influenced by such an example.

The void created in Varlet's life by his father's pursuit of saintliness was no doubt easily filled by his early mentor, the abbé Daguesseau and his family. The abbé's eldest brother, the celebrated Chancellor, though in a high position of state, was noted for his integrity and devotion to the common weal as well as for his rare distinction of character and other-worldliness, denoting an intense spiritual life that was often to be re-marked among Jansenist worthies and was highly prized.[62] It may be that because of such connections, Varlet was later deemed guilty by association where Jansenism was concerned.

But his recourse in 1711 to the kind offices of a relative, Jean-Henri Tremblay, and to the Missions étrangères, both known for their anti-Jansenist stance,[63] should belie such an imputation, while Varlet's train-ing at the seminary in the rue du Bac should have stifled any nascent Jansenist proclivities in him. The over-riding impression we have of Varlet before he set out for North America is one of single-minded devo-tion to spreading the gospel of Christ through missionary activity. Thus it happened that in September, 1713, when he was absent in the wilderness, the Bull *Unigenitus*, condemning Quesnel for his interpreta-tion of Arnauld's Jansenism, was promulgated in Rome and published in France. Distance and timing prevented him from accepting (or rejecting) it and, so, from admitting (or denying) his doctrinal approval of any or all Jansenist vagaries prevailing at that time. Nor would Varlet ever make a statement in this connection. Although in his various works he cannot help but deal with such important matters as grace and salvation which concerned him personally, nowhere, to our knowledge, does Varlet treat formally of those sticking points of contemporary theology: faith, works, predestination, etc.

When we come to the errors which Varlet is known to have committed after his consecration as Bishop of Babylon, the fault cannot be imputed uniquely to him. What about the responsibility of those who had con-secrated him "incognito"?

---

[62] See Taveneaux, *La Vie quotidienne*, p. 104. Villemain, in his *Tableau* (Paris, 1868), 1: 212, even went so far as to declare that the Chancellor was indeed a Jansenist.

[63] See Malcolm Hay, *Failure in the Far East*, and Launay's *Histoire de la Société des Missions étrangères*, I: 446 f.

(The reasons for this enforced incognito are not clear, even at this late date. While it is true that the Popes could, as with the creation of Cardinals named *in petto*, proceed, for reasons known only to themselves—and to the Propaganda?—to name bishops and archbishops "incognito" except where impossible because of the political terms of one Concordat or another, and while it is also true that Ascalon and Babylon were still considered *in partibus infidelium* until *after* Varlet's consecration, his case presented no such difficulties. Since 1632, under the tolerant rule of the Safivids, his predecessors had been named without becoming involved in international scandal or creating difficulties of any sort. The problem of the intemperate haste enjoined on Varlet at the time of his nomination, consecration, and departure for the Middle East is likewise unclear and hard to explain.)[64]

What also of the directives from the Propaganda that he should occupy his See with the greatest expediency, not to mention the delay in forwarding to Paris the Brief exhorting him to swear allegiance to the Bull *Unigenitus* in the presence of the Nuncio? Insofar as it is possible to determine at this time, the least one can say is that the suspension was published in great haste, without sufficient examination of the facts.[65] Varlet's case was lost in advance, having been judged out of hand by those in Rome who, to achieve their ends by any means, were eager to see their own candidate named to the prestigious See of Babylon and were attempting to discredit the name and career of this unknown and naïve prelate, without special interests in Rome ready to defend him. In this perspective, the slights, real or pretended, to the Nuncios in both Paris and Brussels take on a different cast, even if there may be no legitimate defense of his subsequent activity in Amsterdam on the outward voyage.

On the other hand, for one so zealous in his enthusiasm, so devoted to missions, who had scarce returned from his first exhilarating experience with conversion and the salvation of souls in the North American forests, and who had not even seen fit to bid goodbye to family and friends in his eagerness to comply with the will of his superiors, who knows but what, faced with the sadly diminished state of the Church in the United Provinces and with the doubtless cogent and insistent arguments of church-

---

[64] Van Kleef (*IKZ*, p. 95-97) attempts to explain the incognito by reason of the Papacy's desire to have Varlet confirm catechumens and consecrate priests in countries on the way to Hamadan that were in the hands of the Turks, but his argument does not bear close scrutiny.

[65] The reason for this condemnation was not, however, as F. Péret would later claim (VII: 148) that Varlet had not subscribed to the Bull *Unigenitus* before his departure for Canada; the Bull was not published until 8 September 1713, when Varlet was already in the New World.

men there, Varlet was not simply acting in response to his emotions in an unthinking, sentimental manner? Or is it that already, by 1720, the word "Jansenist" had changed meaning, not so much in the minds of those who professed to follow the teachings of the *Augustinus*, as in the minds of those (the Curia, the national synods, the Jesuits) who wished for complete regimentation—and hence, domination—of religious orthodoxy, substituting, and giving precedence to, political considerations over all others? Certain it is, in any event, that such are the arguments Varlet would later invoke in his two *Apologies* to defend himself. At the same time, there is no overt and proven act of his which might be labelled schismatic until after his return to Amsterdam at the beginning of 1721, though many a critic, both eighteenth-century and modern, has claimed otherwise. His errors were errors of judgment, technical in nature, and had nothing to do with belief. With his return to the Dutch capital, the problem turns not on doctrine but on discipline.

Yet, once Varlet realized his precarious situation within the hierarchy, that stubbornness of character and recalcitrance noted earlier, in conjunction with his training, sufficed to push him even further into opposition to both Church and State and to develop a legalistic, if not outright political, bias for his defense. According to the outline suggested by Préclin and Tapié,[66] it is easy to see how Varlet adapted certain characteristics of eighteenth-century Jansenism to his own use, however much doing so meant exposing himself to a great ill for a lesser. Some of these were as second nature to him, once the thorny problem of refusing the Bull *Unigenitus* were put into the background before it, too, became a political issue in 1730.

Like so many of his contemporaries, to whom the climate of the Regency offered a propitious occasion for manifesting their dissatisfaction with the established Church in France, Varlet sought first of all his own justification, through freedom of expression, a means which until his time had not properly been within the purview of the priesthood. In the situation then developing, a number of his brethren believed that it was only necessary for a synod to denounce the iniquities of the Bull *Unigenitus* and to appeal to a future General Council of the Church in order to set matters right. This spontaneous opposition to the Bull helped weld a new alliance between clergy and Parlement, creating yet another variant of Gallicanism, stronger than Bossuet's (because it went against the established power of both Church and State), and adapted, after the end of Louis XIV's reign, to different circumstances.[67] To this move-

---

[66] *Le XVIII° siècle*, p. 392-394.

[67] For a succinct and cogent explanation of this term in the eighteenth century, see van Kley, op. cit., p. 22, n. 63, and note 46 supra. See also J. Boulenger, *The Seventeenth Cen-*

ment Varlet contributed no little support, both wittingly and unwitting-
ly. His attitude can be recognized most clearly in his defense of Monsignor Soanen, Bishop of Senez, who was suspended in 1727 for his
reiterated—and frequently telling—appeals to a future Council and who
became, in the eyes of many, a martyr through official condemnation and
exile to La Chaise-Dieu. Varlet composed and published several epistles
to this saintly prelate which demonstrated his approval of the Bishop's
stance while confirming his own opposition to the Bull *Unigenitus*.

   Basking in the approval of Monsignor Caylus, the respected and
powerful Bishop of Auxerre, Varlet was not content merely to affirm the
postulates of the new Gallicanism. He went further and proclaimed his
adherence to the tenets of the canonist Nicolas Travers who had earlier
advanced the idea that since priests are ordained to serve the whole
world, their power to administer the sacraments cannot be limited to a
certain specified area, whether parish or diocese. This egalitarian sentiment, if allowed by the Church, would have enabled the Bishop of
Babylon to receive the revenues from his diocese and would have
validated his confirmation of the faithful and his consecration of four
archbishops in the United Provinces, quite outside his jurisdiction. It
would also have absolved all those who had made their confession to him
from any sin for having done so to a priest, like him, under Papal inter-
dict.[68] A further consequence, known as "richerism," would likewise
have appealed to Varlet. In fact his penury alone would have prompted
his support for, fiscally, if the priesthood were to become a sort of ecclesiastical workingmen's union as Edmond Richer had claimed as early
as 1612, then Varlet would have been allowed to receive the revenues
from his See in Asia and, so, repair the state of his dilapidated finances.[69]

   Subsequently, however, his role as an Appellant was most clearly
defined by his attitude toward the miraculous cures that were said to have
been effected on the tomb of Archdeacon Pâris in the cemetery of Saint-
Médard from 1727 to about 1734.[70] This popular expression of faith soon
gave rise to all sorts of excess of religious fervour on the part of a group
known to history as the Convulsionaries. If Pâris himself had been a
Jansenist, we do not know for certain that his followers were, although

---

tury (New York, 1920), p. 284: "Many French prelates resented the Bull *Unigenitus* as
papal interference with the Gallican church, and Jansenism merged with a revival of the
Gallican movement."

   [68] The abuse of this last situation in France would lead to the notorious history of the
"billets de confession" between 1749 and 1757, but as this controversy developed only
after Varlet's death, it need not detain us here. See van Kley, op. cit., p. 229-231.

   [69] On Varlet's finances, see van Kleef, *IKZ*, p. 150-151.

   [70] For the latter date (1734) which does not necessarily conform to that commonly
assigned to the end of this incident, see Barbier's *Journal* for 1734.

they and their works were taxed with Jansenism. Into this fray Varlet came hard on the heels of his idol, Monsignor Soanen. Yet he was not enthusiastic about the Convulsionaries; indeed he could not countenance their folly, since unbelief, which was spreading more and more, used them as a weapon against the true miracles of the Gospel and against Christian miracles in general. Varlet did not go so far as would Hume in his *Enquiry* to condemn, nor the *Nouvelles ecclésiastiques* of 24 December 1731, to equate, these scenes of unedifying display with the works of Christ himself.[71] Instead, in at least two of his published epistles, he protested to Monsignor Soanen that the Convulsionaries were stripping Jansenism of its prestige. Nonetheless, as a true believer and as a reasonable man, Varlet was careful to distinguish between the miracles of Holy Writ and modern elucubrations which might pass for a similar manifestation of divine intervention in human affairs, but which could not qualify as miracles on the basis of either theology or dogma. Yet despite his determined mediation between one extreme and the other, Varlet has often been grouped with those apologists of the Convulsionaries who would subscribe to such utterances as the following: "C'est aujourd'hui écouter la voix de l'Eglise, ou, ce qui est la même chose, la voix de l'Evangile et de la tradition apostolique, que d'écouter la voix des miracles de M. de Pâris que d'écouter la voix de la Doctrine et de la Loi dans laquelle il est mort."[72]

Incidental to this attitude was another which Varlet is said to have shared with self-proclaimed Jansenists of his own time—though on what grounds we do not know—figurism.[73] This method of scriptural interpretation was not new, and it was not unfamiliar to Jansenists of the first generation, like Pascal;[74] but it was given new life by Fathers Duguet, Legros, and Etemare (the latter Varlet's "légataire universel"), clerics whose importance for the intellectual life of the disloyal opposition in the eighteenth century is considerable, though unstudied. And since, according to this source, Pâris himself was said to have been a figurist, what better way of announcing to one and all that the incidents and personages of the Bible are indeed but prefigurations of future events and characters in the history both of the Church and the world? Already, in 1731, this teaching had begun to take root among the Convulsionaries. Then figurists reckoned that the war between the Saints and the Beast of the

---

[71] Hume, *Enquiry into the Human Understanding* (1747), sect. 10, and the *Nouvelles ecclésiastiques*, 24. xii. 1731, p. 104.

[72] Préclin-Tapié, op. cit., p. 392.

[73] See especially Pastor, op. cit., 35: 451, and, more recently, van Kleef, *IKZ*, p. 196-198.

[74] See the *Provinciales*, no. xi, and the *Pensées* (Brunschvicg ed.), nos. 570-692, passim.

Apocalypse had begun with the Royal Edict of 24 March 1730, giving the Bull *Unigenitus* force of law in France. Curiously, this aberration was not peculiar to dreamers from among the common people. LaRoche, editor of the *Nouvelles ecclésiastiques*, and Bishop Colbert of Montpellier, along with Soanen himself, subscribed to this strange identification. And though there is no published proof of Varlet's approval or practice of figurism that the present editor has seen, he once more appears to have been included in this group—and condemned—by reason of his acquaintance with these eminent recruits to the figurist camp.

But the culmination of the reproaches against the Bishop of Babylon is perhaps best seen in those conversations he had in Schemacha with Isaiah, an Orthodox Bishop, in which his heterodoxy first found coherent expression.[75] Later, that same naïve zeal as had once fired his missionary enthusiasm would force him to give concrete form to this burgeoning sense of ecumenicism when he undertook to consecrate the first of a series of archbishops for the Church in the United Provinces. Whatever the formal arrangement of the ceremonies may have been, we must remember that the first was not canonical, in that it did not take place in a church or other consecrated spot. Even though succeeding acts may have seemed fitting, proper, and sufficient to the participants, who knows what this first lack of compliance betokened for the others? In addition, since 1724, a notorious innovator, Jacques Jubé de la Cour,[76] formerly of Asnières in the Paris suburbs, and envoy of Archbishop Barchman-Wuytiers to the court of Saint Petersburg to prospect the possibility of a union between the Churches of the two countries, had been resident in Amsterdam, where Varlet came into his ken. Through close association Varlet could appreciate his ideas on liturgical reform such as: saying the Mass in French, with the secrets repeated aloud; celebrating the Mass without crucifix or candles; administering the Eucharist under two forms, etc., all of which sound familiar enough to those who observe the working of Vatican II today. Yet this sort of activity could only reinforce the independent tendencies of one like the Bishop of Babylon, who, as time went on, became more and more closely identified with a body already in schism from Rome. And such was the nature, the size, and the importance of Varlet's role in the United Provinces that he is rightly considered the Moses, sometimes even the Saviour, of the Old Catholic Communion (Roomsche Katholieken der oude Klerizij). Thus, through such proclivities as have just been hastily reviewed above: gallicanism, appellantism, egalitarianism, developing richerism, convulsionism, figurism, ecumenicism, and liturgical reform, Varlet was indeed in opposition to

[75] See the *Inventaire de Port-Royal*, no. 3753.
[76] See the *Inventaire de Port-Royal*, nos. 4141-4152.

the established Church of his time. He knew it and, after 1723, applied much of his energy and all his training and intelligence to defending these positions with vigour and no small effect. Yet despite the fact that each of these movements had one or more Jansenist participants, never did Varlet admit—nor his opponents convincingly prove—that he was a Jansenist himself. What then is the reason for such an oversimplified classification of this man?

From the multiplicity of arguments that might be invoked (ultramontane bias, anti-schismatic criticism, jealousy, refusal to admit misjudgment, etc.) there remains but one which would have some weight and validity today as in the eighteenth century: preferment.[77] Preferment, that is, in the sense that the end of the pontificate of Clement XI (Francesco Albani, 1700-1721), a weak Pope, saw considerable disaffection among members of the Curia, and, even before his death, much jockeying for position. In this struggle for power, the pro-French (or international) faction, seemingly in the ascendant since about 1705, was ultimately thwarted by those who would seek to reinforce an Italian (or specifically ultramontane) point of view without coming into the open and declaring their intentions publicly. The result was that though Varlet was nominated, approved, and even consecrated as a protégé of the French party, there was another candidate waiting in the wings for just such an oversight as his failure to visit the Nuncios in Paris and Brussels (both, we would point out, Italians themselves), one who in occupying the See of Babylon could also expect the approval and co-operation of his neighbour, the Dominican Bishop of Isphahan (also an Italian). For, as the Italian faction had earlier succeeded in usurping the Portuguese right of nomination to the latter diocese, so they were attempting to abrogate a similar right in the former held by the French since 1638.[78] Ancillary considerations such as this are essential, however unedifying they may seem in underlining the politics of religion, if we wish to come to grips with the problems of the Papacy in the eighteenth century and ultimately with those of any established institution at the crucial moment when the decadence that will at last destroy it sets in. For, once Varlet was in the United Provinces, the Curia did not hesitate to charge an Italian with responsibility for the See of Babylon, despite arrangements with the French which would have perpetuated their right to nominate bishops there. Although the See was not provided with a bishop (at last, a French national) until after Varlet's death in 1742, why did the Curia delay?

---

[77] For a complete appraisal of this statement from an orthodox point of view, see J. Vidal in *Revue d'Histoire des Missions*, x (1933), p. 364-366.

[78] See van Kleef, *IKZ*, p. 95-97, and A. Huonder, *A Chronicle of the Carmelites in Persia*, 2 vol. (London, 1939), vol. I, p. 549-552.

After 1724, Varlet had been anathematized and condemned and was no more deemed worthy to perform episcopal functions, while in his physical and spiritual isolation from Rome he no longer presented a threat to the hierarchy, which nonetheless on at least one occasion attempted to liquidate some of Varlet's problems (and their own) through a financial settlement.[79] In this apparently internecine struggle it is easy to see how the Bishop of Babylon was but the pawn of forces greater than he could envision in his enthusiasm and willingness to spread the Gospel of Him who is Love and, so, found another preferred, even as he undertook to carry out the Biblical charge of "Go ye into all the world. . . . ''[80]

Another reason for the oversimplified view of Varlet which has prevailed until now is undoubtedly to be found in the nature of his associations. As mentioned before, abbé Daguesseau, Cardinal Noailles, Bishop Isaiah in Caucasian Albania, Bishops Colbert and Soanen in France—to name only a few—were perhaps not the surest guarantors of Varlet's orthodoxy, despite his traditional, if not reactionary, stance in attempting to determine what was just and unjust, for example, in matters of missionary activity, liturgical reform, usury, or miracles. On the other hand, it would be difficult indeed to ignore the fact that Varlet's own father, however genuine his inspiration, was a member of a small group of enthusiasts who had to be disbanded for their strange, if single-minded, devotion to the perfection of the individual self, guided only by an inward light. We might therefore be justified in conjecturing about Varlet's destiny, predetermined, as Péguy would later claim for us all, "avant que nous ayons vingt ans.''[81] In this perspective, Varlet was bound to spend his life on the periphery of whatever endeavour he undertook. He was a part—yet for all his success or importance, still only a part—of that greater Service to which he was called. He was the victim of circumstances beyond his control, the prisoner of his own naïveté and reasonable attitude, orthodox, but unimaginative and unrealistic. In the words of Maximin Deloche's nice psychological portrait:

> Toute sa correspondence confirme pareille mentalité. Varlet s'y révèle sous le même aspect d'un simple et modeste, quelque peu timide, sans vues générales, malgré sa culture, apôtre convaincu, fervent et passionné, d'une conscience scrupuleuse, dépourvu de tout esprit d'initiative, et même peu curieux, fait surtout pour être guidé, ce qui donne la clef de sa conduite dans la seconde partie de sa vie.[82]

---

[79] See J. Vidal in *Revue d'Histoire des Missions*, x (1933).
[80] See *Mark* 16:15, *Matthew* 28:19, etc.
[81] "L'Argent," in *Œuvres complètes*, II (Pléiade), p. 1099.
[82] Deloche, op. cit., p. 42.

Precisely because of this dubiousness, the final reason for History's view of Varlet results from his own personality. His training had been excellent, as even a brief perusal of his writings, both published and manuscript, demonstrates. Yet his scholastic excellence (in dealing with things) seems to have been accompanied by a fatal lack of perception (in dealing with people) that refused to admit to error. In turn, his querulousness was reinforced by an argumentative nature that could only bode ill for so delicate an enthusiast. Such a precarious balance between sensitivity and selfishness derives perhaps from that same need to be loved which, when frustrated, first sent Varlet off to the Indians in the heartland of America, filled with the zeal of a born proselytizer. And this same disproportion in his makeup is what accounts, in the pages which follow, for the tone that varies from one of benign concern to one of subdued petulance. The range and variety of expression is never very great, but in the limits afforded by this correspondence we can gain a nicer, more balanced view of the man, his *persona* and its importance—more at any rate, than had previously been admitted—and at the same time be witness to the politicization of Jansenism in the eighteenth century and the development of such a sensibility as is frequently connected only with a later generation.[83] To quote Deloche again:

> Le caractère intime de ces lettres n'est pas seulement précisé par les liens étroits des destinataires. . . . La forme s'y ajoute: le style est lâche, sans artifice, ni prétention. Sous ce rapport, elles contrastent même singulièrement avec celles que l'auteur écrira [officiellement], lorsque le frottement de la vie sociale l'aura affiné. . . . Ce qui a intéressé Varlet et ce qu'il fait connaître, c'est la vie matérielle proprement dite; à ce point de vue, ses relations, non destinées à la publicité, se juxtaposent heureusement [avec celles d'autres de ses contemporains] dont elles comblent plus d'une lacune. . . . On voit ainsi à la fois et l'intérêt de ces documents et la confiance qu'on peut leur faire.[84]

Quite apart from historical considerations, therefore, these letters are valuable and moving, simply as human documents. The themes of family, finances, and the future, which form the burden of Varlet's contribution to this exchange, recur with almost predictable regularity, so that the content, by and large, is not remarkable. But the life—and the story suggested behind the façade—is.

The early letters are full of the fire of the dedicated zealot, unfortunately couched in the platitudes of the seminary. There seems to be none in which he does not ask his correspondents to pray for him while reassuring them that they are daily in his prayers. Nor is there any from which he omits bits and pieces of practical advice and edifying exhortations. Varlet

---

[83] See especially letter no. 47, infra.
[84] Deloche, op. cit., p. 42.

seems to be dominated by one feeling: he loves his family. He says so repeatedly, stressing how important their letters are to him, how he wishes they would write more, how long it is since he has had news from home, how they can make sure their letters reach him safely and swiftly, and more of the same monotonous effusions, lightly coloured by his own brand of piety. Thus, whenever he takes up his quill, he frequently repeats himself. Yet the proselyte ends his life in poverty, dying in a borrowed shirt while his library brings the incredible sum—for the time—of nearly three thousand florins. There is something admirable about an individual who cannot afford to clothe himself but who will buy a book. The most moving letter of all, one where his humanity breaks through his rather reserved, austere, and scholarly nature, is the one in which he recounts the attempts to get him to return to France.[85] He refuses, because this would mean a compromise (and he had gone too far down the road to complete independence), so that despite age, condition and financial situation, he will not treat with those who have hurt, nay, worse, maligned him. His religion seems to grow deeper and more personal (though never lyrical), while his family appears as a group of greedy cheats, always engaged in lawsuits (mostly to deprive him of his inheritance), and the younger generation is a failure, his niece unhappily married, his nephew virtually feeble-minded, and both a disappointment. All this is accompanied by the misery of those near and dear to him while he contemplates his own death, an exile in a foreign land, with none of his kinsmen by his side as the end approaches. Such details make this a tragic story, but it is to some degree the story of Everyman, begun in enthusiasm and idealism, and ending in loneliness and disaffection.

Although most of this interpretation does not actually appear in the letters, it is to be perceived behind them, informing our appreciation to such a degree that it might conceivably inspire the reader with a sense of life truly in keeping with the Pascalian background to which Varlet has so often been linked. Yet we cannot help reflecting that such an attitude does not take into sufficient account the changes wrought by time in Jansenism.[86] Sainte-Beuve notwithstanding, that movement in the eighteenth century is still largely uncharted, though useful correctives are beginning to appear in the work of such scholars as Emile Appolis, Bruno Neveu, René Taveneaux, and Dale van Kley. We are, nonetheless, in need of more detailed studies, not only of the different phases of the movement, but also of the various personalities like Dominique-Marie Varlet, associated with it. In such a perspective—and such a hope—the

---

[85] See letter no. 47, infra.
[86] See van Kley, op. cit., p. 10-41, passim.

present edition has been prepared as a tool that might ultimately lead to the knowledge and understanding which the study of this important topic demands.

For various reasons, it has been deemed best to present the following correspondence in a diplomatic edition. Spelling, grammar, and punctuation have been strictly reproduced, according to the originals, now in the possession of the Bancroft Library of the University of California at Berkeley. In the text of each letter, superscriptions, numbered consecutively, refer to the end of each letter where they will provide corrections, full expansion of abbreviations, modernized spelling according to a consistent (if not universally recognized) form, and a minimum of textual commentary. Substantive notes are as brief as is consistent with clarity and the needs of the modern reader, being added only in hopes of elucidating the text.

The titles in English at the head of each number have been added by the present editor. In certain letters an attempt has been made to reproduce sigla relating to ecclesiastical custom (i.e., the sign of the cross at the beginning of no. 65) or to financial symbols (i.e., £ for "livres" in no. 69). Dates and salutations are transcribed and placed exactly as they appear in the originals, but complimentary closings have been simplified and systematized in their alignment, to be read as a single, separate paragraph. Such arrangements have been necessary in order to reduce the innumerable *sic* of such editions as this to a manageable proportion, reserving the Latin adverb for truly exceptional cases.

Among the various signs employed, two parallel strokes (//) indicate the end of a page; S/ means that the name following is a holograph signature, while names in brackets ([]) at the end of certain letters indicate an unsigned autograph, and N.S. means "No Signature." Brackets are also used in the body of some letters in poor condition to indicate holes, tears, or undecipherable words. The initials DMV refer throughout to Dominique-Marie Varlet, Bishop of Babylon (1678-1742).

Finally, thanks must be expressed to the Bancroft Library of the University of California at Berkeley and especially to its Director, Dr. James Hart, who first undertook to procure this collection and who has authorized this publication of material under his control.

For various details gleaned from their respective competencies, I am also indebted to my colleagues Professors Wallace Chafe, Arnolfo Ferruolo, John Polt, and W. E. Rex, III, all of the University of California at Berkeley, and to Professor Frank Bowman of the University of Pennsylvania. For particular favours at a crucial point in my research, thanks are due to my former teacher, Professor Jean Darbelnet of Laval University, Quebec, and to W. Aderman Carney, Esq., of San Francisco. I have incurred no inconsiderable debt to the kindness of MM. André Gazier, Bruno Neveu and R. P. Jean Guennou in Paris, to S. E. Monsignor Lourdusamy in Rome, and especially to Dr. K. van der Horst at Utrecht. After several fitful starts, Linda Conley and Lori McCracken, by their intelligence and assiduity, assured the excellent presentation of this work. The editor hopes that whatever its shortcomings, they will not detract from the usefulness, nor discourage the proper utilization, of this correspondence as a tool for further study—and a better appreciation—of Dominique-Marie Varlet, along with Jansenism and the Church of Utrecht in the eighteenth century.

CALENDAR OF THE CORRESPONDENCE

The following list includes, in chronological order, all the items acquired by the Bancroft Library of the University of California at Berkeley in 1974. Each item is numbered consecutively and presents:

1) the name of the writer, in brackets if unsigned;
2) the date, or approximation of the same;
3) the place where written (when known);
4) the addressee;
5) the address, in as exact a transcription as possible, with a slash-mark indicating the end of a line;
6) the overall dimensions—in centimetres—of the *paper* on which the text is written;
7) in parentheses, the dimensions—in centimetres—of the *page* on which the text is written;
8) the number of pages to the letter.

An asterisk indicates documents which are not properly correspondence. In such cases, numbers 4 and 5 above are replaced with a brief indication of the nature of the contents.

1. DMV 18.xii.1712. "au Semin. des miss. Etr." [Paris]. A Mademoiselle/ Mademoiselle Varlet/ A Conflans (his mother). 22.5 × 17.5 (11.25 × 17.5), 2 p. Published by Deloche; see Bibliography, part E.
2. DMV. 27.xii.1712. Angers. A Mademoiselle/ Mademoiselle Varlet au coin de/ la rue de Nevers au bout du pont/ Neuf/ A Paris (his mother). 22.5 × 18 (12.75 × 18), 1 p.
3. [DMV.] 31.xii.1712. Nantes. No address; to his mother. 27.5 × 18 (14.25 × 18), 2 p.
4. DMV. 2.i.1713. Nantes. A Monsieur/ Monsieur Olivier/ A Paris (his brother-in-law). 22.5 × 17 (11.25 × 17), 2 p.
5. DMV. 9.i.1713. Port-Louis. A Mademoiselle/ Mademoiselle Varlet au coin/ de la rue de Nevers au bout du pont Neuf/ A Paris (his mother). 22.5 × 17 (11.25 × 17), 2 p.
6. DMV. 16.i.1713. Port-Louis. A Monsieur/ Monsieur Varlet chez Mr./ Olivier Procureur au Chastelet/ rue de la Truanderie/ pres St. Eustache/ à Paris (his brother). 22.5 × 17.5 (11.25 × 17.5), 2 p. Published by Deloche; see Bibliography, part E.
7. DMV. 25.i.1713. Port-Louis. No address; to his mother. 23 × 17.5 (11.5 × 17.5), 3 p.

8. DMV. 7.ii.1713. La Rochelle. A Mademoiselle/ Mademoiselle Varlet au coin/ de la rue de Nevers au bout/ du pont neuf/ A Paris (his mother). 20 × 16 (10 × 16), 2 p.

9. DMV. 20.ii.1713. La Rochelle. A Mademoiselle/ Mademoiselle Varlet/ en sa maison au coin de la rue/ de Nevers au bout du pont neuf/ A Paris (his mother). 22.5 × 16.5 (11.25 × 16.5), 2 p.

10. DMV. 28.ii.1713. La Rochelle. A Mademoiselle/ Mademoiselle Varlet/ A Paris (his mother). 22.5 × 17.5 (11.25 × 17.5), 1 p.

11. DMV. 28.ii.1713. La Rochelle. A Monsieur/ et Mademoiselle Olivier/ rue de la truanderie/ A Paris (his brother-in-law and sister). 22.5 × 17.5 (11.25 × 17.5), 1 p.

12. DMV. 13.iii.1713. Brest. A Mademoiselle/ Mademoiselle Varlet/ au bout du pont neuf au Coin de la rue de Nevers/ A Paris (his mother). 22 × 16.5 (11 × 16.5), 1 p.

13. DMV. 19.iii.1719. Compiègne. A Mademoiselle/ Mademoiselle Varlet/ au Coin de la rue de Nevers au/ bout du pont neuf/ a Paris (his mother). 23.5 × 17.5 (11.75 × 17.5), 1 p.

14. DMV. 25.iv.1719. Amsterdam. A Monsieur/ Monsieur Varlet procureur/ au parlement au bout du pont neuf/ au coin de la rue de Nevers/ a Paris (his brother). 35 × 23.5 (17.5 × 23.5), 1 p.

15. DMV. 17.vi.1719. Pétersbourg. A Mademoiselle/ Mademoiselle Varlet au coin de la/ rue de Nevers au bout du pont neuf/ a Paris (his mother). 23 × 17.5 (11.75 × 17.5), 1 p.

16. DMV. 23.iii.1720. Chamaké (Schemacha). A Mademoiselle/ Mademoiselle Varlet au coin/ de la rue de Nevers au bout du pont/ Neuf a/ a Paris (his mother). 34 × 23 (17 × 23), 1 p.

17. DMV. 29.v. 1721. [Holland.] A Monsieur/ Monsieur Olivier procureur/ au Chastelet rue de la truanderie/ a Paris (his brother-in-law). 36.5 × 23 (18.5 × 23), 2 p.

18. Tremblay. 12.vi.1721. [Paris.] à Monsieur/ Monsieur Olivier procureur/ au chatelet rüe Truanderie/ a Paris. 22 × 17 (11 × 17), 1 p.

19. Tremblay. 14.vi.1721. [Paris.] à Monsieur/ Monsieur Olivier procureur/ au chatelet rüe Truanderie/ a Paris. 22 × 17 (11 × 17), 2 p.

20. DMV. 26.vi.1721. [Holland.] No address; to his brother-in-law and sister. 23.5 × 18.25 (11.75 × 18.25), 2 p.

*21. Tremblay. 21.vii.1721. [Paris.] Attestation in re: Jean-Achille Varlet. 35.5 × 23.5 (17.75 × 23.5), 3 p.

22. DMV. 15.ix.1721. [Holland.] A Monsieur/ Monsieur Olivier procureur/ au Chastelet rue de la Truanderie/ a Paris (his brother-in-law). 26.5 × 19 (13.25 × 19), 2 p.

23. Chastellain. [20.]x.1721. Paris. Monsieur/ Monsieur Olivier/ Laisné procureur au Chastelet/ rüe de la grande Truanderie/ a Paris. 27 × 18 (14.5 × 18), 2 p.

24. DMV. [1721.] [Holland.] a Monsieur/ Monsieur Olivier procureur/ au Chastelet rue de la truanderie/ a Paris (his brother-in-law). 22.5 × 16.5 (11.25 × 16.5), 2 p.

25. DMV. 18.i.1722. [Holland.] a Monsieur/ Monsieur Olivier procureur/ au Chastelet rue de la truanderie/ a Paris (his brother-in-law). 26.3 × 18.75 (13.75 × 18.75), 2 p.

26. DMV. 11.iii.1722. [Holland.] a Monsieur/ Monsieur Olivier procureur/ au Chastelet rue de la truanderie/ a Paris (his brother-in-law). 22.5 × 16.75 (11.75 × 16.75), 2 p.

27. DMV. 13.viii.1722. [Holland] A Mademoiselle/ Mademoiselle Olivier/ rue de la truanderie/ A Paris (his sister). 33.5 × 22 (16.75 × 22), 2 p.

28. [DMV.] 13.xi.1722. [Holland.] A Monsieur/ Monsieur et Mademoiselle/ Olivier rue de la truanderie/ A Paris (written to his sister only). 23 × 17.75 (11.5 × 17.75), 2 p.

29. [DMV.] 24.i.1724. [Holland.] A Monsieur/ Monsieur Olivier/ Procureur au Chastelet rue/ de la truanderie/ A Paris (his brother-in-law). 35.73 × 22.75 (18.25 × 22.75), 2 p.

30. [DMV.] 5.xi.1724. [Holland.] A Mademoiselle/ Mademoiselle Olivier/ a Paris (his sister). 23.5 × 18 (11.75 × 18), 2 p.

31. [DMV.] 19.i.1725. [Holland.] No address; to his brother-in-law and sister. 23.5 × 17.75 (11.75 × 17.75), 3 p.

32. [DMV.] 12.iv.1725. [Holland.] a Monsieur/ [tear]sieur Olivier [tear]/ au Chastelet rue/ [tear]nderie proche les [tear]/ A Paris (his brother-in-law). 35.5 × 23.5 (17.75 × 23.5), 2 p.

33. [DMV.] 17.xii.1725. [Holland.] Pour/ Mademoiselle Olivier (his sister). 22.5 × 18.25 (11.25 × 18.25), 3 p.

34. [DMV.] 3.i.1727. [Holland.] No address; to his brother-in-law and sister. 23 × 18.25 (11.5 × 18.25), 2 p.

35. [DMV.] 17.ii.1727. [Holland.] Pour ma Sœur/ Olivier. 23 × 18.25 (11.5 × 18.25), 2 p.

36. [DMV.] 6.ii.1728. [Holland.] No address; to his brother-in-law. 23 × 18.75 (11.5 × 18.75), 3 p.

37. [DMV.] 6.ii.1728. [Holland.] A ma sœur Olivier. 23 × 18.75 (11.25 × 18.75), 3 p.

38. [DMV.] 11.iii.1729. [Holland.] a Mademoiselle/ Mademoiselle Olivier/ a Paris (his sister). 23.5 × 19 (11.5 × 19), 3 p.

39. [DMV.] 11.iii.1729. [Holland.] No address; to his brother-in-law. 23.5 × 18.75 (11.75 × 18.75), 3 p.

40. [DMV.] 19.ix.1729. [Holland.] a Monsieur/ Monsieur Olivier pro-
cureur/ au chastelet rue de la truanderie/ pres les halles/ a Paris (his
brother-in-law). 37.25 × 23.5 (19 × 23.5), 1 p.

41. [DMV.] 3.iii.1730. [Holland.] A Mademoiselle/ Mademoiselle
Olivier (his sister). 23.5 × 19 (11.5 × 19), 2 p.

42. [DMV.] 3.iii.1730. [Holland.] No address; to his brother-in-law.
23.5 × 19 (11.75 × 19), 2 p.

43. [DMV.] 2.ii.1731. [Holland.] No address; to his brother-in-law.
23.5 × 18.5 (11.5 × 18.5), 2 p.

44. [DMV.] 24.xi.1731. [Holland.] a Monsieur/ Monsieur Olivier/ a
Paris (his brother-in-law). 24.5 × 20 (12.25 × 20), 2 p.

45. [DMV.] 4.ii.1732. [Holland.] No address; to his brother-in-law.
24.5 × 20 (12.5 × 20), 2 p.

46. [DMV.] 29.i.1733. [Holland.] No address; to his brother-in-law.
24.5 × 20 (12.5 × 20), 2 p.

47. [DMV.] 21.xii.1733. [Holland.] No address; to his sister. 18.75 ×
23 (full sheet), 2 p. Published by Deloche, but dated "31.xii.1733";
see Bibliography, part E.

48. [DMV.] 7.iii.1734. [Holland.] No address; to his brother-in-law.
23.25 × 18.5 (11.5 × 18.5), 2 p.

*49. Qualenbrinck. 11.iii.1734. [Utrecht.] Will of DMV, plus deposi-
tion, dated 1.viii.1742. 37.5 × 22.75 (18.75 × 22.75), 3 p.

50. [DMV.] 29.i.1736. [Holland.] No address; to his brother-in-law.
23.75 × 19.5 (11.75 × 19.5), 3 p.

51. Roquette. 6.ii.1736. Rouen. No address; to Antoine Olivier. 33.5
× 22 (11.75 × 22), 1 p.

52. [DMV.] 9.ii.1737. [Holland.] a Monsieur/ Monsieur Olivier/ Procureur au/ Chastelet rue de la/ Truanderie/ a Paris (his brother-in-
law). 23 × 18.75 (11.5 × 18.75), 2 p.

53. [DMV.] 16.ii.1737. [Holland.] a Mademoiselle/ Mademoiselle
Olivier (his sister). 22.75 × 18.75 (11.5 × 18.75), 2 p.

54. DMV. 22.ii.1737. [Holland.] a Monsieur/ Monsieur Olivier/ Procureur au Chastelet/ a Paris (his brother-in-law). 23 × 18.5 (12.75
× 18.5), 1 p.

55. [DMV.] 16.vi.1737. [Holland.] No address; to his sister. 37.5 ×
22.75 (18.75 × 22.75), 3 p. (page 2 torn).

56. [DMV.] 20.vi.1737. [Holland.] a Mademoiselle/ Mademoiselle
Olivier/ chez Me Olivier Procureur/ au Chastelet rue de la
Truanderie/ Paroisse S. Eustache/ a Paris (his sister). 22.75 ×
18.75 (11.5 × 18.75), 2 p.

57. [DMV.] 10.iv.1738. [Holland.] a Monsieur/ Monsieur Olivier/
procureur a Chastelet/ rue de Truanderie/ pres les Halles/ a Paris
(his brother-in-law). 37 × 23 (18.5 × 23), 2 p.

58. Roquette. 14.v.1738. [Paris?] à Monsieur/ Monsieur Olivier Lainé Procureur/ au Chatelet rue de la Grande/ Truanderie/ A Paris. 33.5 × 21.75 (16.75 × 21.75), 1 p.

59. Roquette. 6.viii.1738. [Paris?] à Monsieur/ Monsieur Olivier Procureur au/ Chatelet/ A Paris. 27 × 19.27 (13.75 × 19.27), 1 p.

60. [DMV.] 11.vi.1739. [Holland.] No address; to his brother-in-law. 38.25 × 22.75 (19.25 × 22.75), 2 p.

61. [DMV.] 30.xii.1739. [Holland.] a Monsieur/ Monsieur Olivier procureur/ a Chastelet rue de la Truanderie/ quartier s. Eustache proche des/ halles/ a Paris (his brother-in-law). 23 × 18.5 (11.5 × 18.5), 2 p.

62. Villiers. 17.v.1742. Utrecht. No address; to Antoine Olivier. 30.5 × 19 (15.25 × 19), 3 p.

*63. Anonymous. N.p.n.d. Two fragments. 17 × 21.5, 2 p.; 11.5 × 18.25, 1 p.

64. La Noix. 30.v.1742. Rhynwyck. à Monsieur/ Monsieur Olivier l'ainé/ Procureur au Chatelet, rüe de la grande/ Truanderie, prez St. Eustache/ à Paris. 31.75 × 20 (15.9 × 20), 2 p.

65. Villiers. 31.v.1742. Utrecht. No address; to Antoine Olivier. 22.9 × 18.5 (11.5 × 18.5), 4 p.

*66. Lohof. 4.vi.1742. Utrecht. Burial certificate of DMV. 37.5 × 22.75 (18.5 × 22.75), 2 p.

67. Villiers. 4.vi.1742. Utrecht. No address; to Antoine Olivier. 23 × 18.75 (11.5 × 18.75), 4 p., plus 1 p. 11.5 × 18.75.

68. Villiers. 2.viii.1742. Utrecht. No address; to Antoine Olivier. 36.25 × 22.75 (18.25 × 22.75), 3 p.

*69. Thiery. [19.x.1742.] Paris. Extract in re: DMV. 26.5 × 18.5, 1 p.

70. Villiers. 18.xi.1742. Utrecht. No address; to Antoine Olivier. 37.5 × 23.75 (18.75 × 23.75), 3 p., plus 1 p., 18.75 × 23.25.

*71. Anonymous. N.p.n.d. Notarial opinion in re: DMV. 17.5 × 23, 2 p.

72. Villiers. 28.iii.1743. Utrecht. A Monsieur/ Monsieur Olivier l'ainé/ Procureur au chatelet/ rüe de la grande Truanderie/ proche St. Eustache/ a Paris. 37 × 23 (18.5 × 23), 3 p.

73. Villiers. 14.vii.1743. Utrecht. A Monsieur/ Monsieur olivier L'ainé/ Procureur au chatelet/ rüe de la grande Trüanderie/ pres de Saint eustache/ a Paris. 37 × 23 (18.5 × 23), 2 p.

74. La Cour. 22.xi.1743. N.p. A Monsieur/ Monsieur Olivier L'Ainé Procureur au/ Chatelet Rue de la grande Truanderie/ Paris. 24 × 18.5 (12 × 18.5), 2 p.

75. Villiers. 6.ix.1745. Utrecht. A Monsieur/ Monsieur olivier L'ainé/ Procureur au chatelet, rüe de la/ grande Trüanderie prez St. Eustache/ a Paris. 37.75 × 23.25 (19 × 23.25), 3 p.

DOMESTIC CORRESPONDENCE OF DMV

1. DMV to his Mother

Ma très chère et très honorée mère[1]

La precipitation avec laquelle je suis obligé de partir des demain ne me laisse pas le tems d'aller encor une fois vous dire aDieu; peutetre que la providence veut en cela epargner ma faiblesse qui auroit de la peine a soutenir cette separation: rien ne m'encourage davantage a entreprendre l'œuvre sainte a laquelle Dieu daigne m'appliquer que l'exemple de votre vertu et de votre soumission a ses adorables volontez, rien ne merite une plus grande reconnoissance que l'honeur et la grace qu'il veut bien faire a un aussi mauvais ouvrier que moi de me donner de l'ouvrage dans la vigne.[2] Je vous prie instament de joindre vos prières avec les miennes afin de le remercier de la faveur singuliere qu'Il me fait, et lui demander pour moi la fidelité à correspondre a ses graces, en sorte qu'en travaillant au salut des ames du prochain, je ne neglige point la miene. Je vous demande une seconde grace c'est de conserver votre santé avec tout le soin possible; je vous prie de me donner la consolation de m'en mander souvent la disposition pour me tirer de la seule inquietude que j'emporte avec moi et que je conserverai en quelque lieu que je sois. Tant que je respirerai je ne cesserai point d'offrir mes foibles prieres pour la conservation d'une santé si chère et pour obtenir de Dieu qu'il vous comble// de ses graces.

Je suis/Ma très chere et tres honorée Mère/Votre tres humble et tres/obeissant serviteur et fils

S/Varlet

au Semin. des miss. Etr.[3]
ce 18 Dec. 1712

Je salue tres humblement ma chere tante.

Il est encor du a Echarcon[4] a Mr. Canet[5] 18. Livres pour les voitures qu'il m'a faites. Je crois devoir encor au meme lieu 7 ou 8 francs a un nommé Iret (?). Je vous prie de leur faire venir cet argent sur mon compte a votre commodité. Je vous prie assui a votre commodité de donner à mon beau frere environ 20 Ecus pour payer Mr. Cenard procureur a l'officialité qu'il a occupé pour moi dans l'affaire d'Echarcon.

[1] For family relations of DMV, see the Genealogical Table. Note 18th century usage in matters of formal address, reflecting rather curiously the state of relations between parents and children. Varlet was 34 at the start of this correspondence and his mother possibly near 60 years old.

[2] As would be normal with such a personage, the Bible and its lessons are never far from the thoughts of DMV in this correspondence. The present allusion is to Matt. 20-21. See also Mark 12, Luke 20.

[3] Religious society established in 1658, rue du Bac, Paris, where it is still located. Cf. Launay, *Histoire de la société des missions étrangères*, 3 vol. Paris, 1894.

[4] Village near Essonnes some 8 kilometers SW of Corbeil-Essonnes (S-O).

[5] The names of all persons and pertinent information may be found in the index at the end of this correspondence.

2. DMV to his Mother

Ma tres chere mere,

Je suis arrivé hier ici en tres bonne santé grace au Seigneur et a vos saintes prieres, a eté si heureux que j'ai tout lieu d'esperer que la suite sera de meme. La protection de Dieu est si visible sur mon voyage, quelle me marque bien que je suis en cela la sainte Volonté. Lui etant aussi parfaittement soumise que vous l'etes, je ne doutes pas que vous ne soyez tres tranquile et que vous ne rendiez a la souveraine bonté de fideles actions de graces de ce qu'il daigne m'appeler a un si sainte ministere. Je me confie beaucoup sur le secours de vos prieres, je vous prie de bien menager votre santé pour laquelle je ne cesse d'offrir a Dieu mes foibles prieres et suis avec le plus profond respect

Ma tres chere mere/Votre tres humble et/tres obeissant serviteur et fils

S/Varlet

a Angers le 27 dec. 1712

Je salue mes tantes mes freres et sœurs et cousins, je n'ai pas le temps de leur ecrire, je le ferois dès que je serois au port Loüis.[1] J'oubliois de vous marquer qu'en passant a Blois ou je dinai vendredi je vis mon cousin Lanoi [Lannoy] qui m'apprit la mort de Mademoiselle Bourillon enterrée le dimanche precedent.

[1] Port at entrance to the harbour of Lorient in Lower Brittany, developed in 17th century for the Atlantic trade.

3. DMV to his Mother

Ma tres chere et honorée mere

Je vous souhaite pendant la nouvelle année ou nous entrons demain toute sorte de prosperitez spirituelles et temporelles, que nostre sauveur repande sur vous de jour en jour de nouvelles graces, et vous donne de nouvelles consolations, que vous unissant a Luy deplus en plus, et vous conformant en tout a sa sainte volonté, vous acqueriez de nouveaux mérites, je vous prie de demander a dieu pour moy touttes les graces qui me sont necessaires pour me rendre digne de son ministere, auquel il m'a appellé; je suis arrivé icy hier en bonne santé, graces au seigneur, je compte de me remettre aprèz la feste[1] en chemin, pour aller au port Louis, qui n'est pas fort eloigné d'icy. Vous ne scauriez me faire plus de plaisir que de conserver soigneusement vostre santé, et de m'en mander souvent des nouvelles jusqu'au temps de l'embarquement. mon adresse sera chez Mr de Surville au port Louis. J'ay trouvé un papier qui regarde Leglise Décharcon qui n'est pas d'une grande utilité, mais je n'en ay que faire, ainsi je vous prie de le faire venir a Mr Le curé Decharcon par la première occasion. J'écris a Mr Duval au mont valerien,[2] je vous prie de la lui faire venir; j'aurois bien voulu//aller dire adieu a tous ces messieurs, mais vous scaviez que je n'en ay pas eu le temps. resalue ma chere tante et toutte la famille, j'écris a mes freres, ma sœur et ma tante La grange. Je suis avec le plus profond respect

Ma tres chere et tres honorée mere/Vostre tres humble et obéissant serviteur/et fils.

N.S.

A Nantes ce 31 xbre. 1712

[1] Feast of the circumcision celebrated 1 January.
[2] Eminence to the W of Paris to which DMV refers below (''ces messieurs''). Formerly there was established here a religious community (to which DMV's father retired and where he died in 1709). Site today of an important military and radio installation.

4. DMV to his Sister and Brother-in-law Olivier

mon tres cher frere et ma trez Chere Sœur (car il ne faut pas separer ce que la grace unit si etroitement)[1]

Les plus grands eloignemens n'affoibliront jamais l'attachement qui me lie a vous, la grace aussi bien que la nature en a serré les nœuds puisque si vous m'avez toujour donné des marques du meilleur naturel du monde, j'ai aussi bien des fois reconnu combien votre pieté est pure et sincere. Si quelque chose avoit eté capable de me faire rester dans ma patrie çauroit ete la satisfaction d'etre pres de parens que tout contribue a me rendre si chers. Mais le service de Dieu doit l'emporter sur tout, et nulle consideration en doit nous empecher de nous soumetre a sa sainte volonté qui ne m'éloigne a present de la veüe de mes proches que pour me la rendre un jour d'une manière plus solide et plus durable. C'est donc avec les sentimens de l'amitié la plus tendre que je vous souhaite au commencement de cette nouvelle année que Dieu repande de plus en plus sur vous et sur votre famille ses graces et ses benedictions, et que la fidelité que vous aurez a y correspondre vous en attire encor de plus grandes. Je vous prie de ne point m'oublier dans vos prieres et d'en faire souvenir vos enfans que je porte tous dans mon cœur. Je ne saurois assez vous recommander ce que j'ai de plus cher au monde c'est ma mere, je sai bien qu'elle ne vous est pas moins chere; ainsi je suis assuré que votre premiere attention sera//toujours d'etre sa consolation, son conseil et son support. Je l'ai priée de vous donner sa commodité sur le revenu de mon titre de quoi payer le procureur de l'officialité. Vous ne sauriez me faire plus de plaisir que de me mander la plus souvent qu'il sera possible l'Etat de votre santé, et de m'apprendre que Marie anne fait de grands progrès dans la Science du Salut et dans la vertu car il n'y a que cela de souhaitable. J'en dis autant de Manon, que Dieu acheve de delier sa langue pour chanter ses louanges. Je n'oublie pas mes petits neveux et je souhaite de tout mon cœur qu'ils croissent de jour en jour en grace aussi bien qu'en age. Je crois partir d'ici demain pour aller au port Louis. Recommandez a Dieu le succès de mon voyage. Je salue Mr et Me Olivier pere et mere et leur famille me recommande a leurs prieres et suis

Mon tres cher frere et ma tres chere sœur/Votre tres humble et tres obéissant serviteur/et frere

S/Varlet

A Nantes ce 2 Janv. 1713

[1] Souvenir of phraseology of the marriage ceremony, invoked probably because of the recent marriage of Marie-Anne Varlet with Antoine Olivier.

5. DMV to his Mother

Ma très chère et très honorée mère

J'ai eu l'honeur de vous ecrire de Nantes et a toutte la famille pour vous souhaiter une heureuse année. Je suis arivé ici le jour de l'Epiphanie[1] en tres bonne santé, elle n'a jamais eté meilleure, je m'y etois bien attendu, le meilleur de tous les medecins en prend soin ces jours et vos saintes prieres m'attirent les benedictions. Je vous prie de me les continuer. Rendez moi la justice de croire que vous etes le premier et le continuel object des miennes. La veille de mon depart je donnai a mon Cousin Lanoy [Lannoy] un petit paquet de livres pour rendre a Mr Bouché [Boucher] apparement qu'il la oublié car Mr Bouché [Boucher] a été au seminaire[2] redemander ces livres. Prenez bien soin de votre santé et me croyez

Ma tres chere et tres honorée mere,/Votre tres humble et très obéissant serviteur et fils.

S/Varlet

Je salue tres humblement ma chere tante
au port Louis ce 9 Janv. 1713

[1] Religious feast of January 6.
[2] Seminary of the Missions étrangères, rue du Bac, in Paris.

6. DMV to his Brother, Jean-Achille

J'ai reçu, Mon tres Cher frere, les deux dernieres lettres que vous m'avez ecrites. On ne peut pas etre plus sensible que je le suis aux temoignages d'amitié que vous m'y donnez. Je suis tres edifié des pieux desseins que vous me marquez avoir conceu, je vous exhorte autant que je la puis a les soutenir et a profiter de la grace qui les a fait naitre, et a racheter le tems que vous regrettez de peur que ces moments de grace ne reviennent plus s'ils etoient negligez. Mon eloignement ne doit pas etre un obstacle a leur execution, Paris est plein de secours pour aller a Dieu et pour faire de grands progres dans la vertu. Si les mondains y trouvent une grande porte pour se perdre, les gens de bien y peuvent avoir touttes sortes de facilitez pour entrer dans la voye du Ciel. Prenez ce parti la, Mon cher frere, si votre lettre est sincere. Les sentimens que vous avez vous accuseront au jugement de Dieu si vous ne les suivez pas et si vous ny perseverez pas. Car que sert a l'homme de gagner tout le monde s'il part son ame.[1] A l'egard du voyage de Mississipi,[2] je ne vous le conseillerai pas et ne vous en dissuaderai pas non plus. Je ne vous le conseille pas parce que je sai que ces sortes de voiages sont aussi dangereux a ceux qui cherchent l'argent qu'ils sont salutaires a ceux qui cherchent des ames. Je ne vous en dissuade pas de peur que vous ne m'accusiez d'etre indifferent a l'egard de votre Etablissement que je souhaite etre tres avantageuse et tres chretien. Pour les Ecclaircissemens que vous demandez je vous dirai que Mr Le gouverneur est plein d'esperance de la reussite de cette entreprise ici il a receu depuis peu des//nouvelles de ces païs la par un homme qui en vient, tout y est disposé parfaitement pour le trafic de Mr Crozat, mais pour y faire quelque chose, trois precautions sont necessaires. 1) il faut y etre envoyé par Mr Crozat et en etre bien apuyé 2) estre d'une conduite admirable tant accause des occasions qu'on y trouve de se perdre qu'accause des espagnols qui meprisent fort les etourdis; 3) savoir entendre et parler espagnol. voila de la matiere a vos reflexions. Croyez qu'il n'y a personne au monde qui vous aime aussi sincerement que moi qui suis

Mon tres cher frere/Votre tres humble et tres obeissant/tres obeissant serviteur

S/Varlet

au port Louis ce 16 Jan. 1713

Faites je vous prie mes excuses a ma mere ma tante et ma cousine de ce que je ne leur ecris pas car comme jachevois cette lettre le recteur du port Louis m'est venu voir et m'a occupé toutte l'apres dinée et l'heure de la poste presse ce sera pour le 1ᵉʳ ordinaire. Faites mes complimens a mon beaufrere et a ma sœur.

---

[1] Allusion to the story of Nicodemus, Matt. XIX. "part" for "perd"

[2] From France, DMV would go to Santo Domingo, Havana and Mobile, Alabama (Fort Louis) before ascending the Mississipi valley to "the country of the Tamaroas", site of his mission-post. Since the city of New Orleans was not founded until 1718, the center of proselytizing activity in the South was at Mobile, Alabama, founded in 1710 (see A. Launay, *Histoire de la société des missions étrangères* I:446). Louisiana was separated from Canada at 40⁰ latitude in 1717.

7. DMV to his Mother

Ma tres chere et tres honorée Mere[1]

J'ai receu la lettre que vous m'avez fait la grace de m'écrire en datte du 7ᵉ Janvier. Je suis tres sensible a la bonté que vous m'y temoignez et tres édifié de la resignation ou vous etes a la volonté de Dieu. Nous ne sommes au monde que pour travailler a la faire, et vous savez que nous ne pouvons pas etre plus honorez que d'etre employez au service des ames que J.C.[2] a racheté de son sang, je vous prie de vouloir bien lui demander qu'il me rende fidele a la vocation a laquelle il daigné m'appeller par la misericorde. Sa protection paroist si visiblement par la maniere dont il m'a rendu la santé qu'il y a tout a esperer pour la suite, puisque etant parti de Paris tout languissant je suis arivé ici plus vigoureux que je ne me suis veu depuis longtems. J'avois emporté un petit pot de quinquina de Conflans[3] mais je n'en ai pas eu besoin et ne m'en suis pas servi quand le grand medecin s'en mesle les remedes et les precautions ne sont pas necessaire. Ainsi vous avez tout lieu d'etre tranquile. //Je vous prie de travailler le plus soigneusement que vous pouvez a conserver votre santé, et de prier Dieu pour moi et pour le succez de notre mission sans aucune inquietude. Nous n'attendons que le vent pour sortir du port; j'ai eu bien de la joye d'apprendre que vous aviez eté saluer Mr Le Cardinal.[4] Je suis bien sensible a ses bontez et bien touché de lamitié que tous ces Messrs de Larcheveche me temoignent. Je vous prie de me recommander aux prieres de tous nos amis. Je suis bien aise que Mr abdalnour vous ait eté voir. c'est un bon pretre. je me recommande a ses prieres. Je crois que vous aurez eu la bonté de rendre a Mr Pascal les 4 volumes de St. Jerome[5] que j'ai laissé a Conflans a cette intention, afin qu'il les puisse rendre au Libraire a qui il m'a temoigné qu'ils n'avoient pas eté payé. Je lui devois environ pour dix frans d'autres livres et le St Jerome. J'avois acheté vingt francs. Dittes lui je vous prie que Je me recommande bien a ses prieres et a celles de Mlle Pascal. Je n'ai guere manqué les ordinaire[6] qui se sont presentez pour vous ecrire. Je ne sai si vous aurez receu touttes mes lettres. Je manderai a Mrs des missions etrangeres ce que vous me marquez quoique cela ne soit pas necessaire car ce sont des messieurs tous pleins de charité d'honestete et de desinteressement et vous pouvez conter qu'en tout ce qu'ils pourront vous rendre service ils le feront tout de grand cœur. J'ai deja eu l'honeur de vous marquer que vous etiez le premier objet de mes prieres. Je vous prie d'etre persuadé que je m'aquitte de ce devoir avec toutte l'ardeur dont je suis capable et que je suis avec le plus profond respect

Ma chere mere/Votre tres humble et très obéissant/serviteur et fils

S/Varlet

Je salue tres humblement ma tante Prevost mes freres et ma sœur ma tante la Grange et ma cousine Lanoi [Lannoy] et Treteau et me recommande a leurs prieres. Je vous ai ecrit que j'avois veu a Blois mon cousin Lanoi [Lannoy] et qu'il m'avoit apris la mort de Mlle Bourillon.//

Mon frere ma mandé que mon cousin Lanois [Lannoy] le[7] marioit sans me marquer aucune circonstance. Je prie Dieu que ce soit pour son avantage.

Je viens de recevoir votre letre du 16e Janv. elle m'afflige en m'apprenant que vous ne reposez pas. Que votre foi mette fin a vos inquiétudes, et quand vous etes tentée de vous inquieter Lizez et meditez Le ps. 90e *qui habitat*[8] a complies et vous y trouverez Le remede a tous vos troubles. Ceux qui vous ont dit l'accident du guide et des bourses devoient vous dire que cet accident ne me regardoit pas, j'en ai ete spectateur mais je n'en ai pas souffert. Mes hardes ont eté un peu mouillées ce n'est pas un grand malheur. Les bourses de cuir ne contenoit que des pastilles pour des malades, elles ont eté perdues, on a pesché les bourses mais on ne me les a pas encor fait venir, Je ne m'en inquiette pas elles ne contiennent plus rien qui me soit fort necessaire. Je suis bien aise que Mr Bouché

[Boucher] ait receu les livres. Je le prie bien de m'excuser si je ne les lui ai pas reportez et je me recommande a ses saintes prieres aussi bien qu'a tous les Mrs de la paroisse.[9] L'embaras du depart pour lequel il faut preparer ici milles choses est cause que je n'ecris pas a la moitié des persones aqui je souhaiterois ecrire. ayez la Charité d'y suppléer.

au Port Louis ce
25e Janv. 1713

[1] Above the salutation, another hand has added: Port Louis, 25 Janvier 1713.

[2] "Jésus-Christ".

[3] Community to E of Paris, now a part of the metropolis, where DMV had his first parish in 1708 and where, until 1713, his mother resided. For further details about family addresses, cf. van Kleef, *IKZ* 53 p. 84.

[4] According to this reference, the Cardinal de Noailles was indeed DMV's patron.

[5] The first mention in this correspondence of DMV's books to which he was greatly attached and by which he set such great store. Cf. Deloche p. 44 and van Kleef *IKZ* 53, p. 98 n.2.

[6] Should be plural.

[7] "le" for "se".

[8] "ps" for "psaume" Beginning of Ps 90 in the Vulgate, but of Ps 91 in more recent editions.

[9] Perhaps the parish of St. André des Arts to which DMV's mother had recently returned to live, but more likely, given what DMV has mentioned in the body of this letter, his first cure at Conflans.

8. DMV to his Mother

Ma tres chere mere

Je vous ecris ces mots a la hate pour ne point manquer l'heure de la poste pour vous dire qu'étant parti du port Louis le dernier Janvier nous avons eté obligez par les vents contraires de relacher ici. Je crois que la providence l'a permis affin que j'eusse moien de vous marquer que ma santé se soutient mieux sur la mer qu'en France et que j'ai eprouvé que le plus efficace de tous les remedes est de faire la volonté de Dieu et de chercher premièrement le roiaume de Dieu et la justice. Priez le seigneur qu'il me continu[1] ses graces. Nous serons ici environ 8 ou 10 jours apres quoi nous continuerons notre voiage. Je salue mes freres ma sœur mes tantes ma cousine Meunier mes autres cousins et Cousine[2] et tous no//amis et suis avec tout le respect possible

Ma tres chere mere/Votre tres humble et très obéissant serviteur/et fils

S/Varlet

a La rochelle
le 7e fevr. 1713

[1] "continue"

[2] Should be plural.

9. DMV to his Mother

Ma tres chere et honorée Mère

Je profite de l'occasion qui s'est presentée de venir a terre et qui est rare pour vous ecrire et vous marquer que Dieu me fait la grace d'etre en parfaite santé. J'espere que les vens qui jusqua present ont eté contraires deviendront favorables par le secours de vos prieres et que le reste de notre navigation sera heureux. Je vous prie d'avoir un grand soin de votre santé et de n'entrer dans aucune inquietude a mon sujet; on est bien quand on est entre les mains de Dieu et qu'on se livre a lui sans reserve. Vous avez assez de foi pour n'avoir pas besoin qu'on vous represente ces motifs de confiance. Je salue mes freres et ma sœur ma tante et ma cousine, ma tante Prevost mes cousins et cousines Mr et Me Pascal Mlle Delaunai [de Launay] Mr et Me Martin tous nos amis me recommande a leurs prieres. Si je reste quelque tems a terre je pourrai ecrire a quelqu'un mais comme//je pourrai peutetre retourner ce soir au vaisseau je commence par le plus pressé en vous ecrivant. Je suis avec le plus profond respect

Ma tres chere et honorée mère/Votre très humble et très obéissant serviteur/

S/Varlet

a La Rochelle ce 20e fevr. 1713

10. DMV to his Mother

Ma tres chere et tres honorée Mere

La divine providence me retient jusqua present ici par les vens qui sont toujours contraires et je profite de ce sejour pour vous demander le secours de vos prieres afin que Dieu repande la benediction et sur mon voiage et sur touttes les entreprises ou son service m'engage. Ma santé est toujours graces a Dieu tres bonne. Je vous prie d'avoir bien soin de la votre surtout pendant le tems du Careme ou nous entrons demain. N'entreprenez rien audessus de vos forces. Le jeune et l'abstinence, lorsqu'un temperament aussi foible que le votre ne permet pas de l'observer exactement, peut etre remplacé par d'autres exercises de pieté au jugement d'un directeur capable. Je vous prie de me recommander en particulier pendant cette sainte quarantaine aux prieres de nos parens et

amis, des Ecclesiastiques de la paroisse et surtout de mes freres de ma sœur de mes tantes et de ma cousine Meunier de Nicole.
Je suis

Ma tres cher mer[1]/Votre tres humble et tres obeissant serviteur

S/Varlet

a la Rochelle ce 28e fevr. 1713

[1] "mer" for "mère"

11. DMV to his Sister and Brother-in-law Olivier

Mon tres Cher frere et Ma tres chere sœur

Le peu de tems que j'ai ici pour descendre a terre dans la situation ou nous sommes d'etre toujours prets a partir pendant que nous restons toujours ici depuis 3 semaines que les vents contraires nous y retienent est la cause de ce que je n'ai pas encor pu vous ecrire. Mais ma mere vous aura communiqué apparement les letres que je lui ai ecrites depuis que le mauvais tems nous a obligé de relascher a La Rochele. Dieu me fait la grace d'etre dans une fort bonne santé. Je souhaite que la votre soit toujours parfaite. Redoublez pour moi vos prieres dans ce saint tems de Carême ou nous entrons demain, afin que le Seigneur m'accorde une navigation heureuse et qu'il me donne les lumières et les forces necessaires pour reussir dans les entreprises ou son service m'engage.[1] Je salue mon frere, le peu de tems que j'ai m'empeche de lui ecrire en particulier. Ce sera pour un autre ordinaire si je reste en ce païs ce que je ne souhaite pas.
Je suis tres sincerement

Mon tres cher frere et ma tres chere sœur/Votre tres humble et tres obeissant serviteur

S/Varlet

a la Rochelle ce 28e fevr. 1713

[1] A discreet allusion to Ps 27.

12. DMV to his Mother

Ma tres chere et tres honorée mere

Je vous ai ecrit 3 fois de la Rochelle ou nous avions relasché en premier lieu. Nous y avons eté un mois et nous en partimes le 8e du mois. Le mauvais tems nous a encor obligé de relascher ici. Dieu ma fait la grace de me porter parfaitement bien jusqua present, mais j'ai appris que vous aviez eté indisposée, on m'a marqué en meme tems que votre indisposition n'avoit pas eu de suite, je crains bien que le Careme ne vous echaufe. J'ai deja eu l'honeur de vous prier par une letre de vous menager et de ne point entreprendre audessus de vos forces. Je reïtere cette priere, votre temperament foible veut etre menagé, Je vous demande cette grace avec toutte l'instance possible. Je salue mes freres ma sœur, mes tantes, cousins et cousines et suis avec tout le respect imaginable,

Ma tres chere mere/Votre tres humble et tres obeissant serviteur

S/Varlet

à brest ce 19ᵉ mars 1713

13. DMV to his Mother

a Compiègne ce 19ᵉ mars 1719

Ma tres chere mere

La precipitation avec laquelle il ma fallu partir hier pour profiter d'une bonne occasion qui doit me conduire jusqua mon Eveche[1] m'a empeché d'avoir l'honeur et la consolation de vous aller dire adieu dans les formes. Mais je sais que vous avez trop de zèle pour la gloire de Dieu pour trouver a redire que je quitte tout pour me metre en etat d'executer sans aucun delai les ordres de Dieu. Le commencement de notre voiage est jusqua present fort heureux. J'espere que les suites seront de meme. Surtout etant soutenu de secours de vos prieres j'espere que Dieu nous préservera de tout danger, benira nos travaux et nous metra en etat de travailler utilement a ammener a la foi tant de peuples qui segarent. Si vous voulez me faire ecrire pendant le voyage faittes le incessament et adressez vos lettres au seminaire,[2] d'ou on me les fera venir. Je salue mon frere et ma sœur et suis avec un profond respect

Ma tres Chere mere/Votre tres humble et tres obeissant serviteur

S/Varlet
Ev. de bab.[3]

---

[1] DMV was named Bishop of Ascalon and Co-Adjutor of Babylon by Clement XI 17 September 1718 just after his return from America. Since his consecration in 1719 had to be "incognito" he was anxious to leave for Persia to occupy the See of Babylon, as he had been urged to do by the Curia, which explains in part the haste and secrecy with which he left Paris, as described in this letter.

[2] The Seminary of the Missions étrangères, rue du Bac, in Paris.

[3] "Evêque de Babylone", the first time DMV so signs himself in this correspondence.

14. DMV to his Brother, Jean-Achille

a Amsterdam ce 25ᵉ avril 1719

Depuis mon depart de Paris Mon tres cher frere, je n'ai veue que deux de vos lettres. Je ne sai pas si vous m'avez encor ecrit d'autres letres. Je rends graces a Dieu de l'heureux acouchement de ma sœur.[1] Je prie N.S.[2] de faire par la grace que cette petitte enfant conserve toujours l'Inocence quelle a receue dans le St. bapteme. Je n'ecris pas cette fois a ma chere mere puisque vous n'avez pas encor juge a propos de lui donner ma letre et de lui apprendre mon depart. Je vous prie d'en prendre tous les soins possibles. A l'Egard de la fille qu'on vous propose pour epouse c'est bien jeune pour vous que dix huit ans.[3] Mais ce que vous devez encor plus considerer et rechercher particulierement dans celle que vous choisirez c'est une grande pieté, une grande modestie un grand eloignement de lesprit du monde et des compagnies du monde. cela vaut mieux que les plus grands biens et sans cela une femme en depense bientost plus qu'elle n'en a apporte. Ainsi si c'etoit celle dont vous m'aviez parlé qui etoit elevée dans la vanité je vous conseillerois de ni[4] point penser. Nous sommes prests a nous embarquer apres avoir attendu ici plus de 3 semaines. Le vent est tres favorable. Je ne crois pas que je puisse recevoir de vos nouvelles sur la route car je crois que nous serons plus tost a Petresbourg que vos letres n'y seroient. Vous avez l'addresse de Mr Le Chevalier[5] vous n'aurez qu'a metre mes letres dans son paquet. Il est en peine de n'avoir point receu de reponse aux letres qu'il vous a ecrit de la Haye peutetre n'avez vous point receu son paquet parce qu'il avoit mis l'addresse a la rue guenegaud[6] aussi bien qu'au paquet qu'il vous ecrivit hier. Vous n'aurez qu'a l'envoyer demander a la poste. Il a receu tous les paquets qu'il attendoit dela cour ainsi rien ne nous arreste plus. Il vous recommande son fils. Je vous le recommande aussi. Je n'ai pas le tems d'ecrire a ma sœur et a son mari. Faites leur mes excuses. Faites mes compliments a tous nos parens et amis recommandez moi a leurs prieres. Je suis de tout mon cœur

Votre fre[7]

S/Varlet E.D.B.[8]

---

[1] Probably the birth of Manon Olivier, the second daughter of Marie-Anne Varlet and Antoine Olivier.

[2] "Notre Seigneur"

[3] This is undoubtedly Mlle de Valle.

[4] "ni" for "n'y"

[5] Le chevalier Padéry, recently named consul at Shiraz, with whom DMV was travelling to the Near East.

[6] Understandable confusion, since the rue Guénégaud is around the corner from the Varlets' normal Paris domicile, "au bout du Pont Neuf, au coin de la rue de Nevers".

[7] "fre" for "frère"

[8] "Evêque de Babylone"

15. DMV to his Mother

a Petersbourg le 17ᵉ Juin 1719

Ma tres chere et tres honorée mere

Quoique notre voyage soit extremement lent Dieu le permettan ainsi il a cependant ete jusqua present fort heureux. Dieu nous a donne une fort douce navigation. Les gens de ce païs ci sont si peu expeditifs qu'il nous retienent ici depuis pres de 3 semaines pour faire ce qu'ils pouroient faire en 2 jours. Nous sommes sur le point de partir pour achever notre voiage. Voila la plus belle saison. J'espere que nous le ferons agreablement par le secours de vos prieres. Ayez bien soin je vous prie de conserver votre santé quoique je n'aye pas receu de nouvelles de notre famille depuis 2 mois. J'ai cependant apris par une letre de Mr Le Chevalier Monier ecrite a Mr notre Consul que mon frere est marié.[1] Je ne doute pas que ce mariage ne se soit fait par votre choix et par consequent que nous n'ayons tout lieu d'en benir Dieu et qu'il n'ait apporté a ce sacrement touttes les dispositions les plus propres a attirer les benedictions celestes et a lui faciliter le moyen d'etre heureux et en ce monde et en l'autre. Permetez moi de le saluer en particulier et son epouse car je n'ai pas le loisir de leur ecrire. Je salue tous nos parens et nos amis. Dans ce moment on m'avertit qu'il faut partir. Je n'ai que le tems de cacheter cettre letre et ne puis ecrire ni a ma sœur ni a ma tante ni a ma cousine. Je suis avec un profond respect

Ma tres chere Mere/Votre tres humble et tres obeissant serviteur

S/D.M. Eveque de babilone

---

[1] Marriage with Mlle de Valle alluded to in the previous letter.

16. DMV to his Mother

a Chamaké[1] le 23ᵉ mars 1720

Ma tres chere mere

Je ne sai si vous aurez receu touttes les letres que j'ai eu l'honneur de vous ecrire. Je ne l'ai pas fait aussi souvent que j'aurois desiré, mais dans un si long voiage il est impossible de trouver des occasions d'ecrire en france si ce n'est fort rarement. Je suis extremement inquiet de votre santé car il y a pres d'un an que je n'ai appris de vos nouvelles. Je ne sais quand j'aurai cette consolation. Dieu ma fait la grace de me conserver la santé pendant tout le voiage. Je vous prie de l'en remercier. Il y a pres de 6[2] mois que nous sommes dans cette ville qui est la premiere de perse que l'on trouve apres avoir passé la mer Caspiene. Je ne sai quand nous en partirons. On nous fait esperer que ce sera bientost.[3] Voila la belle saison qui nous donne lieu d'espere un voiage agreable. Priez sil vous plaist notre Seigneur qu'il y donne la benediction afin qu'il reussisse pour la gloire et le salut de ces pauvres peuples, qu'il leve tous les obstacles a leur conversion, afin qu'ils puissent etre eclairez de la lumiere de la foi.[4] Le peu de tems que j'ai pour ecrire ne me permet pas d'ecrire a mon frere a Mr et Ml Olivier ma sœur. Je les salue. Je prie Dieu sans cesse qu'il vous donne une santé parfaite et touttes sortes de consolations spirituelles et suis avec un profond respect

Ma tres chere mere/Votre tres humble et obeissant serviteur

S/Dom. Marie Eveque de babilone

[1] Modern Schemacha (Azerbaidjan SSR) not far from Baku and the Caspian Sea, in 18th century still part of Persia.

[2] Rather, 5 months.

[3] DMV would leave Schamacha shortly after this letter was written, but not in the direction of Babylon. The Carmelite Bishop of Ispahan (*not* a Dominican, as in van Kleef, *IKZ*, p. 157; see Vidal, *Rev. d'hist. des missions*, p. 364) had been alerted to the danger of enthroning a Jansenist in the See of Babylon, and, rather than provoke a crisis, DMV withdrew to Europe.

[4] Undoubtedly reminiscences of Acts ii and xvii, as well as of Eph. ii and I Cor. iii. An allusion to his conversations with the Orthodox Bishop of Caucasian Albania on the possibility of uniting Eastern and Western Catholics.

17. DMV to his Brother-in-law Olivier

Le 29e mai 1721

Il y avoit longtems Mon tres Cher frere que je souhaitois avoir de vos nouvelles. Enfin il y a 15 jours que j'ai receu votre letre du 23e mars, c'est la seule que j'aye receue depuis mon depart de Paris. Les embaras et la fatigue du voiage m'ont empeche de vous repondre plus tost. Comme la providence de Dieu a permis que je me sois un peu approche de vous j'espere recevoir plus souvent de vos letres. Mais comme je ne sai pas si je pourai aller a Paris, du moins si tost, il faut travailler a terminer les affaires de la famille en mon absence. Mrs du seminaire[1] ont ma procuration aussi ample qu'on puisse souhaiter, ainsi je n'y suis point necessaire. Vous me confirmez (mais bien en abregé) la nouvelle de la mort de ma mere et de mon frere que j'avois deja receu des le mois de Janv avec beaucoup de douleur et de surprise.[2] Je dis surprise par rapport a la mort de mon frere car pour ma mere dans l'etat de foiblesse de corps et d'esprit ou je l'avois laissée en partant je ne m'attendois pas qu'on put la conserver longtems. Je vous remercie des soins que vous en avez pris apres la mort de mon frere en la retirant chez vous. Vous n'avez pas eu long tems cette consolation puisquelle est morte au bout d'un mois. Je crois quelle a receu du juste Juge la recompence de la sincere pieté qu'on a veu constament briller en elle tout le cours de sa vie. Mais les obligations immenses que nous lui avons exigent de nous des prieres ferventes, afin que Dieu lui remete tout ce qui pouroit retarder la jouissance du bonheur eternel. J'espere aussi que Dieu aura fait misericorde a mon pauvre frere, ne l'oublions pas dans nos prieres et aprenons d'une mort si prematurée, combien nous devons faire peu de fonds sur la vie presente, et le mepris que nous devons faire des biens de ce monde.[3] Je prens aussi beaucoup de part a la perte que vous avez faitte de Mr votre pere. Je n'ai pas manquée de me souvenir de lui au Saint autel. Je suis ravi d'apprendre que vous et votre famille soyez en bonne santé. Je prie Dieu de vous combler de ses graces, et de faire croitre vos enfans (qui me sont tres chers) dans la vertu et la Science du Salut. Je prends toutte la part imaginable a vos peines qui viennent du malheur des tems et du derangement des affaires du roiaume et qui vous sont communes avec bien d'autres.[4] Il m'est d'autant plus facile d'entrer dans vos peines que j'en eprouve moi meme de semblables et que je me trouve fort a l'Etroit.[5] Un voiage de plus de deux ans ne se fait pas sans de grands frais. Cependant je n'ai pas receu un Sol du revenu de mon Eveché qui est tres peu de Chose et ne sai pas si j'en recevrai. Vous savez que quand je suis parti de Paris on ne m'a pas payé les arrerages de mon titre qui m'etoient dus de quelque années et me sont encor dus. Je fus donc obligé d'emprunter 4000 pour mon voiage. Je les dois encor. Il ma fallu encor faire d'autres emprunts en chemin pour subsister; et voyant que je ne recevois rien j'ai eté obligé de renvoyer le seul Ecclesiastique que j'avois et me reduire a rester seul avec un domestique. Je vous fais ce detail afin que vous connoissiez mes besoins et que cela vous porte a travailler a me faire toucher de l'argent incessament ce qui m'est du d'arrerages payera une bonne partie de mes dettes et mon revenu suffira pour ma subsistance. Pour ce qui est du testament dont vous parlez c'est une chose toutte nouvelle pour moi. Mr Tremblai ne m'en a rien ecrit parce que aparament ce testament ne regarde que la Sepulture de ma mere ou pareilles autres menues dispositions que je crois que vous n'aurez pas manqué d'executer a la letre. Car si ce testament touchoit la disposition du bien de la famille il seroit evidemment nul, tant par l'inhabilité ou ma chere mere etoit les dernieres années de sa vie pour rester, que parce quelle s'etoit (comme vous savez) privée du pouvoir//de disposer du fonds de son bien par la transaction quelle passa avec nous tous au mois de Sept. 1709 apres la mort de mon pere. Cet acte regle nos partages et la succession de ma mere d'une maniere a ne laisser aucune difficulté ni aucun doute. C'est cette transaction que l'on doit appeller la derniere volonté de notre mere, puisque par cet acte elle renonce au pouvoir d'avoir jamais une autre volonté sur la disposition de son bien. Sur ce pied la il est facile de finir les Choses comme vous dites a l'amiable, puisque nos affaires sont sans difficulté et que le tuteur de mon neveu ne peut pas en disconvenir lorsqu'on lui fera voir les choses. Mr Tremblai s'etant plaint a moi que vous ne lui donniez pas connoissance des affaires, je lui ai repondu que je vous avois toujours reconnu bien intentionné, éloigné de touttes sorte d'injustice. J'espere que vous ne me ferez pas mentir et que bien loin de m'obliger a quitter ces bons sentimens vous m'y confirmerez et que les temoignages reciproques d'amitié serreront de plus en plus les deux nœuds de l'union et de l'amour fraternele. Il n'y a personne qui le desire plus ardement que moi. Je chercherai toujours les occasions de vous marquer a vous a ma chere sœur et a toutte votre famille avec quelle tendresse je suis dans l'amour de N.S.J.C.[6] tout a vous

S/Varlet E d B.[7]

[1] Seminary of the Missions étrangères, rue du Bac, in Paris.
[2] Mme Varlet had died early in 1721; her son, DMV's brother, Jean-Achille Varlet had died in mid-1720.
[3] Allusion to, among other texts, Matt vi:19, 20.
[4] Allusion to the disastrous state of French finances after Law's bankruptcy (1720) and which continued to be endemic throughout the 18th century and, indirectly, one of the causes of the Revolution.
[5] DMV's impecunious situation is largely what motivates the following correspondence. His lack of revenue from episcopal benefices would be complete after 3 march 1730 when, he was deprived by law (both civil and ecclesiastic) from making any claim against the See of Babylon. Cf. van Kleef *IKZ* 53, p. 85 n.1, 99 n.2, 150 n.3, 223.
[6] "Notre Seigneur, Jésus Christ".
[7] "Evêque de Babylone".

18. Tremblay to Antoine Olivier

ce 12 Juin 1721

J'ay recu Monsieur, encore une lettre de M de babilone qui me presse fortement d'avancer les affaires. Je vous supplie de me mander si vous voulez les faire regler a l'amiable ou a la rigueur et si vous estes pour le parti. Si nous dresserons un compromis et mettrons chacun nos pieces pour mettre les avocats en estat de juger. J'ay les pieces qu'il me faut hors le testament que vous ne m'avez pas communiqué. Je suis très parfaitement Monsieur, votre tres humble et tres obeissant serviteur.

S/Tremblay

19. Tremblay to Antoine Olivier

Je vous suis tres obligé, Monsieur de vos honnestetez mais pour commençer quelque chose qui soit comme il faut, Je crois que nous devons nous assembler chez Mad. Devalle, et regler ensemble le compte de ce que vous avez receu, et convenir de la maniere de regler l'affaire du testament et le partage et faire vendre ce qui reste de meubles qui se gastent. Vous pouvez prendre sur cela vos mesures avec M de Valle et me mander quand//vous voudriez faire cette assemblée et je m'y trouveray. Je suis tres parfaitement Monsieur votre tres humble et tres obeissant serviteur

14 Juin 1721

S/Tremblay

20. DMV to his Sister and Brother-in-law Olivier

le 26ᵉ Juin 1721

Mon tres cher frere et ma tres chere sœur

Il est vrai que Je ne suis pas fort eloigné de france comme vous l'avez facilement connu par la date de mes letres. Cependant Je ne sais pas quand Dieu permetra que j'aille a Paris et que Jaye le plaisir de vous voir.[1] Ainsi il faut terminer les afaires comme si J'etois a mille lieues d'ici. Mr. Tremblai a tous les pouvoirs pour cela. Il est bon meme avant que nous nous revoyons que touttes les difficultez soient levées, et tous les sujets de peine evanouis. J'espere que cela sera dans peu, fondé sur les dispositions ou je vous vois a me rendre justice, et a débarasser nos affaires de ce mauvais ouvrage qu'on a mis sur le compte de ma mere contre ses intentions et qui semble n'avoir eté fait que pour troubler la paix de notre famille qui etoit si bien établie. Je crois comme vous le dittes que vous n'y avez pas eu de part, et que vous ne l'avez pas meme sceu. Il y a quelque chose de trop noir dans cette affaire pour que je veuille vous en charger. Je ne l'attribue meme a persone. Dieu connoist la verité et rend justice a tous. Vous savez les justes defiances que j'avois et que je vous temoignai quelques jours avant mon départ en présence de ma cousine. Mais vos affaires vous ont empeché d'y faire attention depuis. Car puisque vous reconnoissez que feu mon frere vous a parlé de testament peu de tems avant la mort de ma mere, et par consequent encor moins de tems avant la siene, puisqu'il est mort le premier, vous deviez veiller à ce qu'on n'opprimât point un absent. Enfin cela peut et doit se réparer. Vous savez bien que Dieu ne punira pas seulement ceux qui font mal mais ceux aussi qui y consentent et qu'on est aussi coupable en retenant le bien d'autrui qu'en l'usurpant. Les sentimens de Religion que vous temoignez avoir me font esperer que vous ne negligerez rien pour détourner de dessus vous et de dessus vos enfans la malediction inséparable attachée au bien d'autrui ravi d'une maniere si criante. Il est vrai comme vous le dites que la minorité de mon neveu fait une difficulté.[2] Mais enfin il y a des juges//qui doivent la Justice aux grands comme aux petits, et qui savent que quoi qu'ils soient les protecteurs des pupiles, il ne leur est pas permis de les favoriser aux depens de la Justice. Le pauvre enfant a besoin qu'on attire la benediction de Dieu sur lui en purgeant son bien de toutte iniquité. Ainsi Je crois qu'on ne poura pas se dispenser de s'addresser aux juges. Mais la chose sera sans difficulté quand vous témoignerez, comme vous y etes obligé, ce que vous savez, qui est que quand ma mere auroit pu disposer de son bien elle étoit depuis quelques années absolument et notoirement incapable de le faire, et qu'ainsi Elle peut avoir innocement mis la fausse date qui paroist dans ce pretendu testament. Cela vaut beaucoup mieux que d'en venir aux affreuses verifications de quelque fausseté commise de propos délibérée. Croyez qu'on ne peut pas etre plus sensible que Je le suis a vos peines. Je voudrois etre en Etat de faire en sorte que vous ne vous sentissiez pas de la misere du tems. Mais apres tout considerez que Je ne vous demande pas un sol du votre. Je ne demande que ce qu'il a plu a la divine providence de me donner par la voye du monde la plus légitime qui est l'heritage paternel. Vous ne sauriez me faire plus de plaisir que de me donner souvent par vos letres des marques de votre amitié, et des nouvelles du succez d'une afaire dont le bonheur de notre famille dépend. Je vous prie de saluer ma belle sœur de ma part, et de croire que Je suis avec la plus tendre affection en N.S.J.C.[3] tout a vous.

S/Varlet. E. d.b.[4]

---

[1] DMV would return briefly to Paris on 21 July 1721, but would be forced to go into hiding almost at once because of threats on his life.

[2] Jean Achille Varlet had had a posthumous son "Pierre" by Mlle de Valle who would ultimately help to settle these thorny financial questions in 1757, being, like other members of his immediate family "procureur au Châtelet". See Rijksarchief, nos 4031, 4032.

[3] "Notre Seigneur Jésus Christ".

[4] "Evêque de Babylone".

21. Attestation in re: Jean-Achille Varlet

Nous soussignez Jean Henry Tramblay pretre procureur de la maison de Messieurs des Missions Etrangeres etably a paris Rue du Bac par-

roisse St Sulpice y demeurans fondée de procuraon[1] de Messire Dominique Marie Varlet Eveque de Babilonne, Antoine Olivier procureur au
Chatelet et Marie Anne Varlet mon[2] Epouse que j'othorise demeurans
rüe de la Grande Truanderie paroisse St Eustache, et Charles de Valle et
Catherine Maret mon Epouse, aussy de moy autorisée, tuteur
coniointemt[3] de Pierre Varlet fils mineur et unique heritier de feu Me[4]
Jean Achiles Varlet procureur au parlement demeurans Rüe de Nevers,
psse[5] St. Andre des Arts. Led.[6] Seigneur Eveque de Babilone et lad.[7]
demoiselle Olivier frere et sœur de leur chef et Led. Mineur Varlet leur
nepveux par representation de feu M. son pere, heritiers chacun par un
test[8] de deffunte dle[9] Marie Vallée venue au jour de son deces du Sr.[10]
Achiles Varlet leur mere et ayeule, Reconnoissons que de nôtre commun
consentement, l'inventaire fait apres le deces de ladite veuve Varlet par
Lauverjon et son Confrere No.re[11] le [blank]//[12] et jours suivans, ensemble tous les titres et pieces preventoires par celuy dont nous Olivier et ma
femme avions estez Chargez es le Testamens de la deffunte ont estez mis
ce jourdhuy es mains de Mere[13] Antoine Chatelain avocat en parlement
demeurans Rüe haute feüille, dont nous sommes convenus pr[14] notre
Seul arbitre, a l'effet de nous regler sur touttes les Contestations que nous
avons et que nous pourrons avoir es dit homs,[15] tans[16] au Sujet de L'acte
en forme Egalement fait entre lad. feüe demoiselle veuve Varlet, led.
Seigr.[17] Eveque de Babilone nous dit Olivier et ma femme, et led. deffunt
Jean Achiles Varlet, devant le Chanteau et son Confrere No.re le vingt
deux Septembre 1709, du Testament fait par lad. deffunte dle veuve Varlet, qu'au sujet de sa succession, et de celle dud.[18] feu Sr. Varlet son
mary, comme aussy pour les partages desd.es[19] successions suivans d'un
chacun de nous esd.[20] nom y sera fondez, afin d'entretenir la paix et
amité entre nous et sortir d'affaire a l'amiable par la voye de la Douceur
et Sans proces, promettans d'en passer par tous ce qui sera reglez et deci-
dez par led. Sr Chatelain, et d'aquiesser a Son jugemens arbitral comme
a arrest de Cour Souveraine sans pouvoir le Contester ny en interpeler
appel, a faire de trois mil Livres//[21] de dedis contre le contrevenans, qui
ne pourra etre reputée peine comminatoire sous quelque pretexte que ce
soit lesquels trois mil livres seront payées par le Contrevenans aux aque-
rans au paravans la premiere contestation, et pour donner du temps suf-
fisans au Sr Chatelain pour rendre son jugement arbitral sur lesd.[22] titres
et pieces et sur nos Memoires nous luy avons accordé jusque et Compris
le mois de novembre prochain a conter de ce jourdhuy sans que neant-
moins le deffaute de fournir nos memoires puisse Empecher led. Sr Chatelain de rendre son jugement arbitral auparavans led.[6] mois de novembre
prochain, et pour l'Entiere Execution des presentes et pour recevoir lecture de la Sentence arbitrale qui interviendra, nous avons Elu nos domi-

cilles dans nos demeures cy dessus declarées auquels lieux Tous lesquels titres et papiers mis es mains dud.[18] Sr. Chatelain ne pourrons etre retirés par aucuns de nous qu'en nos presences et de notre Consentement fait triple entre nous affaire le vingt un juillet mil sept cens vingt et un.

S/Tremblay
Olivier
P. Varlet

Marie anne Varlet
Catherine Maret

[1] "procuration"
[2] "mon" for "son"
[3] "conjointement"
[4] "Maître"
[5] "psse" for "paroisse"
[6] "Ledit"
[7] "ladite"
[8] "testament"
[9] "Demoiselle"
[10] "Sieur"
[11] "Notaire"
[12] In margin in autograph initials "MAV, CM" for "Marie-Anne Varlet, Catherine Maret".
[13] "Messire"
[14] "pour"
[15] "èsdits hommes"
[16] "tant"
[17] "Seigneur"
[18] "dudit"
[19] "desdites"
[20] "èsdit"
[21] In margin in autograph initials "CM, MAV" for "Catherine Maret, Marie-Anne Varlet".
[22] "lesdits"

22. DMV to his Sister and Brother-in-law Olivier

Le 15 Sept. 1721

Mon cher frere et ma chere sœur

Il y a fort long tems que Je n'ai point receu de vos letres. Je n'en ai point receu depuis la derniere que Je vous ai ecrites. Je me suis informé de vos nouvelles autant qu'il m'a été possible et ce que j'en ai apris a souvent eté triste. Lorsque j'ai apris la mort de votre fils cadet j'en ai douté quelque tems, croyant que vous me l'auriez ecrit. Il y a peu de tems que ma cousine ma ecrit la maladie de ma sœur causée par une fausse couche de 2 mois. Cette nouvelle m'auroit cause beaucoup d'inquietude, si je n'avois apris presque aussitost quelle[1] etoit un peu mieux que le 15e etoit passé, ainsi hors du grand danger. Mais cependant Je ne suis pas sans crainte, puisqu'on marque quelle[1] a de la fievre un grand mal de teste des sueurs continuelles et point d'appetit. Je souhaite que vous m'appreniez dans peu son parfait retablissement. Je ne saurois assez exhorter ma sœur a se conserver en tout tems surtout dans ses grossesses. Sa conscience y est engagée puisque en s'exposant a se blesser elle risque la vie et le salut de son fruit. Je suppose que le reste de la famille est en bon Etat, que votre fils fait des progres dans la science autant que son foible temperament le permet. Mariane qui a autour de 15 ans doit avoir fait de grands progres dans la Vertu, elle doit etre d'un grand secours a sa mere, mais aparement quelle a oublié quelle[1] a un oncle dans le monde, c'est ce que Je trouve un peu Etrange. J'ai eté un peu indispose ces jours-ci d'une fievre double tierce. Quoi quelle n'ai duré que huit jours elle n'a pas laissé de m'affoiblir beaucoup. J'en suis presentement quite graces a Dieu et Je commence a reprendre mes forces. J'ai apris que vous avez signé un compromis pour remetre nos affaires a l'arbitrage de Mr Chastelain.[2] Je crois que vous lui aurez envoyé les memoires necessaires pour terminer tous les differens en sorte que l'on puisse dans peu finir les partages. Je prie le Seigneur de vous combler de graces et suis tres cordialement

Mon cher frere et ma chere Sœur/Votre tres humble et obeissant serviteur

S/Varlet

[1] "qu'elle"
[2] Reference to procedural arrangements of document no. 21 preceding.

23. Chastellain to Antoine Olivier

Jay receu de Monsieur Levesque de Babilone, Monsieur mon cher cousin, un pacquet contenant une Lettre et un memoire pour moy, et une letre pour vous qu'il me prie de vous faire rendre. Vous la trouverez icy incluse.[1] Je me presse de regler votre affaire, jay tout vu, Jay des memoires de Monsieur de Babilone, et de Monsieur devalle, Il n'y a que de votre part que je nay rien. Ayez agreable de m'envoyer vos pretentions, ou bien de prendre la peine d'avoir une conference avec moy. Vous m'avez dit au calvaire[2] qu'il y avoit la question prealable du testament//[hole] mais comme le compromis porte que je reglerai les dificultez et que je feray le partage, et que je rendray une sentence arbitrale, il ne me paroist pas que je puisse decider separement la question du testament, ne pouvant aux termes du compromis rendre qu'une sentence arbitrale. D'ailleurs par les pieces que Jay entre les mains et que Jay parcouru, il seroit dificile de faire un partage, il faudroit d'autres pieces et d'autres eclaircissemens. J'espere que vous voudrez bien me faire reponse, afin qu'on ne m'impute pas d'avoir laissé écouler le tems du compromis sans vous tirer d'affaire. Monsieur de Valle est venu icy aujourd'huy, la[3] esté longtems avec moy permettez de saluer madame votre epouse et Madame votre chere mere, et croyez moy vostre tres humble et tres obeissant serviteur

S/Chastellain

Paris ce 20 Octobre 1721

[1] This letter follows.
[2] On the occasion of one of the several family funerals of the year 1720-1721.
[3] "la" for "il a".

24. DMV to his Brother-in-law Olivier

Il est fort triste Mon tres cher frere que depuis le tems que ma chere sœur est malade elle ne soit pas encor retablie. Veillez a ce quelle se conserve dorenavant avec de grandes attentions afin que de pareils accidens n'arivent pas. Vous me marquez que ma sœur ma ecrit beaucoup de fois. Cependant je n'en ai receu que deux. Les autres aurioent elles ete perdues? Vous avez dites vous consenti volontiers a vous rapporter a Mr Chastelain de nos affaires. Ce n'est pas assez que ce consentement, il faut soutenir cela en fournissant a Mr Chastelain vos memoires. Il se plaint de ce que vous ne lui en avez donne aucun pendant que les tuteurs de mon neveu lui ont fourni les leurs, cependant le tems presse de juger. Je vous prie de les lui envoyer incessament autrement le consentement que vous avez paru donner ne serviroit qu'a prolonger nos partages et me laisser plus longtems dans le besoin. Ne differez donc pas a me donner cette marque de votre bonne volonté. Rien ne me prouvera mieux que vous n'avez aucune part dans un testament qui met une si grande tache dans la famille et qui est si indigne de ma mere. J'ai bien remercié Dieu//d'avoir enfin delivré ma cousine des persecutions auxquelles elle etoit exposée. Vous voyez qu'il ne faut qu'avoir confiance en Dieu, qu'apres nous avoir eprouvé il nous delivre, et que sa Providence veille pour frapper les oppresseurs et soulager ceux qui souffrent l'oppression.[1] Je vous recommande le soin des affaires de ma cousine; elle se trouve dans de grands embaras. Je ne sais point encor combien de tems Je serai eloigné ni quand je pourai avoir le plaisir de vous voir et ma chere soeur. Vous marquez a la fin de votre letre que Je vous ferai plaisir de presser Mr Chastelain de nous regler. Il na pas besoin d'etre pressé; il n'attend que vos memoires, Je l'ai pressé et Il me repond que vous ne lui avez rien envoyé. Faites le donc Je vous prie incessament. Je ne vous demande rien que de juste. J'ai receu la letre de ma niece, voici la reponse.[2] Je n'en ai point encor veu de mon neveu Olivier. Je suis tres sincerement Mon tres cher frere

Votre tres humble et tres obeissant seviteur

S/D.M. Varlet EdB[3]

[1] Reminiscence of Luke xvi, as also perhaps of Luke i or Matthew xxii, etc.
[2] This letter is missing from the present correspondence.
[3] "Evêque de Babylone"

25. DMV to his Sister and Brother-in-law Olivier

Le 18e Jan. 1722

Mon tres cher frere et Ma tres Chere sœur

Il y a quelques jours que Jai receu votre letre du 4e. Je suis tres sensible a touttes les marques d'amitie que vous m'y donnez, et aux bons souhaits que vous faites en ma faveur. Je prie Dieu de vous donner dans cette nouvelle année touttes les graces et les benedictions qui vous sont necessaires afin que vous attachant uniquement a lui vous evitiez tout ce qui pouroit lui deplaire, et que vous vous appliquiez serieusement a vous sanctifier en remplissant tous les devoirs de la religion et surtout en donnant a vos enfans une education si chretiene que vous en recueilliez les fruits et par la consolation qu'ils vous donneront et par la recompense que vous en recevrez en l'autre vie. Je fais reponse a ma niece. Pourquoi mon neveu ne m'a-t-il pas aussi ecrit? Dieu soit beni de ce que nos affaires sont enfin terminées de ce que vous avez donné les mains a touttes les propositions d'accommodement. Je n'ai point encor veu le Jugement mais sur le recit que l'on m'en a fait, il me paroist bon. J'espere que vous continuerez a marquer l'amitié que vous avez pour moi en executant l'accord avec autant de droiture//que vous en avez eue pour terminer ce petit different[1] que Dieu a permis que[2] s'elevast entre nous afin de nous donner occasion de nous unir plus que jamais. Je ne sais pas ce qui a pu vous deplaire dans cette affaire. Etant absent Je ne pouvois donner d'Ecclaircissemens a l'arbitre que par Ecrit. Je ne crois pas autant que Je m'en puis souvenir qu'il y eut aucun mot qui vous touchast. Ce n'est pas moi qui avois mis la piere de scandale qui nous divisoit.[3] J'etois obligé de travailler avec moi d'une maniere qui fait connoistre vos bonnes intentions dont j'etois persuadé meme avant que j'en visse les effects. Mr Tremblai ma envoyé l'argent que vous lui avez remis et dont j'avois grand besoin. Il est bon de liquider les comptes de chacun une bonne fois affin que lors qu'on recevra son revenu par quartiers comme cela se doit, on ne donne pas des quitances a compte mais toujours d'une maniere determinée. Je n'ai point receu de letre ni de nouvelle cette année de ma belle sœur. Je lui ecrirai au premier jour. Je suis avec une veritable et tendre affection mon tres cher frere et ma tres Chere sœur

Votre tres humble et obeissant serviteur

S/D.M. Varlet Ev. dB.[4]

[1] "différend"

[2] "que" for "qui"

[3] From the Book of Genesis on (the story of Cain and Abel), stoning has had a highly metaphoric significance in interpreting the Bible. See, especially in the New Testament, John viii, Matt xxiii and Acts vii. According to L. von Pastor, *History of the Popes*, 35: 450-451, DMV was a believer in figurism. Cf. also van Kleef *IKZ* 53, p. 198 n.2.

[4] "Evêque de Babylone"

26. DMV to his Brother-in-law Olivier

Le 11e mars 1722

J'etois inquiet Mon tres cher frere de l'etat de votre santé, parce qu'il y a longtems que je n'ai eu de vos nouvelles. Lorsque J'ai apris par une letre que Je viens de recevoir que vous avez eté considerablement malade; heureusement j'apprens votre guerison en apprenant la maladie; cela m'épargne une nouvelle inquietude. J'aime mieux ne vous ecrire qu'une courte letre que de manquer l'heure de la poste pour vous exhorter a conserver votre santé en ne vous laissant point accabler par le travail. Donnez moi souvent de vos nouvelles soit par vous soit par ma niece ou par votre docteur dont Je n'ai point encor veu l'Ecriture, et qui cependant doit deja etre avancé. Il y a fort longtems aussi que Je n'ai eu de nouvelles de ma belle sœur et de son fils.//Je Dieu[1] dans ce saint tems de quareme de vous combler de ses graces, et de vous disposer a celebrer dignement la solemnité de paques. Je suis avec un sincere et parfait attachement

Mon tres cher frere Votre tres humble et obeissant serviteur

S/D.M. Varlet Ev. de Bab.[2]

[1] "Je prie Dieu..."

[2] "Evêque de Babylone"

27. DMV to his Sister Olivier

Le 13e aoust 1722

Je ne sais Ma tres chere sœur si vos letres ont ete perdues, mais il y avoit plus de 6 mois que Je n'en avois receues, lorsque J'en ay receu enfin une sans date ces Jours ci, avec des letres de mon neveu et de ma niece. Vous pouvez juger de la Joye quelles m'ont causée, vous aimant aussi tendrement que Je fais. Ma santé est assez bonne graces a Dieu. Je suis bien aise de ce que nos comptes sont enfin finis, et Mr Tremblai a eu soin de me faire tenir la portion qui m'est echeue du partage qui a ete fait. Il est vrai que la somme est reduite au tiers en sortant du royaume, mais c'est un effect de la facheuse situation des affaires, en quoi il n'y a autre chose a faire qu'a se soumetre aux ordres de la divine providence. Je ne vous marque cela que pour vous faire connoitre la raison qui m'avoit fait ecrire a ma belle sœur qu'il falloit eviter les depenses superflues dans un tems ou l'on manque du necessaire. Je sais bien que quand Je n'en parlerois pas vous et mon cher frere estes assez prudens pour ne pas faire de depenses inutiles, car pour celles qui sont absolument necessaire il faudroit etre bien deraisonable pour y trouver a redire, on se feroit un tort considerable en negligeant de les faire. Je suis pesuadé qu'en representant a ma belle sœur et au tuteur de mon neveu les choses paisiblement ils ne s'opposeront point a ce qui se trouvera necessaire.//Quel age a mon neveu Olivier?[1] Pourquoi ne va-t-il point encor au college? Il faut tacher, sans le surcharger de travail, qu'il ne perde point son tems. Si vous le metiez dans quelque bonne pension Lemulation des autres ecoliers l'encourageroit peutetre. Mr Felix[2] cet Ecclesiastique qui a fait le voiage avec moi, s'est remis depuis son retour a Instruire des enfans; il a bien de la piete et du talent. Voiez avec mon frere s'il ne conviendroit point de lui confier l'education de votre fils. Je ne puis pas en juger de si loin mais je vous conseille d'aller voir de ma part a votre loisir Mr Poquet [Pouquet] un des directeurs du Seminaire des Miss. Etr.[3] pour le consulter sur ce qu'il y auroit a faire de mieux pour donner a votre fils une bonne education. C'est un homme tres experimenté et tres sage. Priez le de vous aller voir et de vous donner conseil apres avoir veu le petit homme, et vous ne pourez pas mieux faire que de suivre ses avis. Faites en sorte que mon neveu et ma niece profitent de mes Letres, ne negligez rien pour leur Instruction et pour former leur esprit, ayez soin qu'il[4] s'appliquent a la Lecture et faites leur rendre compte en conversation de ce qu'ils auront leu. Cela les enhardira et leur formera le jugement. mais surtout recourez a Dieu afin qu'il repande sa benediction sur vos travaux pour les faire fructifier. Je suis persuadé que de votre côté vous etes plus exacte que jamais et a la Lecture et a l'oraison et a tous les exercices de piete tels que la frequentation des Sacrement,[5] etc. Je n'i apris que par la letre de ma niece que Me votre belle mere demeure avec vous. Je m'en rejouis. C'est une grande consolation reciproque. Je vous prie de la saluer de ma part aussi bien que mon cher frere. Priez Dieu pour moi avec toutte la famille et soyez persuadée du tendre attachement avec lequel

Je suis ma tres chere sœur Votre tres humble et obeissant serviteur

S/D.M.V. EdB[6]

---

[1] Another subject, along with finances and his inheritance, of great concern to DMV, attested by the numerous and frequent references to his nephew Olivier in the following letters of this correspondence.
[2] "Nom de guerre" of Jacques Jubé, also called "de la Cour".
[3] "Séminaire des Missions étrangères".
[4] "il" for "ils"
[5] "Sacrements"
[6] "Evêque de Babylone"

28. DMV to his Sister Olivier

Le 13e nov. 1722

Ma tres Chere sœur

Je viens d'apprendre par une letre de ma chere cousine qu'il vous est arrivé un facheux accident, mais en meme tems que Je vous temoigne ma douleur de ce mal, Je vous felicite et rends graces a Dieu de ce que la Chute n'a pas ete aussi funeste quelle auroit pu etre sans une protection particuliere de Dieu. Ayez soin de ne rien negliger pour vous retablir. Je prie notre Seigneur de benir les remedes afin que vous obteniez une parfait guerison. J'aprends avec Joie que vous avez mi mon neveu chez Mr Felix et qu'il y est content. Dieu en soit beni. J'espere qu'il y profitera. C'est une bonne Ecole et pour l'Etude et pour la pieté. La bonne methode du maitre et l'Emulation le feront avancer et Je crois qu'en notre consideration, il en prendra un soin particulier. Je lui ecrirai un autre Jour pour le lui recommander.// J'apprens que Mr Launai [Launay] ne fait pas bien ses affaires. Je suis persuade que mon frere ne negligera rien afin qu'un si gros loyer ne periclite pas. Je salue tres humblement mon tres cher frere et toutte la petite famille a qui Je souhaite mille benedictions et suis etc.

N.S.

29. DMV to his Sister and Brother-in-law Olivier

Le 24e Janv. 1724

Mon tres cher frere et ma tres chere sœur

Il est vrai qu'il y a longtems que Je n'avois eu de vos letres. Vos 2 que j'ai receues avec celles de mes neveu et niece m'ont fait d'autant plus de plaisir. Je sais bien que vos affairs sont grandes et nombreuses. Au reste Je vous suis bien obligé de ce que vous vous interessez a ma sante en vous en informant de temps en temps comme aussi du soin que vous prenez de mes affaires, dont Mr Tremblai me rend fort bon temoignage comme je vous le marquois dans la letre que j'eus l'honeur de vous ecrire les premiers Jours de cette annee. Je suis tres sensible aux bons desirs que votre amitie pour moi vous met dans le cœur en ma faveur. Tout ce que nous pouvons faire de mieux en cette vie ci c'est de faire la volonté de Dieu c'est a cela principalement que nous devons aspirer.[1]

Je suis tres touché de touttes vos peines et de touttes les pertes pour lesquelles il plaist a Dieu de vous eprouver; J'en suis d'autant plus penetré que j'en juge par ma propre experience, car vous savez que je suis moi meme dans un Etat tres triste selon la nature, puis que tout ce que j'ai pour subsister passe par vos mains, et vous savez aussi qu'avant qu'il arrive jusqua moi il est diminué des deux tiers. Je me flatte toujours que les Especes pouront etre reduites a leur valeur naturelle et ce qui ne suffit pas aujourdhui poura suffire allors.

Je suis bien aise de ce que mon neveu va enfin au college mais il n'est guerre avancé pour son age. Il faut qu'il travaille soigneusement pour reparer le tems perdu. Quoi qu'il soit delicat, il n'est pas necessaire qu'il s'eforce, il suffit qu'il employe bien son tems et qu'il n'en//perde pas. S'il pouvoit prendre goust a l'etude allors il se porteroit de lui meme mais pour cela il faut qu'il soit des premiers et au dessus de son ouvrage. Il faut qu'il s'applique a la Version et a bien expliquer les auteurs sans neanmoins negliger la composition Latine. Je ne me soucie pas beaucoup qu'il soit en pension, il y en a peu de bonnes, et des pensions ordinaires ne feroient que le gaster. Je suis bien touché de la mort de ma cousine Le Lievre, apparement sa mere se porte bien, la voila donc chargée de ses petits enfans car selon les apparences le pere n'aura pas le moyen de les elever. Avez vous des nouvelles de la famille Treteau; que font ils a Blois? Je n'en entends rien dire depuis que vous m'avez apris la mort de leur pauvre mere. Je prie Dieu de tout mon cœur de vous remplir de ses graces et de ses consolations spirituelles et suis tres parfaitement mon tres cher frere/et ma tres chere sœur Votre tres humble et tres/obeissant serviteur, etc.

N.S.

¹ Discreet reworking of Christ's teaching in John iii.

30. DMV to his Sister Olivier

Quoique¹ je ne vous ecrive pas souvent Ma tres chere sœur, Je ne vous oublie pas et J'ai soin de m'informer soit a Mr Tremblai soit a ma belle sœur soit a ma cousine de ce qui vous regarde et ils m'en rendent compte. Jai sceu que mon frere a ete malade mais heureusement j'ai appris son retablissement. Vous ne sauriez me faire un plus grand plaisir que de m'ecrire le plus souvent quil vous plaira. Car vous pouvez vous persuader qu'apres Dieu il n'y a rien qui me touche si fort au cœur que ce qui vous regarde. Ainsi si vous vouliez m'ecrire plus souvent vous pouriez demander mon addresse a M. Tremb.²

C'est un grand embaras que celui des massons³ ou vous etes, mais cela passera et vous aurez l'agrément de demeurer dans une maison renouvellée ou il n'y aura de longtems rien a faire. Ce que vous me dites de mon neveu me fait plaisir puisqu'il employe si bien son tems et qu'il aime fort la lecture. Il faut esperer qu'il avancera plus qu'il na fait; Je suis bien aise que vous lui ayez donné un repetiteur qui est un Ecclesiastique de merite. J'apprendrai toujours tres volontiers des nouvelles du progres de ses etudes. Puisqu'il aime la lecture il faut lui metre dans ses heures de loisir d'excellens livres entre les mains, tels que le Catechisme de Montpelier, les figures de la Bible de roiaumont,// et apres cela vous feriez bien de vous faire rendre compte de ce qu'il auroit lu par maniere de conversation.⁴ Cela lui formeroit le Jugement, vous pouriez faire de meme avec vos filles. Je m'étone que mon neveu a son age n'ait point encor fait sa premiere communion. Il depend beaucoup de vous de l'en rendre capable par vos bonnes instructions et par votre vigilance. Je crois cependant que vous ne manquez pas a ce que vous devez la dessus. Les souhaits que vous faites pour moi me touchent fort, mais il faut etre soumis a la volonté de Dieu, c'est pour la faire que nous sommes au monde. Nous n'avons point ici bas de Cité permanente. C'est au ciel que nous devons travailler a nous etablir.⁵ Demandez a Dieu dans vos prieres qu'il daigne graver profondement ces veritez dans mon cœur. Saluez de ma part mon frere et me croyez tres cordialement votre etc.

N.S.

Le 5ᵉ nov. 1724

¹ Above the incipit another hand has written "5. 9bre 1724".
² Tremblay
³ "maçons"
⁴ Interesting commentary on the instruction of the young in the 18th century, though not perhaps remarkable in a religious school nor in a family with DMV's connections. The "Catéchisme de Montpellier" composed of Pastoral Instructions by Bishop Colbert, arranged by the Oratorian Pouget in 1702, was particularly favoured of the Jansenists.
⁵ Reminiscent of Biblical exhortations in Matt xxv, Luke xvi, Rev xxi, etc.

31. DMV to his Sister and Brother-in-law Olivier

Mon tres cher frere et Ma tres chere sœur[1]

Je suis tres sensible aux marques d'amitié que vous me donnez dans vos letres, et aux souhaits favorables que vous me faites au commencement de cette année. Je prie Dieu aussi de mon cote de vous combler de ses graces, et de vous donner plus de repos cette année que la derniere. C'est un grand embaras que d'avoir a reparer une maison de fond en comble, outre l'embaras c'est une grande depense qui ne laisse pas d'incommoder lorsque cela survient sans qu'on s'y attende. Je suis fort edifié de vous voir si resigné à la volonté de Dieu qui permet ces accidens pour votre bien spirituel qui est de beaucoup préferable au temporel. Il faut prendre garde que l'air et l'humidité du nouveau batiment ne vous incommode. J'apprens avec bien de la joye que vos enfans vous//donnent de la satisfaction et que vous en concevez de bonnes esperances et qu'ils sont en bonne santé. Mon neveu est en une bonne ecole. Il doit bien profiter des bons soins de son regent. Je suis bien aise de voir par vos letres qu'il commence a aimer les bons livres puis qu'il vous a demandé le catechisme du Concile de Trente. Si ces[2] en latin que vous le lui avez donné il aura lieu d'y profiter pour la langue en meme tems qu'il y apprendra la religion. Il est vrai que le Catechisme de Montpelier auroit eté plus a sa portée mais l'un n'empeche pas l'autre car cest un livre a avoir dans une maison et a lire en famille pour l'utilité de tous les enfans; comme vous savez que chez feu mon pere on faisoit tous les soirs une lecture commune. Jai cru vous faire plaisir d'ecrire a M. Theru [Thiery] une letre de recommandation pour mon neveu. Je vous l'envoye ouverte afin que vous la fassiez rendre//apres l'avoir cachetée.[3] Je vous suis bien obligé des soins que vous continuéz a prendre de nos affaires communes, M. Tremblai a soin de m'en rendre un compte exact. Mes affaires sont toujours dans le meme etat. Heureusement je me porte assez bien graces a Dieu; continuez je vous prie a m'aimer a prier Dieu pour moi et a croire que je suis tres veritablement Mon tres cher frere et ma tres chere sœur

Votre tres humble et tres obeissant serviteur

N.S.

Le 19 Janv. 1725

Je vous prie d'assurer de mes respects Madame votre mere et vos freres et sœurs

---

¹ Above the salutation and to the right another hand has written: 19 Janvier 1725.
² "ces" for "c'est"
³ This letter is lacking from the present collection.

32. DMV to his Sister and Brother-in-law Olivier

Le 12ᵉ avril 1725

Mon tres cher frere et ma tres Chere Sœur

Vos letres m'ont fait un tres grand plaisir. J'etois en peine de votre santé. Je craignois que les embaras du bastiment et l'humidite ne vous eut incommodé. Mais j'apprens que votre santé est bonne, dont je rends graces a Dieu. Je suis bien aise que mon neveu ait ete juge digne de faire sa premiere communion a Paques. Voici un petit mot que je lui ecris pour le congratuler et l'exhorter a etre fidele a conserver une si grande grace.

J'ai une extreme peine de n'avoir pas pu vous faire tenir l'ecrit que vous souhaitez,¹ j'ai d'autant plus de desir de le faire et de vous donner cette satisfaction que vous l'avez trouvé bon et que plusieurs de vos amis en pensent de meme. Croiez que je n'aurois pas attendu que vous m'en eussiez demandé. Si j'avois pu le faire et je vous aurois prevenu tres volontiers. Mais rien n'est si difficile que de faire entrer ces sortes d'ouvrages. Il n'en est passé qu'un tres petit nombre dont je n'ai pas ete le maitre, j'attends tous les jours la nouvelle qu'un autre petit nombre puisse penetrer jusqua vos quartiers. Aussi tost J'auray soin que vous en ayez ou bien je ne le pourai en attendant je prierai ma cousine de vous preter le sien et de vous donner aussi la liberté d'en donner la lecture aux personnes qui vous le demandent.//Je vous prie aussi de faire la dessus mes excuses a Mr Thery [Thiery] et de lui marquer que si je puis je lui en procurerai lorsqu'il y en aura occasion. Je me recommande a vos prieres et salue touttes votre famille et suis tres sincerement en N.S.J.C.²

Mon tres cher frere et ma tres Chere Sœur/Votre tres humble et tres obeis. serviteur

N.S.

---

¹ Probably a Jansenist work; if the lines immediately following are to be put in true perspective, quite likely a copy of DMV's first *Apologie* which had appeared at the end of 1724.
² "Notre Seigneur Jésus Christ".

33. DMV to his Sister Olivier

Le 17ᵉ Dec. 1725

L'inquietude que vous me temoignez ma tres chere sœur avoir de ma santé, marque votre bon cœur dont je suis bien convaincu; assurez vous je vous prie d'une parfaite correspondance de ma part. Car je n'ai pas ete sans inquietudes sur votre sante. Surtout dans les embaras et fatigues de votre batiment dont vous etes enfin bien debarassez. Pour eviter ces peines mutuelles, il faut tacher de nous ecrire plus souvent l'un a l'autre; il arrive toujours quelque inconvenient qui retarde les letres, par exemple votre letre est dattée du 3ᵉ octob. Cependant il ny¹ a pas long tems que je lai receu, et cela donne quelque occasion d'impatience. pour eviter cela cette fois ci je vous l'addresserai en droiture. Ma santé est grace a Dieu assez bonne. Vous m'avez fait un tres grand plaisir de m'informer des etudes de mon neveu, vous savez combien j'y prends de part. J'ai eté content de sa letre. C'est une bonne nouvelle que vous m'apprenez qu'il commence a etre fort et capable de supporter la fatigue et qu'il a de l'ardeur pour aller de bon matin profiter des soins d'un bon repetiteur. J'espere quil aura la meme ardeur pour profiter//dans la vertu car cest le principal sans quoi le reste n'est rien. Il est en bonne Ecole pour apprendre les sciences et la religion, car Mr Dupuis qui est presentement son regent, est une personne d'un merite excellent en toutte maniere. Voici une letre de recommandation pour lui.² Vous la cacheterez et lui envoyerez si vous la jugez a propos. Ce que vous me dites de la misere m'etoit deja connu par les nouvelles publiques. C'est un fleau tres affligeant, cependant on dit que le blé diminue un peu de prix. Jai bien de la joie que ma cousine vous ait fait avoir un exemplaire de l'ouvrage dont vous parlez et que vous l'ayez gouté, et que vous l'ayez montre a vos amis. J'aurois voulu vous en pouvoir procurer assez pour en faire present aux persones que vous considerez mais cela na pas ete possible.

Je suis ravi d'apprendre que votre famille soit en bonne sante et surtout mon cher frere dont la sante vous est si necessaire. Je vous prie de l'assurer de mon sincere et parfait attachement et de la reconnoissance que j'ai des soins qu'il se donne pour moi. Je prie notre seigneur de vous donner toutte sorte de grace spirituelle et temporelle pendant le cours de cette nouvelle annee ou//nous allons entrer. Je suis en peine de la sante de ma cousine. Je n'ai receu qu'une letre depuis son retour de la campagne, et elle me marquoit qu'elle relevoit d'une maladie assez considerable. Trouvez bon que je recommande ses proces a mon frere si elle en a encore pendans au chastelet. Lorsque vous me ferez le plaisir de m'ecrire aprenez moi des nouvelles de ma cousine Treteau, je nen ai rien oui³ depuis la mort de sa mere, j'estime fort sa vertu. Dites moi aussi des nouvelles de ses freres, et de ma cousine Lanoi [Lannoy] et sa famille. Je me recommande a vos prieres et suis etc

N.S.

1 "ny" for "n'y"
2 This letter is lacking from the present correspondence.
3 "oui" for "ouï"

34. DMV to his Sister and Brother-in-law Olivier

Le 3e Janv. 1727

Mon tres cher frere et ma tres chere sœur

Vous vous plaindrez sans doute de mon long silence et vous aurez raison. J'en suis moi meme confus et dois vous en faire des excuses. Mais ne l'attribuez pas sil vous plaist a aucune indifference ou aucun oubli; vous ne me rendriez pas justice. Croyez qu'il n'y a personne qui prenne tant d'interrest a tout ce qui vous touche et qui vous aime plus sincerement que je le fais. Mais j'ai eté si accablé d'ouvrage toutte l'année derniere que je n'ai presque pas eu de moments libres.[1] Je jouis presentement, graces a Dieu, de quelque loisir et j'en profite pour repondre a vos letres et vous assurent qu'on ne peut pas vous souhaiter plus de benedictions spirituelles plus de consolations et de prosperités que j'en demande a Dieu pour vous et pour toutte votre famille. Je prie sans cesse la divine misericorde de daigner benir et faire reussir les soins que vous prenez d'elever chretienement et de soutenir votre famille, afin qu'a mesure que vous chercherez avant touttes choses le royaume de Dieu et sa justice, il vous accorde le reste comme//par surcroist selon sa parolle.

J'ai de l'empressement d'apprendre les progres que fait mon neveu dans ses etudes, s'il employe bien cette seconde année de troisieme comme je l'espere il sera fort dans le reste de ses etudes et il travaillera avec plus de goust et de succes. Je vous envoye un mot de letre de recommandation pour M. Dupuis que vous cacheterez.[2] J'ecris aussi a ma niece Marie anne. Comment se porte votre derniere? Elle a eté bien infirme ci devant. Dieu pardonne au Mr Delaunai [de Launay] le tort qu'il nous a fait, il ne devoit pas en agir ainsi.[3] Je suis surpris d'apprendre que le second etage de notre maison est vacant. Voila bien des pertes que je porte cette année. Dieu en soit beni. Je crois qu'il n'y a pas de faute de vos soins conoissant votre affection pour moi. Je vous prie de me les continuer et d'etre persuadé du sincere attachement avec lequel je suis mon tres cher frere et ma tres chere sœur

Votre tres humble et tres obeissant serviteur

N.S.

[tear] l'honeur de saluer tres humblement Me[4] votre mere Mr[5] vos freres et votre bonne sœur [tear] pieuse.

[1] Probably because of the recrudescense of anti-Jansenist activity in Rome and in France after publication of the acts of the Lateran Council (1725).
[2] This letter is lacking from the present collection.
[3] About this time DMV's relative M. de Launay went bankrupt, as will be seen from the next few letters in this correspondence.
[4] "Madame"
[5] "Mr" for "Messieurs"

35. DMV to his Sister Olivier

Le 17e fevr. 1727

Je me mettois en devoir Ma tres chere sœur de repondre a votre paquet du 19 du mois passe que j'ai receu en son tems lorsque j'ai receu a l'ouverture de votre lettre du 9e du present mois la triste nouvelle de la mort de notre chere tante. Elle est passee bien viste a une meilleure vie car je n'avois pas appris qu'elle eust aucune nouvelle indisposition. Ma cousine est sans doutte dans une grande affliction, nous la partageons avec elle mais cela ne la soulage pas. et cette perte est venue la frapper dans une facheuse circonstance dans le tems d'une maladie considerable dont elle n'etoit pas remise. Vous me marquez quelle est retombée malade d'une fluxion de poitrine et vous ne dittes pas s'il n'y a point de danger. Cela ne laisse pas de m'inquieter. Je vous suis obligé de tous les souhaits avantageux que vous me faites. A l'egard de mon cher neveu quoi qu'il paroisse encore foible il faut l'encourager a bien faire le reste de cette année. S'il peut devenir un peu fort dans cette classe, Il n'aura plus de peine dans//le reste de ses etudes. Je prie Dieu qui lui a donne la bonne volonte de lui donner la facilité pour la faire valoir. J'ai bien de la joie que ma plus petitte niece se fortifie et aprene a ecrire. Je vous prie de faire payer exactement les loyers car je souffre beaucoup des retardemens apres les pertes de la banqueroute de Delaunai [de Launay] et des appartemens vacans. Je me recommande a vos prieres et suis Votre etc.

N.S.

36. DMV to his Brother-in-law Olivier

Le 6e fevrier 1728

Je suis tres sensible mon tres cher frere a l'amitié que vous me marquez dans la letre que j'ai receue de vous. Rien ne me fait plus de plaisir que d'apprendre de vos nouvelles, et M. Tremblai lorsqu'il m'ecrit ne manque pas de me donner cette satisfaction mais cela me fait tout un autre plaisir lorsque je recois par vous meme des temoignages de votre souvenir. J'ai ete souvent prest a vous ecrire mais des affaires impreveues, des voiages ou des infirmités men ont oté ou le tems ou le moyen.

Je suis souvent attaque de maux de teste qui m'empechent de m'appliquer a ecrire. grace a Dieu jen suis bien soulagé par une saignée que je me suis fait faire il y a quelque tems. J'ai bien de la joye d'apprendre que toutte//votre famille est en bonne santé et que Manon se fortifie apres avoir ete si infirme. Quoi que mon neveu soit foible dans sa classe il ne faut point perdre esperance du succes et attendre tout de son assiduité au travail et de la benediction de Dieu. Il est bon de l'encourager. J'ai la consolation d'apprendre qu'il fait ce qu'il peut et qu'il est d'une conduite sage et reglée. Son ancien regent M. Dupuis m'en a ecrit depuis peu en ces termes. Je ne connois pas le regent qu'il a presentement mais j'ecrirai a M. Dupuis pour le prier de le lui recommander.

C'est une chose facheuse pour moi que la banqueroute que le Sr Delaunai [de Launay] nous a fait et les frais inutiles que l'on a fait en consequence pour eviter ces inconveniens. Je vous prie davoir attention de ne pas laisser accumuler loiers sur loyers de peur que les gens ne souffrent et ne devienent insolvables. Continuez je vous prie vos bons soins//pour mes affaires. Je suis bien oblige a M. Poisot de son souvenir. Faites lui en mes remerciemens. Je me recommande a vos prieres et suis avec l'affection la plus sincere

Mon tres cher frere/Votre tres humble et tres obeissant serviteur

N.S.

37. DMV to his Sister Olivier

Le 6e fevrier 1728

Il est vrai Ma tres chere sœur qu'il y a long tems que je ne me suis donné la consolation de vous ecrire et je suis tres sensible à l'amitie qui vous porte a vous en plaindre. Je rens raison de ce retardement dans la lettre que jecris a mon frere. J'espere que ma santé qui est un peu meilleure me donnera moien detre plus exact a entretenir un commerce qui m'est si doux. J'ai receu un peu tard la letre que ma niece m'a ecrite vers la fin de l'année passée, je lui ai fait reponse par ma cousine qui m'avoit fait tenir la letre. Je crois, quoi que je n'en aye pas de nouvelle quelle aura ete rendue. Je prie notre Seigneur de vous combler//dans cette nouvelle année de ses benedictions et en particulier de benir les efforts que fait mon cher neveu pour se rendre digne de vos soins et repondre a vos desirs. La bonne conduite doit vous consoler du peu de succes qu'ont eu jusqu'ici ses etudes. Puisque son repetiteur qui est honneste homme et habile vous exhorte d'avoir patience et qu'il vous fait esperer que la facilite poura venir il faut patienter et donner toujours bon courage a l'etudiant. Il n'est pas necessaire que tous les hommes soient docteurs, ni qu'ils aient le meme degre de science, les etudes sont toujours utiles a tout. Elles ouvrent lesprit rendent laborieux et capable d'application pourveu qu'on supporte de bon cœur comme il paroist qu'il fait; on doit attendre le reste de Dieu. Le principal qui ne peut pas se suppleer, c'est la piete Dieu soit beni de ce qu'il lui fait la grace de s'y porter.//J'ai ete bien aise d'apprendre des nouvelles de mon cousin Treteau, je ne savois pas qu'il fut[1] a Paris. Je ferai reponse a son billet un autre jour car je n'ai pas le tems aujourdhui.

Je vous prie de recommander a mon frere le soin de mes affaires et de me conserver une part dans votre amitie et dans vos prieres et de croire que je suis avec un attachement inviolable en NSJC.[2]

Ma tres chere sœur/Votre tres humble et tres obeissant serviteur

N.S.

[1] "fût"
[2] "Notre Seigneur Jésus Christ"

38. DMV to his Sister Olivier

Le 11e mars 1729

Si je repons tard Ma tres chere sœur a votre letre ce nest pas par oubli ni par negligence, mais les affaires impreveues et quelque voiage que jai ete oblige de faire non obstant la rigueur de la saison m'en ont oté le tems lorsque je voulois suivre en cela mon inclination. C'est sans doutte un grand embaras qu'une maladie aussi dangereuse que celle qu'a eue ma chere niece Manon. Vous avez agi prudemment de fermer la communication a l'air contagieux de la petitte verole, dont mon cher frere qui na jamais eu ce mal auroit ete plus susceptible. Dieu soit beni d'avoir par sa misericorde preservé le chef de votre famille, et gueri cette bonne enfant. J'espere que cette maladie aura emporte ses autres infirmités et que comme elle est douce et docile elle vous donnera bien de//la satisfaction.

Presentement que vous etes delivrée de cet embaras, ayez donc soin de votre santé car mon frere se plaint que vous vous fatiguez trop par la peine que vous vous donnez dans votre menage. L'attention et la vigilance sur le menage est deja un assez grand travail. Vous devez vous faire soulager dans le reste.

Puisque le repetiteur rend bon temoignage a mon neveu et que sa conduite est toujours bonne il faut etre content. Il seroit bon qu'il fit sa philosophie. Cela forme lesprit et n'est point inutile quelqu'etat qu'on embrasse. Ce n'est meme qu'apres la philosophie qu'on est capable de choisir un etat. Les commencemens en sont epineux et difficiles. s'il a un bon repetiteur il surmontera ces difficultés, et trouvera plus de goust dans sa seconde année dont les matieres//sont plus agreables. Continuez a m'aimer et a me secourir de vos prieres aupres de Dieu et soiez persuadée qu'on ne peut etre avec une plus sincere affection que Je suis ma tres chere sœur

Votre tres humble et tres obeissant serviteur

N.S.

39. DMV to his Brother-in-law Olivier

Le 11ᵉ mars 1729

Je suis tres sensible Mon tres cher frere au temoignage annuel que vous m'avez donné de votre amitie. Je nai pas manqué de renouveller avec une plus grande ardeur au commencement de cette année, les vœux que j'offre tous les jours au Seigneur pour vous et pour toutte notre famille afin d'obtenir de sa misericorde qu'il vous comble de ses graces, et qu'il vous conduise dans la voye qui menne au veritable bonheur.

Les reproches que vous me faites sur la rarete de mes letres me sont tres agreables puisque c'est une preuve de votre sincere amitié. Soiez persuade que si mes letres vous font plaisir, je n'en ai pas mois[1] a recevoir les votres. Et je vous promets que j'aurai soin de menager le tems, qui s'envole avec une extreme rapidité, pour vous donner de tems en tems de mes nouvelles. Quoique//je ne manque pas touttes les fois que j'ecris a M. Tremblai de le prier de vous assurer de mon invoilable attachement. Ce monsieur a soin de me rendre compte de l'application que vous avez a veiller a mes affaires domestiques. Je vous en suis tres obligé.

J'ai bien de la consolation d'apprendre la satisfaction que vous donne vos enfans et surtout ma chere niece marie anne; il est vrai qu'elle est en age detre pourveue et puisque Dieu l'appelle a l'Etat du mariage J'ai bien de la joie que vous ayez des veues pour lui procurer un parti avantageux. Je prie Dieu de verser ses benedictions sur vos bons desseins, afin qu'ayant trouvé un mari selon le cœur de Dieu elle puisse se sanctifier dans cet etat.

Je rends graces a Dieu de ce qu'Olivier continue a se conduire sagement dans un age qui est expose a bien des perils. Cest le principal;//pour les etudes lorsqu'il fait ce qu'il peut et qu'il employe bien son tems on a lieu detre content. Letude nest pas inutile quoi qu'on n'y fasse pas les progres qu'on pouvoit desirer. Pourveu qu'il ne se degoute pas, en continuant a s'appliquer il poura avec le tems aquerir plus de facilité.

J'ai appris que Manon a eu la petitte verole et que Dieu la conservée, et quelle est guerie de cette dangereuse maladie, qui servira a ce que jespere a afermir sa sante et a la delivrer de ses autres infirmités.

Continuez mon tres cher frere a m'aimer et croyez qu'on ne peut etre plus parfaitement que je suis/Mon tres cher frere/Votre tres humble et tres obeissant/serviteur

N.S.

Voici un mot de letre que je vous prie de faire rendre a mon cousin Treteau. Il m'avoit envoye une addresse mais de peur qu'il n'ait change de demeure, je vous l'envoye.[2]

---

[1] "mois" for "moins"
[2] This note to Treteau is lacking from the present collection.

40. DMV to his Brother-in-law Olivier

Le 19e Sept. 1729

Connoissant vôtre bon cœur Mon tres cher frere et votre amitié pour moi, Je me reposerois survos bons soins pour mes affaires et ne croirois pas necessaire de vous en ecrire, si mes besoins ne me pressoient pas de le faire. Je vous prie de considerer que nous touchons au commencement d'octobre et je n'entends point encore parler du quartier qui devoit etre payé au commencement de Juillet, cependant j'ai une pension a payer. Mr. Trem[1] m'avoit fait entendre que Je le recevrois au mois d'aoust mais j'apprends par une lettre du 7e de ce mois que ce monsieur est allé a la campagne pour un mois voyez ou cela nous rejette. Vous savez ce que le retardement des payemens de Launai nous a couté. Je me recommande donc a vos bons soins. Vous priant si M. Trem na pas encore receu ce terme de le lui donner aussitost qu'il sera de retour. Ma santé par la grace de Dieu est aussi bonne qu'elle a ete depuis longtems. Je ne cesse de prier Dieu pour vous et pour votre famille que je salue de tout mon cœur particulierement ma tres chere sœur. Je suis tres affectueusement Mon tres cher frere/Votre tres humble et tres obeissant/serviteur

N.S.

---

[1] "Tremblay"

41. DMV to his Sister Olivier

Le 3e mars 1730

Je vous suis tres sensiblement oblige ma tres chere sœur des bons souhaits que vous avez faits en ma faveur au commencement de cette année, et de l'interrest que vous voulez bien prendre a ma santé. Elle est presentement assez bonne graces a Dieu au commencement de l'hiver j'ai eu une fievre un peu opiniatre mais comme elle etoit petitte elle ne ma pas affoibli, apres quelques mois je lai chassée avec le quinquina, qui nest gueres a la mode en ce pais.

J'ai bien de la joye dapprendre que vous vous portez bien. Je prie Dieu de conserver votre sante qui est si necessaire à votre famille. Je prie Dieu de repandre les benedictions sur les soins que vous vous donnez pour elever et etablir vos enfans. Je souhaite que vous reussissiez d'une maniere utile pour leur salut, et le votre. Dieu est un bon pere. Il nya qu'a metre sa confiance en lui, et il fera naitre les occasions les plus favorables.[1] Je me recommande a vos prieres et suis avec un veritable attachement.

Ma tres chere sœur/Votre humble et obeissant/servit.[2]

N.S.

---

[1] Echo of Rom. vii:26.
[2] "serviteur"

42. DMV to his Brother-in-law Olivier

Le 3e mars 1730

Je suis tres sensible Mon tres cher frere aux temoignages d'amitié que vous me donnez dans votre letre que j'ai receue a la fin de Janvier, mais je n'ai pu trouver qu'aujourd'hui le tems dy faire reponse. Je vous prie d'etre assuré que je ne vous oublie point et que l'absense quoi que longue n'affoiblit en aucune maniere la tendre amitié que j'ai pour vous et pour toutte votre famille. Si je ne vous en donne point plus souvent des marques par mes letres ce n'est que de peur de vous causer de la depense et de l'embaras. Je ne cesse point de prier dieu qu'il repande ses benedictions sur vos travaux et qu'il veuille bien vous inspirer ce que vous devez faire pour l'Etablissement de vos enfans.

Je vous suis tres oblige du soin que vous prenez de mes affaires. Je vous prie de continuer. Les quartiers[1] retardent bien je n'ai pas encore//entendu parle de celui echu le 1er janvier. Je crois qu'il ny a pas de faute de diligence de votre part, mais ces retardemens sont toujours facheux car cest par la que la banqueroute de Delaunai [de Launay] est venue, et etant aussi a l'etroit que je suis, Je n'ai pas besoin de perte. Car je crois que vous savez bien que je n'ai aucun secours ici, et que l'argent venant de France diminue de moitié lorsqu'on le recoit ici ou tout est extrememement cher. Je me confie sur vos bons soins et suis avec un attachement inviolable

Mon tres cher frere/Votre tres humble et obeissant serviteur

N.S.

[1] Quarter-rents were income on investments payable 4 times a year: December, March, June and September. Frequently these terms bore the name of important religious feast-days that fell on or near the duedate, thus: Noël (25 December), l'Annonciation (25 March), St. Jean (24 June) and St. Michel (29 September).

43. DMV to his Brother-in-law Olivier

Le 2 fevrier. 1731

Je suis fort sensible Mon tres cher frere aux temoignages d'amitié que vous me donnez au commencement de cette année et aux souhaits favorables que vous faites pour moi: vous etes bien persuadé comme je crois que de mon coté je ne cesse de demander a Dieu qu'il vous comble de ses benedictions vous et toutte votre famille n'ayant rien plus a cœur que votre sanctification.

Vous m'annoncez une affaire importante que vous avez conclue et achevée. C'est le mariage de ma chere niece. Il paroist par tout ce que vous men dites et par le caractere du mari tels que vous me le representez que vous avez serieusement examiné touttes les circonstances de cette affaire afin que votre fille puisse etre heureuse dans cet engagement. Je ne doutte pas que vous n'aiez porte votre principale attention sur l'esprit de religion et de piete qui pouvoit paroitre dans cette persone car c'est la le fondement de tout edifice chretien; et ce qui peut rendre un mariage vraiment heureux. Je prie Dieu de repandre les graces sur ces 2 epoux afin qu'ils travaillent a se sanctifier, eux et la famille qu'il plaira a Dieu de leur donner.

Il est vrai que les quartiers viennent un peu tard comme vous le remarquez dans votre letre. Mais je suis persuade que vous faites de votre mieux. Je vous remercie des soins//que vous vous donnez pour cela. Je vous prie de me les continuer et de croire qu'on ne peut etre plus sincerement

Mon tres cher frere Votre tres humb. et tres obeiss. serv.[1]

N.S.

Je vous prie de faire tenir ce mot de lettre au cousin Treteau.[2] Il mavoit envoyé son addresse mais depuis ce tems la je crains qu'il n'ait change de logis et que ma letre ne fut[3] perdue.

[1] "très humble et très obéissant serviteur"
[2] This note is lacking from the present correspondence.
[3] "fût"

44. DMV to his Brother-in-law Olivier

Le 24 nov. 1731

Je vous felicite Mon tres cher frere de votre nouvelle qualite de grand pere. Vous m'apprenez que la petite fille et sa mere se portent parfaitement bien. J'en rends graces a Dieu de tout mon cœur et le prie de verser ses benedictions et ses graces sur les deux familles et faire la grace a ma niece d'elever cet enfant dans la crainte et l'amour de Dieu afin quelle le serve chretienement et saintement. Vous ne pouviez me faire plus de plaisir que de me mander cette bonne nouvelle en detail, puis que je m'interresse tres particulierement a tout ce qui touche votre chere famille.

En recevant votre letre j'ai aussi receu le quartier de la St. Jean.[1] Il a un peu tardé mais c'est l'absence de M. Tremblai qui en a ete cause. Je compte que le quartier du 1er octob. suivra bientost. Je vous aurois fait plustost reponse mais pour ne vous point charger de ports de letres j'ai voulu attendre qu'j'eusse occasion d'ecrire a M. Tremblai. Je salue tres affectueusement ma chere sœur, ma niece, son mari et toutte votre//famille et suis avec un sincere attchement

Mon tres chere frere Votre tres humble et tres/obeissant serviteur

N.S.

---

[1] Religious feast the 24th of June, commonly used to indicate the second quarter of the fiscal year.

45. DMV to his Brother-in-law Olivier

Le 4e fevrier 1732

Je vous suis obligé Mon tres cher frere des temoignages de votre souvenir et de votre amitié que vous me donnez dans le paquet que vous m'avez addresse et que j'ai receu sur la fin du mois dernier. J'y apprends avec Joye que vous et votre famille etes en bonne santé. J'ai soin de m'en informer touttes les fois que j'ecris a M. Tremblai et il ne manque pas de m'en rendre compte tous les 3 mois en m'envoyant mon contingent comme il a fait a la fin de l'année derniere. Soiez persuade que je vous ai toujours a l'esprit et dans le cœur et que je vous presente souvent a Dieu au Saint autel afin qu'il verse sur vous les abondantes benedictions et qu'il vous fasse la grace de le servir sans que l'embarras des affaires vous fasse jamais negliger l'affaire qui est la seule necessaire et a laquelle touttes les autres doivent se rapporter.

Je suis bien aise que vous ayez mis votre seconde fille en pension chez les filles de la croix de Ruel [Rueil] pour la disposer a faire saintement sa premiere communion. Je prie dieu de lui faire la grace de//se disposer si bien a une action si importante que ce soit pour elle une source de grace dont elle puisse gouter les fruits tout le reste de sa vie. Je vous addresse le paquet pour mon neveu et ma niece Monslafere [Mons. La Fère][1] parce que j'ai egaré leur addresse mais comme vous les voiez souvent il vous sera facile de le leur remettre. Je vous demande la continuation de votre amitie et la continuation de vos bons soins pour mes affaires et suis tres parfaitement

Mon tres cher frere/Votre tres humble et tres obeissant serviteur

N.S.

Voici un mot de letre que je vous prie de faire tenir au cousin Treteau[2]

---

[1] An example of 18th century polite usage; though both husband and wife are intended, only the husband's title is used.
[2] This insert is lacking from the present collection.

46. DMV to his Brother-in-law Olivier

Le 29. Janvier 1733

Il n'y a que peu de Jours mon tres cher frere que j'ai receu votre paquet datté du 1er du mois. Ainsi n'attribuez pas le retardement de ma reponse a aucune negligence. Je n'ai pas de plus grand plaisir que de recevoir de vos letres et d'y repondre; mais les letres doivent passer par diverses mains avant que d'etre mises a la poste. C'est ce qui cause le retardement.

Les pensées sur la mort que j'ai recues dans votre letre m'edifient fort, c'est la pensée la plus utile qu'un chretien puisse avoir, puis que comme dit le sage si nous pensions toujours a notre derniere fin ce seroit un excellent preservatif pour nous garantir du peché.[1] Car lors qu'on fait reflexion au suites de la mort et a l'incertitude de ce moment decisif rien n'est plus capable de nous detacher de l'amour des biens perissables. J'ai eté fort touché de la mort de votre bonne mere. A l'age de soixante et dix neuf ans, il n'y a rien de surprenant; c'est un age qu'on ne passe guerre et qu'on atteint rarement. Mais elle etoit dun excellent temperamment et etoit encore forte pour son age puis qu'on dit quelle alloit encore de son pied voir votre sœur religieuse a l'autre bout de Paris. Mais une mort si subite dans l'espace d'une demie heure ou vous n'avez pas eu le tems de receuillir ses derniers soupirs est ce qui frappe le plus. Cependant comme elle avoit beaucoup de pieté, quelle revenoit alors de l'Eglise ou elle etoit tres assidue il y a lieu de croire que sa mort n'a pas ete impreveue et qu'elle s'y etoit bien preparée.//Je n'ai pas manqué aussitost que j'ai appris cette triste nouvelle de celebrer la Ste Messe pour le repos de son ame et de continuer souvent depuis.

J'ai bien de la joye d'apprendre que vous continuez a etre content de la conduitte de mon neveu votre fils; sil ne fait point un progrès aussi grand que vous le souhaiteriez on ne doit pas l'en blamer puis qu'il fait ce qu'il peut et qu'il employe bien son tems. Je vous remercie de tous les bons souhaits que vous faites en ma faveur de mon coté je prie Dieu sans cesse de vous combler de ses graces et de ses benedictions, et de vous conserver une santé qui est si necessaire a votre famille. Au reste il en est le pere encore plus que vous ainsi on doit avoir une grande confiance dans sa bonte paternelle.[2] Je suis avec un tendre attachement

Mon tres cher frere/Votre tres humble et tres obeissant serviteur.

N.S.

[1] Cf. Ecclesiasticus ii, et seq.
[2] Souvenir of Rom iv:16.

47. DMV to his Sister Olivier

Le 21 Dec. 1733

Il y a trop longtems Ma tres chere sœur que je dois une reponse a la letre que vous mavez ecrite au sortir de l'embaras d'un demenagement et d'un perilleux emmenagement preste a vous aller delasser a votre maison de campagne. Comme cette absence interrompt ordinairement notre commerce reciproque de litre[1] par la difficulte de la correspondance, j'ai attendu le retour et insensiblement cela m'a conduit à aujourdhui. Je n'alleguerai pas mon demenagement car il est bien different du votre,[2] il est vrai d'un coté que vous demeurez ou vous voulez, mais non pas moi premiere difference, de l'autre coté votre demanagement entraine de grands embarras, le mien n'en donne qu'un fort petit. Mais enfin il faut s'arranger dans son petit lieu, faire connoissance avec ses nouveaux hostes. Mais le grand empechement ce sont les affaires continuelles et desagreables qui m'assiegent et ne me laissent jouir d'aucun repos d'esprit, affaires dont je n'apperçois point la fin, meme dans le plus grand eloignement ou la veue humaine puisse s'etendre. Ne croyez pas que ce que je vous dis là ait aucun rapport a la fable qu'on vous a contée que j'allois prendre la place de mon defunt ami.[3] Les gens les moins instruits de ce qui se passe ici ont coutume de vous aller conter leurs songes; mais vous ferez bien de n'y faire point de fond. Le fait est que le defunt ne m'a legé que les plus tristes de ses affaires et celles qui l'ont tué, il en seroit arivé autant de moi si Dieu ne m'avoit pas assisté. Mais mon cœur est presentement un peu plus au large qu'il n'etoit, mais ce n'est qu'un peu car je regrette encore souvent les bois de l'amerique.[4] Mais dans cet état d'ennui, devineriez vous bien la tentation que j'ai eue a combattre? des personnes puissantes et respectables me sont venu offrir de m'ouvrir une porte pour retourner en France en me sollicitant vivement d'accepter ce parti. Je leur ai avoué que je ne souhaitais rien tant que de sortir d'ici, mais que ce ne seroit jamais, Dieu aidant, par une porte ou il faudroit laisser sa conscience et son honeur.[5] La negotiation a fini par des reproches tres durs qu'il ma fallu essuier etc. Je vous assure d'une chose que depuis six mois que les grands assauts durent je n'ai pas eu un moment ou j'aie eu tant de joye que j'en ai a present ou j'ai le tems et le plaisir de repandre mon cœur dans le votre. Car la moindre et la moins difficile de mes affaires a ete cette ridicule negotiation qu'il a fallu traiter bien serieusement a cause du respect du aux negotiateurs. que de reflexions tristes inquietantes, que de letres mesurées il a fallu ecrire! Vous jugez bien que ceci ne doit point etre communiqué. Parlons maintenant d'autre chose. Vous avez trouvé un nouveau monde a votre campagne. Etes vous bien// contente de ces nouveaux voisins? Pour moi j'ai receu depuis peu l'affligeante nouvelle que Le mouton est serieusement malade, il me l'ecrit lui meme en me disant aDieu jusqu'au jour de l'eternité. Vous savez combien est grande et sensible pour moi une telle perte. Je le recommande a vos prieres. Pour ce qui est de ma santé je vous en ai parlé pour ce qui regarde l'esprit qui a bien ete en convulsion et qui y est encore mais pour le corps qui en a fort senti le contre coup, cela va mieux presentement, peu de ressentiment de fievre, les maux de teste moins frequens, j'en attribue la 1ere cause a Dieu qui ne nous charge pas au dessus de nos forces,[6] la cause 2e est peutetre la meme qui fait quelque fois qu'une grande frayeur fait perdre la fievre. Donnez moi s'il vous plaist des nouvelles de votre sante. J'aurai une grande inquietude de moins, pourveu que j'apprenne comme je le souhaite qu'elle soit bonne. Voici un petit mot pour M. Votre mari.[7]

Je suis etc.

N.S.

---

[1] "lettres"

[2] Allusion to DMV's recent removal to the Orvalist house at Rijnwijk.

[3] At the time of Barchman's death, rumours were rife that DMV would succeed him as Archbishop of the schismatic church at Utrecht.

[4] Curious, but enlightening remark about DMV's missionary career in his "voyage de Mississippi" (1713-1718).

[5] With the virtual end (in September 1732) of public discussion and scandal resulting from official persecution of Jansenism in France, DMV would have been able, on condition of certain accommodating statements and gestures, to return to Paris and his family. But his intransigence was such that he would not perform merely perfunctory acts and so remained in Holland where, after the failure of his talks with the French and Portuguese ambassadors at Zeist (15-16.xi.1733), he received word of his excommunication.

[6] Echo of Rom. viii.

[7] This enclosure is lacking from the present collection.

48. DMV to his Brother-in-law Olivier

Le 7e de mars 1734

La multitude des mes affaires m'ont empesche mon tres cher frere de vous remercier plustost des marques d'amitie que vous m'avez données au commencement de l'année par vos lettres et celles de votre famille. Votre lettre ma[1] édifié parce que elle me fait connoitre que vous vous occupez des pensées de l'eternite d'une maniere particuliere. C'est en effect l'essentiel et le moien d'attirer la benediction de Dieu qui nous ordone de chercher premierement le roiaume de Dieu, nous promettant que le reste nous sera donne par surcroist.[2] Ce 10e dernier et les reparations dont vous me parlez m'incommoderont, car vous savez sans doutte que je n'ai rien autre chose pour subsister que ce que vous m'envoyez. Mais il faut se soumettre aus ordres de Dieu. Je vous suis toujours bien oblige des soins que vous continuez a prendre de nos affaires. Je rends graces a Dieu de ce qu'il inspire une bonne conduite a votre fils, puis qu'il travaille selon ses talens vous avez lieu detre content, on ne doit pas demander des personnes plus quelles[3] ne peuvent. Si Manon est docile, obeissante, et pieuse il faut lui pardonner sa vivacité M. Olivier.//Cela se changera en bien avec l'age et les bons soins de sa mere. Je vous recommande tous les jours a Dieu et toutte votre famille. Je suis bien obligé a M. Bizot et son souvenir, je vous prie de l'assurer de mon estime singuliere. Je me recommande a ses prieres et suis avec un attachement inviolable

Mon tres cher frere/votre tres humble et tres obeissant serviteur

N.S.

[1] "ma" for "m'a"

[2] Cf. Matt vi, 33.

[3] "quelles" for "qu'elles"

49. Last Will and Testament: DMV

Minuté sur un sceau de cinq florins	Seal
G. C. Qualenbrinck	Province
NotE. Publ.[1]	Utrecht

Par devant moy, George Chrestien Qualenbrinck, Notaire de la Cour de Justice de la Province d'Utrecht,[2] demeurant à Utrecht, et admis à l'exercice du Notariat par Le venerable Magistral de cette Ville, en présence des temoins sousnommez, Comparut en propre Personne, Monsieur Marie Dominique Varlet François, Evesque de Babilone, demeurant à present à Schonauwen[3] dans cette Province, connû auz temoins sousnommez, étant sain de corps et d'esprit, Lequel, voulant disposer de ses Biens temporels en vertu d'un Octroy de la susdite Cour du 5e de ce mois, a declaré et declare par ces presentes de Laisser ses Biens patrimoniaux, qui sont en France, à ses Heritiers naturels; Et quant aux effets Mobiliers qui sont en ce Paÿs ici, tant à Schonauwen qu'à Rynwyck,[4] Livres, meubles, argent monnoié, et non-monnoié, Il Legue tout à Monsr d'Ettemar [Etemar], Ecclesiastique, demeurant à Paris, et à Monsr Willemaers l'ainé, demeurant à Amersfort,[5] substituant Le Survivant à L'autre en cas de mort de L'un des deux; De plus Le Testateur//nomme pour Executeur de ce Testament Monsieur Devilliers, François, demeurant presentement à Utrecht. Enfin Monsr. le Testateur charge ses dits Legataires de payer ses dettes, qui se trouveront a l'heure de sa mort, et aussi qu'ils Aÿent soin de payer les frais de L'enterrement. Enfin Monsieur Le Testateur a declaré que tout ce qui est ecrit cy-dessus est sa derniere volonté, Laquelle il veut que subsiste et sortisse son plein effêt apres sa mort, soit comme Testament, Codicile ou telle autre disposition, selon qu'elle puisse Le mieux valoir; aussi fait et passé à Schonauwen en presence de Messieurs Jacques Jubé de La Cour et Martin Baudrier dit Ferrand, comme temoins de foy et d'age competent, qui ont signé La Minute de ces presentes avec Monsieur Le Testateur, et moÿ Notaire ensemble, dans mon Prothocol L'onzieme de Mars l'an Mille sept cent trente quatre, Le matin environ huit heures.

Quod attestor
GC Qualenbrinck
Note. Publ.

Nous, Grand Bailliff Bourguemaitres//et Echevin de La Ville d'Utregt, Certifions que George Chrestien Qualenbrinck, qui a signé l'acte cy-dessus, est Notaire publicq, admis par la Cour Provinciale d'Utrecht, demeurant dans cette ville, et admis à l'exercice du Notariat par le Venerable Magistrat de cette Ville. Et que foÿ doit ettre attribuée à tous les actes qui sont passées devant lui et deux temoins. Et qu'ici en Ville ne réside ni Ambassadeur ni aucun autre Ministre de sa Majesté le Roÿ de France. En foÿ de quoÿ nous avons fait mettre le Cachet de cette Ville et signer par notre Secretaire, le 1e août 1742.

T. Beeldsnyder Matroos.

SEAL
CITY OF
UTRECHT

[1] "Notaire public". Under the accompanying seal there is written in another hand in Dutch: Senden.
[2] Utrecht: Provincial capital, Bishopric, and university city in Central Holland on the Old Rhine, some 22 miles SSE of Amsterdam.
[3] Schonhauwen: the second ward of the city of Utrecht, site of a Carthusian House frequented by DMV from 1727 to 1733.
[4] Rynwyck (Rijnwick) town some 12 miles SE of Utrecht on the Old Rhine, site of a Cistercian foundation frequented by DMV after 1733.
[5] Amersfoort town some 10 miles N of Utrecht, seat of an Old Catholic seminary whose documents are now to be found in the Rijksarchief at Utrecht.

50. DMV to his Brother-in-law Olivier

Le 29e janv. 1736

Je n'ai receu Mon tres cher frere, votre letre qu'hier apres midi et j'irai demain lundi au matin chez le notaire pour faire expedier la nouvelle procuration conformement au modele que vous m'avez envoyé, dont je vous suis fort obligé. Il est vrai que j'aurois du vous demander ce modele d'abord, mais je croiois les notaires de ce païs ci plus habiles qu'ils ne le sont, d'ailleurs M. Tremblai m'avertit si brusquement l'été dernier qu'il ne vouloit plus etre mon procureur sans me dire alors qu'il signeroit encore pendant quelque tems les quittances que je crus qu'il ny avoit pas un moment a perdre pour envoyer une nouvelle procuration. Je tacherai que cette derniere procuration soit en etat de partir avec ce paquet. J'ai bien de la joye que vous ayez fait affaire avec M. Tremblai pour le remboursement de la rente que je lui payois. Si je ne vous l'ai pas proposé plus tost cest que j'avois lieu de douter que vous fussiez disposé a la faire, parce que je sais que les persones de votre profession ont besoin d'argent comptant et vous ne pouviez pas ignorer que je payais encore ma part d'une rente dont notre maison a toujours ete chargée depuis le jour que nos pere et mere en ont fait laquisition, ainsi je pensais que s'il vous est convenu d'en faire le remboursement vous me l'auriez declaré. D'autant plus que vous ne pouviez douter que dans l'etat ou je suis n'ayant pour subsister que mon patrimoine dont vous connoissez la médiocrité, je ne fusse tout a fait hors d'etat de fournir une pareille finance.//Je ne vous amuse de touttes ces reflexions que pour vous assurer que je suis comme j'ai toujours eté disposé a vous faire tous les plaisirs dont je suis capable. Je viens de chez le notaire et lui ai donné votre modele aujourd'hui [illegible] lundi, il ma[1] promis de me donner aujourd'hui la procuration toutte légalisée pour partir ce soir par la poste.

Vous avez bien fait de prendre une maison de campagne pour vous delasser de votre travail, puisque vous etes sujet des douleurs de la goutte, Dieu le permet afin de faire penser de plus pres a la mort. J'espere cependant qu'il prolongera vos jours et je l'enprie pour le bien de votre famille qui a besoin de vous. Je suis content de votre fils. Il me paroist que son ecriture est meilleure que ci devant. il est sage mais il n'a pas de vivacité. Ce n'est pas sa faute, on ne doit demander de lui que ce qu'il peut. La bonne conduite que tient ma niece dans son menage ou elle a deja 4 enfants me fait plaisir. Mais il n'y a point dans cette vie ci de satisfaction sans croix. C'est pour son bien spirituel que Dieu la fait passer par les epreuves qu'elle a a souffrir. Je tacherai d'ecrire a ma sœur et a vos enfans. Ma santé pour le reste du corps est assez bonne; mais il y a pres d'un an que je suis attaqué d'une fistule a un œil; c'est ce qui a fait que je n'ai gueres ecrit l'année dernier. Cela va mieux depuis quelque tems quoi que je ne sois pas gueri apres avoir ete 6 mois de suite//dans les remedes ce qui a couté beaucoup comme vous pouvez le penser. Je vous prie de me continuer vos bons soins pour mes affaires et de me croire Mon tres cher frere

Votre tres humble et tres obeissant/Serviteur

N.S.

Voici les letres pour la famille que je vous prie de faire rendre a la famille.[2]

---

[1] "ma" for "m'a"
[2] These letters are lacking from the present collection.

51. Roquette to Antoine Olivier

a Rouen ce 6 Fevrier 1736

Je vous envoie, Monsieur, le paquet que j'ai recu hier, avec ma nouvelle procuration en forme. Le cachet vous paroitra entamé parce que la cire s'est colée d'une enveloppe sur l'autre, mais il ny a rien eu d'ouvert, et j'ai eté obligé dy laisser en cachet volant celui de mon enveloppe. J'espere être de retour à Paris pour le jour des cendres;[1] ainsi mon eloignement ne retardera point le paiement des rentes sur la ville, et l'arreté de vos comptes. Permettës moi de faire mes tres humbles complimens a Madame Olivier, et a Monsieur votre fils. Je suis tres parfaittement, et avec respect

Monsieur/Votre tres humble et tres obeissant serviteur

S/de Roquette

[1] "Mercredi des cendres" or Ash Wednesday, the beginning of Lent.

52. DMV to his Brother-in-law Olivier

Le 9 fevr. 1737

Je suis toujours tres sensible Mon tres cher frere aux temoignages de votre amitie qui m'est tres chere. Ma sante est assez bonne, a l'exception des yeux dont je suis fort incommodé. J'ai, comme je crois vous lavoir ecrit une fistule a l'œil gauche depuis deux ans. J'ai ete pour ce mal longtems entre les mains des medecins ce qui m'a beaucoup couté et le mal a resisté a tous les remedes en sorte que j'ai pris le parti de ne plus rien y faire que pour adoucir un peu le mal sans esperance de guerison et de prendre patience; je ne laisse pas de travailler tout doucement, ce qui ny[1] fait pas de bien, mais on ne peut pas demeurer a rien faire et il faut servir l'Eglise selon son pouvoir. Je vous ai envoyé lannée passée des fruits de mon travail. vous devez avoir receu depuis peu un autre ouvrage de moi moindre que le premier mais pas moins important.[2] Vous avez bien fait de prendre une petite maison a la campagne pour votre sante qui en a besoin.

Je souhaiterois que votre gendre vous donnat plus de satisfaction, j'espere que la patience et la douceur de sa femme le gagnera.

Pour votre fils vous devez en etre content quoiqu'il ne seconde pas tout a fait votre ardeur pour son avancement. Vous devez etre persuadé qu'il fait ce qu'il peut. et vous etes trop equitable pour lui demander rien qui soit au dessus de ses forces. Je vous prie d'assurer M. l'abbé [hole] de mon estime et de la reconnoissance que j'ai de son souvenir. Voici des lettres pour toutte votre famille.[3] Je prie Dieu de vous combler de ses graces et de vous faire reussir dans touttes vos entreprises — autant que ce sera pour sa gloire, en sorte que le soin des affaires temporelles ne vous fasse pas perdre de veue les eternelles. Je suis avec un tendre attachement dans l'amour de notre Seigneur

Mon cher frere/Votre tres humble et tres obeissant/Serviteur

N.S.

[1] "ny" for "n'y"

[2] The first is probably DMV's *Lettre... à Msgr l'évêque de Montpellier* (1736) about the condemnation of miracles supposedly performed in the cemetery of St-Médard on the tomb of archdeacon Pâris in 1727. The second is composed of three letters entitled *Réponse... à Msgr l'évêque de Senez*, dated 1736, published 1737, concerning anti-Jansenist activity in France following the suspension of Msgr Soanen, Bishop of Senez, by order of the Council of Embrun, called by Cardinal Tencin.

[3] These letters are lacking from the present collection.

53. DMV to his Sister Olivier

Le 16 fevrier 1737

C'est une grande consolation pour moi Ma tres chere sœur lors que je puis recevoir par vous meme des nouvelles de votre sante et des temoignages de votre souvenir et de votre amitié car dans le reste de l'année j'ai soin de m'en informer de M. l'abbé de R.[1] Il me paroist que Dieu vous conserve une assez bonne sante cest un grand tresor. La mienne est assez bonne de puis quelque tems graces à Dieu, a l'exception des yeux, dont je suis toujours incommodé depuis deux ans qu'il m'est venu une fistule a un œil. Mais c'est la volonte de Dieu, il faut s'y soumettre. Je vois avec action de grace que vous avez assez de satisfaction de vos enfans. votre fils se porte au bien. Il fait ce qu'il peut on ne doit pas lui en demander d'avantage. Votre fille ainée porte avec courage douceur et patience les difficultés de son menage et les peines qui s'y recontrent. Dieu est plus sage que nous, il a permis pour son bien qu'elle eut des degousts et des peines dans ce monde de peur qu'elle ny attachât son cœur. J'espere qu'a force de soufrir de recourir a Dieu dans la priere elle obtiendra quelque jour la conversion de son mari. Pour la plus jeune je me persuade que sous vos instructions elle est bien formée à la [hole]//

Je vais faire reponse a la letre qu'elle m'a ecrite.

Je n'entends point de nouvelle de ma cousine. Je lui ai ecrit bien des fois par l'addresse ordinaire sans recevoir de reponse. Ne la voyez vous pas quelque fois; si vous la voyez dites lui que je suis inquiet de son etat. J'ai apris par ma belle sœur (dont le fils est toujours malade) qu'on avoit ete obligé de faire a notre maison des reparations necessaires et que cela diminuera le quartier courant. Quoique cela me viene assez mal parce qu j'ai eté obligé de faire des depenses pour mes incommodites j'ai donné a un seul medecin cent cinquante francs. Mais enfin il faut se soumettre a la volonte de Dieu. Je le prie de tout mon cœur de vous combler de ses graces, et de vous faire croitre vous et votre famille de plus en plus dans son amour. Je suis

Ma tres chere sœur/Votre tres humble et tres obeissant/Serviteur

N.S.

[1] "Roquette"

54. DMV to his Brother-in-law Olivier

Le 22 fevrier 1737

Il y a peu de jours Mon tres cher frere que je vous ai ecrit et a toutte la famille. Voici l'occasion qui me porte a le faire encore aujourdhui. Il y a ici un de mes plus intimes amis qui a un neveu a paris, il voudroit lui faire prendre quelque connoissance des affaires. Pour cela M. l'abbé de Roquette a cru qu'on ne pouvait mieux faire que de le mettre pendant trois mois en pension chez vous pour travailler a votre etude; je vous prie de me faire l'amitie de le recevoir chez vous avec une pension aussi modique qu'il vous sera possible. Je crois que vous en serez content. Pendant le peu de tems que je l'ai vu il m'a paru fort sage et fort raisonnable. Comme il n'a pas beaucoup de tems a demeurer chez vous je vous prie de l'avancer autant qu'il sera possible. Je salue tres particulierement toutte votre famille et suis

Mon tres cher frere/Votre tres humble et tres obeissant/Serviteur

S/Dominique

55. DMV to his Sister Olivier

Le 16ᵉ juin 1737

J'ai receu depuis peu de tems Ma tres chere sœur votre letre du 23 avril. Elle a été longtems en chemin et n'est pas venu en poste aussi n'avez vous pas pretendu qu'elle vint par la post. Je repondra d'abord de cette derniere letre apres que je vous aurez dit que j'ai receu exactement la grosse letre du 3 avril dernier. Mais plusieurs voyages que j'ai faits m'ont oté le tems d'y repondre. Je vous suis tres obligé de l'avis que vous me donnez du remboursement de la dette d'Halluin.[1] Je suis tres disposé a recevoir le rembourcement tel que vous me le marquez. Je vais ecrire a la persone qui a ma procuration et qui doit etre revenu d'un long voyage qu'il a fait, afin qu'il consente en mon nom a tout ce qui sera necessaire. Mais ne faut il pas que je donne une procuration speciale pour cela. Il faudroit que mon beau frere en ce cas m'en envoyat un modele. Car les nottaires de ce pays ci ne sont pas fort habiles. et mon nottaire quoiqu'il soit advocat avoit si mal fait ma derniere procuration generalle qu'il a fallu la recommencer jusqu'a 3 fois avec les frais que vous pouvez juger. Cela me coutta 20 ou 25 francs. Il est vrai qu'on trouve rarement ce monsieur chez lui. Mais le nottaire chez qui il demeure recoit les paquets et les lui envoye quant a l'addresse dont vous me parlez. J'aurois ete inqiet de la maladie de ma sœur que vous m'apprenez si vous ne me marquiez qu'elle est hors d'affaire.

J'apprends par votre letre du 3 avril commencée le 3 mars que vous avez les deux ouvrages dont je vous ai fait present avec les deux letres que je vous ai ecrites.[2] J'etois en peine de ne point recevoir de reponse sur tout cela. Cela etoit cause que je n'ecri [hole] plus dans l'incertitude du succès. A l'egard de mon [hole] ne m'empeche pas decrire moi meme quoi que cela [hole] penible qu'auparavant. Mais je vois que vous etes [hole] incommodée de la vue que je ne le suis mais c'est un ma [hole]//

J'apprens encore que vous avez une autre grande incommodité qui vous empeche de m'ecrire si ce n'est avec bien de la difficulté, c'est un mal que vous avez au bras et un tremblement a la main droitte, qui provient d'une chute que vous avez faitte. Mais ma chere sœur ne pouriez vous pas lorsque vous ne pouvez m'ecrire prier la demoiselle qui vous rend mes letres, de m'ecrire en votre nom? Je sens bien que ce n'est pas la meme chose mais cela est toujours quelque chose dans le cas de l'impossibilité ou d'une grande difficulté. Je vois que Dieu vous eprouve par des croix de touttes sortes mais il vous fait la grace de vous soutenir par de grandes consolations. Votre grand livre c'est la croix de N.S.[3] et c'est un livre bien eloquent, qui dit tout au cœur de celui qui sait y lire. J'ai bien de la joye que vous ayez prevenu ma belle sœur pour l'engager a vous aller voir. Ces petits esprits ont besoin detre prevenus par des manieres polies, il faut avoir egard a leur foiblesse. Ce que vous me dittes de ma sœur et de son mari de leurs bonnes manieres me fait un tres sensible plaisir. Ma niece Marie anne est bien a plaindre et le seroit encore plus si elle n'avoit pas pere et mere. Je suis charmé autant que vous au moins de tout ce que vous avez la bonté de me raconter de mon grand neveu. Car pour ce brillant qui lui manque, et qui pouroit servir a satisfaire son pere, a quoi est il bon qu'a etre un sujet de tentation et un obstacle au vrai bien. Pour le petit il est bien a plaindre tant a cause de ses infirmites qu'a cause de la difficulté naturelle qu'il a a prononcer la langue. Cependant j'ai bien de la joye d'apprendre qu'on l'eleve tres chretienement, aussi bien que de ce que vous [hole] de la pieté solide du beaupere de ma belle sœur [hole] nsible a la peine que votre amitié vous a fait prendre [hole] tant de nouvelles les unes interressantes les autres [hole] assaisonnées de reflexions utiles et edifiantes.//Pour ce qui est de votre grande croix, il n'y a que Dieu qui puisse remedier a vos peines, vous vous etes jettée heureusement entre les bras d'un bon pere. Perseverez dans les sentimens que vous exprimez et soyez seure que vous ne presenterez pas inutilement a Dieu le sacrifice d'un cœur contrit et humilié et que ce bon pere ou vous delivrera de cette Epreuve, car il sait convertir a lui les cœurs qui en sont les plus eloignes, ou bien il addoucira cette croix par l'onction de sa grace, en sorte que vous direz comme St. Bernard,

Mon amertume est tres douce.[4] Je prie Dieu de mon cœur de vous faire la grace de sentir que tout coopere au bien spirituel et eternel des elus.

Je suis, etc.

N.S.

[1] Halluin, town in the north of France on the Belgian frontier (part of metropolitan Lille) where the family of Varlet (and probably his Jansenist inclinations) had their origins. Cf. his connections with the de Lannoys, formerly lords of nearby Roubaix.

[2] See no. 52 bove.

[3] "Notre Seigneur"

[4] St. Bernard, "Sermo Super Cantica Canticorum" in Migne, *Patrologia Latina* CLXXXIII 169. This work of devotional literature had a vast influence especially among religious contemplatives; cf. J. Leclercq, *The Love of Learning* (NY 1961) p. 15-17.

56. DMV to his Sister Olivier

Le 20 Juin 1737

Il n'y a que peu de tems Ma tres chere sœur que j'ai receu une letre de ma cousine mais qui etoit d'assez ancienne datte. Elle me mandoit que vous aviez ete dangereusement malade. Cette nouvelle m'auroit inquieté si elle ne m'eut marqué en meme tems que vous etiez hors d'affaire. Et comme il y a longtems que cela m'a ete ecrit, je compte que vous etes presentement entierement retablie. Jen rends graces a Dieu de tout mon cœur et le prie de vous conserver la santé et celle de mon beau frere qui est si necessaire a sa famille et dont les bons soins pour nos affaires communes nous sont si utiles. Ma cousine ma marqué aussi qu'on doit travailler le mois prochain a faire le remboursement de la rente d'halluin. J'ecris a M. l'abbé de R.[1] pour le prier de donner les mains en mon nom a tout ce que mon frere Olivier jugera a propos. Mais je vous prie de lui demander s'il n'est//point necessaire que j'envoye pour cela une procuration speciale en cas que cela fut necessaire, je prie mon frere de m'en envoyer le modele a cause du peu d'habilete de nos nottaires. Je prie Dieu de vous combler vous ma tres chere sœur mon frere et toutte votre famille de ses plus precieuses benedictions et suis

Votre etc

N.S.

[1] "Roquette"

57. DMV to his Brother-in-law Olivier

Le 10e d'avril 1738

Si je n'ay pas repondu plustot Mon tres cher frere a votre paquet du commencement de l'année qui m'a ete rendu exactement cela vient de ce que j'etois dans une compagne un peu eloignée du lieu de mon sejour ordinaire ou j'avois laissé votre letre et celles de la famille. Ma santé est assez bonne graces a Dieu, j'espere qu'avec la belle saison qui aproche elle se fortifiera de plus en plus. Vous voiez que j'ai recouvré la liberté d'ecrire que je n'avois pas depuis quelque mois a cause de la grande maladie que j'ay eue l'ete dernier. J'ay toujours un peu mal aux yeux c'est pourquoy je suis obligé de les menager. Je ne saurois assez vous remercier de tous les bons soins que vous prenez pour nos affaires communes. Je recois a tous les quartiers les rentes que vous prenez la peine de recueillir et d'envoyer a M. labbé de Roquette qui me les fait tenir comme il vient de m'envoyer le quartier de janvier.

Il y a peu de semaines que j'ai reçu votre letre du 16 mars par laquelle je vois que vous avez terminé heureusement l'affaire d'halluin ,[1] et vous m'envoyez un modele de la quittance que je dois donner. Je suis venu en consequence a la ville aussitot apres les festes, j'ai fait venir un nottaire qui s'est conforme au modelle que vous avez envoye, j'ai signé ce matin la minutte de la quittance. Il m'a promis de m'apporter cette apres dinée l'expedition legalisée et scellée en sorte qu'elle poura partir aujourd'hui par la poste. Je suis mon tres cher frere

Votre tres humb. etc.

N.S.

Ma sœur m'a mandé que vous aviez perdu Me votre sœur la religieuse// qui est morte il y a pres d'un an comme c'etoit une bonne religieuse il y a lieu de croire quelle est allée recevoir la recompense de ses bonnes œuvres c'est la plus grande consolation qu'on puisse avoir. J'ai apris aussi la mort de M. de Valle beau pere de ma belle sœur qui vous etoit fort uni, je prends part a la perte que vous avez faite de ce bon ami. il etoit aparement d'un age assez avancé.

[1] See letter 55 above, n.1.

58. Roquette to Antoine Olivier

+

Madame Varlet[1] que je vis hier, m'a appris, Monsieur, que les reparations de la rüe de Nevers auxquelles on travaille actuellement sont plus considerables que je ne pensois, et qu'il y en a même qui ne sont pas absolument necessaires. Je croirois, Monsieur, que cette depense iroit tout au plus a deux cent livres pour la part de Monseigneur l'Evêque de

Babylone, et supposé que cela monte plus haut je me trouverai dans la necessité de le prevenir pour scavoir son sentiment sur cette depense extraordinaire; il auroit sans doute demandé de remettre les reparations qui ne sont point urgentes a un autre temps afin de ne pas absorber tout d'un coup plusieurs quartiers de son revenû qui n'est pas considerable. C'est sur quoi je vous prie de donner vos ordres a l'architecte, et de me croire parfaittement

Monsieur, Vôtre tres humble et tres obeissant serviteur

S/de Roquette Pr. de St. Himer[2]

ce 14e Mai 1738

---

[1] Probably the widow of Jean-Achille, Mlle de Valle.
[2] "Prieur de St. Himer" (modern St. Ymare) Seine Inférieure, arrondissement of Rouen, site of an abbey known as "le Port Royal normand".

59. Roquette to Antoine Olivier

+

J'auray l'honneur de vous voir, Monsieur, afin de prendre des mesures pour l'arrangement des comptes que Madame Varlet retarde, en ne voulant point les signer. Il sera peut être à propos que j'en ecrive a Mr. L'Evêque de Babylone, nous verrons ensemble ce qu'il conviendra faire pour accelerer cette affaire qui feroit de la peinne et causeroit de l'incommodité a Monseigneur de Babylone, si le retardement des comptes retardoit longtemps le paiement de l'argent qui lui est dû, et dont il a besoin. Je suis parfaittement, Monsieur,

Votre tres humble et tres obeissant Serviteur.

S/de Roquette

ce 6 aout 1738

60. DMV to his Brother-in-law Olivier

Le 11e Juin 1739

Mon tres cher frere

Jai reçu aujourdhui une letre de M. lab.[1] de Roquette avec une lettre de change de 71 florins somme qui repond a celle de cent cinquante et une livres sept sols trois argent de france qu'il a reçus de vous. Dont je vous remercie. Il m'apprend en meme tems que toutte notre famille se porte bien dont jai une grande joye et jen rends graces a Dieu de tout mon cœur.

J'ai un assez gros paquet a vous ecrire en reponse a vos paquets du commencement de l'année mais M. l'ab. de R.[2] etant presentement en Normandie pour 6 semaines J'ai cru devoir attendre ce tems la pour vous faire reponse plutot que d'envoyer un gros paquet se promener dans ceste province pour y aller trouver cet abbé et etre par lui renvoyé de la [illegible] mais en attendant j'ai cru devoir vous ecrire directement ce mot de lettre pour vous tirer de l'inquietude ou votre amitié vous jette vous et ma chere sœur au sujet de ma santé.

Il est vrai qu'il y a longtems que je n'ai écrit. j'ai eté attaqué a noel dernier d'une maladie a peu pres pareille a celle que j'avois eu le mois auparavant [blank] j'en fus soulagé par le secours//de trois saignées du pied et de quelques autres remedes, en consequence de quoi un habile medecin francois que nous avons ici ma defendu toutte application et tout travail de la teste voila pourquoi je suis reste en repos jusqu'a paques sans permettre qu'on me parlat d'aucune affaire.

Mais dans la semaine de paques, lorsque je croiois avoir la liberté de reprendre le soin de mes affaires, etant allé a Utrecht ou j'entendis parler de quelques affaires [hole] et un peu affligiantes, je sentis une grande disposition a retomber malade, c'est pourquoi comme on n'est jamais mieux pour etre mal que chez soi je pensois a quitter tout soin et toutte affaire pour m'en revenir dans ma retraite, lorsque je perdis tout a coup connoissance, on me crut prest a mourir on m'administra le Sacrement de lextreme onction on me fit une bonne saignée a la main a cause de l'extreme difficulté qu'il y a de me saigner au bras, cela me rendis la connoissance, et avec quelques autres remedes qu'on me fit ensuite, ma santé revint peu a peu mais on me recommande extremement de menager ma teste voila les sujets de mon silence mais apres ce long repos surtout apresent que Dieu par une providence particuliere a oté tous les sujets dinquietude que j'avois j'ai l'esprit tres [hole] plus au long je n'ai pas voulu [hole] suis avec beaucoup de reconnais [hole]

N.S.

¹ "l'abbé"
² "Roquette"

61. DMV to his Brother-in-law Olivier

Le 30e dec. 1739

J'ai ete Mon tres cher frere, quelque tems fort inquiet sur votre santé n'ayant pas receu de reponse d'une letre assez longue et assez detaillée que je vous ai écrite l'ete dernier. Je vous l'avois ecrite en droiture parce que l'absence de M. l'ab.[1] de Roquette qui etoit alle en Normandie m'otoit la facilité de me servir de lui. Il y a environ un mois qu'en m'envoyant le dernier quartier cet abbé me mit en grande inquietude en m'ecrivant que vous n'aviez pas receu mon paquet. Mais il m'a tranquilisé depuis peu en m'ecrivant que ma letre etoit receue. Vous avez vu par cette lettre l'etat languissant ou il a plu a Dieu que j'aye ete pendant une grande partie de cette année. Cest ce qui ma oté la facilité de vous ecrire plus souvent et d'ecrire au reste de la famille. Voici une nouvelle année qui va commencer. Je vous la souhaitte heureuse et remplie des graces des benedictions du ciel. M. lab[2] de roquette m'informe par ses letres du soin que//vous prenez de mes afaires dont de[3] vous suis tres obligé. Les revenus de cette année ont ete un peu plus courts que de coutume parce qu'il a fallu reprendre le prix des reparations que vous aviez eté obligé de faire a notre maison. J'espere que l'annee prochaine sera plus heureuse, d'autant plus que les longues maladies engagent dans de grandes depenses, et que Jai ete oblige de prendre a mon service un domestique pour me soulager, ce qui ne se peut pas faire sans frais comme vous pouvez bien juger.

N.S.

[1] "l'abbé"
[2] "l'abbé"
[3] "de" for "je"

62. Villiers to Antoine Olivier

[All in a notarial hand.]

17 may 1742

Monsieur,

J'ai l'honneur de vous donner avis que *Le 14 de ce mois* a onze heures du matin, Dieu a appellé a Lui l'Illustrissime et Reverendissime Seigneur Dominique Varlet Eveque de Babylone. Vous n'ignorez pas que depuis une attaque d'apoplexie qu'il eut il y a quelques années, il a toujours été dans un état d'infirmité habituelle. Elle etoit considerablement augmentée depuis plus d'un an et enfin quelques jours après avoir reçeu les derniers sacremens, il est allé reçevoir dans le ciel la recompense due a tous ses travaux apostoliques, a son zele pour la verite et a la sainteté de sa vie. C'estoit vraiment un prelat digne des premiers siècles et dont la mémoire sera toujours en benediction auprès des gens de bien, mais surtout dans L'Eglise catholique de ces Provinces dont il a été le Restaurateur.[1]

Monseigneur l'Eveque de Babylone m'a fait l'honneur de me choisir pour Executeur de son Testament et c'est en cette qualité que je suis actuellement occupé à disposer tout ce qui est necessaire pour son enterrement qui se fera demain a Utrecht avec toute la sollennité convenable a sa dignité et a la veneration que tout le monde avoit pour lui. Le saint corps demeure encore exposé dans la chapelle de Rhynwick ou l'on ne cesse d'offrir le saint sacrifice, et aujourd'huy M. l'Archeveque y est allé exprès pour y dire une grande messe des morts. Il fera la meme chose//plusieurs jours de suite dans la principale eglise catholique d'Utrecht.

Vous serez informé, Monsieur, par la copie ci-jointe du Testament de Msgr l'Eveque de Babylone de la disposition qu'il a faite de ces biens. Vous scavez mieux que moi en quoi consistent ceux qu'il laisse a ses parens et heritiers naturels. A l'egard de ses effets mobiliaires qu'il lègue aux deux personnes nommées dans son Testament, vous n'ignorez peut-etre pas qu'il etoit d'une extreme simplicite dans ses petit meubles et jusque dans les marques de sa dignité. Une crosse d'ebene garnie d'yvoire en faisoit un des principaux ornemens. Ainsi il n'y a gueres que les livres qui soient de quelque prix. Cependant j'ai fait mettre le scellé sur tout ce qu'il pouvoit avoir dans les deux maisons de Schonauw et de Rhynwick ou il residoit alternativement pour se partager entre les Chartreux et les Orvalistes.[2] Et afin de vous donner, Monsieur, une preuve sensible du respect et des egards que je conserve pour la famille de ce saint Prélat, j'attendrai vostre reponse pour le faire lever. Si meme vous jugez apropos d'envoier a quelqu'un dans ce païs une procuration pour assister de votre part a la levée du sçellé et pour prendre connoissance de tout, j'agirai tres volontiers de concert avec lui pour l'execution des dernieres volontés du respectable Defunt.

Les frais de son enterrement et le payement de ses dettes emporteront a peu de choses pres, la valeur de ses effets mobiliaires. Il y a un memoire de ce qu'on a avancé pour lui les dernieres années de sa vie qui monte à deux mille florins, c'est a dire a plus de quatre mille livres argent de france: ce que vous n'aurez pas de peine a comprendre en faisant attention aux depenses extraordinaires qui ont dû etre les suittes de ses longues infirmités pendant les quelles on n'a rien negligé pour soulager et pour conserver le plus longtems qu'il a eté possible un Prélat qui etoit si pretieux et si necessaire à L'Eglyse. J'attens l'honneur de votre reponse et suis avec beaucoup de respect,

Monsieur/Votre tres humble et tres obeissant serviteur

S/Villiers

a Utrecht Le 17. Mai *1742*
Mon adresse est a *Mr. de Villiers chez M. Kemp sur le Mariplaats a Utrecht//*

Copie du Testament de Monseigneur l'Eveque de Babylone[3]
Je reçois dans ce moment Monsieur votre lettre du 10 mai. Celle-ci vous apprendra pourquoi on ne vous a point envoié la procuration, mais je suis bien mortiffié que ceux a qui vous vous estes addressé ne vous ayent point fait reponse.

[1] For the role of DMV in the "Jansenist" movement and in establishing the Chapter at Utrecht see a) *Nouvelles Ecclésiastiques* 1742 p. 105-108, and "Introduction" to this correspondence; b) L. von Pastor, *History of the Popes*, London, 1941f, especially vol. 34 p.60-61 and 286-288.

[2] Two religious foundations, the former an order of hermits founded by St. Bruno at La Grande Chartreuse (Dauphiné, France) in 1084, noted for its austerity and for the manufacture of chartreuse liqueur; the latter a branch of the Benedictines established in the 12th century at Orval in the Belgian Ardennes, well-known throughout the Low Countries. The establishment at Schonauwen was Carthusian, that at Rijnwijk Orvalist.

[3] There follows a complete and accurate transcription of the text of no. 49.

63. Two fragments[1]

A. Je trouve dans Edrise [Edrisi] une route de Bagdad a Racaa par Mausel dans laquelle on rencontre une ville de Karch a 60 m.[2] de Tharthar mais la distance de Bagdad a Tharthar n'est point marquée. Il paroist que cette route se fait le long du tigre et sur la rive occidentale a 33 m. apres cette ville de Karch en remontant le Tigre on trouve une ville noee[3] Saun Mr de l'Isle met un Sarsar a 13 m. de Bagdad que juge[4] estre le Tharther d'Edrise [Edrisi] le t. arabe se prononçan coe[5] un s. dans plusieurs mots usage[6] qu'ont aussi les juifs d'allemagne pour un des t hebr.[7] je juge que cette ville de Karch est Chale et que celle de Saun est Resen ou EinvaResen va est un arte[8] persan que les sarrasins auront retranche mal a propos du nom de Resen et moyennant cela Sum ou Daun sera la Rhisena de Ptolemee que Monsieur d'Anville ne//veut point voir. Mr de l'Isle met sa ville de Sarsar de sus farsangues trop loin de Sarsar en supposant sa farsangue de 28 au degre egale a 3 M. d'Edrise [Edrisi]. je ne scais point si Karch est sur le Tigre ou a quelle distance la ville de Chala de Monsieur d'Anville est mise dans la meme posin[9] par M. de l'Isle sous le nom de Galula. Je ne pense pas que ce voyage de Tharthar a Saun se fasse par eau//

B.[10] Je prie Monsieur d'Anville de ne point faire relier l'allemagne que je n'aye vu les pays et la suisse il faudra necessairement coencer[11] l'Allemagne par le Rhein[12] mais j'aurois bien euvré[13] d'y inserer la suisse outre la Souabe et la baviere Je renvoye le P la Barthe [Labat] il semble selon luy qu'on tire du vin des Dattes mais c'est un arbre trop connu pour qu'on ne le sceust pas d'ailleurs si cela estoit.

---

[1] The place of these 2 fragments in this correspondence is uncertain. In as much as the 2 hands are readily distinguished from those of other correspondences, it would seem that they may come from other portfolios, even though the first may relate to DMV's journey to Persia in 1719-1720.

[2] "milles"

[3] "nommée"

[4] "que *je* juge"

[5] "comme"

[6] "mots *d*'usage"

[7] "hébraïque"

[8] "article"

[9] "position"

[10] In margin by another hand: fils du Régent.

[11] "commencer"

[12] Which is to say that a map of the Rheinland should be bound at the beginning of an atlas of Germany.

[13] "œuvré"

64. Lanoix to Antoine Olivier

Monsieur

Je reçu hier au soir 29. votre lettre dattée du 20. Dez le grand matin j'ai envoyé demander l'extrait mortuaire que vous souhaités Legalisé, car *quelqu'un des interessés* à l'hoirie en recevra un bientot, non Legalisé, mis à la poste lundi 28. D'abord que je l'aurai, je l'enverrai par exprès à Utrecht à Mr De Villiers, qui l'ayant fait mettre en état vous l'enverra jeudi. Je fais toute la diligence possible pour vous témoigner avec quel empressement je souhaitte de pouvoir vous être utile en quelque occasion; et combien j'honore Mr Dela cour [de Lacour] a qui je fais mes très respectueux complimens, et dont je souhaitte ardemment le retour, si le sejour de Paris Le met dans La moindre inquietude; nous serions ici tous au desespoir, s'il lui arrivait le plus petit chagrin, car nous le regardons comme notre patriarche et bon ami.[1] Il a confondu la premiere procuration que j'envoyai à Mr. De Roquette avec celle que vous demandiés, et que Msgr ne pût pas faire ni signer. Je ne vous parle pas de la mort precieuse et douce de ce saint Prelat, vous en verrés sans doute bientôt la relation imprimée.[2] Vous aurés reçu aussi la copie de son testament.[3] Quant à ses effets, Mr De La cour [de Lacour] vous en dira plus que moi; Je crois que sa bibliotheque qui est belle et choisie, quelques armoires et tables font tous ses effets; il a tellement aimé La pauvreté et son revenu etoit si modique, qu'il a manqué La fin de chemises, je Lui en ai prêté des miennes et il est mort dans une de[4] quatre que j'avois empruntées de Mr Savoye, pendant qu'on blanchissoit les siennes, qui pendant Les deux//derniers mois ne suffisoient pas parce que son état demandoit de changer souvent de Linges et de matelats, étant mort sans fievre, mais d'un épuisement qui insensiblement malgré tous nos soins, nous L'a enlevé pour une vie plus heureuse; il a été plus content et plus tranquile dans Sa pauvreté et Ses souffrances que les plus riches et Les-plus opulents Evéques de france. On a mis le Scellé sans frais de justice sur les deux portes de ses chambres de Rhynwick ou il est mort, et de Schoonau, ou sont sa plus belle bibliotheque et Ses vieux habits. Mr De Lacour vous dira qu'il portoit un surtout depuis 12. ans qui étoit si dechiré et si rapiecé, que lui étant[5] tres commode pour son état; il y a trois mois que je lui en fis faire un neuf, pour me tirer de la honte que j'en avois. Comme nous ne sçavons pas au juste son âge, Je vous prie de me L'écrire simplement; il y a environ deux ans qu'il me dit qu'il etoit né en 1678. cependant nos Messieurs Le croient plus âgé; je serois bien aise Si les nouvelles ecclesiastiques[6] disoient exactement son âge, vous pouvés Le rectifier en parlant à quelqu'un ou à Mr De La cour [de Lacour], pour la faire sçavoir à celui que personne ne connoit.

J e suis plein de respect et d'estime pour tous ceux qui vous appartien-nent et à Msgr L'Eveque de Babilone, je vous prie de les en assûrer.

J'ai l'honneur d'être avec une parfaite consideration/Monsieur, Vôtre tres humble, obeissant Sr.[7]

S/Delanoix [de Lanoix]

à Rhynwick Le 30 mai 1742

[1] Jubé dela Cour, at great personal risk was apparently absent in Paris when DMV died. The use of this pseudonym "De la Cour" by the author of this letter is but one indi-cation of the continuing threat to French priests within the Church at Utrecht.
[2] As in the anonymous *In obitum illustrissimum...DMV Babylonensis Episcopi*, etc(Ultrajec-teum, 1742)and in the *Nouvelles ecclésiastiques* 1742, p. 105-108 and 185-188.
[3] See no. 49 above and no. 75 below.
[4] "de" for "des"
[5] for "qui lui était"?
[6] The notice in the *Nouvelles Ecclésiastiques* 1742 p. 105-108 does not mention DMV's age, though his exact birth and death dates are given.
[7] "Serviteur"

65. Villiers to Antoine Olivier

Utrecht ce 31 may 1742

je viens de recevoir, + Monsieur, une Lettre que Mr de La noix vient de m'envoier de Rhynwyck pour vous adresser avec un extrait mortuaire de Msgr de Babilone, extrait qui est Signé des echevins et du secrétaire de Geide[1] village a deux lieües d'icy d'ou depend la maison de Rhynwyck.

Comme cet extrait mortuaire est en flamand et que je crains qu'il ne vous sera pas d'une grande utilité, jay eté sur le champ consulter un notaire avocat qui parle françois, le priant d'en dresser un Acte en cette langue, mais il m'a répondu que cela etoit inutile, qu'il ne pouvoit dans cette acte que donner une traduction françoise de l'extrait mortuaire et qu'on avoit bésoign en justice d'un original qui fut entendu; il m'a dit d'ailleurs que le Magistrat d'Utrecht ne legaliseroit//point cet extrait mortuaire, ne connoissant point les signatures des echevins de Geide; sur cela je me suis informé avec d'autres personnes, sur la maniere dont on pourroit s'y prendre; et jay appris que le Marguiller de léglise Ste Marie ou le crieur public donneroit ledit extrait mortuaire en françois et que Mr le Bourgmaistre voudroit bien le Légaliser en cette langue; jay donné ordre qu'on fît venir le crieur public, mais supposé qu'il donne cet extrait en françois comme je viens de dire; je ne saurois, Monsieur, vous l'envoier que l'ordinaire prochain. je suis faché de ce contretems, si vôtre lettre m'eût été adressée je vous l'aurois envoié du lundi dernier; car votre Lettre du 20 pour Mr De Lanoix a resté quatre jours chez Mr Savoye qui etoit a Amsterdam, et n'a eté envoiée que mardi dernier a Rhynwyck. en attendant jay l'honneur de joindre a cet extrait une gazette de cette ville, qui dans l'article d'utrecht du 16, parle de la mort de Mgr de Babilone. peut etre cette gazette servira-t-elle, a vous obtenir//du moins quelque delai.

jay eü l'honneur, Monsieur, de vous ecrire le 17 de ce mois pour vous annoncer la mort de notre illustre Prelat; on fit le lendemain 18. l'enterrement avec la solennité qui convenoit. le St corps fut porté par Seize ecclésiastiques françois dont la plupart etoient pretres ou religieux, il y eut un grand concours du peuple et prez de cent personnes en habit et manteaux noirs; le corps a eté mis dans un caveau prez du cercueil de Madame la Princesse d'Auvergne dans le cloitre de l'eglise de Ste marie;[2] Mgr l'Archéveque a officié ici pontificalement, et fait l'éloge funèbre le 22 de ce mois, la pluspart des Pasteurs ont deja fait ou feront aussi un Service Solemnel; on a imprimé un poeme flamand de cinq cent vers[3] qui contient la vie de Mgr de Babilone dont la memoire sera en benediction dans ces provinces.

j'attendrai, Monsieur, l'honneur de vôtre réponse avant de lever le sçellé qui a eté//mis sur les effets du defunt; si vous, Monsieur, ou quelqu'un de la famille voulés y etre present, cela nous fera beaucoup de plaisir; sinon, vous aurés la bonté d'envoyer une procuration a qui vous jugerés a propos; je me ferai un plaisir de concourir a tout ce qui pourra vous en faire et a temoigner a la famille du respectable prelat, le respect infini que jay toujours eu pour luy depuis que jay eu l'honneur de la connoitre.

les principaux effets qu'il laisse sont ses livres; ils ont couté bien de l'argent, mais vous savés, Monsieur, que quand on les vend aux encheres, ce n'est pas la meme chose que quand on les achete chez le libraire—quand on en aura fait l'inventaire, il faudre apparament imprimer le catalogüe avant de proceder a la vente.[4] on aura soin de vous l'envoier, Monsieur, afin qu'on retire de ces livres pour l'argent qui se pourra, et qui servira a payer les frais funeraires et acquitter les dettes. jay l'honneur d'etre avec bien du respect, Monsieur

Votre tres humble et tres obeissant Serviteur

S/Villiers

[1] Geide (modern Ede), important center some 25 miles E of Utrecht in the province of Gelderland, in whose legal jurisdiction lay the village of Rijnwijk.

[2] Born princess of Aremberg of the celebrated family of the same name, she married François-Égon, prince of Latour d'Auvergne (of the dukes of Bouillon) about 1685. After the death of her husband she devoted herself to good works, became interested in the Jansenists of Utrecht, and went to live in this city where she died and was buried, revered by her co-religionists. The church was destroyed in 1803 and the tombs from the cloister destroyed or moved to the present Oud Katholiek Museum.

[3] See *Ter Gedagtnisse van den door lugtisten en hoogwaerdigsten Heer Domenicus-Maria Varlet, bisschop van Babylonien*, etc [Utrecht, 1742]. A copy of this work was most kindly supplied by Dr K. van der Horst, archivist at the Rijksarchief, Utrecht.

[4] So far as we know, this catalogue was never printed; though see no. 4044 of the Amersfoort inventory in the Utrecht Rijksarchief and van Kleef, *IKZ* 53 p. 223 n.2.

66. Burial certificate of DMV

SEAL CITY OF UTRECHT[1]

Je sousigné Jaque Lohof Juré Crieur d'enterrement de la Ville d'Utrecht, Certifie par le present acte que le 14 du Mois Mai 1742 est decedé à Rhynwyk Monseigneur Dominique Marie Varlet Evêque de Babylone, et que son corps a été enterré par moi dans l'Eglise de St Marie a Utrecht le 18 du dit mois de Mai 1742. Fait a Utrecht ce 4 Juin 1742.

S/Jaque Lohof

Nous grand Bailliff, Bourguemaitres et Echevins de la Ville d'Utrecht, Certifions que Jaque Lohoff, qui a donné et signé la certification cy dessus est un Crieur d'enterrement juré, et admis dans la Ville d'Utregt, et qu'ainsi les certificats donnés et signés par lui dans cette qualité meritent toute croyance et sont recus partout; Ne residant en cette Ville ni Ambassadeur, ni aucun autre Ministre//de sa Majesté le Roÿ de France. En foy de quoy nous avons fait mettre le Cachet de Cette Ville et Signez par Notre Secretaire, la presente, le 4 Juin 1742

S/T. Beeldsnyder Matroos

SEAL OF PROV. UTRECHT

[1] Under the accompanying Seal there is written in another hand in Dutch: Senden.

67. Villiers to Antoine Olivier

J'ai[1] recu avanthier, Monsieur, avec bien de la reconnoissance la lettre obligeante que vous m'avez fait l'honneur de m'ecrire conjointement avec tous les principaux parens de Mgr. l'eveque de Babilone. Je vois avec plaisir dans cette lettre les marques d'estime, d'attachement et de veneration que vous avés tous pour la memoire de cet illustre Prelat, et les dispositions sinceres que vous témoignés d'entrer dans ses veües et d'executer ses dernieres volontés, dont l'equité et la justice ont eté les guides. Msr.[2] le gros [Legros] a recu en meme tems la procuration que vous avés eü la bonté de luy envoier; je suis bien aise que vous ayés choisi un homme de ce merite pour agir en votre nom et soutenir vos interets; j'agirai tres volontiers de concert avec luy pour que tout se fasse selon les regles et//de maniere que vous soies content et les autres interessés; jay ecrit a Paris a Mr. l'Abbé d'ettemar [Etemare] un des legataires, et des qu'il aura envoié sa procuration, on procedera a l'ouverture du scéllé et a la Confection de l'inventaire en presence du Mr. legros [Legros] et des deux legataires ou leurs procureurs; il me semble que ce qu'on doit principalement eviter, ce sont les frais de justice qui sont icy fort grands, et qui absorberoient les fonds; s'il y avoit par exemple deux Committaires avec un Secretaire ou greffier, l'inventaire des livres emporteroit beaucoup de tems, et les séances des Committaires avec leur greffier couteroient beaucoup. Ma pensée est donc, Monsieur, que cet inventaire se fasse de concert, qu'on prenne deux personnes affidées pour écrire sous la dictée de Mr. le gros [Legros] en ma presence et celle des deux legataires ou leurs procureurs; on trouvera facilement dans chaqune des deux maisons de Schoenaw et de Rhynwyk quelques amis qui se pretera[3] sans frais a cette œuvre et des que//l'inventaire sera fait on vous en enverra, si vous souhaittés, une copie qui sera visée de nous tous.

A l'egard de la vente des effets, je ferais de mon mieux pour qu'ils soient portés au plus haut prix, il est indubitable que les frais qu'on fera soit pour le catalogue des livres, soit pour les encheres devront etre pris sur les deniers qui proviendront de la vente; si vous desirés, Monsieur, de garder quelques effets du St.[4] Prelat, comme sa croix pectorale, son anneau, sa crosse, ayés la bonté de me le marquer, afin que je voie avec Mr.[5] Les legataires, ce qu'on pourra faire pour obliger, car pour moy en particulier, je vous prie, Monsieur, d'etre persuadé de ma bonne volonté a vous rendre tous les services qui dependront de moy.

Jay l'honneur de vous envoier l'extrait mortuaire, tel que vous le souhaittés, c'est a dire, en françois et bien legalisé.[6] Jay eü soin//qu'on mit *Dominique Marie*, et non *Marie-Dominique*; Si cette faute est dans l'original du testamens, elle me semble corrigées[7] par la signature de Mgr de Babilone luy même, qui certainement a signé au bas du Testament, *Dominique Marie*; si vous en desirés, Monsieur, une expedition authentique je vous l'enverrai volontiers, et je prendrai les frais de cette expedition ainsi que de l'extrait mortuaire, que je vous envoie, sur les effets du defunct.

Il est vrai que jay en main un testament spirituel qui est fort beau, et digne d'etre donné au public, je ne sai point cependant n'y quand, n'y ou on l'imprimera, je suis plus porté a croire que ce sera a Paris, et qu'il fera une des feüilles des nouvelles ecclesiastiques;[8] je me ferai un plaisir de vous en envoier deux exemplaires, mais s'il devient public a Paris, vous pouvrés[9] l'avoir sur les lieux et epargner le port qu'il vous en couteroit en vous l'envoiant d'icy; Si on ne l'imprime point en entier, j'aurai soin de vous en envoier dans la suite deux copies bien couvertes en attendant vous trouveréz cy joint un extrait des dernieres paroles de ce testament, qui ont trait a ses biens temporels. Je prens la liberté d'assurer icy de mes tres humbles respects Madame vôtre epouse Madame Miget, et Monsieur Varlet. Jay lhonneur d'etre avec bien de respect, Monsieur, votre tres humble et tres obeiss. serviteur

S/Villiers

a Utrecht ce 4 juin 1742//

Copie des dernieres paroles du testament spirituel de Mgr l'eveque de Babilone en datte du 2d. fevrier 1741

Il ne me reste plus que de remercier les amis si genereux qui ont jusqu'icy contribué par leurs aumones a entretenir les serviteurs de bien refugiés en ce pays. J'espere qu'ils auront la charité de continuer cette bonne œuvre, et j'y consacre volontiers ce qui pourra me rester icy d'effets apres les frais funeraires, et l'acquit de mes dettes, conjurant les Seculiers et les Reguliers d'honorer toujours par leur conduite l'eglise catholique dont ils sont membres, de répondre par la Sainteté de leur vie a celle de la Cause pour laquelle bien leur a fait la grace de souffrir, ou de

sacrifier quelque chose, de vivre dans une parfaite union, et de se souvenir de moy dans leurs prieres.

Fait a Utrecht le 2d. fevrier 1741.

<hr>

[1] Above the incipit, another hand has written toward the right margin: 17 juin 1742, répondu à M. Devilliers.
[2] "Monsieur"
[3] for "se prêteront"
[4] "Saint"
[5] for "Messieurs"
[6] See no. 66 above.
[7] for "corrigée"
[8] See *Nouvelles Ecclésiastiques* 1742 p. 185-188 and Appendix 4 of the present edition.
[9] for "pourrez"

68. Villiers to Antoine Olivier

Monsieur[1]

Jay recu vers la Saint Jean[2] la lettre que vous m'avés fait l'honneur de mécrire le 14 de juin. Le lundi 2d juillet Mr. le gros [Legros] et moy nous nous rendimes a Rhynvyk ou Mr. Willemaer l'un des legataires se rendit la même jour, nous y procedames a la reconnoissance et a la levée du scellé et des le lendemain matin nous commencames l'inventaire des effets, meubles et livres de feu Mgr l'eveque de Babylone, lequel inven-taire nous continüames jusqu'au vendredy 6e juillet au soit,[3] que nous etablimes le Procureur de la maison pour commissaire et garde des effets dont nous avions fait l'inventaire, nous partimes le même soir pour Schoonaw ou nous avons continué l'inventaire jusqu'au 15 de juillet; nous n'avons trouvé parmi les papiers de Mgr de Babylone, ny testament ny codicille ny aucune autre derniere disposition, n'y aucun contract ou billet d'obligation.

Parmi la multitude des papiers assez inutiles pour ses affaires tempo-relles, nous y avons trouvé plusieurs collections manuscrites de la main du respectable Prelat, qui prouvent sa profonde erudition sur toute sorte des matieres, la plupart des autres ecrits regardent les missions etrange-res, nous avons rangé tous ces papiers que nous avons conservés en trente cinq paquets ou liasses que nous avons renfermés dans un armoire; Si Messieurs de justice s'en etoient meslés, je croi que la seule visite des papiers les auroit occupés pendant deux mois, et que le seul inventaire des livres et de ces papiers auroit absorbé le fonds de tout le mobilier qui est icy; nous avons pris a Schoonauwe et a Rhynvyk deux secritaires qui ne nous ont rien couté, et nous en sommes quittes pour la depense de bouche que Mrs.[4] le gros [Legros] Willemars et//moy avons faite pen-dant quinze jours dans les deux maisons ou nous avons travaillé avec assiduité pendant quatre seances chque jour depuis les six heures du matin jusqu'a la nuit.

Je me propose, Monsieur, de faire la vente, de concert avec Mr. le gros [Legros], des petits effets qui sont a schoonaw immediatement apres la fete de l'assomption, et de ceux qui sont a Rhynvyk, apres St. Bernard,[5] supposé qu'il y ait des achetteurs pour ces petits meubles; on ne vendra point ny les croix pectorales, ny l'anneau, ny la mitre, ny la crosse, ny le calise, et Mrs. les heritiers ou legataires en disposeront comme ils jugerons a propos.

A l'egard des livres qui sont le principal objet, on travaille actuellement a mettre en ordre et dans leur rang ceux qu'on a trouvés a Schoonaw et a Rhynvyk, et a n'en faire qu'un catalogue, afin de les faire prises et estimer par deux libraires dont Mr. le gros [Legros] et moy conviendrons; on verra ensuite le meilleur party qu'on pourra prendre pour les vendre au plus haut prix.

Jay mis a part, monsieur, pour vous etre envoiés dans l'occasion 1.° deux Cachets de Mgr de Babylone, l'un grand et l'autre petit, que je crois etre tous les deux d'argent; 2.° une petite plaque de cuivre pour graver ses armes, cela regarde naturellement la famille de Mr. Varlet, 3.° trois exemplaires du poeme flamand dont je vous ay parlé.[6] 4.° trois autres exemplaires d'un poeme latin, qu'un chartreux a composé sur la mort de Mgr. de Babylone, et qui est fort estimé desconnoisseurs;[7] il y a icy une personne qui dans quelque tems doit aller a Paris, si vous jugés a propos, Monsieur, que je luy confie ces peices avec les cachets pour vous les apporter, je le feray volontiers, sinon je vous les enverrois par la route de Bruxelles, ou par telle autre voÿe qu'il vous plairra m'indiquer.

Comme vous m'avés marqué, Monsieur, qu'une expedition en forme du testament du defunt vous feroit plaisir, et qu'elle vous est même necessaire, jay l'honneur de vous l'envoier aujourdhuy; elle a même retardé cette lettre de quelque jours,//parceque le notaire etoit en campaigne, et je n'ay point voulu vous ecrire a deux fois pour ne pas multiplier le port des lettres;[8] je prendrai les frais de l'expedition, comme vous le dites fort bien, sur la vente des effets.

Je vous envoie aussi, Monsieur, un billet de Mr. le gros [Legros] qu'il m'a remis, il y a quelque jours pour vous envoier quand je vous ecrirois.[9]

A l'egard des frais que jay fait, ou des dettes que je connois, je ne saurois aujourdhuy, Monsieur, vous en donner un memoire exact. Ce que je sai c'est que pour les seuls frais funeraires jay depensé jusqu'icy plus de six cent florins, et jay lieu de croire qu'avec les articles que je n'ay point encore payés, il se monteront tous ensemble prez de huit cent florins; il a eté juste et convenable de faire rendre au Prelat les honneurs deüs a sa personne et a sa dignité.

Pour ce qui est des dettes, ou des depenses qu'on a fait icy soit pour les frais des dernieres maladies, soit pour les gages et nourritures des domestiques pendant quatre ans, jay eu l'honneur de vous marquer que ces depenses alloient a deux mille florins, outre quelques autres depenses particulieres; il seroit juste aussi de faire quelque present a Mr. le medecin qui la[10] servi gratuitement pendant plusieurs annees et qui s'est donné bien de la peine ainsi que Mr. de Lanoix pretre qui luy a rendu des services essentiels pendant ces dernieres années; il seroit aussi fort juste de donner quelque gratification a Mr. de Rhynvyk et a Mr. de Schoonaur qui ont fait plusieurs frais a l'occasion de Mgr., ou des visites qu'il leur a occasionnées, mais vous verrés, Monsieur, dans la suite avec Mrs.[11] les legataires ce qu'on pourra faire a ce sujet quand on aura retiré le prix de la vente des effets.

Mr. le gros m'a communiqué le billet sur lequel est fondée votre creance; je souhaitte qu'il y ait assés de fonds pour satisfaire tout le monde, et je feray de mon mieux pour qu'on en retire tout l'argent qu'on pourra.

Je prens la liberté d'assurer des mes respects Madame votre epouse, et Madame vôtre belle sœur, je salüe tres humblement Mr votre fils et Mr. Varlet neveü, et jay l'honneur d'etre avec bien du respect.
Monsieur
Votre tres humble et tres humble et tres obeissant serviteur

S/Villiers

a Utrecht ce 2d. aoust 1742

[1] Above the incipit, another hand has written, toward the right margin:
2 aoust 1742.
[2] Religious feast of 24 June commonly used to indicate the second quarter of the fiscal year.
[3] for "soir"
[4] "Messieurs"
[5] Religious feasts, the first 15 August, the second 20 August.
[6] *Ter Gedagtnisse*, etc. See above no. 65, n. 3.
[7] *In obitum illustrissimum...DMV Babylonensis Episcopi...*, See above no. 64, n. 2.
[8] A necessary courtesy in a time when postage was paid by the addressee.
[9] This note is lacking from the present correspondence.
[10] for "l'a"
[11] "Messieurs"

69. Extract in re: DMV

Du Registre des Insinuations du Chastelet de Paris a Esté ce qui suit:

aujourd'huy 19 8bre 1742 Est comparu Mr antoine olivier Laisné procureur au chastelet tant pour luy a cause de Ladame son Epouse que pour jacque varlet mineur son neveu heritiers Beneficiaires en La succession cy apres, Lequel nous a declaré et di[1] ses noms et que dans La Succession de M. Dominique Marie Varlet Eveque de Babilonne decedé le quatorse may 1742 Il n'y a aucun autre Bien Immobilier sujet au centieme denier situez dans paris que Le quart du total d'une maison sise a Paris Rue des amandiers Butte Saint Roch de valleure de 22 500 £. Et le Tiers d'une autre maison sise quay de conty au coin de La rue De nevers de valleure de 1600 Livres La Totalite 2100 Revenant des dites sommes a celle de 38 500 £ quand Le centieme denier de laquell Somme Led. Sr.[2] comparant nous a payé 462 £ compris Les quatre Sols pour Livre[3] La presente declaration pour Satisfaire aux Edits Et a signé, ladite Somme payée dans deniers dud.[4] Sr. comparant

S/Thiery

NB l'original de cette quittance Est Renferme dans mon petit coffre noir Estant dans mon Estude avec les autres [hole] de m d [illegible].[5]

---

[1] for "dit"
[2] "Ledit Sieur"
[3] for "livrer"
[4] for "dudit"
[5] It is possible that the end of this postscription should read: ... avec les autres papiers de M. Dominique-Marie Varlet.

70. Villiers to Antoine Olivier

Monsieur[1]

J'eus l'honneur de vous ecrire au commencement du mois d'aoust et de vous envoier une copie authentique du testament de feu Mgr Léveque de Babylone; depuis ce tems ayant trouvé une occasion favorable d'une personne qui retournoit a Paris, je l'ay chargée de vous remettre, Monsieur, *les deux cachets d'argent du Prélat defunct, une plaque de cuivre pour graver ses armes, trois exemplaires d'un poeme flamand, et autant d'un poeme latin a la loüange de Mr. votre beaufrere:*[2] je suppose, Monsieur, que vous les avés receus quoique je n'en aye eu aucune nouvelle jusqu'icy.

Je vous marquois dans ma lettre que de concert avec Mr. le gros [Legros] votre Procureur, je me disposais de faire une vente entre amis des effets de Mgr de Babylone; je l'ay faite en effet a Schoonaw le 16 du mois d'aoust, et a Ruynvyk le 21 du même mois: j'y ay vendu ce que je trouvois dans ces maisons, appartenant au Prelat, ses hardes, armoires, tables, chaises, etc, et il faut avoüer que tout cela s'est vendu au dela de ce qu'on l'auroit vendu en ville dans une vente publique, outre qu'on a epargnée le port et les droits du crieur public, les petites choses ont eté plus vendües a proportion, que les effets plus considerables, un petit cordon par exemple, une bourse, une ceinture ont eté portés beaucoup au dela de leur prix; cela m'a déterminé a vendre aussi entre amis de concert avec Mr. le gros [Legros] quelques livres qui regardent le Jansenisme et la Constitution[3], livres qui ne peuvent entrer en france et qu'on donne icy a la barrière dans les ventes publiques; j'en ay tiré de l'argent, et jay l'honneur de vous envoyer, Monsieur, un memoire qui contient le montant des sommes que ces trois ventes ont produis; ensemble des depenses que jay faites,//Vous y verrés qu'il m'est encore deu plus de quatre cent florins, mais jay en main pour me rembourser en partie deux medailles d'or des Princes de Brunsvyk-Lunebourg, frappées en 1689. Les orfevres de cette ville les estiment cent dix huit florins chacune: je tacheray d'en avoir quelque chose de plus; mais jusqu'icy je n'ay pas trouvé a les vendre; les gens de ce pays aiment mieux de l'argent courant pour leur commerce ou leur usage: je croi qu'apres que j'en aurai retiré le prix, et que j'aurai reçu les 194 14 16 que Mr de Roquette a remis depuis longtems pour etre envoies icy je serai remboursé des frais a une centaine des florins pres. Il me restera comme jay eu l'honneur de vous l'ecrire, les croix pectorales, l'anneau, un calice, la mitre, la croce[4] et un petit gobelet d'argent marqué aux armes du deffunct, lesquels effets je conserverai jusque ce que vous soies convenu avec Mr. les legataires.

Il reste encore la belle biblioteque de Mgr de Babylone; j'avois pensé que des particuliers pourroient l'acheter en gros, ou acheter les livres en detail, mais on m'a fait remarquer qu'il y a trop d'inconveniens a prendre ce party, et qu'il vaut beaucoup mieux suivre la regle commune qui est de vendre ces livres au plus offrant et dernier encherisseur dans une vente publique. Par cette voie on suit la regle, et l'ordre comun qui s'observe icy, on est a l'abri de tout[5] reproche et de tout soupçon, on ne peut pas dire qu'on aye[6] eu des preferences pour personne, ou qu'on n'a pas pris les moyens convenables, Mrs les heritiers, ny[7] les legataires ne peuvent se plaindre qu'on suive la regle et on ne se trouve point exposé a avoir de discussion avec ceux qui achetent; le crieur public et le libraire qui preside a la vente sont responsables de tout, et c'est a eux a percevoir les deniers des acheteurs, et a les contraindre a leur depens. On ne sauroit estimer au juste la valeur des livres. Quelques libraires la//font monter a 2500 florins, d'autres a trois mille; il est vrai que les livres aujourdhuy ont beaucoup diminué de leur prix, mais comme ceux de Mgr de Babylone sont de tres bon gout et qu'ils sont bien conditionnés, je me flatte que la vente ira au dela de trois mille florins tout frais payé; je ferai de mon mieux pour qu'elle soit portée le plus haut qu'il se pourra; on travaille actuellement a en faire un catalogue par ordre de matieres, qui sont bien fait, on doit le presenter ensuite a Mr. le Recteur magnifique de cette université, puis on l'imprimera pour etre distribué dans differentes villes, et divers pays: j'en enverrai un nombre d'exemplaires a Paris et j'aurai l'honneur de vous en adresser, Monsieur, une douzaine d'exemplaires, afin que les amis qui en voudront, puissent envoier des commissions pour acheter les livres qu'ils souhaiteront. Plusieurs libraires de ce pays temoignent deja de l'empressement, et demandent quand est-ce que se fera la vente? mais on ne sauroit la faire qu'apres pâques,[8] il faut attendre la belle saison, et donner le tems de prendre les arrangemens necessaires pour procurer des acheteurs a la vente.

Comme vous avés souhaitté, Monsieur, d'avoir une copie du testament spirituel de Mgr de Babylone, je prens la liberté de vous en adresser une copie, afin que vous soiés un des premiers qui en ayt, comme il est juste.

Mr le gros [Legros] m'a dit qu'il alloit vous ecrire au sujet de 2200 et tant de livres que vous demandés, et que Mrs les legataires font quelque difficulté de vous alloüer, et qu'il vous feroit remettre sa lettre par le canal de Mr de Lacour.

Vous voulés bien me permettre, Monsieur, d'assurer icy de mes respects Madame vôtre épouse, et toutte votre chere famille sans oublier Madame et Monsieur Varlet, et de vous prier d'etre bien persuadé de l'attachement sincere que je conserverai toute ma vie pour la famille du defunct, et de l'inclination que jay a vous obliger en particulier, et a vous temoigner dans toutes les occasions combien parfaitement jay l'honneur d'etre

Monsieur Votre tres humble et tres obeissant serviteur

S/Villiers

Utrecht ce 18 9bre 1742//

jay recu pour la vente des effets faite a Schoonauwen le 16 aoust 1742, deduit les frais	119	fl
pour la vente faite a Rhynwyck le 21 aoust deduit les frais, la somme de	140—5	
la vente des quelques livres faite a Schoonauwen le 9 oct. deduit les frais, monte a	134—15	
reçu d'ailleurs en argent monnoyé quatre pieces d'or et quelques autres effets. la somme de	210—	
TOTAL	602—[9]	
jay deboursé pour les frais funeraires compris en 28 articles jusqu'a ce jour le 18 nov. 1742 la somme de	193—19	

pour frais de l'inventaires auquel Mr le gros [Legros], Mr
Willemaer et moy avons vaqué depuis le 2 juillet jusqu'au 16
et pour les copies du catalogue des livres, la somme de   61—02

pour quelques dettes pressées   185—

pour port des lettres jusqu'a ce jour   9—18

TOTAL   1047—14[10]

reçu cy dessus   602—

reste deü   445—14[11]

pour me rembourser en partie de ces 445 fl 14 jay encore a main deux
medailles d'or que les orfevres de cette ville estiment cent dix huit florins
chacune; je tacherai d'en tirer quelque chose de plus.

[1] Above the incipit, another hand has added toward the right margin: Répondu le 30
9bre.
[2] For the Flemish poem see above no. 65, n. 3 and, for the Latin poem, no. 64, n. 2.
[3] The Bull, *Unigenitus*, condemning Jansenism, promulgated 8 September 1713, the
cause of much difficulty in the Roman Catholic Church in France throughout the 18th
century.
[4] for "crosse"
[5] for "toute"
[6] for "ait"
[7] for "ni"
[8] In 1743, Easter fell on 16 April.
[9] Should total: 603 fl 20
[10] Should total: 1054 fl 53
[11] Should total: 448 fl 39

71. Notarial opinion in re: DMV

Le Conseil qui a vû une Copie du Testament de Dominique du 11
mars 1734, et du Billet ou l'obligation du même Dominique du 19 aout
1729, Estime qu'Antoine Coheritier ne peut reperter ce qui luy est dû,
des legataires nommés par le Testament de Dominique 1e.[1] C'est une
regle de droit d'interpreter la Volonté au Testateur de telle maniere
qu'elle s'eloigne le moins qu'il est possible du droit commun
    1.° 13 *Cod. de hared. justit.*[2] porte que les legataires ne sont point obligés
de payer les dettes du deffunt. Ainsi quand le Testateur charge ses legataires de payer les *dettes qui se trouveront a l'heure de sa mort*, cela se doit
entendre seulement des dettes courantes, non des dettes Capitales, soit
personnelles soit réelles, et cette interpretation n'est point forcée, mais
fondée sur la signification//du terme *dettes*

2.° On ne peut point nier que Dominique n'ait voulu gratifier ses legataires, et ainsi il ne peut être presumé avoir voulu les charger d'une dette ancienne qui absorberoit tous ou presque tous les legs.

3.° la Somme que demande Mr Antoine ne luy est point düe a proprement parler, C'est la rente qui luy est düe, il a ordre et est en droit de prendre cette rente sur le tiers de la maison de Dominique, ainsi il doit s'adresser au proprietaire de cette maison, et non aux legataires, *quippe res transir cum suo onore*[3]

4.° la Charge de payer les dettes ne peut s'entendre que des dettes dües a des tieres personnes, non de celles qui sont dües aux heritier, parce que c'est chose inoüie dans le droit ancien que la même personne puisse être créancier et heritier 1.75 ff de Salut.[4]//

5.° Il est vray que par le droit nouveau le 22. S.g. *Cod de jure Deliverandi*,[5] au heritier sous benefice d'inventaire retient le droit de concourir avec les autres créanciers du défunt, mais comme cela est une exception de la regle commune, il n'est nullement probable que Dominique y ait pensé, surtout parce que cette exception ne peut avoir lieu qu'aux dépens de sa mémoire. ainsi la prétention de M. Antoine en cas qu'il veüille se declarer heritier sous benefice d'inventaire, seroit fondé sur la supposition la plus outrée, scavoir que Dominique ait voulu charger ses legataires qui par le droit commun n'y sont nullement obligés, de payer ses dettes dües a ses heritiers, qui pour noircir sa memoire, ne veulent se declarer heritiers que sous benefice d'inventaire.

6.° la nature mûre des biens legués demontre que les legataires ne sont obligés qu'a payer tout au plus les dettes simplement personnelles, etant plusieurs fois decidé en france "haredun mobilieun soleun ad as alienum mobile, immobilium vere successorem ad immobila defuncti delecta creditoribus prastenda obligatum esse, uti testateur embertus Enchirid. jur. gal. verbo bonoi. differentia cirea medium argurtrans de Consult. Britan. art. 219. gloss. 8. N.S."[6]

7.° le dette düe a S.[7] antoine n'est pas a proprement parler une dette de Dominique, mais une charge qui luy reste de la Succession de feüe Madame sa mere

8.° enfin MM. N. n'etant legataires que des biens mobilier[8] d'hollande, il est plus que probable que Dominique ne les a voulu charger que du payemant des dettes qu'il pourroit contracter en hollande, et nullement de celles qu'il pourroit avoir en france.

---

[1] "légataire"
[2] "livre 13 *Codex de haereditatum justitiae*"
[3] "Certainly the item is transferable with its income".
[4] "livre 75 ff *de Salutate*".
[5] "le 22 Statutum generale *Codex de jure Deliverandi*"

⁶ The notary's Latin should read: "haeredun mobilium solum ad as alienum mobile, immobilium vere successorem ad immobilia defuncti delecta creditoribus praestenda obligatum esse, uti testatur Imbertus Enchiridion juris galiae verbo bono differentia cirea medium arguturans de Consultatiore Britannica articulo 219. glossario 8 nova serie." Meaning: "Before an heir to the estate of a person unrelated by blood can enter into his inheritance, and in order to secure the real property in his inheritance from the estate of the deceased, he must, by right, pay creditors from levies on the personal property only, as witness Imbert in *Enchiridion juris galiae*, arguing from *Consult. Britan.* article 219 note 8 with favourable comment for a reasonable distinction (between real and personal property)."
⁷ "Sieur"
⁸ for "mobiliers"

72. Villiers to Antoine Olivier

28 mars 1743¹

Monsieur,

Jay recu dans le tems la lettre que vous avés pris la peine de m'ecrire le 30 novembre dernier; je n'ay eü depuis ce tems là rien d'important a vous mander.

Je me donne l'honneur de vous ecrire aujourdhuy, Monsieur, pour vous donner avis qu'enfin le catalogue des livres de feu Mgr l'eveque de Babylone est en etat d'etre imprimé, que Mr. le Recteur de cette université apres l'avoir gardé plus de trois semaines a accordé la permission de l'imprimer, et d'exposer les livres a une vente publique. On est convenu qu'elle se fera en ville le 29ᵉ du mois de may prochain, et les jours suivans; ce 29ᵉ May est le lundi avant pentecôte, et nous ne l'avons pas differée plus loign, parceque les livres se vendent mieux dans ce pays entre Paques et pentecote; c'est alors qu'on a de l'argent,² et que les Pasteurs et autres se remüent d'avantage.

On tachera de se donner tous les mouvemens qu'on pourra pour que les livres soient portés au plus haut prix; ils sont tous bons, bien choisis, et bien conditionnés; ce sont la plupart des livres de theologie, de droit, d'histoire, et des langues etrangeres, et ces sortes des livres se vendent beaucoup mieux en ville, et a moins de frais, qu'en france ou//dans les autres villes de ces provinces; des que le catalogue sera achevé d'imprimer, ce qui sera a la fin du careme, j'aurai l'honneur, Monsieur de vous en adresser quelques exemplaires ainsi qu'aux amis, et a quelque libraires de Paris, afin que ceux qui voudront acheter envoient leurs commissions a quelques personnes connües de ce pays; je croi que je me servirai de la voie de Bruxelles pour envoier ces catalogües a Paris.³

Jay fait savoir a Mrs les legataires vos intentions, Monsieur, au sujet des croix Pectorales et autres ornémens episcopaux du Prelat defunct, et ils m'ont repondu qu'on pourroit convenir de tout cela en même tems qu'on conviendroit de ce qui vous est deü, en attendant je les garderai exactement, et ne m'en désaisirai point.

La personne a qui je donnai l'an passé les deux cachets d'argent pour vous les remettre, Monsieur, je nomme Norblin; je ne sai s'il vous aura remis enfin ce paquet. Desque j'eus appris par votre lettre du 30 novembre que vous ne l'aviés pas reçu je luy fis ecrire par un ami d'icy, et cet ami n'ayant point eu de réponse, je luy ecrivis moy même le 11 janvier de dernier. Je n'ay aucune de ses nouvelles, peut etres serés vous plus heureux que moy pour en avoir. Ce Mr. Norblin avoit resté icy quelques mois et avoit acheté plusieurs livres, et offrait même d'en acheter a la vente qu'on feroit de ceux de Mgr de Bab.—il me laissa en partant son adresse qui est telle *a Monsr. Auzon chez Madame Dumas, Rue du Chaume a coté de la merci au Marais, pour Mr Norblin d'egligny.* Ayez la bonté, Monsieur, de vous informer chez cette dame Dumas, ce qu'est//devenu le Sr. Norblin d'egligny; je ne comprens rien a cela, car d'un coté il nous a paru honnete homme, il etoit connu de plusieurs amis qui l'ont veü icy devant a Paris, et d'un autre coté le paquet n'est pas d'une si grande importance ou d'un prix a etre volé, quoique l'on pouvoit faire un fort mauvais usage de ces cachets qui ne sont bons d'ailleurs que pour une famille. Je crus vous faire plaisir, Monsieur, de vous les envoier en profitant d'une occasion qui se presentoit naturellement, il promit de vous l'en rendre exactement, et je n'aurois jamais soupconné qu'il eut manqué a sa parole; peut etre trouvera-t-il le moyen de se justifier du retardement de vous les remettre?—je luy ferois encor ecrire par les amis qui sont icy, et si j'en recois quelque nouvelle je ne manquerai pas de vous en informer.

Je prens la liberté, Monsieur, d'assurer icy de mes respects Madame votre epouse, Madame et Monsr. Varlet, et toute votre illustre famille. Jay l'honneur d'être tres parfaitement

Monsieur/Votre tres humble et tres obeissant/serviteur

S/Villiers

a Utrecht ce 28ᵉ mars 1743

---

[1] Above the date, in another hand toward the right margin is written: Mr. noblen Degligny/Rue des Noyers au coin de celle des anglois au 3ᵉ; followed in a third hand by: une maison neuve.

[2] Because of the payment either of second quarter-term or of the first half-year benefices.

[3] See above, no. 64, n. 4.

73. Villiers to Antoine Olivier

Monsieur[1]

Je ne dois pas differer plus longtems d'avoir l'honneur de vous ecrire: j'attendois une réponse finale de Monsr. L'Abbé d'etemare [Etemare] un des legataires, sur la proposition que vous avies faite de prendre des croix pectorales et autres joyeux pour partie du paiement de ce qui vous est deü; d'abord on ecrivit que Mr d'etemare [Etemare] etoit malade a la campagne ou il prenoit le lait; enfin il a ecrit luy même, il y a peu de jours qu'il luy paroisoit que ces effets conviendroient mieux a Monsr. Varlet comme chef de la famille, et portant le même nom que le defunct, et qu'il a appris que Madame Varlet sa mere etoit un peu fachée de ce que dans une autre occasion vous avies retenu, Monsieur, les tableaux de la famille, du reste il semble que cet Abbé s'en rapportera a l'avis de Mr. le gros [Legros], et de luy marquer vos intentions au sujet de ces effets et du paiement de votre dette, je crois aussi que vous pouviés vous accomoder a ce sujet avec Mr Varlet, s'il souhaite quelqun de ces effets, et que vous pouviés peut etre luy en ceder une partie au prix dont on seroit convenu.

La vente de la Biblioteque de feu M. Léveque de Babylone s'est faite icy en ville aux encheres le 29 du mois de May et les jours suivans;//elle s'est montée a trois mille sept cent florins, je n'en ay point encore reçu l'argent, mais je le recevrai sans doute bientôt: il y a environ cinq cent florins des frais, ainsi il restera pour les dettes et pour les legataires trois mille deux cent florins, ce qui fait environ six mille cinq cent livres argent de france; j'aurais souhaitté que la vente eut monté plus haut, mais il faut considerer que les livres sont aujourdhuy en tout pays a tres bon marché; j'eus l'honneur de vous envoier dans le tems, Monsieur, six exemplaires du catalogue des dits livres de feü Mgr L'eveque de Babylone, ils etoient adressés a Mr etienne Savoye Libraire rüe St Jacques a l'esperance[2] et on m'a marqué de Paris que ces exemplaires vous avoient eté remis quoi qu'un peu tard.

Je me suis donné bien des mouvemens pour m'informer ce qu'etoient devenus le Sieur Norblin, et les deux cachets d'argent que je luy avois donné l'an passé pour vous remettre, Monsieur: enfin je viens d'apprendre que ces deux cachets d'argent avec la petite plaque de cuivre etoient entre les mains d'un curé du Diocese de Sens oncle dudit Sr Norblin, et que ce curé ne sachant a qui les remettre, en avoit parlé a Monsr. Pothouin le fils avocat au parlement qui en a ecrit icy a un de ses amis. Je luy ay fait faire aussitôt reponse qu'on devoit vous remettre lesdits cachets d'argent avec la plaque de cuivre; ainsi, Monsieur, si l'on ne vous les remet vous pouvés vous adresser vous même a Monsr Pothouin l'avocat: Si je puis vous rendre quelque autre service, vous me trouverés toujours, Monsieur, tres disposé a vous obliger, et a vous temoigner dans toutes les occasions, combien je suis, Monsieur, et a toute la famille—

Votre tres humble et tres obeissant serviteur

S/Villiers

a Utrecht ce 15 aoust 1743

¹ Above the incipit toward the right margin another hand has added: 14 aoust 1743.
² Probably because Savoye's shop sign bore the symbol of an anchor for "Hope".

74. La Cour to Antoine Olivier

22 9bre 1743

Monsieur

Des que vous le jugerez a propos le fils de Monsieur Gerz partira de Rouen pour se rendre auprès de vous. Monsieur + Madame Gerz vous font leurs remerciemens que vous vouliez bien le recevoir chez vous; comme un des amis de Monsieur votre fils leur a marquée qu'il etoit à propos de vous offrir quelque chose de plus que les 400 a raison de son droit, ils vous païerons 450 de pension; et comme ce sont des personnes pleines de générosité vous ne perderez rien au surplus. Je n'aurois pas manqué de vous aller rendre visite aujourdhui si je n'etois indispensablement réténu d'ailleurs. Vous aurez la bonté de donner, s'il vous plait vos ordres pour le depart du jeune homme qui est tout a fait aimable; et je le ferai savoir sans delai des aujourdhui.

Quand¹ a l'affaire d'hollande j'ai ecrit de bonne encre et je ne croi pas que dix ou douze jours se passent que je ne vous porte reponse cathegorique.

J'ai confere ici avec quelques personnes tout recemment au fait//de ce qui se passe la bas. J'ai vu par les details des faux frais de la vente des livres, des dépenses extraordinaires qu'on a été obligé de faire pendant des années entieres où il a fallu deux Domestiques à feu Monseigneur l'Evêque de Babylone votre frere, autres dépenses indispensables sans compter les Pompes funebres de transport de Rhynwyk où il est mort, à Utrecht pour y être injumé en terre Sainte dans un caveau fait exprès auprès de Madame la Princesse d'auvergne née Duchesse d'arembert, dans les cloîtres de la grande Eglise de Sainte Marie.² Ces sortes de dépenses sont tout autremens couteuses dans ces païs Heterodoxes que dans ce païs ci; mais on le devoit à la dignité la memoire d'un si Saint et d'un si Respectable Prelat par sa science et par ses immenses travaus.

Quoiqu'il en soit vous ne pouvez mieux faire assurement que de me confier le fini de cette affaire par le devouement et le zele avec lequel je veux être toute la vie plein de respect

Monsieur

Je prie Madame Olivier et M votre fils d'agréer mes complimens./Votre très humble et très obeïssant serviteur

S/J. De la Cour

[1] for "quant"
[2] See above no. 65, n. 2.

75. Villiers to Antoine Olivier

Monsieur[1]

Je suis bien surpris de n'avoir reçu aucune de vos nouvelles depuis longtems. Vous savés, et jay l'honneur de vous l'ecrire que je conservois quelques effets precieux de feu Monseignr. L'eveque de Babylone comme croix Pectorales, anneau, Mitre, Crosse, etc. Monsr. Varlet son neveu me fit prier, il y a deja quelque tems de les luy remettre; le secretaire de la ville vint m'en parler de la part de Messrs les Bourg-mestres et je luy repondis que des que Mr Varlet seroit d'accord avec vous, Monsieur, je remettrois volontiers ces effets a celuy ou ceux dont on conviendroit. Je vous supplies, Monsieur, de vouloir bien convenir entre vous, il me semble que vous pourriés partager et luy ceder quelqu'un des effets. Il y a par exemple trois croix pectorales, il pourroit en avoir un et peut etre deux. Je croi qu'il faut se hâter, je suis infirme, je suis vieux, je puis mourir dans peü et dans ce cas je ne sai ce que deviendront ces effets: je ne puis güeres les laisser qu'au Pasteur chez qui je loge, mais jay veü mourir dans peu de tems deux Pasteurs dans la maison: il est vrai que celuy d'a present est jeune, mais il est fort delicat, et est souvent malade; ayez la bonté, Monsieur, de me marquer ce que vous voulés que je fasse.

Il y a longtems que l'argent provenant de la vente des livres est consumé. Comme avant la mort de Mgr l'eveque de Babylone, le Bureau luy avoit fait des grosses avances il a eté remboursé par cet argent, mais vous n'y perdres pas beaucoup, Monsieur, ces effects ne laissent pas que de valoir: il y a surtout une des trois croix qui est de grand prix. Je presente mes respects a Madame votre epouse, a Monsr. et a Madame Varlet, et suis avec bien du respect.

Monsieur Votre tres humble et tres obeissant/serviteur

S/Villiers

a Utrecht ce 6 Septembre 1745
mon adresse est a M. Devilliers sur le Mari-plaatz. a Utrecht
Tournez la feüille//

p.s. comme je n'ay jamais reçu reponse a la lettre que je vous ecrivis
Monsieur, le 14 aoust 1743, et que peut etre elle a eté egarée, je transcri-
rai icy l'article qui regardoit les deux cachets d'argent que je vous avois
envoié l'année precedente.

"Je me suis donné bien des mouvemens pour m'informer ce qu'etoient
devenus le Sieur Norblin, et les deux cachets d'argent que je luy avois
donné l'an passé pour vous remettre, Monsieur: enfin je viens d'apprendre que ces deux cachets d'argent avec la petite plaque de cuivre etoient
entre les mains d'un curé du Diocese de Sense oncle dudit Sr Norblin, et
que ce curé ne sachant a qui les remettre, en avoit parlé a Monsr.
Pothouin le fils avocat au parlement qui en a ecrit icy a un de ses amis. Je
luy ay fais faire aussitôt reponse qu'on devoit vous remettre lesdits
cachets d'argent avec la plaque de cuivre; ainsi, Monsieur, si l'on ne
vous les remet pas dans peü, vous pouvés vous adresser vous même a
Monsr Pothouin l'avocat."

Je vais joindre dans un papier separé une liste plus etendüe des effets
qui restent de feu Mgr l'eveque de Babylone//
Copie[2]
Liste des quelques effets appartenant icy devant au feu Mgr l'Eveque de
Babylone

1.   Il y a trois croix pectoralles L'une qui est tres Belle, Et qui est d'or
pesan plus de 64 agnels en hollondois, ou [illegible][3] En françois, on croit
qu'il a un medalion mouvant de La rouge croix, on y Lit *en Etiquete* cette
croix a appartenu autre fois a corneille Jansenius Evesque d'ypres; Les
Deux autres croix sont d'une pron[4] medievale elles sont de vermeil,
L'une est plus grand Et cest celle que Mgr de Babylone portait ordinairement, L'autre est petite et contient quelques reliques.
2.   un anneau d'or massif [illegible] avec En chasse une pierre precieuse
Bleüe qu'on croit etre une Turquoise
3.   une mître Brodée Sur un fond Blanc a fleurs enduit avec passements
aussy dor, Ensemance de perles Sur chaque fleur, dont il manque a peu
pres la moitié des perles.
4.   un Baton de crosse de Bois d'Ebène au[5] façons, Surmontée de trois
pieces avec 6 niv[6] ole d'argent d'Environ six gros chaque niv[6] ole Et Enri-
chie de Belles peices d'yvoire Le haut de la crosse tout d'argent Pesant a
peu pres Deux marcs cinq onces deux gros, ainsy Lavaleur de [hole] La
crosse peut aller a trois marcs une once six gros.//

5.   un petit calice d'argent doré en dedans avec sa petite Patene et une petite cuillere de mesme ce petit calice a esté cydevant a Mr Arnaud qui le donna a Mr Ernest[7] et Mr Ernest en fit present a Mr L'Eveque de Babylone.

6.   une petite Boëtte d'argent pour mettre La hostie

7.   une gabelle d'argent au nom du prelat

8.   une tabatiere d'argent d'or En dedans

9.   La Bulle du Pape[8] pour l'Evesché d'ascalon, et La coadjutorie de L'Evesché de Babylone.

---

[1] Above the incipit, toward the right margin, another hand has added: repondu le 30 juin 1755.

[2] All that follows in another hand.

[3] "assolans"?

[4] "production"?

[5] for "aux"

[6] for "nivéoles"

[7] Prince Ernest of Hesse-Rheinfels (1623-1698), friend and correspondent of Antoine Arnauld and Leibnitz.

[8] Clement XI. The original is today in the Rijksarchief Utrecht, no. 3626.

HISTORICAL CALENDAR (1668-1743)

1668 — Peace of Clement IX (Rospigliosi) between Church and State in France

1670 — Pope Clement X (Altieri)

1672 — War between France and the United Provinces

1676 — Pope Innocent XI (Odescalchi)

1678 — Treaty of Nijmegen between France and the United Provinces (10.viii)

1679 — dispersion of the "hermits" of Port Royal, closing of the schools

1680 — Arnauld flees to Brussels

1682 — Articles of St-Germain sanction political Gallicanism (16.iii)

1685 — Quesnel at Brussels
— beginning(?) of the hermitage on Mt. Valérien
— Revocation of the Edict of Nantes (22.x)

1688 — Antonius Heinsius tolerant grand pensioner of Holland

1689 — Pope Alexander VIII (Ottoboni)

1690 — condemnation by Pope of "philosophic sin"

1691 — Pope Innocent XII (Pignatelli)
— War between France and the United Provinces

1692 — definitive version of Quesnel's *Réflexions morales*

1693 — reconciliation of Louis XIV and the Papacy

1694 — Arnauld dies at Malines (8.vii)

1695 — royal edict accentuating differences between the upper and lower clergy (11.iv)
— Noailles approves Quesnel's *Réflexions morales* (22.vi)
— Noailles becomes archbishop of Paris (xii)

1697 — Quesnel arrested in Brussels (30.v)
— abrogation of the Articles of St-Germain by Louis XIV
— treaty of Rijswyk between France and United Provinces (30.ix)

1700 — Pope Clement XI (Francesco-Albani)

1702 — war between France and the United Provinces
— suspension of Pierre Codde, bishop of Sebaste, serving in Holland (3.iv)
— first volume of Jesuit *Lettres édifiantes et curieuses*

1704 — Chinese rites condemned by Pope

1705 — end of the Peace of Clement IX, after 37 years
— the Jesuits banished from Holland (20.v)

— *Vineam Domini*, bull against the "respectful silence" of the Jansenists (15.vii)

1708 — Fr. le Tellier confessor to Louis XIV with great influence

1709 — Port Royal closed (29.xi)

1710 — Port Royal destroyed (22.i)

1713 — treaty of Utrecht between France and United Provinces (11.iv)
— *Unigenitus*, bull against quesnellism (8.xi)

1715 — edict of king in favour of Jesuits (iv)
— death of Louis XIV (3.ix)
— regency of the Duke of Orleans, "Polysynodie" (4.ix)
— Noailles heads the "Conseil de conscience" (12.ix)
— imprisoned Jansenists set free

1716-1718 — candidates suspected of Jansenism cannot be made bishops

1717 — appeal by the bishops of Boulogne, Mirepoix, Montpellier, and Senez ("the four Bishops") against the *Unigenitus* (1.iii)

1717-1718 — more than 3,000 priests give expression to a new form of Gallicanism by appealing against the *Unigenitus*
— *Pastoralis Offici*, bull against Jansenist appellants (8.ix)
— end of "Polysynodie" (24.ix), beginning of Dubois ministry which with that of Fleury, until roughly 1733, continues government policy
— Daguesseau in disgrace, a Jansenist setback
— Noailles appeals against the *Unigenitus*
— the government refuses to recognize the bull *Pastoralis Offici*, 35 bishoprics vacant

1719 — the Pope yields by naming several "Jansenist" bishops (25.v)
— the Regent (and the government) accept the bull
— death of Quesnel at Amsterdam (2.xii)

1720 — appeal by the bishops of Bayeux, Lorraine, Montpellier and Senez against the *Unigenitus*
— death of Heinsius

1721 — Pope Innocent XIII (Conti)

1723 — death of Dubois

1724 — Pope Benedict XIII (Orsini-Gravosa)

1725 — Lateran Council condemns Jansenism
— convulsionist "miracles" begin in parish of Ste-Marguerite (Paris) (3.v)

1726 — canonisation of Gregory VII unleashes Jansenist resistance
— Fleury becomes prime minister
— Bishop of Senez severely criticizes the king (viii)

1727 — death of Archdeacon Pâris, "miracles" worked on his tomb until, roughly, 1734

— Council of Embrun suspends and exiles the bishop of Senez (ix)
— "Consultation of 30" defends Senez (xi)
1728-1803 — *Nouvelles ecclésiastiques*, influential Jansenist journal
— death of Noailles
— appellants harried out of the land
1729 — dispersion of hermits at Mt. Valérien by Archbishop of Paris
1730 — Pope Clement XII (Corsini)
— *Unigenitus* becomes civil law, beginning of a struggle between king and Parlement (24.iii)
— alliance between Jansenists and Parlement
1733 — temporary peace between king and Parlement (brought about by the War of the Polish Succession) with a few Jansenists named to bishoprics in the South
1734 — development of anti-episcopal feeling, liturgical innovation, figurist tendencies, and the acceptance of richerist principles among the clergy
1735 — canonisation of Vincent de Paul unleashes greater resistance to the papacy (16.v)
1738 — the Parlement of Paris condemns the Pope for sedition (4.1)
1740 — Pope Benedict XIV (Lambertini)
1742-1753 — clandestine Jansenist law-school at St-Josse (Paris)
1742 — *Ex quo Singulari*, bull ending Chinese Rites controversy (9.viii)
1743 — death of Fleury, personal reign of Louis XV

CALENDAR OF THE LIFE OF DMV (1678-1742)

1678 — born in Paris at home of parents, rue de Nevers, parish of St-André des Arts (15.iii)

1698 — studies at the Sorbonne

1706 — ordained priest at St-Magloire Seminary (Oratorian)
— Doctorate in Theology from the Sorbonne (8.vii)
— assistant priest in several parishes of the Paris region

1708 — pastor at Conflans, living with mother

1709 — death of father, aged 51 (ix)

1711 — received into the Société des Missions étrangères

1712 — leaves for America but does not sail (26.iii)

1713 — finally departs from Brest (20.ii) travels, via Santo Domingo and Havana, arriving Mobile (6.vi)

1714 — first trip to wilderness of North Mississippi and Alabama (15.iv-13.v)

1715 — leaves for the Illinois (Tamaroas) via the Mississippi, with La Mothe-Cadillac (7.iv)
— named Vicar-General in Canada (6.x)

1716 — differences with Jesuit missionaries in the Illinois

1717 — leaves the Illinois for Quebec (25.iii) via the Mississippi, Fort Mackinac and the Great Lakes
— arrives at Quebec (11.ix)

1718 — leaves Quebec for France (29.ix)
— named Bishop of Ascalon (i.p.i.) cum Babylon (27.ix)
— returns to La Rochelle (13.xi) and Paris (29.xi)

1719 — Curia demands acceptance of the bull *Unigenitus* (18.ii)
— consecrated *incognito* in the chapel of the Missions étrangères by Massillon, Bishop of Clermont, Matignon, Bishop of Condom, and Mornay, Co-Adjutor of Quebec (19.ii)
— leaves for Brussels on way to Persia (18.iii) arriving in Amsterdam (2.iv)
— confirms some 600 neophytes (17-23.iv)
— leaves Amsterdam aboard the *Koningsbergen* under Captain Pietersen (25.iv) for Reval (19.v) and St-Petersburg (31.v-20.vi)
— declared suspended by Clement XI (7.v)
— travels by boat to Moscow (6.vii-25.vii), Kazan (18.viii), Astrakhan (10.ix), and Niazova (9.x-26.x), to Schemacha in Persia (1.xi)

1720 — informed of his suspension by Father Bachou, a Jesuit (15.iii)
— leaves Schemacha (6.v) for Astrakhan (18.v), Moscow (30.x) and St. Petersburg (15.i) by land
1721 — death of mother, aged 61
— returns by land via Danzig (24.iii), Berlin (23.iv-2.v) and Hamburg (8.v) to Amsterdam (16.v-9.vii)
— arrives Paris (21.vii)
— in hiding at Regennes with Archbishop Caylus (viii)
1722 — returned in secret to Amsterdam (ii)
— Memorandum to the Curia (19.iii)
— consultation with the Canonist Gibert (xii)
1723 — *Appel à la Cour Pontificale* (15.ii) [pub. 1724]
— under pressure to return to France (and there to be arrested)
— election of Cornelis Steenhoven to be archbishop of Utrecht (27.iv)
1724 — *Plainte...à l'Eglise catholique, Lettre à Benoît XIII* (6.vi) [pub. 1724]
— *Suite de l'appel...* [pub. 1724]
— DMV consecrates Steenhoven, assisted by Dean van Erckel and Canon Dalenvort at Keizersgracht 160, Amsterdam, a private dwelling (15.x)
— *[Première] Apologie* [pub. 1724]
1725 — *Seconde Lettre à Benoît* XIII (15.i) [pub. 1727]
— Brief of Benedict XIII against DMV (21.ii)
— *Mémoire pour l'Eglise et Clergé d'Utrecht* (15.iii) [pub. 1725]
— Steenhoven dies (3.iv)
— Cornelis Barchman-Vuytiers elected to succeed Steenhoven (15.v)
— arrival in Holland of Carthusians and Orvalists
— plot to kidnap DMV (21.vi)
— *Lettre... à Monseigneur l'évêque de Montpellier* (12.vii) [pub. 1740]
— second brief of Benedict XIII against DMV (23.viii)
— consecration of Barchman-Vuytiers by DMV (6.xii)
1726 — *Seconde Plainte... à l'Eglise catholique* [pub. 1726]
1727 — leaves Amsterdam for Schonauwen
— *Seconde Apologie* [pub. 1727]
— discussions about usury in Church at Utrecht (viii)
— *Lettre... à Monseigneur de Senez* (12.xi) [pub. 1728]
1731 — *Lettre à un Docteur* (2.ix) [pub. 1731]
1733 — death of Barchman-Vuytiers in arms of DMV (13.v)
— election of Theodore van der Croon to succeed Barchman (22.vii)
— suffers from the first of a series of strokes (20.vii)

— *Lettre aux missionnaires du Tonquin* (25.x) [pub. 1734]
— DMV removes to Rijnwijk (xi)
— consultations with da Cunha and Fénelon at Zeist (15-16.xi)
— convulsionist "miracles" at Polsbroek (xii)

1734 — Testament of DMV (11.iii)
— accompanied by Jubé de la Cour, DMV retires to Zwolle in dispute over usury (iii-vii)
— consecration of van der Croon by DMV in cathedral at Utrecht (28.x)

1735 — Brief of Clement XII against DMV (17.ii)
— *Réponse à une lettre de Monsieur de Senez* (5.ix) [pub. 1737]

1736 — *Lettre à Monsieur de Montpellier* (7.vi) [pub. 1736]
— *Lettre...sur les erreurs avancées* (5.x) [pub. 1740]

1737 — *Lettre... à Monsieur de Montpellier* (7.vi) [pub. 1742]

1738 — quarrel at Utrecht over a Co-adjutor (through 1739)

1739 — death of van der Croon (8.vi)
— election of Pieter Jan Meindaerts (2.viii)
— Brief of Clement XII against Jansenism (6.x)
— consecration of Meindaerts by DMV in cathedral at Utrecht (18.x)
— DMV suffers from several strokes (xi-xii)

1740 — severe stroke (25.xii), Soanen dies the same day

1741 — Brief of Benedict XIV against DMV (24.i)
— Spiritual testament of DMV (2.ii)

1742 — death of DMV at Rijnwijk (14.v)
— interment at St. Mary's, Utrecht (18.v)
— Pontifical Requiem with Meindaerts presiding in cathedral at Utrecht (22.v)

1752 — DMV's works placed on the *Index* (2.ii)

1757 — final settlement of DMV's estate with his relatives and heirs

APPENDIX III

GENEALOGICAL TABLE
to illustrate the accompanying correspondence.

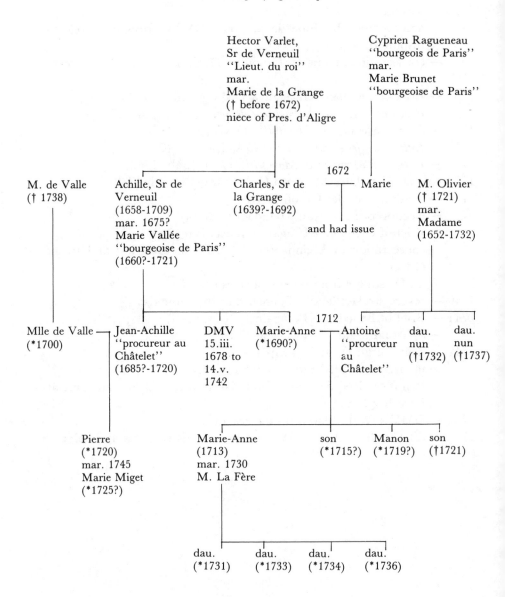

Sources: *Documents du minutier central*, p. 85-278, passim.
La Chesnaye-Desbois, *Dictionnaire de la noblesse*, vol. xii "Lagrange".

SPIRITUAL TESTAMENT OF DMV

[21 February, 1741]

†Au nom du Père et du Fils et du Saint-Esprit.†

Considérant devant Dieu que mes infirmités et divers accidents dont j'ai été attaqué depuis quelques années, m'avertissent de ne m'occuper que de l'éternité, et du soin de me préparer à paraître devant le Souverain Juge des vivants et des morts, qui est en même temps mon Rédempteur et mon Sauveur, je me prosterne en esprit et m'humilie le plus profondément qu'il m'est possible devant Dieu, pour lui rendre grâce de ses bienfaits, et pour lui demander par les mérites de Jésus-Christ, et par l'intercession des Bienheureux Anges et de tous les Saints, particulièrement de la Sainte-Vierge, le pardon de tous mes péchés, la grâce de vivre et de mourir dans son amour, et la gloire à laquelle j'ai la confiance qu'il a daigné me prédestiner avant tous les siècles.

Je crois aussi devoir rendre compte à son Eglise des sentiments dans lesquels je désire vivre et de mourir, d'autant plus qu'il est de mon devoir d'expliquer et même de corriger quelques démarches dont on pourrait abuser; et que par rapport aux autres que je n'ai faites que pour me conformer à son esprit, j'ai demandé son Jugement par des Actes d'Appel dans lesquels je persiste.

Je déclare donc premièrement que par la grâce de Dieu je veux vivre et mourir dans la foi et dans l'unité de l'Eglise Catholique Apostolique et Romaine, au Jugement de laquelle je soumets tout ce que j'ai écrit; que j'embrasse avec une docilité sans réserve toutes les décisions qu'elle a faites, ou qu'elle fera à l'avenir sur le dogme; que je révère les Lois de sa discipline comme la règle que l'on doit suivre; que je regarde Notre Saint Père le Pape comme le premier des Vicaires de Jésus-Christ, et le Siège de Saint-Pierre comme le centre de l'unité Catholique; que je crois qu'il n'est jamais permis de s'en séparer, et qu'on doit rechercher par tous les moyens légitimes la Communion immédiate avec le Saint-Siège, lorsque la malice des hommes empêche qu'on n'en jouisse actuellement et parfaitement.

Je déclare en second lieu que quand je souscrivis en Sorbonne en l'année 1702 le Formulaire du Clergé et la Censure de M. Arnauld,[1] ce

---

[1] Prescribed by an Arrêt du Conseil, 23 April 1661, against Arnauld's distinction between "le fait et le droit".

fut par défaut de lumière, et sur de mauvais conseils que je suivis avec trop de docilité. Je n'ignorais pas dès lors que l'Eglise même n'est pas infaillible sur des faits récents, contestés, obscurs et douteux, indifférents à la Religion, et qui sont l'objet de la critique et non de la foi. Je savais par conséquent qu'elle ne peut en exiger la croyance en vertu de sa seule autorité; que le fait de Jansénius était de cette nature; qu'ainsi on ne pouvait être obligé de le croire et d'en attester la croyance; que tout ce qu'on pouvait exiger des particuliers à cet égard, était qu'ils ne s'élevassent point contre le Jugement que le Pape Alexandre VII et quelques Evêques avaient porté sur ce fait;[2] et que cela était incontestable, non seulement par les principes de la foi, mais encore par tout ce qui s'était passé lors de la Paix conclue sous le Pape Clément IX avec le concours des deux Puissances.[3] Mais c'est de ces principes même qu'on abusa pour me faire illusion. On me persuada qu'il était si notoire que l'Eglise se contentait sur le fait de Jansénius d'une soumission de respect et de discipline, qu'il n'y avait point lieu, surtout depuis la Paix de Clément IX de regarder la souscription du Formulaire comme une marque de croyance. Ce sentiment était alors aussi commun qu'il était commode, et les Syndics même déclaraient aux Candidats que l'intention de la Faculté n'était point de rien exiger de plus que le silence respectueux.[4] On étendait ce principe jusqu'à la souscription de la Censure de M. Arnauld. La Faculté, disait-on, n'a point prétendu proscrire la doctrine ni le langage des Saints Pères. Il est toujours permis de dire qu'on ne peut faire le bien sans la grâce efficace. La Faculté a entendu la proposition de M. Arnauld dans le sens d'une impuissance absolue et antécédente, ou au moins dans le sens d'une privation d'un pouvoir surnaturel dans les Justes. C'est dans ce sens qu'on doit prendre la Censure; tout ce que la Faculté demande, est que ses membres condamnent avec elle cette erreur, et qu'ils ne s'élèvent pas contre son Jugement, sous prétexte qu'elle aurait mal pris le sens de M. Arnauld.[5]

---

[2] Reference to the bull *Regiminis apostolici* (15 February 1665) and to the appeal to a future Council by the bishops of Boulogne (de Langle), Mirepoix (de Labroue), Montpellier (Colbert), and Senez (Soanen), in 1717.

[3] The Peace of Pope Clement IX or, Peace of the Church, lasted from 1668 to 1705, seconded by both the spiritual and temporal powers.

[4] An attitude that was condemned by Clement XI in the bull *Vineam Domini*, 16 July 1705.

[5] Note from the *Nouvelles ecclésiastiques*: Dans la première proposition de fait, M. Arnauld dit qu'il a lu exactement le livre de Jansénius, et qu'il n'y a point trouvé les propositions condamnées par le feu Pape [Innocent X], et néanmoins que comme il condamne ces propositions en quelque lieu qu'elles se rencontrent, il les condamne dans Jansénius, si elles y sont. IIe Proposition de droit: La grâce sans laquelle on ne peut rien, a manqué à St Pierre dans sa chute.

C'est dans cet esprit et sur ces assurances que j'ai signé; mais je reconnais que j'ai mal fait. La proposition de M. Arnauld qui regarde le droit est tellement consacrée dans la Tradition, que, comme l'a remarqué M. Bossuet Evêque de Meaux, la condamner, c'est livrer tous les Pères au Jansénisme.[6] De plus, la Censure à laquelle je souscrivais, condamne aussi la première proposition de ce Docteur, qui concerne le fait de Jansénius. Or ceux-mêmes qui m'engageaient à souscrire, reconnaissaient qu'il était indubitable qu'ainsi que l'énonce cette proposition, l'Eglise ne pouvait exiger sur un fait tel que celui de Jansénius qu'un silence respectueux. Condamner cette proposition, c'était fixer la souscription du Formulaire à signifier la croyance du fait. C'était même faire de cette croyance un devoir indispensable, non seulement pour ceux qui signaient, mais encore pour tous ceux qui savaient que les V Propositions avaient été condamnées comme extraites de Jansénius, et dans le sens de cet auteur.[7] D'ailleurs, indépendemment de cette Censure, les paroles même du Formulaire marquent la croyance du fait, et celui du Clergé porte que Jansénius a mal expliqué la doctrine de Saint Augustin. Je ne devais donc pas signer purement et simplement le Formulaire, puisque je ne croyais pas ce fait, et qu'il me paraissait au moins douteux. La Paix de Clément IX peut bien autoriser les inférieurs à signer avec explication, et elle doit engager les Supérieurs à se contenter des signatures expliquées, que ce Pape a admises avec beaucoup de prudence; mais elle en'autorise point à signer ce qu'on ne croit pas, ni par conséquent à souscrire purement et simplement une Formule qui exprime la croyance d'un fait sur lequel on est dans le doute. Enfin rien n'était plus opposé à la conduite des IV Evêques que cette souscription que je faisais en Sorbonne.[8] Ces Prélats avaient souscrit et fait souscrire avec explication, et je souscrivais purement et simplement. Ils avaient expliqué le dogme même et la condamnation qu'ils faisaient des V Propositions, en déclarant que c'était sans donner la moindre atteinte à la doctrine de la grâce efficace par elle-même; et en souscrivant le Formulaire, je souscrivais en même temps à une Censure qui donnait réellement atteinte à la nécessité de cette grâce; puisque s'il n'était pas vrai que sans elle on ne peut rien, elle ne serait pas nécessaire pour tout acte de piété chrétienne. Ces Evêques expliquant la soumission qu'ils rendaient aux Constitutions sur le point de fait, la faisaient consister à ne point contester la décision; et c'est ce que je condamnais avec la Faculté en souscrivant à la Censure.

---

[6] Bishop Bossuet made this observation in his *Censura et declaratio conventus generalis cleri gallicani congregati in palatio San-Germano...*, Paris, 1700.

[7] Condemned in the bulls *Cum Occasione* (31 May 1653) and *Ad Sacram* (16 October 1656).

[8] The appeal mentioned in note 2 above.

C'est pourquoi j'ai retracté cete souscription, que j'ai eu le malheur de faire sur de faux principes, et dans un âge où il n'était pas étonnant que je me laissasse éblouir. J'en demande pardon à Dieu et à l'Eglise. Je réclame à la Paix de Clément IX à laquelle j'aurais dû me conformer. Je regrette qu'en signant purement et simplement on ait donné lieu à l'annéantir, et je me joins à feu MM. les Evêques de Montpellier et de Senez,[9] qui ont interjeté appel au Saint Siège et au futur Concile, du violement de cette Paix si juste et si précieuse, à laquelle on donne atteinte, soit en exigeant des souscriptions pures et simples, soit en condamnant celles qui sont conformes aux Procès-verbaux des IV Evêques.

Rien ne fait mieux voir la nécessité des précautions que prirent ces sages Prélats dans l'affaire du Formulaire, que la Constitution *Unigenitus*.[10] Ce décret met en évidence que les adversaires de la grâce faisaient condamner sous les termes vagues et équivoques du sens de Jansénius, puisque on a fait dire à Clément XI que celles des CI Propositions qui regardent la grâce, renferment le sens condamné dans les V Propositions proscrites par Innocent X et par Alexandre VII.[11] Cela seul devrait suffire pour empêcher de souscrire sans explication les Bulles que Clément XI explique si mal, et pour engager à rejeter absolument cette dernière.[12] Mais elle renferme d'ailleurs une multitude d'autres défauts qui ont été exposé en différents Ecrits;[13] et j'en ai été si frappé d'abord que j'ai toujours évité de donner la moindre marque d'approbation à ce Décret, qu'on tenterait en vain de réconcilier avec le dogme, la discipline, ou le langage de l'Eglise. C'est apparemment ce qui commença à me rendre suspect aux Officiers de la Cour de Rome, lorsque je partis pour me rendre en Perse, comme mon devoir m'y obligeait.

Je leur devins bientôt odieux par l'engagement où la divine Providence me mit de rendre quelque service à l'Eglise de Hollande que cette Cour voulait priver de ses droits, et gouverner par des Ministres précaires et destituables, comme elle fait les nouvelles Missions. C'est déjà un grand abus que de ne point fonder les nouvelles Eglises, comme ont fait les Apôtres, et les hommes Apostoliques de tous les siècles, en y établissant des Pasteurs ordinaires, pour y conduire un troupeau dont ils soient les Chefs, avec une juste subordination au premier des Pasteurs, et à l'Eglise

---

[9] Charles-Joachim de Colbert de Croissy, bishop of Montpellier, and Jean Soanen, bishop of Senez. See their *Acte d'appel de Msgrs les évêques de Senez et de Montpellier par lequel renouvellant et confirmant l'appel par eux interjeté le 1er mars 1717…*, s.l. [1727]

[10] Bull promulgated against 101 propositions from Pasquier Quesnel's *Réflexions morales* (1668) by Clement XI on 8 September 1713 and which sharply divided opinion in France.

[11] See note 2 above.

[12] Not only the bull *Unigenitus* (see note 10 above), but also the bull *Vineam Domini* (see note 4 above).

[13] See the Bibliography of DMV's writings appended hereto.

Universelle. Mais c'est un abus bien plus criant, que de vouloir renverser ce bel ordre dans une Eglise qui subsiste depuis mille ans, et qui, pour avoir perdu ses biens temporels en conservant la foi, n'en est devenue que plus digne de tous les biens et de tous les droits spirituels. Je ne savais pas tous les démêlés qu'il y avait sur ce sujet par rapport à l'Eglise de Hollande; mais me trouvant dans cette portion du troupeau de Jésus-Christ tandis que j'attendais une occasion de partir pour la Perse, je ne crus pas pouvoir refuser de donner la Confirmation à des Fidèles que me présentaient leurs Pasteurs ordinaires, établis par des Evêques que le Saint-Siège avait lui-même nommés et consacrés. C'est néanmoins ce qui donna lieu à la première suspense qui me fut signifiée en Perse, dont j'ai démontré la nullité dans ma première *Apologie*.[14]

L'impuissance où je me trouvais en conséquence de cette prétendue Censure d'être utile à l'Eglise particulière pour laquelle j'avais été ordonné, m'engagea à revenir en Europe; et ne pouvant me réconcilier avec la Cour de Rome sans trahir ma conscience, je crus devoir fixer mon séjour dans l'Eglise de Hollande. Je lui ai ordonné des Prêtres et quatre Archevêques consécutifs, et n'ai pas cru qu'après avoir consacré une partie de ma vie à aller secourir des Eglises éloignées en Asie et dans le Nouveau Monde, je dusse refuser à une Eglise si voisine de la France une assistance dont elle avait le plus pressant besoin. J'ai cru en cela ne faire que ce que demandait la charité épiscopale.[15] J'ai concerté mes démarches avec les Prélats et les Théologiens les plus dignes d'être consultés. J'en ai rendu compte dans ma seconde *Apologie*;[16] et je désire de tout mon cœur que le Concile au Tribunal duquel j'ai porté cette affaire par un *Appel*[17] canonique, veuille bien en prendre connaissance; et ce n'est pas tant afin qu'il me rende justice, que dans l'espérance que le Concile fera cesser dans l'Eglise de Hollande cette espèce de schisme qui y sépare la plupart des Catholiques des pays de leurs légitimes Pasteurs. Je souhaiterais fort que Notre Saint Père le Pape prévînt sur cela le Concile, et qu'en examinant canoniquement cette affaire, sur laquelle quelques-uns de ses prédécesseurs ont été sans doute mal-informés, il rendît la paix à des enfants qui le révèrent.

Je recommande avec tout l'instance possible et avec toute l'affection dont je suis capable, à M. l'Archevêque d'Utrecht,[18] à MM. du Chapitre, à tout le clergé, et au peuple de ces Provinces, de ne s'éloigner jamais

---

[14] Ibid.

[15] The Netherlands had been without a Roman Catholic bishop since the deposition of Pierre Codde in 1704; Cornélis Steenhoven was the first to fill the void and was consecrated by DMV 15 October 1724.

[16] See the Bibliography of DMV's writings appended hereto.

[17] Ibid.

[18] Pieter-Jan Meindaerts, consecrated by DMV 18 October 1739.

de cet esprit de respect de Notre Saint Père le Pape, de l'obéissance canonique qui lui est due, de l'amour de l'Unité, et de la disposition où ils
sont de tout sacrifier à un si grand bien, autant que la conscience le peut
permettre.

Je crois devoir recommander en particulier à M. l'Archevêque, et le
conjurer très instamment de ne jamais procéder à la consécration d'un
évêque, soit sous le titre d'Evêque d'Haerlem, soit sous celui de Coadju-
teur, ou en quelqu'autre manière que ce soit, que de l'avis et du consentement de tous les Prélats orthodoxes qui honoreront cette Eglise de leur
bienveillance; et qui étant instruits de ses droits, seront touchés de son
état, n'y ayant qu'un esprit de schisme qui puisse jamais porter à en user
autrement.

Je le supplie aussi d'être fidèle à n'ordonner jamais aucun Evêque, ou
aucun Prêtre, et à n'engager même dans les Ordres Sacrés aucun Sujet
qui ne soit bien déclaré contre toute usure, ferme dans les principes qui y
sont opposés, et bien déterminé à ne pas accorder dans la pratique
l'Absolution à ceux qui prêtant à des riches, stipulent qu'on leur rendra
plus qu'ils n'ont prêté; ce qu'on a voulu justifier en ce pays, à titre de
rente racheptable des deux côtés.[19]

Je n'ai point oublié ce que m'a dit feu M. Barchman Archevêque
d'Utrecht[20] étant sur le point de mourir, que si c'était un mal que cette
Eglise n'eût point d'évêque, c'en serait un plus grand encore, qu'elle en
eût un qui serait favorable à l'usure; parce qu'en effet il est plus important de contribuer à conserver dans toute l'Eglise l'intégrité de la foi et la
pureté de la morale, que de perpétuer l'Episcopat ou le Sacerdoce dans
une Eglise particulière. Si je n'ai point pris ces précautions à l'égard des
deux premiers Archevêques que j'ai sacrés, c'est que je ne connaissais
pas le besoin que cette Eglise avait d'être instruite sur ce point. Mais plus
j'en ai été informé, plus j'ai cru qu'il fallait travailler à extirper l'usure;
et si j'ai paru à quelques personnes trop difficile à contenter sur ce point,
lorsqu'il a été question de sacrer les deux derniers Archevêques, je crains
plutôt de n'avoir pas été assez ferme; et je conjure M. l'Archevêque de ne
se point laisser ébranler par les clameurs de ceux qui se plaindraient
qu'on veut introduire un nouveau Formulaire. Il ne s'agit point ici,
comme dans le Formulaire d'Alexandre VII,[21] d'un fait nouveau ou
indifférent à la Religion: il s'agit d'un dogme indubitable qu'il faut soutenir, et d'une pratique pernicieuse qu'il faut extirper. C'est pour procurer de tels biens, qu'on donne à l'Eglise des Pasteurs; et il est indispensa-

---

[19] DMV refers here to the problems raised by E. Richer and "richérisme"; cf. E. Préclin, *Les Jansénistes du XVIIIe siècle et la Constitution civile du clergé* (Paris, 1929).
[20] Cornélis-Jan van Barchman-Vuytiers, consecrated by DMV 30 September 1725.
[21] See note 2 above.

ble de n'en établir aucun dont on n'ait une assurance morale qu'il sera
fermement attaché à la saine doctrine, et puissant pour reprendre ceux
qui s'en écartent.

Quant à MM. du Chapitre, s'ils conservent quelque reconnaissance
des services que je leur ai rendus en me sacrifiant pour cette Eglise,
j'espère que j'aurai cette joie dans le Seigneur, qu'ils se joindront à leur
digne Archevêque, pour extirper l'erreur et l'abus. Quand la plupart
d'entr'eux ont fait profession d'être fermement attachés à ce principe
généralement reçu parmi les Théologiens, qu'il n'est jamais permis
d'exiger du profit du prêt fait à un pauvre ou à un riche, et qu'on peut seulement dans le cas d'un gain que le prêt fait cesser, ou d'un dommage
qu'il cause, demander une juste indemnité, en observant toutes les conditions que les bons Théologiens prescrivent; que ces MM. sans doute
n'ont pas voulu me surprendre par des équivoques: ils ont donc entendu
ce principe comme on l'entend dans les Ecoles, comme l'entendent Saint
Thomas, Hesselius, M. de Sainte-Beuve, le Père Alexandre, *la Morale* de
Grenoble,[22] et en générale tous les bons Théologiens.

Il ne me reste que de les prier de ne s'écarter dans la spéculation, ni
dans la pratique, de ce principe qui est en effet indubitable, et qui appar-
tient à la foi de l'Eglise. La tolérance des Lois civiles, la témérité de quelques Théologiens qui ont entrepris de justifier ce que l'Eglise a toujours
condamné, les vains prétextes de ceux qui trouvent partout un lucre ces-
sant, dès qu'on ne prête pas à des pauvres: l'indocilité des peuples, la
crainte de les voir s'éloigner de leurs Pasteurs, ne sont pas des raisons de
s'écarter de la Règle qui était généralement reçue dans ces Provinces
avant les révolutions. C'est pourquoi je conjure ces Messieurs, tous les
Pasteurs, et les Fidèles même, de détester toute usure, et de se distinguer
des Protestants en ce point, comme en tous les autres sur lesquels Calvin
a innové.

En général on ne saurait trop se défier de cette licence qui est le vice de
ce siècle, et qui fait qu'on s'écarte sans scrupule des sentiments reçus
dans l'Eglise. Les nouveaux Ecrivains que M. de Senez a combattus, ont
donné dans bien des excès, que M. de Laon a aussi relevés dans ses vingt
Lettres.[23] Je me joins à M. de Senez, pour témoigner toute l'horreur

---

[22] St Thomas Aquinas in *Collationes de X praeceptis*; Hesselius (Jan Hessels) in *Brevis et
catholica decalogi explictio* (1567); Jaques de Sainte-Beuve in his *Résolutions* (3 vol.,
1689-1704); Noël Alexandre in *Abrégé de la foi et de la morale de l'Eglise* (2 vol., 1686); and E.
Le Camus, bishop of Grenoble, in *Instructions et Méditations pour la retraite annuelle* (Grenoble, 1698; otherwise known as *la Morale de Grenoble*)—all fulminate against usury, and all
were approved by DMV in his struggle against usury in the Chapter at Utrecht (1727-
1739).

[23] See Jean Soanen, bishop of Senez, *Lettre de Msgr l'évêque de Senez sur les erreurs avancées
dans quelques nouveaux écrits* (1736), and Louis de Clermont de Chaste de Roussillon, bishop
of Laon, *Mandement de Msgr l'Evêque-Duc de Laon* (1718).

qu'un bon Catholique doit avoir de cette hardiesse si pernicieuse à inventer et à défendre des nouveautés; et pour exhorter tous les bons Théologiens à combattre *pour la Foi qui a été une fois laissée aux Saints par Tradition.*

Je bénis Dieu des miracles par lesquels il lui a plu de venir au secours de ses Serviteurs,[24] et de fortifier l'espérance que nous avons qu'il lui plaira de remédier à tous nos maux, en renouvellant la face de son Eglise. Il s'en est fait dans ce pays même, pour attester la vocation et honorer le Ministère des Archevêques que j'ai consacrés. Occupons-nous de ces merveilles, et rendons-y témoignage: c'est le moyen d'en obtenir de nouvelles, et de recueillir le fruit de celles que Dieu nous a accordées dans sa miséricorde. Quant à l'événement singulier des Convulsions, j'ai applaudi aux *Règles* que M. de Montpellier a établies avec tant de sagesse, et après un examen si mûr;[25] c'est à quoi je crois devoir m'en tenir.

Il ne me reste plus que de remercier les amis si généreux qui ont jusqu'ici contribué par leurs aumônes à entretenir les Serviteurs de Dieu réfugiès en ce pays: j'espère qu'ils auront la charité de continuer cette bonne œuvre; et j'y consacre volontiers ce qui pourra me rester ici d'effets après les frais funéraires, et l'acquit de mes dettes:[26] conjurant les Séculiers et les Réguliers d'honorer toujours par leur conduite l'Eglise Catholique, dont ils sont membres, de répondre par la sainteté de leur vie à celle de la cause pour laquelle Dieu leur a fait la grâce de souffrir, ou de sacrifier quelque chose, de vivre dans une parfaite union, et de se souvenir de moi dans leurs prières.

Fait à Utrecht le 2 Février, 1741

(*Nouvelles Ecclésiastiques*, 25 November 1742, p. 185-188.)

---

[24] Allusion to the "miracles" of Archdeacon Pâris in the Cemetery of St-Médard from 1727 to 1734, as well as to those involving Marguérite Périer, Rousse de Mareuil, la femme Boissonade, et. al.

[25] Charles-Joachim de Colbert de Croissy, bishop of Montpellier, wrote about the "convulsionnaires" in his *Réponse...à Mlle Hardouin* (1732) and in his *Copie d'une lettre...du 12 octobre 1733* (1733).

[26] Unfortunately, according to number 49 of the present Correspondence, DMV did not, or could not, make this disposition of funds as he here claims he would.

BIBLIOGRAPHY

A. MANUSCRIPTS

CANADA

Quebec, Archives du Séminaire
Polygraphie 9, no 26 (DMV's Mississippi mission);
Sém. 15, no 68 (powers granted DMV by Msgr. de Saint-Vallier).

FRANCE

Paris, Archives nationales
Série G⁸, 2628 (correspondence with agents of the clergy);
Série L, 20 (Unigenitus — notes of Joly de Fleury);
Série M, 746 (Unigenitus and Jansenism).
Paris, Bibliothèque nationale
Collection Duchesne, no 24 (genealogy of the Varlet family);
Collection Joly de Fleury, folios 563-920 (*avis* and *mémoires*, 1712-1789), 1048-1049 (*lettres patentes*, 1714-1763), 1616 (*actes anciens*), 2491-2492 (Jansenist bibliography);
Fonds français, nos 5751, 10612, 10613, 23441-23458 (Unigenitus), 15801, 17666 (Jansenism), 17762 (letters of D. Thierry de Viaixnes, 1722), 24875-24878 (correspondence of N. Petitpied);
Histoire de France, V: Ld⁴ (ecclesiastical affairs, 18th century);
Nouvelles acquisitions françaises, no 23218 (correspondence of Cardinal de Noailles, 1710-1723), 25538 (letters 1682-1771, formerly Blancs-Manteaux no 77B), 3333-3335 (Jansenism and Parlements).
Paris, Bibliothèque Sainte-Geneviève
no 1965 (letter on the consecration of Barchman by DMV).
Paris, Ministère des Affaires étrangères
Correspondence politique, Hollande, vols 350-354 (French interest in Dutch religious matters);
Correspondence politique, Rome (1714-1739), 761-765 (Appellants).
Paris, Société de Port-Royal
Collection le Paige (devoted entirely to Jansenist documents), esp. no 480 (39) — (letter from DMV on miracles, 1.ix.1734).
Paris, Sorbonne, Bibliothèque Victor Cousin
no. 768-769 (collection of 18th-century autographs; Noailles, Fleury, Joachim Colbert, et al.).
Sens, Bibliothèque de Archevêché
Collection Languet (ecclesiastical affairs, 18th century).
Troyes, Bibliothèque municipale
Collection de l'Oratoire, nos 1013, 1645, 1650-1654, 1818-1823, 1833, 2150-2157, 2168, 2461, 2543 (Jansenist documents by Le Roy de St-Charles and Etemare);
Collection Sémillard, nos 2317, 2318 (Unigenitus); Fonds général, no 2892 (Jansenism).
Vitry-le-Francois, Bibliothèque municipale
nos 100-102 (Jansenism).

ITALY

Rome
[The contents of various collections in Rome that deal with DMV are carefully noted by P. Polman, OFM, in *Romeinse Bronnen IV*, ('s Gravenhage, 1966) and in *Romeinse Bescheiden* ('s Gravenhage, 1959), from which the following numbers are taken]

Romeinse Bronnen: nos 381, 533, 535, 538, 539(i), 554, 555, 612, 652, 679, 682, 684-689,
       692, 695-697, 700, 703, 709, 712, 715, 717(ii), 717(iv), 718, 722, 728, 730(i), 734-
       737, 741-745, 750-752, 755, 757(i), 762, 765(i), 766, 769-772, 780, 790-792, 795,
       798, 805, 807, 808, 811, 815, 817, 818, 823(iv)-831, 834-837, 849, 853, 859, 862-
       865, 870, 874, 883, 889, 893, 894, 921, 930
Romeinse Bescheiden: nos 98, 157, 180, 203, 261, 264, 266-270, 272, 274, 276, 277, 280-
       294, 298, 303, 305, 308, 309, 313, 315-320, 330, 333-337, 341, 342, 345, 373, 375,
       405, 407, 409, 412, 415-422, 425, 429-435, 438, 467-470, 473-477, 482, 679, 717

NETHERLANDS

Utrecht, Rijksarchief
Ancien fonds d'Amersfoort, nos 4044 (catalogue of DMV's Books), 3953, 4093, (DMV's
       death), 3626, 3627, 3753 (documents), 1456, 1606, 1610, 1983, 3009, 3317, 3750,
       3769-3794, 3923, 3933, 3934, 3978, 4043, 4136, 4146, 4151, 4998, 5649, 5815, 5907,
       6514, 6899 (some 169 letters *from* DMV), 2787, 3222, 3260, 3309, 3339, 3632-3749,
       4006, 4030-4032, 4083, 4092, 4137, 4774, 7024 (some 800 letters *to* DMV), 2675,
       3012, 3309, 3629, 3631, 4301, 4302 (documents, will and testaments, etc.).

USA

Berkeley (California), University of California
Bancroft Library, no 74/103Z (letters and documents).

B. PUBLISHED WORKS OF DMV

Arranged in the Order of their Composition

(Editor) Claude Caille, — *Quaestio theologica; quis solus habet immortalitatem* (I *Tim*. 6, v. 16).
       N.p. [Paris], n.d. [Défense dated 8.vii.1706], in-fol.
Appel de Msgr l'évêque de Babylone au Concile général de la Constitution Unigenitus. Haarlem,
       1724, 54 p. in-4. [Dates from 15.ii.1723]
Plainte de Msgr l'évêque de Babylone contre un libelle calomnieux répandu sous le nom de Leurs Excel-
       lences les Cardinaux assemblés en conclave...[avec] *la Suite de l'Appel*. N. Potgieter
       [Amsterdam], 1724, 98 p. in-4.
Apologie de M. l'évêque de Babylone, contenant son Appel au Concile général de la Constitution Unige-
       nitus, et d'un prétendu Acte de suspense [sic] *qui porte le nom de M. l'évêque d'Isphahan*...*avec*
       toutes les pièces qui ont rapport à cette affaire. N. Potgieter, Amsterdam, 1724, xxii and
       98 p. in-4.
Mémoire pour l'Eglise et le Clergé d'Utrecht. Utrecht, 1725. [Dates from 15.iii.1725]
Lettre de M. l'évêque de Babylone à M. l'évêque de Montpellier [Colbert de Croissy], *où il lui*
       marque la part qu'il prend à ses souffrances et le cas qu'il fait de ses ouvrages. [In Colbert de
       Croissy, *Œuvres*, III. 886; dates from 12.vii.1725]
Seconde Plainte à l'Eglise catholique au sujet de trois écrits répandus sous le titre de: Bref de N.S.P. le
       Pape Benoît XIII, le 21 février, le 23 août et le 6 décembre 1725. N.P. [Amsterdam], 1726,
       in-4.
Seconde Apologie de Msgr l'évêque de Babylone, contenant son Appel au Concile général et sa Seconde
       Plainte...*avec plusieurs pièces qui y ont rapport*... N. Potgieter, Amsterdam, 1727, xxxx
       and 511 p. in-4.
Lettre de Msgr l'archevêque d'Utrecht [Barchman-Vuytiers] *et de Msgr l'évêque de Babylone à*
       Msgr l'évêque de Senez [Soanen] *au sujet du jugement rendu à Embrun contre ce prélat*. N.p.
       [Paris], 1728, 29 p. in-4. [The letter is dated 12.xi.1727]
Lettre de M. l'évêque de Babylone aux missionnaires du Tonquin sur la Constitution [Unigenitus], *les*
       miracles [du diâcre Pâris], *et les devoirs d'un missionnaire*. Vve la Fuite, Utrecht, 1734, 13
       p. in-4. [The letter is dated 25.x.1733; see *Nouvelles ecclésiastiques*, 1735, p. 15]

Lettre de Msgr l'évêque de Babylone à Msgr l'évêque de Senez [Soanen] *en réponse à la lettre qu'il lui avait adressée sur les miracles* [du diâcre Pâris]. Paris, 1736, 31 p. in-4. [The letter is dated 5.ix.1735; see *Nouvelles ecclésiastiques* 1736, p. 81-82]

Lettre de Msgr l'évêque de Babylone à Msgr l'évêque de Montpellier [Colbert de Croissy] *pour servir de réponse à l'ordonnance de Msgr l'archevêque de Paris* [Vintimille du Lac], *rendue le 8 novembre 1735 au sujet des miracles opérés par l'intercession de Monsieur de Pâris*. Au Dépens de la Compagnie, Utrecht, 1736, 71 p. in-4. [Dated 12.v.1736; see *Nouvelles ecclésiastiques* 1736, p. 124 & 1742, p. 167]

Lettre de Msgr l'évêque de Babylone à Msgr l'évêque de Senez [Soanen] *au sujet* [de la lettre] *de ce prélat sur les erreurs avancées dans quelques nouveaux écrits*. Utrecht, 1736, 17 p. in-4. Dated 25.x.1736]

Lettre de Msgr l'évêque de Babylone à Msgr l'évêque de Senez [Soanen] *au sujet de la lettre de ce prélat sur les erreurs avancées dans quelques nouveaux écrits, et en particulier dans les notes du P. le Courrayer sur l'histoire du Concile de Trente*. N.p., 1737, 38 p. in-4. [Includes three *Lettres* in reply to an anonymous attack against Soanen, dated respectively 31.x.1736, 5.xii.1736 and 23. xii.1736; see *Nouvelles ecclésiastiques*, 1737, p. 13-14]

Lettre de Msgr l'évêque de Babylone à M. de Montpellier [Colbert de Croissy] *au sujet de l'Instruction pastorale de M. de Sens* [Languet] *contre les miracles*, in *Nouvelles ecclésiastiques*, 1742, p. 167 [Dated 7.vi.1737]

Œuvres posthumes de DMV, évêque de Babylone, où il est principalement traité des miracles, contre M. l'archevêque de Sens [Languet]. Cologne [Paris], 1743, in-4.

C. DICTIONARIES, REPERTORIES, ETC.

Actes et decrets du deuxième concile provincial d'Utrecht. Utrecht, 1764

Analectes pour servir à l'histoire ecclésiastique de la Belgique, 3 vol., Bruxelles, 1903-1904.

Archief voor Nederlandsche Kerkgeschiedenis, 7 vol. 's Gravenhage, 1885-1899.

Bruggeman, J., *Inventaris van de archieven bij het metropolitaan kapittel van Utrecht van de Roomsch-Katholieke Kerk der oud-bisschoppelijke clerezie*, 's Gravenhage, 1928.

Bruggeman/ J. van der Ven, A., *Inventaire des Pièces d'Archives françaises...* (Ancien fonds d'Amersfoort) La Haye, 1972.

Ceyssens, L, *Sources relatives au début du jansénisme et de l'antijansénisme*. Louvain, 1957.

Colonia, P. de, *Bibliothèque janséniste*, 2 vol. N.p., 1731.

Documents du minutier central (ed. Jurgens-Fleury), Paris, 1960.

Dupac de Bellegarde, G., *Recueil de divers témoignages en faveur de la catholicité et de la légitimité des droits du clergé et des chapitres, archevêques et évêques de l'Eglise catholique des Provinces Unies...* Utrecht, 1763.

Fisquet, H-J-P., *La France pontificale*, 20 vol. Paris [1866] Diocese de Paris, vol. 17-20.

Jal, A., *Dictionnaire critique de biographie et d'histoire*. Paris, 1874.

Joanne, A., *Dictionnaire géographique... de la France*. Paris, 1869.

Lalanne, L., *Dictionnaire historique de la France*. Paris, 1877.

Lavaqueray, A., *Les sources du jansénisme aux Archives nationales*, Paris, 1925.

Lefèvre, J. and P., *Documents relatifs à l'admission aux Pays-Bas des nonces et internonces des XVIIe et XVIIIe siècles*. Bruxelles, 1939.

Marion, M., *Dictionnaire des Institutions de la France aux 17e et 18e siècles*. Paris, 1923.

Mozzi, Luigi, *Compendio storico-cronologico de' piu' importanti giudizi portata dalla Santa Sede sopra il Baianismo, Giansenismo, e Quenellismo*, 2 vol. Fuligno, 1792.

[Nivelle, J-A.], *Le Cri de la foi, ou, Recueil des différents témoignages rendus par plusieurs facultés, chapitres, cures, communautés ecclésiastiques, séculières et régulières, au sujet de la Constitution Unigenitus*, 3 vol. N.p., 1719.

[Patouillet, L.], *Dictionnaire des livres jansénistes*, 4 vol. Anvers, 1752. [Sequel to Colonia's *Bibliothèque*, q.v]

Recueil des arrêts rendus dans tous les Parlements et Conseils souverains du royaume au sujet de la Bulle Unigenitus... N.p., 1753, 4 vol.

Romeinse Bescheiden voor de geschiedenis der Rooms-Katholieke Kerk in Nederland, I (1727-1754), (ed. P. Polman), 's Gravenhage, 1959.

Romeinse Bronnen voor de kerklijke toestand der Nederlanden onder de apostolische vicarissen, IV (ed. P. Polman), 's Gravenhage, 1959.

Van Beek, J., *Lijst van eenige boeken en brochuren uitgegeven in de Oud-Katholieke Kerk van Nederland sedert 1700 tot 1751*. Rotterdam, 1893.

Van Lommel, A., *Archief voor de geschiedenis van het aartsbisdom Utrecht*, Utrecht, 1874.

Willaert, L., *Bibliotheca janseniana belgica*, 3 vol., Namur/Paris, 1949-1951.

D. PRIMARY SOURCES

Anonymous. *Acta quaedam Ecclesiae ultrajectinae exhibita in defensionem... adversus scripta... archiepiscopi Mechliniensis.* Trajecta Batavorum, 1737.

Anonymous. *In obitum illustrissimi... DMV Babylonensis Episcopi, cum illi apud Carthusianos in domo dicta Schoonauw prope Ultrajectum solumnitur parentaretur di 21 Junii 1742.* Ultrajectum, 1742.

Anonymous. *Mémoires pour servir à l'histoire du clergé janséniste de Hollande.* N.p.; 1753.

Anonymous. *Mémoire sur l'état présent des refugiés français en Hollande*, Paris, 1728. (A violent attack against DMV and Barchman).

Anonymous. *Ter Gedagtenisse van den doorlugtisten en hoogwaerdigsten Heer Domenicus-Maria Varlet, bisschop van Babylonien. In den heer ontslaepen op Rijnwijk, buiten Utrecht, in het sesen-sestigste Jaer syns ouderdoms. Den 17 Mey*, mdccxlii. [Utrecht, 1742].

Barbeau de la Bruyère, *La Vie de M. François de Pâris, diâcre.* N.p., 1731.

Barbier, E-J-F, *Journal historique et anecdotique du règne de Louis XV* (ed. Charpentier), 8 vol. Paris, 1853-1857 (written from 1718 to 1763).

Bernard d'Arras, *Code des Paroisses*, 2 vol. Paris, 1735. [Necessary for history of liturgical reform].

[Besoigne, J.], *Catéchisme sur l'Eglise pour les temps de trouble.* N.p. [1737].

Broedersen, N., *Quinque tractatus historici de rebus metropolitanae Ecclesiae ultrajectinae*, 3 vol. [Delft/Utrecht], 1729-1763.

Bullarium magnum, 58 vols. Romae, 1733-1768. (Esp. vol. 50-56)

Buvat, J., *Journal de la Régence* (1715-1723), 2.v. Paris, 1865

[Cadry, J.], *Histoire du Livre des Réflexions morales* [de Pasquier Quesnel] *et de la Constitution Unigenitus*, 4 vol. Amsterdam, 1723-1734.

Carré de Montgéron, *La Vérité des miracles opérés par l'intercession de M. le diâcre Pâris*, 2 vol. Utrecht, 1737.

Colbert de Croissy, Charles-Joachim, *Œuvres*, 3 vol. Cologne [Paris], 1750.

Damen H., *Dissertatio de numero episcoporum* [Louvain, 1725].

De Meyere, L., *Historia de rebus ecclesiae ultrajectinae* [Louvain, 1726].

Dorsanne, abbé, *Journal* (Dupac de Bellegarde ed.), 5 vol. N.p., 1756.

Duguet-Mol, J-J., *Journal historique des convulsions.* N.p.n.d.

Dupac de Bellegarde, *Histoire abrégée de l'Eglise métropolitaine d'Utrecht, principalement depuis la Révolution arrivée dans les VII Provinces Unies des Pays-Bas jusqu'à présent.* Paris, 1765.

Fabroni, A., *De Vita et rebus gestis Clementis XII commentarium.* Romae, 1760.

Fleury, C., *Historia ecclesiastica*, 9 vol. Augusta Vindelicorum, 1768 et seq.

Fourqueveaux, J-B-R. de, *Catéchisme historique et dogmatique*, 5 vol., N.p., 1729.

Guarnacci, M., *Vitae et res gestae Pontificum Romanorum et S.R.E. Cardinalium a Clemente X usque ad Clementem XII*, 2 vol. Romae, 1751.

Hoynck van Papendrecht, C., *Historia ecclesiae ultrajectinae a tempore mutatae religionis in foederatio Belgio... cum Refutatio instrumenti capitulationis presbyteriorum ultrajectensium a Constitutione Unigenitus.* Mechlinae, 1725.

La Harpe, Bénard de, *Journal historique de l'établissement des Français en Louisiane*, Nouvelle Orléans, 1834.

Lami, G., "Lettres inedites... à sa famille sur la France du 18e siècle" (ed. Vaussard), *Revue des études italiennes* (1954), p. 72-94.

Le Gros, N., *Lettres théologiques contre le traité des prêts de commerce et en général contre toute usure*, N.p. [1739-1740].

[Lanfredini, G.], *Historia de rebus Ecclesiae ultrajectinis...* Colonia, 1725.

Le Paige du Pratz, *Histoire de la Lousiane*, 3.v, Paris, 1758.

Luynes, C-P. d'Albert de, *Mémoires* (ed. Dussieux and Soulie), 17 vol. Paris, 1860-1865. (Written 1735 and 1737).

Marais, M., *Journal et Mémoires* (ed. Lescure), 4 vol. Paris, 1863-1868. (Written between 1715 and 1737).

Maultrot, G-N./Meyl, C., *Apologie des jugements rendus en France contre le schisme par les tribunaux séculiers*, 2 vol. N.p., 1752.

Montesquieu, C-L. de Secondat de, *Œuvres complètes* (ed. Masson), 3 vol. Paris, 1950. (Esp. vol. II, p. 113, 325-326, 1289-1301.)

Montlauzon, R. P., *Journal du Concile d'Embrun*. N.p., 1727.

Mozzi, l., *Storia delle rivoluzione della chiesa d'Utrecht*, 3 vol. Venezia, 1787.

Nouvelles ecclésiastiques, 76 vol. [Paris] 1728-1803 (esp. in re: DMV — 1731, p. 194; 1735, p. 15; 1736, p. 81-82, 124; 1737, p. 13-14; 1742, p. 49-53, 105-108, 167, 185-188; 1760, p. 188).

Patouillet, L., *Supplément des Nouvelles ecclésiastiques*, 16 t. in 4 vol. N.p., 1733-1748.

Petitdidier, M., *Dissertatio sur le sentiment du Concile de Constance touchant l'infaillibilité des Papes*. Paris, 1721.

[Petitpied, N.], *Lettres touchant la matière de l'usure*. Lille [Utrecht?], 1736.

Quesnel, Pasquier, *Le Nouveau Testament en français, avec des Réflexions morales sur chaque verset pour en rendre la lecture plus utile et la méditation plus aisée*. Paris, 1692. (An earlier version dates from 1668)

Sartre, abbé, *Voyage en Hollande*. Paris, 1896. (Written ca 1725)

St. Simon, Louis de Rouvroy, duc de, *Mémoires* (ed. Boislisle), 41 vol. Paris, 1879-1928.

Soanen, Jean, *La vie et les lettres...* 2 vol. Cologne [Paris], 1750.

[Tencin, P. de, archbishop of Embrun, cardinal], *Institution pastorale et ordonnance... portant condamnation d'un livre qui a pour titre: Histoire du Concile de Trente, 14 août 1737*. Paris, 1738.

[Viaixnes, T. de, OSB], *Etat présent de l'Eglise d'Utrecht*. N.p., 1729

Villiers, L-P Vaquier de, *Lettre d'un prêtre français retiré en Hollande, à un de ses amis de Paris, au sujet de l'état et des droits de l'Eglise catholique d'Utrecht*. Utrecht, 1754.

Van Espen, Z-B, "Casus resolutio...de misero statu Ecclesiae ultrajectinae", in *Opera* (Bruxellas 1768), p. 396-415.

—— *De numero episcoporum ad validam ordinationem episcopi requisito* [Louvain, 1725].

[Van Erckel, J-C], *Causa Ecclesiae ultrajectinae...* [Utrecht], 1724.

Verhulst, P-L, *De conservatione archiepiscopi ultrajectinensis, etc.* [Utrecht, 1725].

E. SECONDARY SOURCES

Adam, A., *Du Mysticisme à la révolte: les Jansénistes au 18e siècle*. Paris, 1968.

Alatri, P., *Profilo storico del cattolicismo liberale in Italia*. Palermo, 1950.

Allo E-B., "Le Jansénisme et sa condamnation", *Nova et Vetera*, 1 (1937).

Amman, E., "Varlet, Dominique-Marie", *Dictionnaire de théologie catholique*, 15:3 (1950), p. 2535-2536.

Appolis, E., *Le "Tiers parti" catholique au XVIIIe siècle*. Paris, 1960.

Armogathe, R., "A Propos des miracles de Saint-Médard: les preuves de Carré de Mont-géron et le positivisme des lumières", *Revue de l'histoire des religions* (1971), p. 135-160.

Aubertin, C., *L'Esprit public au XVIIIe siècle*. Paris, 1889.

Bassieux, L., *Théorie des libertés gallicanes du Parlement de Paris au XVIIIe siècle*. Paris, 1906.

Berliet, J., *Les Amis oubliés de Port-Royal*. Paris [1921].

Bluche, F., *Les Magistrats du Parlement de Paris au XVIIIe siècle*. Paris, 1960.

Bontoux, R., "Paris janséniste au XVIIIe siècle: Les *Nouvelles ecclésiastiques*", *Mémoires de la fédération des sociétés historiques et archéologiques de Paris et de l'Ile de France*, 7 (1956), p. 205-220.

Borkeman, F., *Der Übergang vom feudalen zum bürgerlichen Weltbild*. Paris, 1934.

Brémond, H., *Les Querelles religieuses et parlementaires sous Louis XV*. Paris, 1913.

Cannarozzi, C., "L'Adesione dei giansenisti italiani alla chiesa scismatica di Utrecht", *Archivo storico italiano*, 3-4 (1942).

Carreyre, J., "Jansénisme", *Dictionnaire de théologie catholique*, 8:1 (1948), p. 318-530.

—— *Le Jansénisme durant la Régence*, 3 vol. Louvain, 1929-1933.

—— "Quesnel", *Dictionnaire de théologie catholique*, 13:2 (1950), p. 1460-1535.

—— "Utrecht", *Dictionnaire de théologie catholique*, 15:3 (1950), p. 2930-2446.

Chaunu, P., "Jansénisme et frontière de catholicité", *Revue historique*, 227 (1962), p. 115-138.

—— *La Seconde Période du jansénisme*. Bruxelles/Rome, 1968.

—— "Le Jansénisme. Considérations historiques préliminaires à sa notion", *Analecta gregoriana*, 71 (1954)

Codignola, E., *Illuministi, giansenisti e jacobini nell'Italia del settecento*. Firenze [1947].

Cognet, L., *Le Jansénisme* (Que Sais-je?). Paris, 1961.

Crousaz-Cretet, P. de, *L'Eglise et l'état, ou, les Deux Puissances au XVIIIe siècle*. Paris, 1893.

Dammig, E., *Il Moviemento giansenista a Roma nella seconda metà del secolo XVIII*. Roma, 1945.

Davis, C. M., *History of Holland*, III. London, 1851.

Dedieu, J., "L'agonie du jansénisme", *Revue d'histoire de l'église de France* (1928), p. 161-214.

Delanglez, J., *French Jesuits in Lower Louisiana*. Washington, (D.C.), 1935.

Delbecke, F., *L'Action politique et sociale des avocats au 18e siècle*. Louvain/Paris, 1927.

Deloche, M., "Un Missionnaire français en Amérique au XVIIIe siècle", *Bulletin de la section de géographie, Ministère de l'Instruction publique et des Beaux-Arts*, XIV (1930), p. 39-60.

De Vries, F., *Vredespoigingen tusschen de oud-bisschoppelijke Cleresie van Utrecht an Rome*. Assen, 1930.

Durand, V., *Le Jansénisme au XVIIIe siècle et Joachim Colbert, évêque de Montpellier*. Toulouse, 1907.

Fréret, P., *La Faculté de théologie de Paris et ses docteurs les plus célèbres*, VII. Paris, 1910.

Ferguson, S. K., "The Place of Jansenism in French History", *Journal of Religion*, VII (1927), p. 16-24.

Gagnol, P., *Le Jansénisme convulsionnaire et l'affaire de la planchette*. Besançon, 1911.

Garneau, F-X., *Histoire du Canada*, 2 vol. Paris, 1920.

Gazier, A., *Histoire générale du mouvement janséniste depuis ses origines jusqu'à nos jours*, 2 vol. Paris, 1923.

Gedenkboek, 1723-27 April-1923. Tweede eeuwfest der verkiezing van Cornelis Steenhoven tot aartsbisschop van Utrecht. Utrecht, 1923.

Giraud, M., *Histoire de la Louisiane française*, 2 vol. Paris, 1953.

Godard, P., *La Querelle du refus des sacrements*, Paris, 1937.

Gosselin, A., *L'Eglise du Canada*. Québec, 1912.

Groethuysen, B., *Die Entstehung der bürgerlichen Welt- und Lebensanschauung in Frankreich*, 2 vol. Halle a/Salle, 1927.

Hallays, A., *Le Pèlerinage de Port-Royal*, Paris, 1925.

Hardy, G., *Le Cardinal de Fleury et le mouvement janséniste*. Paris, 1925.

Havings, J-C-A., "*Les Nouvelles ecclésiastiques*" *dans leur lutte contre l'esprit philosophique*. Amersfoort, 1925.

Hay, M. V., *Failure in the Far East*. London [1957].

Honigsheim, P., *Die Staats- und Soziallehren der französischen Jansenisten*. Heidelberg, 1914.

Hooijkaas, A., *Coup-d'Œil sur l'ancienne église catholique de Hollande*. La Haye, 1890.

Ingold, J., *Rome et la France: la deuxième phase du jansénisme*. Paris, 1901.

Janssonius-Beuning, *Geschiedenis der oud-roomsch-katholieke Kerk van Nederland*. La Haye, 1870.

Jemolo, A-C., *Il Giansenismo in Italia prima della Rivoluzione*. Bari, 1928.

Jervis, W. H., *The Gallican Church: a History of the Church of France to the Revolution*, 2 vol. London, 1872.

Julia, D., "Problèmes d'histoire religieuse", *Dix-Huitième Siècle*, V (1973), p. 81-88.

Kirsch, P-A., "Unterdruckungsversuche von Büchern wegen gallikanischer, kurialis-
tischer und jansenistischer Tendenzen", *Zentralblatt für Bibliothekewesen*, XX (1903),
p. 549-579.

Knox, R., *Enthusiasm*. Oxford/London, 1950.

Lacombe, B. de, *La Résistance janséniste et parlementaire au temps de Louis XV*. Paris, 1948.

Lagerwey, E., "De Oud-Katholieke begraafplaats", *Jaarboekje van Oud-Utrecht* (1929),
p. 51-98.

Latourette, K. S., *History of the Expansion of Christianity*, 7 vol. New Haven, 1945.

Launay, A., *Histoire de la Société des missions étrangères*, 3 vol. Paris, 1894.

LeBras, G., *Etudes de sociologie religieuse*, 2 vol. Paris, 1955-56.

LePaysant, N., *Le Port-Royal de Normandie... et son prieur, Henri de Roquette*. Paris, 1926.

LeRoy, A., *Le Gallicanisme au 18ᵉ siècle*. Paris, 1952.

Lesourd, P., *Histoire des missions catholiques*. Paris, 1937.

Lupton, J. H., *Archbishop Wake and the Prospect of Reunion*. London, 1896.

Maan, P., C-J. *Barchman-Wuytiers, Erzbischof von Utrecht, 1725-1733*. Assen, 1949.

Mathieu, F., *Histoire des miraculés et des convulsionnaires de Saint-Médard*. Paris, 1864.

Mateucci, B., *Il Giansenismo*. Roma [1954].

Michaud, E., "Deux Apologies de Dominique-Marie Varlet, évêque de Babylone (1678-
1742)," *Revue internationale de Théologie* (1900), p. 477-503.

Montier, J., "Dissidences catholiques", *Intermédiaire des Chercheurs et des Curieux*, 1960
(Oct.), p. 936f; 1961 (Mars), p. 242f.

Morra, G., *Catechismi giansenisti di Saint-Cyran, Feydeau ed Arnauld*. [Forlì] 1968.

Mousset, A., *L'Etude historique des convulsionnaires de Saint-Médard*. Paris, 1954.

Moss, C. B., *The Old Catholic Movement*, London, 1948.

Namer, G., *L'Abbé Le Roy et ses amis: essai sur le jansénisme extrémiste intramondain*. Paris,
1964.

Neale, J. M., *History of the So-Called Jansenist Church of Holland*. Oxford, 1858.

Neveu, B., "Etemare", *Dictionnaire de biographie française*, XIII (1975), p. 185-186.

Orcibal, J., "Qu'est-ce que le jansénisme?", *CAIEF*, 3-5 (1953), p. 39-53.

Parguez, J., *La Bulle Unigenitus et le jansénisme politique*, Paris, 1936.

Pastor, L. von, *The History of the Popes, from the Close of the Middle Ages. Drawn from Secret
Archives of the Vatican and Other Original Sources*, vol. 33-35, London, 1941.

Pellegrini, C., "G. Lami: le Novelle letterarie e la cultura francesa", *Tradizione italiana e
cultura europea*. Messina, 1947, p. 103-125.

Picot, E., "Varlet, Dominique-Marie", *Biographie universelle ancienne et moderne*, xlii (n.
d.), p. 958-959.

Picot, M-F-P., *Mémoires pour servir à l'histoire ecclésiastique pendant le 18ᵉ siècle*, 4 vol. Paris,
1815-1816.

Pirenne, H., *Histoire de Belgique*, V. Bruxelles, 1920.

Plongeron, B., *Théologie et politique au siècle des lumières*. Genève, 1973.

—— "Une Image de l'Eglise d'après les *Nouvelles ecclésiastiques: 1728-1790*", *Revue d'Histoire de l'Eglise de France*, 16 (1967), p. 241-268.

Polman, P., "De Driehoek van St-Maria", *Jaarboekje van Oud-Utrecht* (1955), p. 51-98.

Préclin, E., *Les Jansénistes du 18ᵉ siècle et la Consitution civile du clergé*. Paris, 1929.

—— "L'Influence du jansénisme français à l'étranger", *Revue historique* (1938), p. 24-71.

—— *L'Union des Eglises gallicane et anglicane*. Paris, 1928.

Préclin, E./Jarry, E., *Les Luttes politiques et doctrinales aux 17ᵉ et 18ᵉ siècles*, 2 vol. Paris,
1955-1956.

Préclin, E./Tapié, V-L., *Le XVIIIᵉ siècle* (Coll. Clio), 2 vol. Paris, 1951.

Prévost, A., *Le Diocèse de Troyes*, 3 vol. Domois, 1914-1926.

Quinsonas, P. de, *Msgr de Laubérivière*. Paris, 1936.

Réjalot, T., "Le Jansénisme à l'Abbaye d'Orval", *Annales de l'Institut archéologique du
Luxembourg*, lxviii (1932), p. 57-196.

Sainte-Beuve, C-A. de, *Port-Royal*, 3 vol. Paris, n.d. [Pléiade].

Séché, L., *Les derniers Jansénistes: 1710-1870*, 3 vol. Paris, 1890.

Sicard, A., *L'Ancien Clergé de France*, Paris, 1912.

Shackleton, R., "Jansenism and the Enlightenment", *SVEC* LVII (1967), p. 1387-1397.

Stella, P., *Studi sul giansenismo*. Bari, 1972.

Tans, J-A-G., "Les Idées politiques des jansénistes", *Neuphilologus* (Jan. 1956), p. 1-18.

—— *Pasquier Quesnel et les Pays-Bas*. Groningue/Paris, 1960.

Taveneaux, R. (ed.) — *Jansénisme et politique*. Paris, 1965.

—— "Le Jansénisme dans le diocèse de Verdun", *Annales de l'Est*, 1 (1950), p. 15-33. Good bibliography.

—— *Le Jansénisme en Lorraine*. Paris, 1960.

—— *La Vie quotidienne des Jansénistes aux 17e et 18e siècles*. [Paris, 1973.]

Thomas, F., *La Querelle de l'Unigenitus*. Paris, 1950.

Tillière, N., *Histoire de l'Abbaye d'Orval*. Orval, 1967.

Van Bilsen, B., *De invloed Zeger-Bernard van Espen op het ontstaan van de Kerk van Utrecht*. 's-Gravenhage, 1944.

—— *Het Schisma van Utrecht*. Utrecht, 1949.

Van de Ven., A. "La Communauté cistercienne de la maison Rijnwijk près d'Utrecht," *Internationale Kirchliche Zeitschrift* (1959), p. 115-139.

—— *Over den oorsprong van het aartsbisschoppelijk kapittel van Utrecht der oud-bisschoppelijke Cleresij*. Utrecht [1923].

Van Kleef, B-A., "Domenicus-Maria Varlet (1678-1742)", *Internationale Kirchliche Zeitschrift*, 53 (1963), p. 78-104, 149-177, 193-225.

—— *Geschiedenis der Oud-Katholieke Kerk*. Assen, 1953.

—— *De Kartuizers in Holland*. Rotterdam, 1956.

Van Kley, D., *The Jansenists and the Expulsion of the Jesuits from France: 1757-1765*. New Haven, 1975.

"Varlet, Dominique-Marie", *Appleton's Cyclopaedia*, vi (n.d.), p. 251.

Vaussard, M., *Jansénisme et gallicanisme aux origines religieuses du Risorgimento*. Paris, 1959.

—— "Autour du jansénisme italien", *Revue d'histoire moderne et contemporaine*, iii (1956), p. 291-303.

Veit, L-A., *Die Kirche im Zeitalter des Individualismus: 1648 bis zur Gegenwart*, 2 vol. Freiburg i/B., 1931.

Vidal, J-M., "la France et l'archevêché latin de Babylone (Bagdad)", *Revue d'Histoire des Missions*, x (Sep. 1933), p. 321-371.

Wrong, G. M., *The Rise and Fall of New France*, 2 vol. N.Y., 1928.

INDEX OF CORRESPONDENTS

Authors

References are to numbered items of the present correspondence. Brackets indicate that signatures are lacking.

Beeldsnyder-Matroos, T., "Grand Baillif et échevin" (Utrecht)   49, 66
Chastellain, Antoine, "avocat au parlement de Paris"   23
La Cour, Jacques Jube de, "prêtre-procureur" (Utrecht)   74
Lanoix, M., priest, (Rijnwijk)   64
Lohof, Jacques, town crier (Utrecht)   66
Qualenbrinck, Georges-Christian, "notaire" (Utrecht)   49
Roquette, priest, "prieur de St-Himer" (Normandy)   51, 58, 59
Thiery, M. "notaire au Châtelet de Paris"   69
Tremblay, Jean-Henri, "prêtre-procureur" (Paris)   18, 19, 21
Varlet, Dominique-Marie, Bishop of Babylon   1, 2, [3], 4, 5, 6, 7, 8, 9, 10, 11, 12, 13, 14, 15, 16, 17, 20, 22, 24, 25, 26, 27, [28], [29], [30], [31], [32], [33], [34], [35], [36], [37], [38], [39], [40], [41], [42], [43], [ç4], [45], [46], [47], [48], [50], [52], [53], 54, [55], [56], [57], [60], [61]
Villiers, Francois de, "notaire" (Utrecht)   62, 65, 67, 68, 70, 72, 73, 75

Addressees

Olivier, Antoine "procureur au Châtelet de Paris", (DMV's brother-in-law)   4, 17, 18, 19, 22, 23, 24, 25, 26, 29, 32, 36, 39, 40, 42, 43, 44, 45, 46, 48, 50, 51, 52, 54, 57, 58, 59, 60, 61, 62, 64, 65, 67, 68, 70, 72, 73, 74, 75
Olivier, Marie-Anne (Paris, DMV's sister)   27, 28, 30, 33, 35, 37, 38, 41, 47, 53, 55, 56
Olivier, M. et Mme, (Paris, DMV's brother-in-law and sister)   11, 20, 31, 34
Varlet, M., (Paris, DMV's brother Jean Achille)   6, 14
Varlet, Marie Vallée (Paris, DMV's mother)   1, 2, 3, 4, 7, 8, 9, 10, 12, 13, 15, 16

Documents

21, 49, 63 A-B, 66, 69, 71

GENERAL INDEX

This list does not include entries for persons named in their quality as correspondents. Such entries may be found in the preceding appendix. References are to numbered items of the present correspondence. Brackets indicate that the person is not named directly.

Abdalnour, M., priest (Paris) 7.

Alexander VII (Chigi), pope in 1655-1667 Intro., App. IV.

Ambassador of the Tsar in Persia see Debenevin.

Ambassador from Poland to the Tsar in 1719 Intro.

Antwerp, bishop of see Franken-Sierstorpff, F. C.

d'Anville, J. B. Bourguignon (1697-1782), famous geographer 63A, 63B.

Arnauld, Antoine (1612-1694), famous Jansenist leader, died in exile at Malines 75, App. IV.

Astrakhan, Orthodox bishop of (1720) Intro.

Augustine, Saint (354-430), bishop of Hippo, celebrated Christian Father App. IV.

d'Auvergne, Marie-Anne, princess, née d'Aremberg (1689-1736) 65, 74.

Auzon, M. (Paris) 72.

Bachou, Jean, S. J., priest at Schemacha in 1719 Intro.

Barchman-Vuytiers, Cornélis-Jan van, archbishop of Utrecht in 1725-1733 Intro., App. IV.

Barnabas Fideli, O. P., bishop of Isphahan in 1719 Intro.

Baudrier dit Ferrand, Martin, priest (Schoonauwen) 49.

Beeldsnyder-Matroos, J. (1694-1757), "Grand Baillif et échevin" at Utrecht 49, 62, [65], 66.

Benedict XIII (Orsini-Gravosa), pope in 1724-1730 Intro.

Benedict XIV (Lambertini), pope in 1740-1758 Intro.

Bentivoglio, Martino, papal nuncio in Paris, 1712-1719 Intro.

Bernard, Saint (1090-1153), mystic, founder of order bearing his name 55, 68.

Bijelevelt, B. J., bishop of Utrecht in 1717-1723, prevented from occupying his see by Dutch authorities Intro.

Bizot, M. (Paris) 48.

Bossuet, Jacques-Bénigne (1627-1704), bishop of Meaux, celebrated defender of orthodox catholicism under Louis XIV App. IV.

Boucher, M. (Paris) 5, 7.

Boullenois, Dom, Benedictine Appellant who led a group of Carthusians to Schoonauwen in 1725 Intro.

Bourillon, Mlle (Paris) 2, 7.

Brunswick-Lunebourg, celebrated German family enjoying princely rank from 1692 70.

Brussels, nuncio in see Santini.

Caille, Claude, French Renaissance theologian, subject of DMV's thesis in 1706 Intro.

Canet, M., carriage-maker at Echarcon 1.

Cardinal, le see Noailles, L-A.

Caucasian Albania, Orthodox bishop of see Isaiah.

Caylus, Charles-Daniel de Tubières de (1669-1754), bishop of Auxerre in 1704 Intro.

Cenard, M., "procureur" (Paris) 1.

Chastelain, Antoine, "avocat au Parlement de Paris" 21, 22, 24.

Clement IX (Rospigliosi), pope from 1667-1669 App. IV.

Clement XI (Francesco-Albani), pope in 1700-1721 13, 75, App. IV.

Clement XII (Corsini), pope in 1730-1740 Intro.

Clement XIII (della Torre-Rezzonico), pope from 1758-1769 Intro.

Codde, Pierre, bishop of Sebaste (i.p.i.), Vicar-Apostolic in the Low Countries until suspended in 1702, deposed in 1704, died 1721 Intro.